The Particle and Philosophy in Crisis

The Particle and Philosophy in Crisis

Towards Mode of Information

Anil Rajimwale

AAKAR

The Particle and Philosophy in Crisis: Towards Mode of Information
Anil Rajimwale

First Published, 2013

Published by
AAKAR BOOKS
28 E Pocket IV, Mayur Vihar Phase I, Delhi 110 091
Phone : 011 2279 5505 Telefax : 011 2279 5641
info@aakarbooks.com; www.aakarbooks.com

Printed at
Mudrak, 30 A, Patparganj, Delhi 110 091

Dedicated to the memory of my father Late Shri D.A. Rajimwale, who introduced me to the interesting world of philosophy, its trends, methods, to its great minds, and who made philosophy look easy. He was an encyclopaedic mind and a voracious reader, with wide sweep and depth of knowledge from philosophy through politics to chemistry.

The book is an insignificant effort to return the debt to him, which cannot be returned, ever.

Contents

Introduction

The present book is the first one of a series of volumes on the most deep-rooted impacts of basic changes in science, technology and communication on philosophy, society, mode of production, concepts of capitalism and socialism, nature of world economy and integrating world, history and future of socialism, world outlook, on Marxism and trends like postmodernism and other questions. I have not numbered the volumes because they are still to be planned as such. But there is a certain order, and the books or volumes will appear before the readers as and when they are ready.

And that should be sooner than later. It is time that we take a broader and deeper look at the world we live in and understand and interpret it properly.

We are most fortunate to live in an era of unprecedented transition, of scientific and technological revolution, which is not only comparable to the great industrial revolution, but is much greater, wider and deeper than the latter.

Among the most important impacts of the ongoing revolution is on science and technology. Electronic technology has become quite common now, which is changing the way we live and think. But before that, the science, in particular physics, has undergone fundamental transformations, in turn causing huge changes in the way we look at the world. The very concept of the 'world' stands redefined.

The two most notable discoveries that have changed science from its classical phase to the post-classical are that of the 'quantum' by

Max Planck in 1900 and relativity, special in 1905 and general in 1916, by Albert Einstein. They and the associated discoveries and theories have overthrown the classical physics, and along with it the established worldview, and have opened a world of quantum mechanics and relativity. Our established concepts about matter and energy apply no longer. Newtonian physics is deposed or left behind, jettisoned, negated, evolving into and replaced by Einsteinian and quantum physics. They have initiated a rapid process of radical change in all the sciences, and are today being transformed into unprecedented and unbelievable forms of technology.

But the point is more serious. It is not a question of physics or mechanics or chemistry alone, which of course it is. It is now a question of *the worldview itself.* The Cartesian worldview created basically during the industrial revolution has been displaced: it is proving inapplicable in one field after another. One after the other, the concepts are getting demolished, to be replaced by new ones or sometimes unfortunately by none at all. The concepts created during centuries and millennia with great care, labour, observation, study and experience are suddenly found to be inadequate and obsolete. The scientists themselves are shocked and surprised. They have taken quite some time to get over their shock! A whole new world opened before them which needs explanation and interpretation afresh.

That is why, the advances in the twentieth century physics and in sciences in general have been accompanied by deep-rooted philosophical discussions and debates, even sharp exchanges. This did not happen before. Earlier, the scientists and philosophers were, generally speaking, separate beings, although common ones are also to be found. And their scientific discoveries did not lead to such debates. Philosophical debates were carried on by others including the philosophers, who used and misused their findings.

But here, in the quantum sciences in particular, philosophical categories began to be debated as to their relevance or correctness or otherwise. Every discovery in the field of particles or waves, atoms and their constituents raised basic questions about the categories of reality, existence, matter, subject and object, causation, time, space, material forms and their concepts and so on. The giants of sciences got involved in the philosophical debates. A.S. Eddington wrote in the 1920s-30s about the nature of physical reality, the much astonished Max Planck, astonished by his own discovery of the quantum, wrote on the physical world and its interpretation; Einstein, Pauli, Born, Bohr, de Broglie, Paul Davies, Stephen Hawkins, Schroedinger, John Bell, Gribbins, Bohm, John Wheeler, and a whole galaxy of extraordinary minds raised more questions about the meaning of reality and existence than they themselves could answer. Instead of following the beaten tracks, they were bold enough to challenge the hitherto established concepts of sciences and philosophy and developed or suggested new ones. They were and are brave thinkers, unlike unfortunately, many others who dare not tread new paths and try to hide behind simplistic interpretations of the 'so-called' established fundamentals.

Niels Bohr and Albert Einstein conducted a three-decade long running 'battle' not only on the nature of the discoveries but on philosophy and worldview itself. They are wonderful debates, the very pinnacle of human thought. Thought never attained such heights as it did now, in the course of these unprecedented exchanges of opinions. It turned out to be those heights where the idea had to survive and develop even, and largely, without experimental proofs!

A whole quantum world opened out, and led to the emergence of a quantum philosophy.

We have made a transition to a philosophical world where the shape and nature of existing philosophy is changed, and it is sometimes even questionable whether it can be called 'philosophy' at all.

The Present Book

So, philosophy itself is in *a severe crisis* today, with its main conceptions falling fast behind and becoming obsolete.

The present book follows the impact of 'the particle' on philosophy and worldview. The 'particle' here represents not just the particular particles; more than that it represents a concept covering new developments in the quantum world, the very opening up of a new world, where events and processes are qualitatively different from those in the classical world in which we lived so far. This particle represents a new world, a radical departure from the world existing so far since the origin of human beings. In some senses 'the particle' reflects the waves and other phenomena like the wave/particle duality, new relations of time and space with matter and energy etc. This particle is different from the atom we so far held to be the constituent part of the world, the very basis of reality. The quantum particle is particle no doubt but its negation at the same time, its instant conversion into waves and 'clouds' the moment you go beyond a certain limit. With this particle we enter the world of rapid motions and transformations, to which the laws and interpretations are no more applicable.

It is a particle that opens up an entirely new world by dissolving itself and inviting new explorations.

The atom, a very old and established reality and concept, explained the classical material world since ancient times. 'Particle' explains the new world because it is the quantum particle representing packs and conversions of energy.

The problem with our thought and philosophy is that we continue to 'hang on to' the atom or the particle, because without this 'something' we find ourselves unable to 'see' and explain the world. We always need 'something' handy to explore and go forward. The entire humanity, history, civilization, culture, thought, philosophy, hung on and depended upon it. We became arrogant in being human beings, and thought that we were going ahead undeterred and comfortably along our path.

The quantum discoveries, the wave/particle dualities, have taken away this 'something'; we have to begin anew.

With the discovery of the quantum, this atom (particle) has disappeared, and the ground on which the philosophy stood has moved away, resulting in a kind of earthquake in the world of thought. The very basis of the world is shaken. Even simple jobs like observation, measurements with measuring rods/instruments, etc. using microscopes, keeping time or using clocks and so on have become problem-ridden as we attain greater speeds. Why? Simply because the instruments themselves undergo transformations at very high speeds and velocities, and also because the instruments are no more our part and assistants; they are being found to both the observers and the observed; they too are revealing to be part of the quantum processes. Consequently, the very concept of 'instrument' changes. The clocks, for example, slow down in space on rockets and at higher velocities. There is a contraction in the measuring rods. The clocks no more help us measure time. The microscope or whatever instrument we are using to 'look at' the particles like the electron, itself interacts, and thus interferes, with the observed 'object'. Therefore, we are unable to find out the real nature of the object we try to observe.

Thus observation itself has become a matter of controversy in the quantum science and quantum philosophy. The meaning of observation changes: Observation means interaction. Interaction means the observed object/process has changed in the course of our observation; then what was its original nature? Such questions lead to a wide range of epistemological problems. How then do we gather/ acquire knowledge? What is knowledge itself?

We are in an epistemological crisis.

In the tangible world it is easy, comparatively speaking, to understand. For example: This is a ball or a sphere or a solid object. It has a certain weight, length, breadth, height, thickness and so on. Even the bacterium under the microscope has these characteristics. I can hold a cricket ball or a football; it will have certain coordinates: distance from the table, height from the surface, it has a left and a right, up and down side to it, it can be made to gain speed by throwing it, it can rebound, it has certain space and certain time also, if you want to be more scientific. It can create certain spaces between itself and other spheres, and can move in time. I can leave the ball on the table or ground, come back the next day, confident that it is there; I can turn my back with the confidence that it will not disappear, and really when I turn back or return the next day I find it still there, with red or white or whatever colour. I can see it in light, and in dark 'I know' it is there! I throw torchlight or switch on the light or the tube and can see it clearly 'as it was' and 'as it is'.

Similarly, we can see an endless number of things and processes, many others we can draw conclusions about on the basis of complicated interrelationships, results, and calculations. We can study complex phenomena and processes repeatedly and draw certain conclusions about them, whether they are price-rise and inflation or chemical organic or inorganic or biological or physical processes or economic, social, political events, and what not. We can see micro-organisms like the bacteria under the microscope, study other living beings.

Down the ages, we have been observing and studying, and philosophizing and generalizing on this basis. Our whole outlook, approach and view is based upon such experiences and drawing of conclusions and formation of concepts. That is how our thoughts and thought processes have evolved. We are used to it.

This is what we call the classical world. It is also called the Cartesian world, after the famous scientist Rene Descartes (1660), who is known in Latin as 'Cartesius'. Hence the term 'Cartesian'. Such a world is also known as Newtonian.

Cartesian/Newtonian world, things are arranged in order, one originating from the other; they are therefore 'historical', the view is 'clear' and going far off 'upto the horizon', things can be seen one after the other, a tree here, rocks there, river, houses, flat or hilly ground and so on and so forth. It can be 'experienced' and is topographical, ontological. Positivism and materialism are closely related to such a world.

This world has its own laws of motion, whether mechanical or dialectical, to be broken up into laws of various fields like the physical, chemical, biological, social, economic and so on. Newton, for example, provided laws of motion of the bodies such as described above, which he also applied to the planets, etc. There are laws of machines, inherent dialectical laws developed by Hegel and Marx, laws and motions of society, production and what not.

The Great Industrial Revolution of the 18th-20th centuries, and events before and after provided scientific proofs and great impetus to the thought process of the classical world.

So, this Cartesian/Newtonian world is quite clear once we understand it. Instruments and appliances and means of production help us reveal new features in objects and society as they, the instruments and means of production, get perfected in the course of time. With the passing of time we more or less 'know' the world.

We become confident of what is what and where. The rocks and trees, houses and spheres and balls are in their place or moving about with this or that speed.

But next we take a new step into the quantum world, and the classical world disappears: No concept or law or notion of the previous era is applicable to this world. Hence the crisis of humanity and human thought itself. We had thought everything is in place.

This is not so with the quantum world! We enter a world where nothing previously developed is applicable and none of our established concepts are working.

Post-classical World

This world is not like the one we have just described, in which we were born and lived, and lived down the ages.

You cannot catch hold of a sphere or a ball and say, it is here. There is no 'is', there is no 'here' here! Can you catch hold of *a* particle, or *the* particles, and say, look here it is and it is going 'there'?! No. Perhaps after a lapse of time, we can after all grasp it or them. But here there is no *lapse of time*, there is only a particular time for a particular moment. Time does not *flow*, as it does on the earth. I cannot be confident that this is the 'atom' or particle I have seen and I will see it again! You can never see the same particle ever in your entire life!

And here lies the root of the crisis of thought and philosophy. You do not know 'its' characteristics; you only know 'the' characteristics that may constitute a particle or wave; the features that you collectively term 'particle-like'. And as you approach the 'particle' it dissolves and resolves into waves or 'clouds' in our popular imagination! The particle is transformed into waves!

There is no right or left, up or down, for a particle or wave. It just flies off, and there is no particular direction or even path for it, like our football or train or river. East, west, north, south have no meaning at all in the outer space. Can you 'catch hold' of the particle and say it is going or coming? That is not possible. The concepts of 'coming' or 'going' do not apply here. And besides, has a particle a 'here' or a 'there'? Does it 'stand' for a certain duration *to enable us to state* that it is and it is here or there? No. This is a very important philosophical and epistemological question as to enabling us to state something with certainty. We state or say something about something only when we can state with a certain amount of certainty!

But there is no 'something' in the quantum world. There are only changes, motions, disappearances there. What appears, appears only to disappear instantly. What appears to appear does not appear at all!

There is no need even to turn your back; you may not be able to see a 'particular' 'thing' or even a process even during observation; no need to wait for tomorrow, because there is no tomorrow in the world of space constituted by the quantum processes!

Epistemological Crisis and Crisis of Epistemology

Now suppose, I want to delve into the world of 'particles', find out what they 'look like' and draw certain conclusion/s. What do I do? I try to observe; how? Very simple: I just take a microscope or whatever instrument there is, and 'look' at the 'moving' (as if it is a moving bacterium!) particle; if necessary, I throw light upon the particle and try to observe. So very simple!

No; it turns out that things and processes in that world are not so simple. The whole exercise is a misconception, a carry over, a burden of the past. We have used terms like 'observe', 'see', 'throw light upon', 'microscope' or 'instrument', etc. These are all inadequate, even inapplicable to the observation of the quantum world.

You throw light upon what? And first of all, what is light itself? It is made up of photons, a form of quanta. So, photon itself is a quantum particle. According to Einstein's photoelectric theory, when you throw light upon, say, an electron, you cause its ejection from a metal plate. When a light particle of certain energy 'meets with' (!) or 'hits'(!) another particle, the course of the latter is changed. Here we will rest a while and ponder upon the *extremely archaic* nature of our expressions conceptual tools. One 'particle' actually never meets with or hits 'another'. At the most we can say they 'interact', to the extent of merging together or repelling each other. Again, this description is highly unsatisfactory.

Thus, it is likely that when our instrument or apparatus throws light on what is supposed to be a particle, it will change the latter. What we are more likely to meet with is the result of quantum reactions, and then we enumerate our observations. Consequently, we do not know what the particle was *before* light hit it. And when it did hit it, the latter was changed, may be both were changed. It is obvious that all this is quite different from our observation of a tennis or cricket balls and their interaction.

As we will mention further on in the book, the particles are all the time popping up and out in space. Therefore there is one chance in a hundred thousand or million to meet an electron or a particle. So, while we try to observe it, we are in effect waiting for its formation and chance passing before the apparatus or whatever. Thus, this 'reality' is quite different from our everyday life. Our instruments themselves consist of particles within the atoms; they may interact with the observed realities, thus not really act as instruments.

Besides, the particle is a dual and highly elusive 'being'. As we shall see, the particle or what we term as 'particle' is actually made up of so many waves, which appear from a certain distance as a particle. In effect we term cloud of waves as particle, the exact opposite!

Wave/particle duality is one of the wonders of nature, particularly of the new world. It defies the existing epistemology and its tools.

Thus, for epistemology, we need certain thought-related tools such as: here, there, object, subject, material form, laws, categories, concepts, etc and certain stability of theirs. But as we speed up we begin to lose them. We lose the very tools that help us comprehend the world. We must see, hold the thing, see it in motion, it should have some space and time, etc. We must have a concept or series of concepts. All these get lost or are distorted or replaced by one another.

Epistemology is thrown into a deep crisis. Without concepts, there can be no epistemology.

Acceleration of Time, Concepts and Thought Process

That is why the present volume begins by tracing the slowdown of time on the earth and consequent thought process, and then gradually goes over to consider the impact of acceleration of time on concepts, philosophy and worldview. This is an absolutely new approach to philosophy, its transformation into non-philosophy, and then the transfiguration into new quantum ('particle') philosophical worldviews drawn and traced mainly along time dimension. The planets in the galaxies are the result of *congealing* of time and space. They are polar opposites of the stars and so-called vacuum of spaces between stellar bodies, where time and space are infinite identified by extraordinarily rapid transformations and motions. Nothing can be stable on the stars and in 'vacuum'; in fact, nothing can 'be' on or in them. Our own sun contains only hydrogen and helium, and no other elements are virtually 'allowed' to form. Waves/ particle duality and rapid energy changes is the reality for them.

This is not so on earth and other planets. That is why the book begins by showing a 'slowdown' of time, and considers it to be the crucial factor for emergence of the conscious being and consciousness on the earth. It is in this state of time and space congealment and exceedingly slow evolution that the events and life have proceeded on its surface. Material life, social-economic life, thought process, philosophy, worldview have emerged in precisely such conditions. Gradually the speed of social development began to gather speed; we 'developed'; our means of production improved, reducing labour and hardship, the industrial revolution took place, our thoughts became richer and varied, philosophy became multi-faceted.

Everything proceeded very well, and we thought we had come to grips with the world and are now proceeding into vast uncharted fields, where we would find things more or less smoothly with ever improving means of knowledge.

Everything was fine *till* that minute 'thing', the quantum, intervened! It upset the cart of our development, particularly of our thought system. This was because with atom and quantum, things suddenly speeded up extraordinarily, in an unprecedented manner, a world of ultra-high speed and exceedingly rapid motions opened up. We were not prepared for it at all. We have evolved in a different setting. The new speeds are unnatural for us, something foreign, un-planetary! They are more star-like, that is our opposites. These and related developments have disturbed the space-time coordinates followed by human society till now. The time coordinate of matter has gone out of control totally, and destroyed the spatial relationship. Earth being too small for the changes, the latter have completely upset thought and society.

Things are not confined to scientific theories; the discoveries are being translated into technology, and thus into everyday life. The two do not square up: Human development till now, and development now onwards. Matter is speeded up as to become energy, a form of matter itself but a form that has time as its determinant. We have begun evolving along a time line. Consequently, our established concepts are falling by the wayside.

Our thought/worldview/philosophy are having to develop and adjust with time, creating a crisis for philosophy and thought itself. Thought is now *bereft* of its tools of knowledge and epistemology.

The book argues that the quantum discoveries have speeded up our development and thus created a crisis for thought. New discoveries and electronics-based technologies have resulted in our lives and thought gaining speed. We have begun the journey more along the time paradigm; the balance or equilibrium between different aspects or sides of reality and matter is upset. Matter has basically the dimensions of time, space and motion. There are other aspects too. So far, our thoughts were created within these confines.

Now, it is **time** that has *gone ahead* in relation to other aspects and dimensions, and is increasingly becoming the determining dimension. It has upset the balance between the dimensions of matter and consequently in the ideas. As we proceed along the time dimension, all the concepts created by and within the other aspects are over-turned, and new ones are created or are needed.

Human thought now is on the path of rapid speed up, and therefore our worldview develops differently. The speed up not only realigns various dimensions; the dimensions themselves are transformed radically. For example, the nature of the particle changes as the building block of the world, the very edifice of our thought and life.

Evolution of 'Particle' and Crisis of Thought

How to understand/comprehend/grasp the 'particle'? Why do we talk of crisis of thought and, consequently, of philosophy? It is very difficult to describe such a particle in ordinary, understandable language, in commonsense terms. Let us take the example of a ball of woollen thread, out of which women weave warm clothes in our houses.

The particles in space are constituted by the waves constantly travelling. It is an instant creation, as we have described while dealing with the standard waves. It is as if the 'threads' of the waves constitute the 'sphere' or the particle and then disappear. Once the threads spread out, the woollen ball disappears. The threads come together in a pattern, and the ball is made. It is an easy transition.

These threads of the waves carry information. If you touch them they disappear. Of course you can't 'touch' them; no such concept exists in the quantum world. The moment you try to touch ('observe') the particle disappears; it loses its wave function. The woollen ball is not made of functions but of tangible threads, but those in space are not tangible objects but energy conversions.

The thought is in crisis because it can't conceive of any particular, tangible clear-cut reality. You can't philosophise.

The evolution of the particle is in fact its disappearance into the vast spaces through conversions into waves.

It is this duality, along with other aspects, that constitutes the vast quantum world. The duality is the dialectics of exceedingly fleeting motions at near-light and light speeds. This is the greatest philosophical question of the present-day 'world', which in fact is endless.

Consider the vastness: the Hubble telescope and other instruments are discovering new realities every day and moment. Our galaxy, the Milky Way, is home to millions of stars and planets; light takes some hundred thousand light years to travel from one end of the Milky Way to another.

How many galaxies do you think exist? *So far,* more than one lakh (a hundred thousand) galaxies have been discovered, and still counting!

'Lighted' Knowledge

Human knowledge is limited only to the lighted, four per cent, of the reality or the world. We know almost nothing about the part of the world where visible light is absent. Our knowledge even about the 'four per cent' is very limited. As for the non-lighted world, we know next to nothing; for example, we know very little about the black holes.

Our entire existence and thought are fashioned by the 'lighted' reality, events, objects, etc, mainly as obtaining on the planet earth. We see the objects mainly because light is reflected from them. We will not here go into details; the question has been discussed in the following pages. When we talk of human beings, society and individual/social consciousness, they are the product in essence of light. Light, alone and along with other events and objects, has determined our being and life cycle as well as social cycle. Motion of the earth is another aspect that has fashioned our lives such as those related to agriculture, etc.

Therefore, our thoughts and being are basically light-oriented and light-guided. All our concepts, social and philosophical, are a product of this fact. Without light there cannot be knowledge, information and consciousness.

This process is upset today as we enter the unlighted world guided and formed by wavelengths beyond the lighted ones. The processes and 'objects' are totally unexpected, and world formed by such wave/particle duality absolutely different from what we are familiar with so far. If we are to explore an entirely new world, we need new tools because the older tools, technical as well as philosophical, are inadequate here. Scientists, and philosophers, are at it. They are talking of string theory, X-ray, gamma ray and other kinds of stars, exotic particles and waves, a world where nothing is standstill, where space and time acquire unexpected turns and twists and bendings and transformations, where particles come and go in a whiz, creating exceedingly momentary existences, yet endless vastnesses. We are on the verge of a massive and giant revolution in thought and consciousness.

A lot of lighted knowledge too is yet to be analysed in greater detail. And here, the relativity of existence and reality emphasizes itself with increasing force. For example, does the colour blue really exist? When we see the blue sky, it is in fact a particular reaction between particular wavelengths and our retina. Hence the colour blue. Out in space this reaction disappears, and with it the various 'colours'.

Human civilization, culture and economy have been guided by sunrise and sunset at particular times. But today, after millennia, we fly into outer space in satellites and space stations, and the concepts collapse; we can observe 'sunrise' and 'sunset' several times in 24 hours. The tools being used on earth are no more usable in space owing to the operation of multiple gravitational forces.

Self-transcendence of Human Thought

Today, for the first time, we can transcend ourselves and look at ourselves. This is no more a philosophical abstraction but a result of the STR and the ICR. Not only have the astronauts and cosmonauts looked at the planet earth from outer space and the moon; they have sent images and pictures of the earth back to us. Manned and unmanned space devices and satellites have sent us millions of images of the earth. We can look at ourselves on the screens lighted from outer space and wonder at the endless expanses opening up due to the extraordinary developments in science, technology and information. It is the first time that the earth and human society appear as a holistic whole and full beings. New dialectics are unfolding between the human society full of contradictions and the human consciousness that has transcended these contradictions. There is a lesson in this self-transcendence. We must work to free humanity of the acute contradictions, which appear more and more insignificant as we proceed into space and the quantum world. This calls for scientific solutions so that we live and think as real human beings by transcending our entire previous history.

This transcendence will create the real human consciousness.

1

Crisis in Philosophy and Philosophy in Crisis

Is there a crisis in philosophy? And is philosophy in crisis? These two are overlapping questions, as also the answers. We may argue that a deep crisis has gripped philosophy; we can also argue that the field and discipline of philosophy itself is in deep crisis. There is not much difference between the two, although there are overlapping areas as well as some uncovered ones, which will be covered in the course of our discussions as we proceed through the book.

May be most people will differ. They may say there could be a crisis *within* this philosophy or that, in this concept or that, and therefore perhaps a crisis in philosophy or in certain philosophical schools, but that there is no crisis in *philosophy as such.*

But the case of this book is that not only is there a crisis within philosophy, whether in this or that field of the discipline, in this aspect and on that question or in particular concept/formulation/s, in particular branches and schools, and even in philosophy as a whole, but also that *the whole of philosophy itself* is today in a very deep crisis, and it will need an entire sea-change for it to come out. There is also a question mark on the relevance and nature of the discipline of philosophy *itself*: whether it exists at all, as we understand it, or do its parameters change drastically as to lead to progressive dissolution. We also have to discuss whether new nature and configuration of philosophy is emerging e.g. as quantum philosophy.

Before we talk of crisis in philosophy and of philosophy in crisis, let us discuss *what is philosophy*. We will often take it that both questions are very similar, though sometimes there may be serious differences between the two posers. That will make it easier to solve the problem of crisis in philosophy and of philosophy in crisis. The two are interrelated, almost the same, but not quite; they are overlapping.

Philosophy has long since dealt with general and abstract questions of life and the world. It is a worldview, which involves the relationship between matter and idea/consciousness, between subject and object. It is an abstraction of the basic questions of existence and non-existence. Therefore, it is a movement away from what we perceive, towards existence/essence in general or towards denial of existence in general. It is a speculation, unconcerned with the concrete forms and dealing with the essence of being. It tries to find out what are we, who are we or who, why, what am I? What is the meaning of my existence and our existence; are we real, or is there a life, real/ unreal, 'beyond'? Are we real or do we become 'really' real after we cease to be? These and such other questions have troubled human beings since time immemorial.

The human brain has never been satisfied with what it sees or perceives, on the surface or just beneath it. This perception does not provide us the meaning of being in existence, of the thing in general, of existence. Human beings have always tried to find the meaning of existence, individual as well as collective, of life. This is what distinguishes the human consciousness. Humans always try to see what they cannot see, try to find out the 'meaning' of this and that.

This way of thinking gave rise to 'philosophy'. For philosophy, what we see is unimportant, useless, immaterial, including the material, tangible, everyday, inessential, superfluous things or happenings. What lies beneath is more meaningful, important, material or ideal. And even more important is what is immaterial, what does not 'exist': abstract and general and that which cannot be 'seen' interests philosophy more than anything elese in the world!

And that is why, philosophy it must move away from the obvious, and must seek the meaning of the non-obvious, must move away from the tangible into the intangible, seek out the abstract, the very essence of the world and of the things in the world and 'outside'. Abstract essence is the core of philosophy. The movement of philosophy is away from the obvious, tangible, concrete, the phenomenal, and into the essence, the abstract, the general. That is the habit of philosophy! That is the real meaning and field of investigation of philosophy. Otherwise, the 'why' of the world cannot be discovered, and we as human beings, cannot justify ourselves. So, philosophy seeks to justify the human's being/consciousness. Therefore, the greater the distance from the concrete, the greater is the true essence, and nearer we reach the truth. To delve into essence is to move away from the expressions of the world and into the world itself.

Thus, philosophy is *antithetical* to the visible, tangible world, even though it is a product of this very world. Abstraction is the opposite of the world. River has no meaning for philosophy, its abstraction, its being or non-being is the only meaning. The moment you discover the river, philosophy *dissolves*. At the same time, the river cannot have an isolated being; it is part and parcel of the general, abstract *being*. River, stone, sky, clouds, humans, I, you – what are they? The question contains the answer. They are not what they appear to be, not what they are. They are not 'they'. They all, put together, are 'it'. For the human brain, 'it' is not what it appears to be, and it is not what it is, really speaking. So, the human consciousness is a doubting being: it does not believe in what the world 'wants' it to believe by simply appearing before it as it is: no, there is something more behind, some abstract meaning. In philosophy, there are virtually no plurals, only singular. They all, put together, are 'it'. There are only abstracts; philosophy is the world of motion of abstracts.

It is synthesis at deeper and the deepest levels. By synthesizing it dissolves the concrete world.

Philosophy, including the materialist philosophy, is the very antithesis of the world, of existence. Even in the materialist philosophy, the concept of matter is an abstraction, materialism is full of concepts, which are generalizations constantly changing. There is no use of the word 'thing' for philosophy. 'At the most', the world and its things and processes help form ideas, nothing more. An idea is superior for human beings or consciousness. And it is not necessary to acknowledge this, because an idea or philosophy considers itself superior already. Any idea in abstraction is philosophy, nothing more, nothing less.

Philosophy thinks abstractly; though in fact it is the brain which thinks, but having done that, the brain can be jettisoned, because it becomes 'superfluous' in the process of abstraction!

Why must idea (philosophy) think, that is, philosophize at all? After all, what you see, is. Why think about it? And not just reflect and leave at that? Because idea must act in opposition to what it thinks. Thinking is separation from the tangible, is denial of reality, it proceeds only in the latter's negation. Idea is the very opposite of reality of what exists. Thought does not exist, idea does not exist, it *does not want* to. *It simply is,* it *permeates* as such. That is what it thinks. This has been the human impression, that has driven human thought in the reverse. That which is does not exist, need not exist, because to exist, it should come into being, and idea never comes into existence, according to its inherent logic, which is in opposition to its actual history, and in opposition it claims that it has always been. To exist is *an inferior act*, to permeate is superior. Idea emanates from a certain stage of matter, but that fact needs to be denied by idea to become eternal, otherwise it can't be idea as per idea. Idea always wants to be ideal, never material, even if it has come into existence from the material at a certain stage of motion.

The problem with idea is that it exists *in opposition* to matter. So, history is opposition, and must be denied. Therefore, it must continuously deny, negate and oppose the material, the existing. The meaning of the material is clear, but idea need not be clear, does not need meaning, it seeks meaning only in the abstract, it need not prove itself, it exists apart from, in opposition to the material; not only that it must now seek to destroy the material to really become abstract, to achieve *full and absolute abstraction.* The question of existence, of what is, arises only after, and in opposition to that which thinks, the idea. The idea really thinks *about,* always about something, but that has really to be denied in order to remain as idea. So, while really it does think about, actually it does not want to *think about*; it only wants to think, in abstraction, in itself, for itself, because it is superior and after that the only reality. Only in this way can it *justify* itself. Philosophy is historical justification of idea. To think about is to do so about that which has given rise to it. But this has to be denied by idea to absolutize itself and to philosophize itself.

Thinking about something is to *fall into* something. Therefore, thought constantly rises above such thinking, to absoluteness. Human thinking never wants to particularize, only to generalize; even when it is thinking about particular, it absolutises the object (river, stone, etc.) to certain general qualities; otherwise it will become the object itself! It moves through and away from the particular, thus jettisoning forms for essence, for essential abstraction. Thought can never be particular because it always goes beyond the concept. It wants to encompass, not limit, absolutize, not particularize, be itself, not something else, be ideal not material, transcend not internalize and stay afloat. And only thus it stays afloat!

Idea: Assertion is Denial

To think is to deny, dissolve what exists. Even the assertion is itself a denial. To say river or tree or stone exists is to deny it exists. 'River exists' means it does not exist! 'River is' means 'it is not'. The statement of 'river' etc. is a concept, and therefore a denial, and thus not the river itself, simply a reflection. We move away and carry away the concept of river, leaving the poor river to itself!

But river, or anything else does not need, never needed, an assertion. Assertion needed *the idea* of the river, etc. Therefore, by saying river exists, one converts it into an idea. It is the point of negation. Therefore, there is an opposition in this assertion. River etc. existed before, even before thought came into being. But to think about it is to incorporate it into a concept, which is an abstraction, and then we *compare* it with the reality of river: whether the river really exists or not, and how or how not. Idea is in constant conflict with reality, object. By saying (asserting) that it is river or stone we in fact question its validity, reality, which was not needed before thought. It just was.

It is only after philosophizing that the contradiction is resolved, because philosophizing is synthesizing, and the object is returned to its 'original' yet transformed state: The river was there as it is now but unseen, and therefore without opposition. Therefore, it was not a 'river', i.e. it was not labelled with an idea of 'river', of existence. It really began to 'exist' only after idea saw it! It remained 'undisturbed' (without the touch of idea and therefore was a pure being), unseen, unlabelled, not physically touched. It is another matter that in the course of our explorations and enquiries, we increasingly interfere with and change the object, say river. But at present we are not concerned with that.

Does a touch with the idea of the subject interfere with the object, the thing, and with matter? 'Interference with matter' we will consider later, because that is abstraction of abstraction.

We are as yet leaving out the consideration of the quantum world.

How does idea know that the object, say the river, existed before? The poser may seem idealist and subjective. Yet it has to be answered. And once it is answered, it is no more subjective, idealist. We know only when we come to know – about river. But suppose we did not 'know', supposing in turn we did not come into being? Then could we really say with certainty that the river existed? There was nobody to say so! The brain and the consciousness did not exist!

It is the series of objects that leads to the constitution of brain, which produces idea as a throwback upon the object as the reflection of the object. Had the series, the motion of the objects not existed, the object would not have been known. So, motion in the object creates self-realization, which also is the other realization.

Thus motion leads to realization and self-realization, and that is the culmination of what existed and exists. Idea changes the object in the sense that the full becomes partial – we have now to understand, which is again a process, and that can only be partial and never full. Idea has to enter the reality of matter. So, for idea, the river is not yet a river, it is becoming a river all the time, never becoming a full river. This was not so earlier, before the rise of idea!

These contradictions are all the time being resolved, but never fully. Matter is full and complete but idea never. Matter in relation to idea is partial, but in itself is full and complete. But matter (object) is rendered incomplete the moment idea tries to grasp it, the motion is incomplete, it moves forward, beyond the grasp of idea, into infinity. An infinite was always there, but grasping, understanding is finite, and therefore has its own infinity: we understand and leave thinking that we have understood, while we actually grasp only the moment, and therefore the incomplete. The finality is a poor reflection; what is thought to be final is actually only a beginning.

The object that is grasped, thus, is a transformed object. It is a philosophized, conceptualized object: an object not because it is an object, but is an object in the presence of the subject, subjectivising the observer as well as itself, because the object came into being only after it gave rise to its opposite, i.e. the subject, an idea-producing object. Matter is all the time channelised through consciousness, thus greatly *limiting* itself. An idea-producing object is not a material form in the strict sense of the term, because it contains its own negation and opposite, and it is these that are grasped, and thus both dissolve as soon as they are grasped.

That is why grasping is an act, which can proceed only in denial: to understand, to accept, is to deny, to refute, is not to accept the existence of reality.

Matter henceforth proceeds under the watchful 'eyes' of the subject, more precisely under the ever deeper critical observation of idea, which often takes recourse to philosophy to grasp (reject! Negate) that which is foreign to it, and is at the same time the polar opposite of it. Idea is something that did not exist earlier, and therefore, matter 'Lived' quite 'peacefully'! But since the idea appeared out of it, it is being 'watched' constantly, being interfered with repeatedly. There is no doubt that the human practice is increasingly changing the shape of the material forms and creating new ones constantly.

But most of the matter is, of course, unchanged and unaffected in the above manner. Yet, interesting questions crop up. Matter is reflected in the brain and cause ideas to emerge. Matter is recreated so to say, in the brain as reflection/s, it is filtered, it must prove itself that it is what it is. It is matter, reality, it is what exists, but how do we know it, except through our brain (ideas)? The brain constantly penetrates matter with the help of idea (which also penetrates the brain), changes it in the course of cognition, uses, increasingly, the more efficient equipment and means of knowledge. Why should idea penetrate deeper, and spread wider, and use the material means as well as tools of knowledge in the form of knowledge)? That is because idea is imperfect. Is matter imperfect? That is the idea of idea. This category comes into existence only after idea emerges. Matter is all pervading. Perfection has no meaning.

So, comprehension and grasping of the world around must first render that world imperfect, incomplete. Comprehension is always imperfect, incomplete.

So, it is a transformed world that is reflected in idea. The world changes in comprehension: that is the inevitable conclusion.

Philosophy, Hegel and Concept of Matter

Marx set up Hegel's philosophy on its feet. In so doing, he did away with philosophy itself, because what was needed was its dialectics. Actually, in Hegel, philosophy is a derivative, a result of the method of dialectics and motion. Hegel's thinking is motion pure and simple, dialectics itself. That is why, we find polar opposites of idealism and materialism in Hegel, in easy and smooth, faintly perceivable transitions from one to the other. Therefore, *philosophy is not important in Hegel.* It is wrong to present him only as a philosopher. He was *a dialectician of the highest order.* Yet, he is the greatest philosopher history has produced. He was in fact ***the greatest abstractionist*** ever. He could abstract generalisation out of any motion. Nothing is stationary in his philosophy. All the concepts are constantly moving towards abstract and pure motion, getting converted into opposites and negations. That again is a tension in his thought that drives thought through the myriad of movement. Concept is his object of analysis (and synthesis). It does not matter whether the concept is material or ideal: part of a materialist philosophy or an idealist one. Its movement is primary, and that is what is analysed in order to discover dialectics. Movement is the rule of the existence. Motion is absolute, reality or idea relative. Motion in Hegel virtually assumes independent, absolute existence. Motion 'of what' is irrelevant in Hegel. That is why, the concepts move unfettered, almost like waves or particles at sub-atomic levels.

What happens when the concept moves? *And why does it move at all?* Because it is seeking out essence all the time. The concept is a changing entity, an abstraction, in fact. *It is an abstraction of motion itself.* Its constant becoming produces the endless phenomena, all the time enriching the essence. The concept is never fully formed, because by the time it acquires full conceptualisation, it is rendered something else; otherwise, it will be dead, and all the motion (motions) will come to a dead stop.

Time and history are the determining results of motion and dialectics. Dialectics is imperfection, the very source of motion. Time stands still in its motion, and motion is nothing but that point which is constantly moving. The stationary point is on the move all the time. There is nothing stationary, and there is nothing that is not converted into time, space and motion. Time is nothing but the measure as well as the reflection of dialectics.

Time slows down on earth; that is why, earth is earth. That is why, and that is how, we are able to talk of 'time'.

Motion is a concept. Of what? Of all that is which is not, moving at a point and it is the point that moves, which is the finest of movement, the minutest one, at the very edge of time, which is constantly receding and changing. How do you grasp a concept? You never catch hold of it because you are always working with it. The concept includes all the possible changes within the possible limits, but it is not possible to draw any perimeter or borderline because it is constantly shifting, moving away. To move away is to follow change, yet the concept all the time resists the movement. It is this tension that keeps the concept in shape, yet the shape is changing all the time, beyond the realm of the idea, rendering idea negated, and thus enriched.

The sciences are the granulated, crystallized forms of motion and of moving concepts. Motion zooms in on motions; therefore, motion disintegrates into motions, rendering it indiscreet. Once you enter the realm of motions, philosophy can't remain intact, because the relationships between matter and idea disintegrates. There is no place for idea, which dissociates into material essences of endless order, to be studied and synthesized by the sciences. Science is conceptualization at discreet levels, but it is also synthesis at non-discreet concept level. Science is the concept of becoming, of emerging and receding. *That is how science replaces philosophy.*

One is forced to study discreet motions because science is concrete. There are so many concretes now. The concept dissociates into the concepts, each of which is whirling around itself and into one another. The human body is nothing but motion of motions, and therefore of concepts of the material discretes.

Thus, the motions do not allow the philosophies to remain as such; the latter must merge with the reality of motions including both material and ideal.

Philosophy is rendered superfluous. Hegel was the last of the philosophers, though not in the strict sense of the term; philosophy was finally dissolved by Marx.

Industrial Revolution and Philosophy

The great industrial revolution of the 18th century began an era of natural sciences and all-round development of technology. Every enquiry now became concrete, ousting philosophical speculation from one area after another.

Why is philosophy not needed? Sciences riding on the new technologies, went deeper into the motions of various natural processes: heat, light, energy, magnetism, electricity, mechanics, biology, chemistry, physics, astronomy and so on.

Even the social fields were transformed into social sciences: economics and politics became sciences; earlier they were not sciences. Even logic, ethics, morality, etc. became sciences. Discoveries were made in growing numbers, almost by the day, and this is truer today in the conditions of the scientific and technological revolution (STR). Ideas emerged anew, not in general but as concrete conclusions and concepts. Concepts covered not general motion/transformation of the being but the concrete motions of concrete events, processes and points. The concept was dissolved into the concepts, the latter crystallizing out of the former.

The industrial world became a world of concepts. These concepts were not speculations and generalizations. They are scientific concepts emerging from concrete reality or realities. Each concept could be shown to have emerged from each concrete reality. Each material reality created concept, moving concept as a reflection of real motion of matter, of material motions. Science is nothing but the study of material motions. It does not *philosophize* at the stage of analysis. Philosophical generalization is needed only at the stage of synthesizing reality, and is thus shifted into the background. Philosophy, *for the first time,* takes a backseat.

New sciences proved incontrovertibly that ideas emerge from matter. Technologies helped this giant leap from speculation to concretization. Science is no doubt a system of concepts. But each concept is born out of concrete material reality, and precisely because of this method it is science. Science has reduced the distance between material reality and idea/concept. The distance continues to be reduced. You need not *speculate* on reality; it is there to be analysed and unveiled.

Science is not so much concerned with the question of the emergence of idea; production of ideas is only a derivative process, which takes the shape of a series of concepts. But the question of relationship of idea with reality or concrete process is not important for, central to scientific investigations.

Therefore, science replaces philosophy in one field after another.

Dialectical materialism (materialist conception of nature and history) discovers that what exists is matter, independent of consciousness. At the same time, matter gives rise to consciousness or idea at a certain stage. Sciences confirm this discovery.

Having discharged this function, dialectical materialism, as well as *philosophy in general, cease, in the main, to exist.* They crop up only from time-to-time to discharge certain functions, to tackle certain philosophical problems. *Philosophy in general is not needed any more.* It has been overthrown by the sciences: *dialectical materialism is the last philosophy, a philosophy that dissolves philosophy.*

Science is the study of dialectics and motion in the material world and in the consequent ideal world. It is not philosophy, because dialectics and study of motion/s is not philosophy.

All the subjects, all the sciences, including the natural and social ones, study concrete fields, and develop concepts as a consequence of these studies and discoveries. They deal with their object/field of study directly. They do not need the help of philosophy and speculation, no intermediary, no intervention.

The question may be posed whether those who study these fields and subjects do not need to follow a philosophy. For their concrete field, no. Abstract generalization is not needed any more. The object is very much there for them to grasp, unless of course they deny the very existence of the object of their study!

The scientists may speculate on other fields, but others are there to study them! So, this philosophy, particularly the idealist one, remains inapplicable. And therefore it is not philosophy. From this point of view, materialism is more applicable: the unknown in a branch of science is taken care of by investigations in that branch. Here again, no philosophy is needed in the speculative sense, because it is dissolved into scientific concepts, methods and technologies.

As established supremacy of matter is in constant flux, time settles down for concrete study. Therefore, change and motions are studied. But study of motion and dialectics is not philosophy at all.

Engels on Philosophy

Frederick Engels went deeper into the relationship between science and philosophy. He traced the development of modern research into nature. "Modern research into nature, which alone has achieved a scientific, systematic, all-round development, in contrast to the brilliant natural-philosophical intuitions of antiquity", dates from the development of modern bourgeois society.[1]

Here already Engels contrasts modern scientific research and natural-philosophical intuition. Natural scientists gradually were coming to realize that nature does not just exist but comes into being and passes away.[2] Various sciences were increasingly pointing to this reality.

In an interesting discussion on the relationship between the natural scientists and philosophy, Engels says that they still work under the concepts and categories from philosophy, which have already become outdated: "They are still under the domination of philosophy". They can't free themselves easily of it, whether bad philosophy or "a form of theoretical thought which rests on acquaintance with the history of thought."[3]

Then Engels makes the most interesting observation: "Natural scientists allow philosophy to prolong *an illusory existence* with the dregs of the old metaphysics. Only when natural and historical science has become imbued with dialectics *will all philosophical rubbish* – other than the pure theory of thought – *be superfluous, disappearing in positive science*".[4]

Philosophy disappears in positive sciences: that is the great revolution in human thought. Significantly, this statement was made way back in the 19th century. Much has changed since then, and science has covered unimaginable areas. The question of philosophy has become clearer than ever before. There is no doubt that *by dissolving philosophy, the industrial revolution has discharged a great historical function.*

With the quantum revolution and the new technological and scientific upsurge, several key philosophical questions are re-emerging, but in a different and changed setting and form. We will have the occasion to discuss them in the later pages.

NOTES

1. Frederick Engels, *Dialectics of Nature*, Moscow, 1976, p. 20. (emphasis added)
2. Ibid., p. 27.
3. Ibid., p. 210.
4. Ibid., p. 210, emphasis added.

2

Slowdown of Time, Thought-process and Flight of Idea/Philosophy

We are faced with the question as to how and why idea emerged. How it flies, moves around, why matter moves in time and space? Why these events happen on earth? The questions have a bearing on the discussions in other chapters. By answering these questions, we will be able to seek their further path in the context of the quantum revolution, their speed up, and discuss the dissociation of matter and its reorganization and transformation. In the present era, thought and matter are undergoing a revolution in their nature.

Here we will discuss things mainly with *slowdown of time* as the centre of the problem, because the crisis in human thought today is basically caused by acceleration of time and the consequent other developments. In the subsequent chapters we will be treating this very question step by step.

Why do we philosophize? Why is there thought-process at all? Why is something that stands totally in opposition to matter, to material reality in motion? Will it, the idea, merge with matter again, and become one with it?

This is a question that logically poses itself at some point or the other. It will have to be answered, at some time.

Let us go into the question of emergence of thought a little more deeply. This question has not been dealt with properly so far, except in derivative form. The 'why' and 'how' of it has not yet been answered or tackled properly. The 'why' of it is far more difficult to tackle than the 'how'.

It is quite clear that the earth and other planets have emerged due to a gradual and progressive slowdown of motions, processes and time: a slowdown of time has led to the emergence of various material processes and forms on the earth – physical, chemical, geological, biological and so on. Motions, and therefore time here, are nothing compared to those in the universe or space and within the atoms, compared to the motions and transformations of the particles. In other words, the material forms must lose their speeds, slowdown in time, to 'create' something; rather, for something to appear, motions have to become more leisurely. The events (processes, points) then happen more and more in an orderly fashion, sequentially. Atomic, electronic and other particulate spins/motions do not have clear sequences. Or, their sequences are too merged, borderless, and without proper 'histories'. Sequential, orderly events have each a certain history.

Thus, the events and developments on earth have moved in a totally opposed manner to that in the outer space. This will have a conflicting bearing in the context of the STR/ICR.

Our mentality, habits and consciousness are conditioned by the sequential history of everything and every object mentioned above.

But we are diverting somewhat from our line of argumentation. A slowdown helps the constituents of various objects, processes, etc. to emerge: the physical, the geological, the chemical, the biological, etc., constituted by the various sequences. A Cartesian, Newtonian world comes into being, and later a world outlook. The laws, categories and concepts crystallize in due course.

At a certain stage of evolution of living beings, their ability to reflect, and then to reflect in terms of ideas, emerge. Reflection is the law of nature. It assumes particular qualities in the living beings. They react and respond to the surroundings in certain ways, which are more active. Biological response to the surrounding events is quite complex. Physical bodies respond too, e.g. rusting of iron. Chemical bodies react in a more complex manner. Rusting also is a chemical reaction. More complex reactions involve a change in chemical, organic chemical and other kinds of configuration. This response is more organized and regular, orderly.

The elements, atoms, and molecules get time to establish bonds. And this takes place at a more leisurely pace. One changes or evolves into another. Electrons are exchanged in fixed number and fixed manner in a fixed situation. Complex but systematic orderly events and transformations take place in the biological systems.

Biological beings are motion of motions at multi-levels. A totality of qualitative changes takes place over millions of years. Chemical changes are taking place all the time.

The brain is a complicated unity of motions. Even the animal brain is highly complicated. It registers objects, events and processes. That means, the reaction and its result lingers on for a long time. This is a very important development in the different evolutions taking place on the earth. The brain is the centre, which can register, investigate, decide to respond. The brain begins to reflect, because of the high concentration of activities and motions. It is a complex of dialectics. Such a complex dialectics must result in qualitatively novel and different ways. With the slowdown of motion and dialectics, the dialectics itself becomes multilayered, highly complex and complicated. The endless inter-relations begin emitting ideas at a certain stage after reacting with the surrounding world. This is a very complex problem that needs to be gone into.

Slow-down of Time and Flight of Idea

What is really idea? Obviously, it is the agitated state of matter of brain when in contact with the surrounding reality. The complex of dialectics at a more relaxed pace needs more and highly complicated interactions for a material form to exist. For example, the biological form is the unity of sub-atomic, atomic, molecular, physical, chemical, biochemical and organic chemical, etc. motions. Any process at these levels is highly involved. Formation of complicated organic chemical molecules and interactions are very involved and proceed in so many states of increasing complexity.

Therefore, slowdown is the key to the complexity and stages of the processes of nature. That is why certain processes take place only on the planets like earth, and not on very hot mercury or 'boiling hot' sun. For ideas to emerge, certain leisurely, stage-wise, multilevel conversions are essential. Ideas may move with the speed of light, yet they lag behind the material processes.

Thus, *time,* or its loss, is a crucial factor in the emergence of earthly objects and processes. This is becoming apparent now after the information and communication revolution and electronics becoming the productive force. We are used to events on the earth, which are orderly, linear, each succeeding the previous one, processes and events being historical and historically determined.

It is such a world that the ideas first meet with. The interaction is further complicated. Idea/s must see and understand things and processes, catch hold of change, motion and dialectics. The problem here is that the idea does not contain the laws, motion and dialectics of matter. Yet it must contain them. It is only their reflection, and gradually acquires them and develops, as also its own dialectics, thus creating a complex whole world of totality of dialectics. Idea is not matter, and that is the greatest problem. Idea is *a break* with matter, it is being released from the latter all the time to really become idea, but never completely. It must *return* again and again to matter. Why, and what for? The problem is that idea is nothing but reflection (of matter). But it is a reflection that is growing and spreading in order to encompass matter. It reflects motion and dialectics, but it does not reflect them flat out. It has to penetrate material dialectics/motion all the time.

By nature, idea is independent, and therefore tries to go as far away as possible, even to the extent of denying the existence of its source. It can travel anywhere, even to the non-existent realities, trying even to be the sole reality. Yet, it is always material reality at its source. It even assumes its own independent source of motion, which is not really independent because it emanates from the activities of the brain through material reflection.

Why does idea travel so far? It is the product of brain activity, and as such has a garbled, imaginary motion. It is image. An image can travel anywhere and nowhere. It exists and does not exist. Images are made of reality and real reactions. The brain produces an endless series of reactions, reflections and images.

Image, imagination, idea cannot do what they really want, what they constantly endeavour-escape from their origin. Idea wants to be what it is: ideal reality, but it is not it: it is not ideal reality but material reality. *And that is why*, it is *no reality at all.* It is its own opposite, acts against itself, upon itself, transcends itself, and therefore returns to itself. It is an itself without its own self, without being itself. It collapses the moment it transcends itself. Transcending is an act of collapsing as well as going far out. But where? *Into what* does it collapse? *Towards* what does it go? The question is pertinent, crucial for the existence/non-existence of idea. Idea has come into being only for a brief moment, it is momentary, matter is ever present. Therefore, idea must collapse or go out into matter. Idea must always travel towards matter, endlessly, without ever meeting it. but idea cannot travel, or travel only briefly, and must take recourse to matter for its existence, its rejuvenation. Idea does not exist, it is constantly produced, reflected continuously, like sunrays reflected from earth.

Word (idea) must be lodged in the brain for its existence: it resides in and issues forth from its opposite. Thus its non-existence itself is existence. 'Word exists' – what does it mean? Where does it exist? In our brain (consciousness). Can the word go out into vacuum and survive? Impossible! The word is a certain configuration in the brain, say, of particles. Word can exist in print of image of electronics. But those again are the configuration of particles, representing something. Therefore, the word does not exist except in representation. But a tree or a brick is not a representation! It is what it is. Concepts flow into matter enriching themselves.

Idea/word/concept must, do, represent what exists, they never represent what does not exist. So, at a certain stage of its development, matter needs representation when its dialectics/time/motion slows down, when its dialectics becomes increasingly complicated; idea therefore represents, is synonymous with, the slowdown of dialectics, when dialectics reaches the verge of mechanics, without really becoming mechanical.

Idea: Withdrawal from Matter

At that moment, idea takes leave of matter.

So, idea is reductionism in time but a complication in space.

Now let us imagine ourselves, rather our idea, in a slow time area. This area will have orderly structure and well-ordered linear, uni- or multi-linear, events. It is full of local histories.

If we are moving rapidly in time, this orderliness of space and its pieces, arrangement of pieces, is not possible. Once things slow down, ordered structures come into existence. Then idea emerges. For it, motion is superficial or does not exist. Idea can't penetrate the surroundings, except touching the surface and returning. Then, gradually, it begins to go deeper than the surface, and 'understand', i.e. generalize, the contents and the essence. The more it penetrates deeper into matter, the more it generalizes.

Idea reduces, slows down, time to grasp, assimilate and encompass matter. Matter must be orderly to reveal itself, and its motions. Thus, motion can be grasped only if it slows down, rapid motions can't be assimilated and reflected at the initial stages of ideas.

Idea moves more rapidly than the world, far too rapidly for it to be able to understand the latter. Idea means that which has no limits. Idea moves instantly, from object to object, in the vacuum, around the earth, out in the space. It has no limits on its movement and nature.

Why is it so? How to explain it? Idea moves–anywhere to anywhere–means what? It means the brain makes copies of the present and past, which then can penetrate/move anywhere. Idea is a copy, a reflection, and therefore freed of the limits of time and space, it transcends all the limit. That only means there is a whole world of images in the brain, yet freed of the limitations of physical brain. Since idea is image, it is material, physical. Yet it moves immaterially.

Idea is constant transcendence of the existing, it is meant to transcend. There has to be something that opposes, denies and turns away from everything other than itself. This other has its own world, where every law must be violated, because idea does not recognize any laws. Time, space, direction, history, motion etc–everything, every concept should be, must be smashed, otherwise, the other cannot prove to be the other.

We the consciousness are all the time withdrawing from matter, as if in an antagonism. These transcendental motions also keep smashing the concepts, which are a hurdle to the motion of idea. Nothing must exist other than idea. We do something because of our ideas, very productive, original ideas–that is how human beings try to dominate nature. Material objects are just resting places, for idea, before it flies off into nowhere–at least tries to. It is here to nowhere. Why does it rest on material points? Because, idea moves through concepts. Concepts must originate, evolve, be completed.

Transcendence is a peculiar act as far as idea is concerned. It is and it is not. Concept is taken as devoid of content, from which it has emerged. That is the only way it can liberate itself from matter and become idea. Having been deprived of content, idea can move anywhere anytime, because it is unbound, freed of limitations. Concept becomes non-concept. Otherwise it will have to depend upon material forms. So, all the concepts must become what they are not, the non-concept, and establish their domain, a denial which is abstraction in the purest form, and therefore the very essence of existence. None can put a finger on it because it is the non-existent, the supreme form of existence. By emptying itself, depriving itself of content, it reduces, that is grows into the very essential abstraction. An abstraction is not bound by time and space, and is therefore dematerialized. Idea, particularly idea in motion, is unearthly, not suited to its limitations. Idea has always *flown away from the earth*, since time immemorial. We hear voice only as reflection, *away from* something.

Thus, slowdown produces an amazing contradiction, refusing to be resolved. The *slowdown produces its anti-thesis, the fastest, instant, speeds.* Only limitation of time-space produces the limitless, unbounded energy, no other. Increase the speeds, and you lose the idea.

Life is bounded, yet it cannot be so. It absorbs the essence of existence into itself, the limitless. Limited life absolutises itself. The absolute, the infinite, is its only limitation. Life becomes the vehicle of transcendence, and idea its form.

That is why, something grows into nothing, at least in appearance. Idea is a nothing, growing out of something. We have already seen that idea is nothing, it does not exist. So, that which is nothing grows out of something. This nothing reflects everything. But nothing grows everything out of nothing; this nothing keeps trying to grow out of nothing.

It is one of the strangest quirks of nature that that which does not exist (idea) moves instantly around the universe, uninhibited. To conceptualise, to abstract, since idea does not exist, it moves and is in motion without limitation, without observing laws, yet reflecting them. Is it motion then? It is abstraction of motion and dialectics.

Had idea existed, its motion would have been full of hurdles, interfered with, cut off repeatedly, inhibited, unfree, slow and orderly, regularized, historicized. But it does not even have speed, it cuts across time, it is instant, is in fact without speed.

Had idea existed, it could not have moved, would have lost motion, yet retained dialectics, and that is why is an instant, and in that instant covers the universe.

How can this be? Is it not a contradiction in terms? How can dialectics be retained and motion be lost? Or, vice-versa; that is precisely the point. Idea is a peculiarity of the universe, a violation of all its laws. It is a negation of everything. The dialectics consists in its being a non-being. Its motion does not affect anything! Idea may hop here to the moon to distant stars to the South Pole in an instant, and yet nothing changes. This is because it is not accompanied by technology. The advent of technology changes everything. And then everything changes from here to the moon to the South Pole. But that is another matter.

How does one analyse the travel of idea to the moon? This travel has motion, has dialectics. Yet, there is no dialectics because it does not travel at all! The dialectics consists of not travelling at all. And since it does not travel, there are no dialectics. The dialectics consists in there being no dialectics. It is the dialectics of being and non-being. It is the dialectics of non-existence, and therefore, there is no motion. The moon remains totally unaffected even if the six billion-plus inhabitants of the planet earth just think about it together! The idea is reflected back from the moon without causing anything at all because it has really not been reflected! What has taken place has not taken place at all! But what has really taken place is a collective thinking, affecting history through materialization of idea.

But idea cannot travel for ever, it has no independent existence; in fact, as we have seen, it has no existence at all. It has no energy of its own, no dialectics, no motion; yet it has all of them. This contradiction takes it far and wide, yet nowhere! It goes far out in the infinite space, yet remains where it is, rooted as it is, without moving a single point and moment. Therein lies its dialectics.

But how is it possible? What is the mystery of thought/idea/consciousness? Consciousness contains a whole world within it that exists outside, but does not exist at all, because it, consciousness, is derived from this world. The limitless consciousness (idea) fall back repeatedly on matter, on what really exists. Non-existence, the other, is not possible without existence, without the 'this'.

Idea is a peculiar culmination of motion of matter: the finite becoming infinite through self-transcendence. While material motion continues, matter comes to an end at a certain point in a qualitative annihilation through reorganization, which from now on looks upon itself by quitting itself. Reality quits (is jettisoned by) reality, which then on engulfs the entire reality. A reflection has no time and space. Its existence solely depends on existence: break the mirror, and reflection simply disappears. But 'break' the reality?! Not possible. It simply does not disappear. It only appears, and disappears only in its appearance. Motion is replaced, in case of idea, by the notion of motion and dialectics. While the mirror reflects the object, does it reflect its laws of motion and dialectics? No.

Does this apply to idea/consciousness? Yes and no. Idea is reflection as well as non-reflection. By travelling afar, it loses contact with dialectics existing outside, the reflections become fainter till they disappear and collapse. Therefore, and that is why, it returns to the material origin in a reassertion of materialist dialectics. Why does the idea/consciousness travel wide? To reconstruct itself, to 'celebrate' its liberation, to go 'wherever' it likes, out into the infinite, because the infinite is the human being's liberation, unfettered endeavour of unfettered freedom. That is the problem. The finite kills idea; the infinite liberates it fully. Therefore, it must reach the end first (!), which is always receding. You can reach the very end of the universe, or galaxy at once, yet you must bounce back in order to really begin the travel, to start reaching it!

Thus, there is double self-transcendence, which now includes the entire universe at the starting point. The stars, and the river and the tree are now inside the brain.

But the star, the tree, the river, etc. are immaterial. The material is subsumed within the idea as concepts and evened out, wiping out their existence. The material becomes immaterial, absolutised, suspended, to fall down any time, which also is a rise up all the time.

Therefore, material is nothing for idea, the ideal, because the ideal is non-material. But, since it is non-material, it has to be material or transformed into the material.

Idea travels out into nothing in search of empty spaces, which are really material spaces. Time is its, idea's, only carrier as well as result, because time must be lost–both expended and done away with, because time is constraints on idea.

Why does idea/consciousness travel out, instantly, away, independent of space and time? This question has not yet been answered. Why does idea need to go out, and far out. This is because of its anti-matter and non-matter character. What is idea/consciousness? It is the negation of matter, its function is to make matter cease function, to deny its very existence. This is natural, appropriate, historical. Idea has, in fact, no other function than to overcome reality. If matter has an independent function, rather existence, why not idea?

Idea is the essence of that which exists, or rather that which does not exist, both being the same thing. That is why it resorts to concepts. If it (consciousness, idea) is the concentrated expression of that which does not exist, this non-existence must be, has to be, expressed through that which is not matter. It does not matter whether matter exists or not.

Image is compressed and inverted matter, in an act of negation and inversion. Suppose, you enter inside a mirror; do the laws operate there? Is the reflection real? Laws do not operate and reflection is a denial, negation of the real. Consequently, you may move frictionless.

Idea is antithetical to the human body, to the brain itself, a denial which is self-denial, to free itself of all the trappings. Idea, so to say, is in the wrong place. Its real place is in the ideal world, the endless conceptual, abstract nothing, where only existence is the non-existence, the transcended existence. It is in and towards the 'not' that idea moves, towards the negative, to render itself positive. It is little realized that, like matter, idea too needs its own existence, which in its case is the negation of existence, thus providing it an advantage over (material) reality. True, idea has emerged, come out of the material; but it has come out in order to leave the material to its natural 'death'. The 'natural' world of idea is the real one from its pole, the only one, and therefore it moves instantly. If it did not move instantly, it would fall back into matter to be annihilated, that is, to be enriched. But it is already enriched, and can move heaven and earth, and therefore is far superior to anything that exists.

Movement of idea is nothing but an achievement of no motion. No reference point, no anything, because it penetrates, comes around, goes far beyond anything that exists, i.e. does not exist. If it has no reference point, nothing exists for it. This self-illusory motion is the most existing one in the universe, rendering the universe non-existing. Idea only moves, that is all, and that means it does not move a single point, because had it moved in this fashion it would have disappeared! Into nowhere! But that does not happen. It comes back to itself, to the site of its own origin, through self-transcendence.

But what is idea, consciousness? An idea is about something, consciousness is of something. Therefore, idea cannot be independent in itself, confined to itself. It is about a material object or about a concept or idea, material or ideal. An idea is an idea because it is not an idea. It is unable to follow its own logic, which, really speaking, does not exist.

If we follow the logic of instant motion of idea, it lives that instant. It covers everything that exists that instant. Since it covers everything that instant, nothing must exist thereafter. But then the job of idea too is over after the instant. But idea exists, wants to exist, for ever. Something or nothing, this or the other must exist for it to exist. In the course of motion, something becomes nothing, and then must become something, for the sake of idea at least. And this must become that or other for the same reason. Otherwise, how will idea propagate, move? The concept must arise as the carrier of idea, which in itself, is a concept. This is conceptual framework, a receptacle for idea, a habitat for consciousness. Concept rolls on loaded with idea. Thus, idea is about and within the concept. It is trapped. Concept steers clear of all that exists, which means nothing exists for the concept. The concept of concept is nothingness, for if there is something, its movement will be hampered, free idea will stop developing, rather start developing, because for development, something must exist. So, the concept of concept is all-embracing, embracing nothing at all. Motion is infinite and instant, and therefore does away with all the conceptualization. To conceptualize is to realize the non-existence of concepts. Idea overcomes concepts, thus absolutising itself. Absolutization and abstraction is a process of withdrawal from the world, including the world of concepts.

Therefore, idea/consciousness is about concepts, their presence or absence. This is the easiest way of dissolution, because dissolution of material form renders dialectics material and process-ridden, steps-ridden. The idea of concept is a conflict where the concept is sought to be transformed into idea. An idea is an infinite concept stretching from nowhere to nowhere, and therefore everywhere. This infinity is instant, and the instant stretches to the forever. This is the only way idea exists, which is nothing but the form of not existing.

But the point is that idea need not exist, for it has not come into existence, it just exists. The human brain simply jettisons consciousness, and consciousness (idea) simply rejects brain, which is too small for it, and therefore it must find a 'better' receptacle if at all, and that is somewhere 'out there'. Idea has never accepted and 'respected' brain, it has always rejected the latter. This has been the main history of human consciousness. So, it has always, all the time looked for a better idea ('brain') or for the Idea. The latter, the idea is an infinitely inflated ego of our consciousness, refusing to be part of anything but the Idea.

Nature of Philosophy

Says Hegel, philosophy does not deal with a determination that is non-essential, but with a determination that is essential.[1] Great words indeed! Incisive ones.

Philosophy is constantly unravelling the essence. "The abstract or unreal is not its element and content, but the real." Philosophy deals with that which has life within itself. It is the process that creates its own moments, and goes through them all. Movement is its positive content and truth.

One point that emerges here is that abstract is unreal, dead. Life, movement is real. Movement is positive, says Hegel. Therefore, philosophy should address motion.

This is one point. Another point. Philosophy does not deal with that abstract which is unreal. The real is that which is in motion.

Here, by implication. Hegel provides a different definition and subject content of philosophy than is normally given. Philosophy is seen to be dealing with process, and not with matter-idea relationship, or with idea to matter or matter to idea relation.

This shows that motion (dialectics) is prime in Hegel's thought, other questions secondary.

Movement of Concept

Concept has a beginning and an end. That is why it is a formed concept. Since it has an end, it must have evolved. We in fact begin with a concept. That is a very low level of material experience, hardly at all. So, while being a great advance, it is, at the same time, a continuous movement backwards *because we deal with a readymade concept.* The constant use of such a concept keeps us behind times and holds back the development of the concept itself. To move forward is in fact to move back. While we move forward in our time, we move back in material time. This is a serious crisis, a crisis of consciousness; consciousness is always in crisis. That is how it develops; it is always, almost, in a critical stage giving way to non-consciousness

Consciousness relapses into the unconscious, the non-conscious, the material: the three are different from each other. This relapse is often a collapse.

So, the concept is in motion. It has a beginning and an end. What is in between? Motion, change and movement. The end is also in motion. Without that it cannot come into being, take shape. Therefore, the concept is always in motion, is changing all the time.

Thus, an important, almost the most important, tool of knowledge and reflection of the material world is the changing concept. It is with this tool that we approach the world, whose reflection it is. Here we come across a whole complicated system of interconnections.

As a tool of knowledge, concept is very complicated, a non-being. The child and the adult begin to know the world through the concepts. It is a tool, a medium to approach the world. We begin with a fully formed concept, a given, not paying attention to its history and limitations. To begin with, the concept helps us to work with the world, yet we do not know what we know. It is only a medium.

We examine the world through it. This empty concept is full of meaning and content, yet it has no meaning apart from the world it is reflecting.

But we do not know whether the concept is real or not, whether reflection or not. It is a given reality for us without our realizing it, it is the world itself for us: a tree, a river, a rock, food, water, etc. That is how we begin our journey: from non-existence to existence, from existence to deeper reality. We are helpless without it/them. Therefore, human beings cannot live as much without concepts as without food. Concept of food is as much a necessity as the food itself (or river or tree, etc.). So, we move from the concept of food to food itself, which can only sustain its carrier (concept). So, the movement is from food to the concept of food to food again.

The object and its concept move in opposite directions, each assuming independent existence, enriching each other all the time, coming in mutual contact from time to time, which is a form of dialectical motion. The concepts evolve into a world of ideas.

Concepts evolve as much forward as back into time and space. What we come across is the end result of a process, the present of the process, that is, the end of it; we always meet the end: the end of the reality, the end-result and develop further.

NOTES

1. See, G.W.F. Hegel, *Phenomenology of Mind,* Para 47 of Preface.

3

Polar Motion of Idea

Philosophy finds its highest (and the last) reflection in Hegel, seeking to dissolve all the individual consciousness in one totalized infinite consciousness, yet which needs, at some point the materiality of the world/existence to seek its own origins and enrichment, and as its receptacle. Idea is now in a free fall, uniting and enriching itself as part of the new found objectivity, thus disintegrating into constituent origins, putting consciousness in deep crisis.

Idea in Polar Motion

Idea in its longer version tries to absolutize the pole it constitutes, both to the concept and to matter. A pole without polar opposition has no reference, and has to create fresh pole/s. Idea moves in polar opposites; yet it tries to shed, negate and grow out of the other pole, absolutize it and itself and thus grow out of polar tension. Solution of the contradiction, detensionization of the tension, absolutizes idea into an all-pervasive non-reality; at least it endeavours to be so. Thus, it is rendered unreal and for it the world itself is unreal.

The absolutized idea is concentrated expression of all the ideas, of the pole that sheds its other, an aim, a destination, which though is no destination, the idea wants to achieve in order to stay afloat. And stay afloat it must, in order to avoid a rapid fall. The fall of the idea is the fall into reality. It is only through knowing that the idea exists. It knows 'something', that is its other, its other pole, which it constantly tries to annihilate, through knowing, and consequently (and simultaneously) identifying with it. Polar annihilation is identification, a recognition of the reality, which in fact is its denial.

The polar movement, the polar alternation and transitions, are complex processes, not only annihilative but also creative. They are constant flip-flop of change of places, producing an intricate pattern of thought-lines.

Idea constantly creates poles, aspects, shades and sides and so on, which may or may not exist. The flight of idea is through its own polar opposites; its fall in flight and unity with reality is through opposition with its cause of origin, the material substratum.

Idea is itself a pole; the longer the version, that is the existence of idea, the greater the need for oppositional poles and tensions, so as to keep it suspended. That is how concepts exist, as they are. But they change and develop as they fall (into reality). So, a fall into reality disintegrates idea (concept), which is not itself then. Its own opposites are not enough. Concept must draw fresh impetus from non-idea to be reconverted into idea.

The longer version remains suspended through internal tension. It must keep on developing on its own, must create fresh poles, must postpone its own disintegration as long as possible, that is, it must conceptualize till infinity.

That is precisely the nature of concept: it tries to maintain itself, remain, keep going, perpetuate itself. A concept is an infinity in itself but it is extremely finite precisely because it is a concept. It remains forever, yet it cannot remain forever, it must evolve in order to remain. It cannot remain without evolving because then it will be dead and stop evolving. But remaining has two forms of existence: one we have just described; the other is remaining as it is, developing, stretching itself into the infinity to encompass and overcome the reality, which is a non-reality for it. It, the concept, stretches itself through tension, whose solution should be postponed for ever. For if the tension is resolved, the concept dives. Thus, the tension is for a suspended stretch of existence, and not for resolution, because that will lead into something else, the opposite, which has already been denied through negation.

That is the life, the living source, the superiority of idea: an idea (reflection) is an idea (separation) because it is an idea (concept). It is an alienated reality and therefore the opposite of it (reality). Motion, that is, abstraction is its life; motion keeps it away from matter, helps develop it, and justify itself through non-justification of non-concept. Therefore it is a non-concept because concept strictly speaking is a reflection of reality. And concept (idea) tries not to reflect, to escape from where it has emerged. Conceptualization is non-conceptualization–the former justifies self-motion, the latter the annihilation of any self-justification, providing self-motion, as now there is no reference point, and therefore no justification. Motion does not need justification. Justification is a relationship with that another which should be converted into this, into non-existence to keep idea afloat. This is the ideal idea, an idea of idea, a conceptual idea, which reflects idea as concept.

From conceptualization to self-conceptualization: such is the movement of idea. From self-conceptualization to self-justification: such is the constant self-motion (existence) of idea. Idea, by its very nature, is self-explanatory, beyond explanation. Explanation is a reference, a relationship of comparison. But that defies the idea of idea. In order to defy explanation, idea must exist, and to exist, it must deny all that exists. In order to preserve itself, it must annihilate all that exists. In order to be self-explanatory, it must deny all connection with reality, and thus assert explanation on its own. His infinity is its dead-point.

As a superior dialectics, idea has to convert itself into reality or existence, its false form. It takes the non-reality of reality from reality, and converts it into its own reality. Concept stretches forward, as dialectics becomes infinite. The longer version becomes infinite. Idea becomes the only reality. It becomes victorious. Yet, it loses everything to reality.

Why do we think? In order not to think. Because if we think, then it would be we, the matter, who would think. In that case, we would not be we. So, we do not think as we are, we think only as we are not. We as concept are detached from we as non-concept. 'We' is the point of contact and self-negation between we as we and we as the other of we, the non-we. Thinking begins only after that: only then we refer to thus freed concept; otherwise, it would be the bodily self that would be referred to.

It is the freed 'we' that does the purest thinking. It is the motion personified, dialectics at the dazzling best. The only problem is that it must stretch infinitely, which really never happens, and which always happens within a concept constantly striving to be the concept.

The beauty of (and problem with) thought is its infiniteness, its ever-presence. And that means it does not exist at all outside itself, and so never goes out of itself. Yet, its whole existence is not within but outside, by bringing down the wall between within and outside. The very question as to where does thought reside is an affront to it!

'Free' Movement of Idea: Negation of Matter

In one form of its existence, idea is a pole to itself, moving out of itself and through itself. Its source and laws of motion reside as itself. Nothing must exist in this world of realities. Otherwise, idea can't simply move freely, it must then come into contact with constant hurdles. Matter, reality, etc. are an impediment to the motion of idea, which moves endlessly if there are no material objects around. Otherwise, idea will have to contemplate, that is slow down its motion, and therefore lose its life as dialectics. Contemplation is confrontation with reality, and that is not necessary for the infinite and timeless concept. Concept has no time. In fact, material existence is not at all essential for the motion of idea; otherwise, how can it traverse the whole universe in no time! At least, that is the inherent nature, the essence, idea considers. Idea means total exclusion of matter, otherwise, it is not needed, as matter/reality already exist.

Reality is essential for idea, but not for its motion. Idea is superficial to matter, and is not needed for its existence at all. But matter comes to life as a concept of idea only after idea has emerged out of it. This peculiar dichotomy affords an independent motion to idea, to concept. Idea by nature is in motion. Motion is its greatest ally. Without motion, there is no idea. Concepts are its stages and states. Infinity equals idea/concept. Its material opposites are replaced by ideal, conceptual poles. Idea by its very nature refuses to be finite. Otherwise, how can it contemplate the distant stars and the nearby rocks *all at once*? Space and time lose their meanings and determinations in concept and are at the same time find their meaning in it. To equalize them, to dissolve the space and time is to deny them their existence into a shapeless idea. Abstraction and absolutization are the most important forms of existence of idea.

Idea cannot exist and operate at mechanical speeds and levels. It is against its nature. Idea is antithetical to matter in every respect. Therefore, its 'escape velocity" is very high! The very first reaction of idea is to escape out, as if liberated. It does operate at mechanical speeds, but only as slow painful reflection. A reflection is no idea in the proper sense of the term. The slowdown of idea, to adjust to the mechanical, excruciatingly slow speeds of the earthly world, is against its very nature and habit. The speeds have virtually come to a standstill on the earth. Hence the complications and complexities in idea. Everything is so slow, so clear, so spread out, both in time and space that idea finds it difficult to discharge its function, that of reflection, which also is too easy at these speeds and in this limited space. Therefore, the very first endeavour of consciousness is to operate at astronomical levels, in opposition to the earthly levels. It is only in developed consciousness that certain earthly order is to be seen.

Therefore, at first, idea expresses the essence of existence as non-existence and non-being. The essential thing for idea is to rise above material forms of the earth, and to meet out and unite with the abstract reality as opposed to the earthly reality.

Human history has been that of conscious adjustments with and of reflection of the earthly material order. It is this order which has been sought to be projected into the celestial bodies.

Idea Comes Back: Determination as Material Reality

Idea escapes from reality, from matter, and goes out into the space, universe, into the 'nowhere'. But where is the nowhere? Idea goes out to what? Why does it have to return at all? Is it ever able to destroy its material pole?

By going out into the space, into the abstract and absolute, idea is actually approaching matter. It has nowhere to go: "from frying-pan to fire", that is its condition! Out into nowhere is the infinite matter, with endless forms of space and time. The nowhere is in fact everywhere, and nothing is always made of something. The empty space in fact is a vast space, made of infinite number of spaces; absence of time is nothing but a particular instant and several particular instants.

Therefore, idea cannot, by any means, travel in vacuum, into nowhere. Its tendency is towards 'nowhere', but since there is no nowhere, it is always moving into somewhere and something. Its 'unlimited' liberation is not absolute liberation, it is actually a liberation *into* something, it is a constant unity with that which is sought to be avoided. Thus idea can exist only in unity with matter, and as a result of matter.

Idea is constantly approaching matter in its endeavour to get away from it. Absolutization and abstraction, acquiring of instant existence unites idea with the essence of matter, dissolving the opposite poles: idea is a pole absolutized (slowdown is a different level of return to matter) equal to and unified with essence as the absolutization of matter. For human beings and their collective consciousness, nothing seemingly exists outside, and everything exists as and through nothing as the essence of existence, because it is supposed nothing needs to exist for consciousness, which has no existence apart from itself. It is thus a collective ego, pitting itself against matter, which it tries to reduce to 'ashes'! For if consciousness is superior, then nothing else needs to exist; once there is the existence, the other is redundant. Yet, collective consciousness is the best reflection of totality of matter in constant motion.

That is how human consciousness proceeds; for it to proceed, it assumes vacuum, absolute nothingness. If it encounters anything, that is set aside as, transformed into forms and concepts of idea/consciousness. Consciousness is always self-defeating, self-contradictory, conscious of itself, because there should be no other.

Yet, it is precisely this other that consciousness flies into, because it is the consciousness, all the time, *of something*. If it is consciousness of itself, then that too is something as the ultimate reflection of the absolutized space-time.

Consciousness, more particularly idea, in its quest for infiniteness, identifies more and more with the infinite reality, without realizing it. Even concept stretches infinitely, thus becoming all-embracing, which is nothing but engulfing of reality in the dissolution of its own pole, which is an unconscious constant search for its other pole infinitely. Polar dialectics of self-justification and abstraction converts these poles into identity, thus seeking for a polar opposite.

Idea thus constantly means its source of origin, enriching itself. Dialectics of motion is such that quest for independence, liberation and abstraction becomes one for truth, which constantly thrusts itself as moments of objectivity 'out there'. Suspense of suspension disintegrates into unity of reality: idea gests a firm material foothold through denial and negation. Dialectics is conversion of opposites. Idea is never able to go out of itself, and out of its material shell. It endeavours to return to itself; in fact, it only succeeds in reflecting what is out there, even if as what is not there. Its denial of reality (matter) is actually an affirmation of the latter.

Absolute absolutization absolutizes the non-absolute, the moment, that is idea, which is just as connection. Thus, this absolutization reveals its relative nature, the non-absolute absolutization, a conversion into the momentary, a momentary infinity, which is only a moment between existence and non-existence. Absolutization is destruction of self-moment, an affirmation of what exists as and through its non-affirmation, which falls flat on the tangible affirmation. The escape is an affirmation of that which should not be, because the escape is from it. Relative absolutization is this; the escape then into something, again a relative absolutization. The absolutization is always relative, and therefore idea is always a non-idea. It is relative to something and there is non-idea for every idea. Therefore, idea is never free, it always moves in and through non-idea.

Idea has everywhere to go and nowhere to go; it returns to itself, i.e. to its material point of origin. Thus, it returns to its self. It thus begins reflecting. The abstract becomes concrete. It had been hovering over the concrete, overcoming all the forms, projections, shapes and motions. It had achieved the unity and dissolution of motions.

Suddenly, it falls into the concrete, loses its momentum. It must now know, and know precisely that which it denied so long. There is no ideal idea. Consciousness is material. Consciousness, by becoming conscious of itself, loses its consciousness, and becomes a material force. Consciousness is 'consciousness' till it is not conscious of itself. In the movement it is conscious, it is transformed into reality. Reality is a negation of its negation. Idea self-transcends into that which does not need idea.

Slowdown of Idea: Fall into Materiality

This is crucial. Idea does need reality, material reality, very badly. But material reality does not need consciousness or idea. This is extraordinary. Idea moves among objects for its own meaning. Human being (brain-mind-idea or consciousness) sits at the bank of the river (water), and contemplates. But the river never sits at the bank of idea and contemplates! Quite extraordinary! Why is it so?! This is because the river does not need consciousness for its existence.

Contemplation is both superior and inferior. It needs reflection, without which it is not. It needs something to be reflected. So, even the fullest idea is empty, and the empty concept is full to the brim of the material reality.

But reflection is only a reflection. It must move, and move into the essence, deeper. And therefore idea must become one with matter, the poles must identify and dissolve. Absolute identity is grasping, assimilation of matter.

Idea must slow down, become richer and thus and through this, must lose its separate identity, which was never separate. By moving away from matter and out, it lost its richness, it was empty comtemplation and speculation. By returning to matter and moving among its forms, it becomes enriched.

Idea thinks about itself, *which is simply not possible.* Thinking about itself is to think about something. But, in abstract, thinking thinks that it is thinking about pure thought, nothing to do with absolute and abstract world, about the world beyond. Thought thus constantly negates itself. Even if you close your eyes, thoughts keep coming (and going), i.e. they keep moving. This movement is floating on and in nothing. If the collective consciousness does the same thing, i.e. keep its eyes closed, idea (s) will keep floating and moving. On and to what ? The idea moves from one object to another. Thus, the objects as resting places of idea as subjects, pure figment of imagination and reflection. As imagination, they do not exist, as reflection they substitute themselves; in both cases they existed, but now, at the moment, need not exist. They have already set the idea in motion, which now des not need any of them; but only their images. An image is an idea but is born out of material non-idea, which is not a formula and abstract 'thing'. Idea is never without a structure, shape and size, and yet it has no structure, shape and size, really speaking.

Contemplation transforms the real into the unreal. Thought never contemplates the object as it is, as material reality. Thought contemplates the object and in the process rejects it, to transform it. To think, about object, is to reject it because the latter is never covered, yet it is covered in its abstract negation, an image taken out of the source. Thought contemplates object not as it is but as it itself proceeds towards it, as it appears to reveal. Contemplation is not an exact copy but a process of revelation. Hence the need to proceed from surface to the essential elements, the totality constituting the essence. If the real remains the real, there is no thought. If the real produces its exact image, as in a mirror, it is dead, without motion.

Idea, thought, has to take recourse to images because subjectivity produces friction and motion. And it is motion that reveals the reality. Motion, in other words, is nothing but a process that reveals the endless reality. Thinking reveals not only what is being thought (about) but also that which is yet to be revealed. Revelation is a subjective process, to which the object yields in the form of thought.

The absence of the objects, their conversion into images, helps idea move from point to point, gather motion and reveal dialectics. Thus, idea has to move from (material) object to object, but not as object; the objects must first be converted into subjective, ideal images/ reflections.

Idea lives and develops in a world of object-caused images, as abstractions, but idea thinks the images are caused by its own superior thinking. It is superior thinking alright but not detached from the material objects or world; rather is dependent on that world. Images create their own world separate from the real world and provide the idea with the justification of its alienation from and opposition to the real world, which is sought to be denied. The abstractions accelerate in motion in an unprecedented manner. In fact abstraction means unlimited motions. Hence the opposition to the tangible. Direct object reduces motion, and thus the operation of dialectics. Dialectics becomes mechanical, revealing hardly anything; even if it reveals something, lot of synthesis is involved. Revelation is analysis, splitting off endless series of aspects and tendencies, unravelling motion.

Withdrawal from matter is its real revelation through the unreal. Material, tangible objects are always a hindrance to the understanding of reality whose concept is split in the idea. The reality of idea and of the real approach each other from opposite directions. In the course of splitting, idea contemplates the idea of the object, and not the object itself. Idea is comfortable with its own image, which in fact is the image of the real. Object is first copied and converted into a comprehensible form, and then contemplated upon. We see objects at the cost of objects, i.e. as images. It is an attempt to justify idea.

That is how, idea has to move around in a world of objects and material reality. It cannot move independently. Independently, idea does not exist. Concept provides a field of activity, a basis, a subjective basis for material activity in converted form. The result is a transformation of the image of the real, which is constantly emitting images.

We 'see' a thing. What we see is an interaction between eye, brain and the objects. Objects interact with objects. Here subjective and objective interact with real objects. Images are objectified. Without objectification, there no is thought-process. But objectification produces subjective images, i.e. an understanding of the object(s). You have to understand the object. Do you deny the existence of the object? Yes and no. No through yes. The object must be made to cease existence to be understood as object. The process imparts absolute existence to idea. Idea admits object by denying it. Idea exists in and through the object. Idea selects an object among many to reside in; therefore, an object, every object (reality) is a receptacle, a residence or habitat of idea. Idea exists because there are so many objects here, there, everywhere, with and without space, now here, now there, not here, not there, present and/or absent. That is how, that is where idea resides, in space and time. Idea needs space first, then time.

But idea is no stationary phenomenon. It must move on. Object first here and then there is too limited a receptacle, narrow space, too narrow for idea, for limited period of time, for a certain fixed period. But if time is instant, idea finds itself nearer to it. But that poses a threat to idea itself by destroying the receptacles.

Idea Among Objects

An idea cannot be an idea if it resides in an object. To say that this is a stone or a river or a tree has no meaning, because for an idea there cannot just be a tree only or trees only. There must be much more, many more. Idea means motion. Therefore, idea means an endless series of objects or processes, ultimately absolutising things.

Idea should be flitting here and there, flitting across beyond time and space. Therefore, it needs an infinite number of objects for free play. Idea must move quickly from one to another, freeing itself of receptacles. In the process it must try to abstract and absolutize itself, become idea in itself, free, without hurdles, needing no space, only time.

This no is yes, because all this happens within the collection, constellation of objects. Idea moves out, yet moves within the habitats in its endeavour to liberate itself, yet remaining easily within the spatial confines, where it collapses and disappears.

But it cannot disappear; in fact, the collapse and the disappearance is the deepening of the content and essence, particularly the latter. Idea moves to the essence, of reality. In ocher words, it goes away from it. Idea, as we said, cannot remain with, reside in one object alone. It is anti-object, its exact opposite, its negation. The moment of negation is that of the generalization, which nothing but the denial of the objective reality. The denial (negation) involves refusal to see (recognize) this tree and that stone, and river that side. We see a tree because so many things exist beside it and beyond, including nothingness which is something unseen as well as something seen and transcended. Every seeing, observation is transcendence. Seeing is seeking another habitat or residence.

But generalisation is a function of idea (concept), and therefore does not reside in the object; generalization takes place outside the object but inside the essence of 'the object/s', but reaching simultaneously the very core or exxence of it, if the object is taken to mean the general concept. Here there is a conflict between the object and its essentiality and generalization. Thus the dialectics of motion of concept/object takes place only in the reality of the essence, in the essential abstraction, and therefore out of everything, thus at the same time residing in everything; concept identifies with the object/s absolutized as the identity of opposites.

In reality, the object/reality cannot be divided into 'this' thing and that, existing 'there' and 'there', etc. Such 'divisions' are no more than tools of knowledge and their function/s created for the sake of our understanding this world. Objective reality or just reality is not so divided, there is no need; it is just one continuous process. The objects and things therefore are no more than moments of thought to reside upon and comprehend. Idea does not stay at the point of comprehension, it never resides in an object; it always emanates out of it. So, thought, idea always generalises, leaves the surface and enters the inner world which is also the world outside, a world outside the thing comprehended. It hopes to unite with the inner-most secrets, the essential motions of reality, and thus move constantly and really, essentially to become idea. Space loses meaning.

Idea in Conflict with Pure Idea

So, the object is just *a reference point* for idea. But idea does not want it, does not 'like' this idea! And wants to get rid of it, and become idea *pure and simple.* Idea has meaning only as 'pure idea', otherwise it is not needed. It makes *no difference* to the material world whether idea exists or not. Similarly, it should make no difference to idea whether the material world exists or not; at least that is what idea aims at, *without ever achieving it,* of course.

In this identity of opposites, idea endeavours to break off, absolutize itself and transcend the region of polar tension.

Hegel says, correctly, that the "production of the universal is abridged"[1] in the process of mediation. As the idea approaches the concrete, the universal, the general, the absolute, and the abstract is abridged and reduced. Idea loses its ideal nature, acquires material nature, because there is no absolute idea, there is only concrete idea, as a conflict of the two, unifying in the evolution of material concept. The subject becomes objectified, as the subject is the carrier of the concept, which is objectified idea, while the object is the receptacle as well as producer of idea.

Idea is itself its own object, as it moves towards itself in a process of the absolutization of the concept. Any concept may be absolutized, because all the concepts have the same nature. It does not matter whether it is the concept of the rock or tree or rivers – or 'something' or 'anything'. Every something has 'anything' within, and every anything is something.

The concept (of, say, stone) has a general nature, and that is why it is infinite, being just a receptacle. Stone is abstracted and absolutized, converted into idea, and unified in and as an absolute, which is a form of its existence. The concept may emerge from a tree or the ground, etc; so, it flies off and acquires motion, such a motion is antithetical to the form and source it has emerged from.

What is the result of the concept of stone? It serves only to launch idea, which then moves on, and onto itself, as the objectification of itself instead of the stone. Ideas do not need real, tangible objects then onwards, they do not want to.

Then where does stone or any other object come in? It is only a reference point in opposite terms. The concept is fixed, as we said elsewhere, uncritically presupposed. What is there to criticize in a 'stone' ?! It is a concept with which we approach the stone. And we find that it is just a stone, not worth a concept. We just give up the stone. But in actual fact, it is the actual stone that is given up for its concept that is carried for ever! The stone is universalized, abstracted and absolutized.

But once it is carried it becomes useless in isolation and useful in unity with concepts. This being must become non-being, and become being as abstraction. It remains while the stone may disappear.

Stone is dissolved in the concept, becoming independent of space and time. Thus, what is uncritically presupposed are subjected to severe criticism, to a point where stone evaporates into absolutely moving concept, which then is the object for itself. Now it is the concept of stone, which is the source of idea-formation (motion of idea). Its material form is jettisoned, replaced by the ideal form.

But stone as idea, in acting as the object is the exact opposite of stone. In the process of acting as object ('objectivity'), it cannot act as an object, since it is the concept of the object. Therefore, this object (that is the concept) is subjected to the laws of motion of the idea (concept), which serve to convert it into absolutized abstraction of 'the concept'. A concept of the concept emerges, which engulfs every other concept.

Concept Loses Boundaries

Stone did not, does not, exist for concept formation. In fact, it does not exist *as stone* until idea comes into being. Stone does not exist, it is just part of the reality that already is. *It does not need idea for its existence*; it just is. It becomes 'real' the moment idea comes on. In nature, the stone is not divided; it gets divided the moment idea touches it; it is the idea and the slowdown of idea that imparts stoniness to stone. It is idea which interferes with the natural flow of the nature and its dialectics. Though idea is the fastest 'thing' in nature, it must slow down in order to understand the material processes. Only then can stone be overcome and comprehended.

In order to understand, idea must go against its own nature, and try to identify with the objects as unity of opposites. It has to slow down at least *towards* the object and its processes. It has to dissect every step, identify every aspect, the endless ones. That is how idea reflects, and is thus able to create an ideal opposite of the material world. Having done that, while doing that, it penetrates the essence of the object/s, which are to a certain extent independent of the time and space of themselves. Essence of the reality is a divergence from the objects, and more and more unites them. Essence of being is different from phenomena of it and of the objects, and therefore identifiable with and easier for idea. Idea takes off again.

What is the essence of stone? It is the material reality that shows continuity of evolution and motion. Essence is something that does not 'exist', is not 'real', but is derived. It is resorted to because the motion of idea is opposite in nature, in the sense that it penetrates the reality, while in reality the essence always expresses itself in phenomenon. Without idea, there is no essence, neither are there phenomena. Idea moves only in these forms, in concepts and categories.

Idea gives up wild movement independent of time and space, and joint-areas within them, becomes part of time and space. It takes the form of concepts. Now, it has to move in between the objects, and therefore grows and develops. Collapse of idea is its concretization. The wildest speculations now begin taking well-ordered shapes. Idea slows down to keep pace with the motion of material reality and its dialectics. There are spaces to be dwelt in time and between spaces. Spatial and time constraints put serious limits to idea and its motion.

But this is the only way it can evolve and develop, otherwise it keeps overcoming itself without matter, which only means non-negation, and which is *a negative negation.*

Once idea resides in objects, it identifies with reality, a historical moment of identity of opposites, of consciousness and matter. Idea enters the *past history* of matter, a course followed in the expressions of phenomena.

Idea unites with something alien to it, and therefore constantly questions its existence to reach the essence, something akin to itself. It can make do with the concepts with constant tendencies of absolutizations. Each and every concept, the idea, has tendencies to go off in any direction in endless projections and possibilities, idea has this tendency of projections of the present into the future, and thus of acquiring its own independence. Idea constantly rises above and deviates from material reality. It must do so in order to maintain its identity, but it must also come back to enrich itself.

Projections are efforts to go ahead of material motion to assert superiority of idea. The asserted self comes out as negation of reality. To understand is to kill motion, even while maintaining, preserving it. Idea must not remain itself in the process of cognition, because it is the non-being of the being.

Becoming provides motion to idea, which also must become. But material reality proceeds through becoming: it is becoming all the time, driven by dialectics. Idea reaches a critical point, falls into crisis, as it becomes.

Matter also becomes. Therefore, becoming is a relationship between poles, both idea and matter give up their polar positions, penetrating each other. How do you know this is concept of matter, of stone, trace etc? Through the collapse of the polar opposites into each other into a synthesized concept, which in fact is a negation of a generalized, projected idea.

Idea can never identify with what exists really; therefore, it identifies with concept/s, which is nothing but piecemeal identities and mergers. Idea is a 'restless soul', and therefore moves from merger to merger. These momentary identifications, of reality, and thus of itself, are the forms of existence of idea.

Concepts replace material reality. Therefore, it is easier to move.

At the same time, it is equally difficult to move. Concept is a fixed entity until it moves. The object, the process, resides in concept in the interregnum that it moves, and moves out of it entirely, leaving behind the dead shell of the concept, of the 'conceptual framework!

This is the problem with concept and idea–it is slowed down, and has to keep pace with the reality, to which it has imparted the final form. Tree is a concept of tree, but the tree has moved on leaving the concept behind. It, the tree or the stone, will always live even without living. The living is the dead, the dead is not dead, it is always living. Reality is rent with serious contradictions. The tree has moved on to become gases, liquid, particles etc., but the concept has not, and must not, otherwise tree will not live (exist), and therefore the world will become incomprehensible (without tree). So, now the idea (concept) must move on: thus, a split takes place between tree and tree with the intervention of idea.

Split Idea and Split Tree

The two trees or the two stones evolve independently. The tree is internalized and imparted an eternal presence by idea. This tree may or may not develop. It may just remain an imprint for ever, an unchanging being, an idea of what existed, past as the present. With the passing of time it becomes something that need not exist or need not have existed, because after all it is just an idea with currently no material basis, an opposite of itself and therefore just a mental construct. The object simply becomes idealized and subjectified, constituting just a speck of consciousness. But the subject cannot remain without the object, idea without matter. In their real absence, the unreal subject becomes the real, the object of thought and enquiry, and are thus is created even while being denied any existence whatsoever. The idea of tree reacts with itself in the absence of the real self. Therefore, this tree, this image of tree can grow, has the potential to grow unhindered. The idea of tree reacts with its own idea, developing and imparting real and unreal projections, in scientific, mysterious and religious forms, even most unimaginable forms, filled with arbitrary content.

This idea takes off once again, due particularly to the absence of material forms, to merge with the generalized content of consciousness.

The real tree, having disappeared, needs scientific investigations to make it real and to really trace its own development. Science therefore cannot fly off; on the contrary it flies in; it becomes part of the object as the subject. The speculative motions are annihilated. *And philosophy begins to collapse.*

The other tree also collapses, but conceptually, without there being an object. Yet, this very collapse is its development, and it evolves in its real form and content, being freed of its ideal and philosophical trappings through science and technology. The idea of the object is replaced by the object itself. The knowledge about tree becomes concrete, detailed and abstract, and enriches the *concept* of 'tree'. The concept becomes material, transits to the opposite pole, and evolves endlessly, not philosophically but scientifically.

This again signifies *the collapse of philosophy*. Idea becomes material, and therefore materially objective and law-governed. In this dialectics of matter and idea, the idea is split and reunited in an effort to overcome it. Such a split is a threat to its very existence, yet this very threat gives it a new lease of life at a higher, synthesized level. The two halves are separate existences, yet they are inseparable. They are torn apart in the course of comprehension, not really. The contradiction of existence takes the form of that between real and the unreal. That is how the contradictions are externalized first and then internalized, because thought must question the reality of the real, then the reality of the relation of the real to the unreal. In that sense, the contradiction of matter is the contradiction of the idea. Contradictory matter is imparted a contradiction external to it even while discovering its internality, while simultaneously denying all the contradictions because contradiction is fully claimed by idea in its effort to rise above the real material contradictions. Matter had been developing on its own. It is killed in order to understand or deny it, and this can only be done by imparting it an ideal contradiction without the intention of imparting the same, trying itself to remain free from all the contradictions. All the attempts of idea to remain free of contradictions fall into insoluble contradictions and only serve to unfold the endless contradictions of its own. Idea thus has no chance to become ideas. This contradictory attempt to free itself of contradictions lands idea into insoluble contradictions!

For idea, matter has no contradiction, and idea itself does not want to have it; it is forced to discover and acquire contradiction from matter, because without that the idea cannot develop! So the external is internalized: but this really cannot be done; so idea becomes but a reflection of the real, and thus the 'external' is really found to be internal.

In that sense, matter did not 'need' contradiction because the question arises only after the arrival of idea on the scene, which *contemplates* matter. It is in the course of contemplation that contradictions are discovered, both in affirmation and denial: the subject both affirms and denies, everything. That is how it proceeds; its very existence is contradiction. It contemplates forgetting its own objectivity Since contradiction itself is contradictory, the role of the subject, particularly of the idea is to deny the contradictory nature of contradiction, which in fact is an affirmation, through which it exists in denials and negations. Negation/denial is the affirmation of the other. Affirming or denying the other dissolves the other, which must then be recast and reconstructed anew, as the other, in a form comprehensible to idea/subject because idea must always have something to *think about*, even while denying that it is thinking about and is it in fact itself is thinking/thought process. Thought cannot take things as they are; they must be reprocessed and transcended, which only enriches matter.

Understanding is Dividing and Synthesizing

When we look at things we divide and contradict them, we contradict them with themselves, with ourselves, with ideas about them. We isolate one object out of so many, and put one different from and in opposition to many. An object does not exist in isolation but we make it do so in order to comprehend it and them. From the point of view of idea, it must exist alone, otherwise it would be nearly impossible for us to understand. Isolation is not existence, it is the conflict of existence, and therefore existence itself is contradictory. Idea has that ability to overcome existence and to tear it out of context.

Separation puts the object in opposition to objects. The object becomes the object of contemplation, even though there can't be contemplation in isolation, but only in general through particular. Idea moves through this and that. This is the difficulty with the concrete: it stands in opposition to the general. Idea unveils the general through particular. Idea comes to know of the object by not knowing the others, and therefore knowing particular against the general. Comprehension, idea cannot hover over the concrete for long, for it must then collapse, and break up into pieces. Knowing proceeds during suspension through not knowing, and only thus can being be known.

Idea escapes into the concepts. Idea touches the concrete but cannot remain there for long as concrete. It must move on to all the objects, particularly those that have been denied existence, and thus constantly lose concreteness. Idea is concept, and therefore always slipping past the concrete and beyond it.

By escaping from the concrete, the concept generalizes the concrete. Concept absolutizes the object, fills it with that which is not there, that is the meaning, replaces it, and thus fully represents it. Concept is the reflection of the concrete, it is an escape, yet it limits the object its essentials, reflecting its motion by stopping it, take only the essential out of the innumerable interconnections. To limit is to generalize, because only the essentials are taken for a general idea of the object, thus bringing all that exists outside the concept to an end.

Looking is contradictory because it non-looks all that can be seen. The process is both biological and philosophical. But that which has been overlooked is included through rejection, which in fact is assertion, an admittance of the fact that all others exist. All others begin to exist in generalization, and the neighbour has really been admitted as existing as part and parcel of the one; one can only exist in many. Existence is dissolved into non-existence to impart it the meaning of existence. Existence is generalized existence.

Science follows a long route to and through existence, while philosophical speculation is instant because it follows abstraction, which at once is in the essence of existence or non-existence of existence.

The conflict is resolved in synthesis.

NOTES

1. Hegel, *Phenomenology of Mind*, Para 33.

4

Science of Dialectics of Motion

How Lenin Rescues Dialectics and Materialism in Hegel. A Study of Lenin's Volume 38

Before we proceed further, we must dwell upon the method of dialectics, which is in operation both in matter and idea. It is the source of motion. Hegel was the greatest dialectician, and Marx and Lenin were dialecticians of the same stature who rescued dialectical method from the Hegelian labyrinthine world of philosophy. Lenin was a great scholar of Hegel, one of the handful who really understood Hegel. He made a Herculean effort to rescue and develop Hegelian dialectics, making an in-depth study of his works. In this context, Volume 38 of Lenin's *Collected Works* is very important.

Here we will have a look at how Lenin dealt with Hegel and his dialectics.

We are bringing out a study and an analysis of Lenin's Volume 38 from his Collected Works for the first time in English. (Earlier it was done in a more limited manner in Hindi by the present author).

Dialectics of Motion of Concept

We always begin with finished and completed concepts. We begin to understand, and not just look at, the world with readymade concepts handed over to us down the centuries. So, the words and the concepts are the depositories of knowledge and experience. But, for us or an individual presently, they are given, and not evolved in the course of experience: tree, river, human being, water, air, food, sky, stars, and so on.

So, we begin our enquiry with the finished 'products', and, in this sense, go backwards as we go forward in our quest for growing knowledge. The concepts are final reflections of material forms, and as such are tools of analysis. But they must be converted into living concepts by really using them as tools of knowledge and thus converted into dialectics, both as tools and as active reflection.

It is theory which rises above the contradictions of matter, and resolves them. Idea is conditioned by matter, which also means it is limited by the latter, and therefore there is a danger of its (idea's) collapse within itself. An age, a situation, sets limits to ideas. The idea may not be able to go beyond, and may surrender. Events may exhaust themselves or may turn out to be different. In such situations, idea (in particular, theory) should be able to overcome, rise above the natural and historical limits and go beyond. This is the active, synthesizing role of theory. Such a role can be played only by idea, particularly theory.

But the finished product is confused with the process itself, with the thing in motion. By conceptualizing, we deconceptualize motion itself. Therefore, we have to move beyond the limits of the concept and show it to be unlimited. We begin with the limited, finished concept; we must move forward towards the evolving concept with no limits and constant motion. Thus the two are the products of two different processes, that too moving in opposite directions. That is what leads us to dialectics, to motion itself. The idea must penetrate the objects, the idea of motion. But the real result is that we want the object to be as we see, as we find it to be. The object remains as it is despite our contemplation. But we do not want the objects to exist at all in motion. We consider ourselves as superior. Our ideas, the final concepts are the final judgment over nature. By so doing we go back instead of forward.

Having begun with concepts, we go into their inner workings. Our concept moves, yet it is taken as stationary, because only a fixed concept can be an instrument–an 'instrument' always is stationary: how can a microscope be changing, developing!

Here arise multiple contradictions. Fixed concept is matter in motion; fixed concept is changing concept. The latter is far more difficult. How can an idea, a concept change? If it changes, how can we understand? Can the tree, as an object, change? Can the tree as an instrument change? The tree or any object as an object may afford not to change, for while; but as an instrument it cannot afford not to change. The object and instrument, with their internal contradictions, are in constant mutual contradiction. The object has to discharge dual and opposite functions.

We have to understand the object as it is and as it is not; as it is actually as it is not; therefore we change it in order to understand it, and in the process change ourselves.

Thought process is basically and ultimately about the object/ objectivity. And, therefore, the object predominates in the direction of ideas, however much the latter endeavour to jettison the former. In fact, jettisoning is also a form of approach to the object.

Marxism and Dialectics

Dialectics is one of the most misunderstood and misused concepts. It has almost always been presented and used mechanically and in a highly dogmatic manner. This applies both to the supporters and opponents of Marxist dialectics. What is surprising is that the Marxists themselves have used dialectics as a formula rather them as a method and a guide to understand and to action.

It is generally the direct followers of Hegel who have used or followed dialectics in a more lively and changeable manner. Very few among all the philosophers, including the Marxist ones, have been able to really master the concept of dialectics and the dialectical method.

Lately, there has been a renewal of interest in dialectics, particularly the Hegelian dialectics. Frankfurt school, trends of Marxism and postmodernism and so on have begun discussing dialectics afresh. One of the major and basic reasons is the unleashing and speeding up of the information and communication as well as the scientific-technological revolution.

There are direct linkages, and growing ones, between the STR and the Hegelian dialectics. This is generally not recognized.

But we will come to these questions elsewhere.

Lenin as a Dialectician: His Treatment of Hegel in Volume 38

A study of Volume 38 of the *Collected Works* of Lenin[1] brings out a rich variety of aspects, interconnections and transformations of dialectics. The volume consists of notes, conspectus of various authors, mainly Hegel, and comments. It is extremely rich. But it has never been properly analysed or even studied.

Very little attention has been paid to Hegel's unparalleled work on dialectics. His works are more the object of criticism and ridicule, at best of simple description, and rather poor presentation.

But hardly any attempt has been made to really understand and master Hegel's philosophy, particularly his dialectics.

This failure to master dialectics has caused, and is causing, a number of problems in theory as well as in practice. In particular, it has resulted in great inadequacy to understand and interpret the world. It is very well to say, following Marx, that one has not only to interpret the world but more particularly to change it.

How much of the world do we really understand, not to mention interpreting it and even less of changing it? The history of the last hundred to hundred and fifty years shows a tendency of progressive inadequacy to understand the motions and changes of the 'world'. Bits-and-pieces attitude to the dialectical method has led to the various inadequate and inconclusive schools and trends of thought. They all together have not been able to constitute a totality, leading to a failure in grasping the world. What is the world like today? – nobody is ready to answer the question. In a world of ever-changing events, when time is becoming a decisive factor, mastery over dialectics has become crucial. The STR, particularly the discovery and application of the quantum processes, unfold ever new aspects of dialectics.

Lenin's volume 38 of his *Collected Works* is one of the most extraordinary of his works, yet also among the most neglected ones. This is quite a surprise. In fact, the volume is a revelation in many ways as a rare work.

Volume 38 is a collection of Lenin's notes, comments and views on some of Hegel's major works. These notes have largely not been used at all. Yet they contain some of the richest ideas on dialectics.

Marxist dialectics is almost always presented as the three laws of dialectics and more particularly as the unity and struggle of opposites, and even more particularly simply as the struggle of opposites; some categories are also mentioned. As a consequence, in the social sphere, Marxist dialectics has been reduced to class struggle alone. This reductionism has deprived the Marxist dialectics of its life source, diversity and movement.

We will deal with the question in greater detail elsewhere.

Lenin has said in his article "On the Question of Dialectics"[2] that "The splitting of a single whole and the cognition of its contradictory parts is the essence (one of the "essentials", one of the principal, if not the principal, characteristics or features) of dialectics. That is precisely how Hegel, too, puts the matter."[3]

The first part of the statement (dividing into two and cognition of the opposite parts) has been widely used and misused out of context, leading to a mechanical and erroneous interpretation of dialectics. Quite often, Lenin himself is responsible for creating a mechanical impression through sweeping statements about society and nature, although if he had time and ambience, he would certainly have been more expressive in a dialectical way. And he really was a great dialectician, both theoretically and practically.

In this quotation, Lenin refers to the quotation from Philo on Heraclitus. It is as follows:

"For the one is that which consists of two opposites, so that when cut into two the opposites are revealed."[4] Philo is commenting here on Heraclitus, who presented an excellent and lively exposition of motion and dialectics, as follows:

"The world, an entity out of everything, was created by none of the gods or men, but war is and will be eternally living fire, regularly being ignited and regularly becoming extinguished...."[5]

Lenin characterized it as a very good exposition of the principles of dialectical materialism.[6]

The point is that seen in the proper context, the concept of dialectics becomes real and livelier, shorn of the mechanical interpretations attached to it later.

So, Lenin's above mentioned description of dialectics has to be taken in inter-connections and entirety. The "splitting" of a single whole is not a mechanical action, consisting of mechanical opposites standing 'in direct opposition to each other'. Rather, they should be taken as tendencies and aspects. Lenin elsewhere does precisely this. Lenin presents a number of examples of identity of opposites from natural sciences making it clear that giving examples is not a correct method. Giving examples could be resorted to only in the interest of popularization. Rather the examples should be seen as exposing laws of cognition.

Differential and integral (mathematics), action and reaction (mechanics), positive and negative electricity, combination and dissociation of atoms (chemistry), class struggle (social science), etc.: they reveal 'identity' or 'unity' of opposites. These opposites are contradictory, mutually exclusive, opposite tendencies in all phenomena and processes of nature (including mind and society)." (pp. 359-60, emphasis in the original) Lenin, as we pointed out just now, talks of opposite tendencies; so the 'splitting' business should be understood as a dialectical method.

Dialectics is in reality the self-movement. This is where Lenin heads to, following Hegel. Development and motion are absolute, continuous, and that is the essence of dialectics. He refers to Marx's *Capital*, which points out the most common contradiction of the commodity society, i.e. exchange of commodities. It reveals the germ of all the contradictions of modern society.

This is an example of the proper treatment and understanding of dialectics. Disclosing objective self-movement is the most important task of philosophy, and of theory, as well as it is best way to apply the dialectical method.

Lenin states that such should be the method of exposition of dialectics ("for with Marx the dialectics of bourgeois society is only a particular case of dialectics").[7] One should begin with what is the most ordinary and simplest, e.g. plant, man, individual, leaf, water, air, and so on. One must be able to show that the opposites are identical: one expresses through the other, e.g. the individual through the particular, and vice-versa. And so on. There is constantly taking place the transition of the one into another (of one opposite into another).

"Thus in any proposition we can (and must) disclose as in a 'nucleus' ("cell", the germ of all the elements of dialectics", and thereby show that dialectics is a property of all human knowledge.[8] The condition for the knowledge of all processes of the world in their interconnections is the dialectical method. In fact, dialectics itself is the science of endless inter-connections. "Dialectics is the theory of knowledge of (Hegel and) Marxism."[9]

In an interesting exposition of dialectics, Lenin spoke on "the dialectics of tumbler" in his speech titled "Once Again on the Trade Unions" (January 25, 1921).[10] Taking a cue from Bukharin's example of aspects of "tumbler on the lectern" in one of the discussions held previously, Lenin explains the difference between dialectics and eclecticism.

The discussion also provides an example of how Lenin could explain dialectics from the merest of objects.

Lenin describes that "a tumbler is assuredly both a glass cylinder and a drinking vessel. But there are more than these two properties, qualities or facets to it." There are infinite number of qualities and 'mediacies' to it, as also "endless inter-relationships with the rest of the world."[11] Lenin goes on to describe some of the innumerable aspects and usage of the tumbler in the course of this highly interesting discussion on the dialectics of a tumbler! The object could be put to any number of usage, be made of so many materials, and in so many shapes.

"Formal logic ... deals with formal definitions", and drawing on what is most common, stops there.[12] When two or more definitions are just taken together and combined at random ("a glass cylinder and a drinking vessel"), it results in eclecticism.[13]

"Dialectical logic demands that we should go further." Firstly, all the possible connections of the object should be examined, and this "we cannot hope to achieve completely". Secondly, dialectical logic should take the object in development and self-movement. It may not be clear in case of objects like a tumbler, "but it too is in flux, and this holds especially true for its purpose, use and connection with the surrounding world."[14]

Thirdly, "a full 'definition' of an object must include the whole of human experience".[15] It should include both the experiences in the form of criterion of truth and practical indicator of human wants. Only then the object exhausts itself (to a considerable extent). That means the truth of the object should be established as well as the endless human wants it satisfies.

Fourthly, Lenin pointed out the statement of Plekhanov, after Hegel, that dialectical logic held truth to be always concrete, never abstract.[16] For this and other reasons, Lenin insisted on a thorough study of Plekhanov's philosophical writings "because nothing better has been written on Marxism anywhere in the world."[17]

These four points did not exhaust the whole notion of dialectical logic.

Thus, Lenin's attitude to dialectics is complex; it is not that simple as is generally made out to be. In other words, he had a highly dialectical and multifaceted, and not a simplified and mechanical, attitude to the events of nature and society. He was highly dialectical in his method.

The subsequent Marxist movement and interpreters (including opponents of Marxism) tore Lenin's statements out of context and rendered them mechanical and lifeless. They ceased to be the instruments of analysis and cognition. The "conflict" and "opposites" aspect was overemphasized to the exclusion of the really lively and dialectical nature, by both the supporters and opponents of Marx and Lenin.

Our discussion, mentioned above, on "On the Question of Dialectics" clears many problems related to Lenin's use of dialectical method.

Dialectics is not limited to 'conflict'. And conflict, too, has several connotations, meanings and endless aspects, not necessarily in the sense of the opposites standing 'face to face' with each other.

Hegel on Dialectics and Lenin's Interpretation

Dealing with dialectics, Hegel brought out its aspects in all their richness, which was hardly ever used by Marxism or other philosophies.

Speaking of the Eleatic School of ancient Greece, Hegel brings out two important characteristics of dialectics, as emphasized by Lenin. First, Hegel says that we find in the Eleatic school, "the beginning of dialectics, i.e. simply the pure movement of thought in Notions".

Second, "likewise we see the opposition of thought to outward appearance or sensuous being, or of that which is implicit to the being–for–another of this implicitness, and in the objective existence we see the contradiction which it has in itself, or dialectics proper..."[18]

Hegel especially notes these two features or characteristics of dialectics.

Pure movement of thought is emphasized here. Similarly, contradiction of thought to outward expression and to objective existence is also brought out. It is clarified that contradiction resides in the dialectics proper.

Lenin explains and interprets these two aspects in greater detail, and reproduces them from the materialist dialectical view: dialectics is the pure movement of thought, i.e. human concepts are not fixed but in eternal movement and flow. One concept flows into another, reflecting the living life. Analysis of concepts always demands study of their movement in interconnections and mutual transformations.[19]

To be more precise, dialectics is the study of the opposition in thing-in-itself, of the essence; at the one time, it was opposition of thing-in-itself to being-for-others: a transition is the "thing", an opposition of essence to appearance. The process goes endlessly deeper from one level of essence to another, and so on.

Thus, it should be stated that there is continuous contradiction within the essence, with boundaries of essence and essences, essences and phenomena constantly shifting.

This is what we usually overlook.

Hegel evolves dialectics further. According to him, dialectics 1) is produced when external movement is different from its comprehension;

II) is "not a movement of our intelligence only, but what proceeds from the nature of the thing itself, i.e. from the pure Notion of the content."[20] Hegel, by implication, differentiates between subjective and objective dialectics.

In the words of Hegel, subjective dialectics reasons from external grounds and does dialectical justice by recognizing that "in the correct there is what is not correct, and in the false the true as well."[21] That means there is a discrepancy between the estimation and existence, and there is continuous approximation of the reason.

Subjective dialectics is also "external dialectics", which regards "objects in such a way that reasons are revealed and aspects of them are shown."[22] Consequently, what was at first thought to be fixed, "is made to totter". The object is scattered, with it its concept, as the idea penetrates further into the object, and multifaceted dialectics is produced.

Once this takes place, a transition to objective dialectics happens. And this is a very important point. As Hegel emphasized, it is "not a movement of our intelligence only" but a revelation of the nature of the thing or the object itself.

This other dialectics is the immanent contemplation of the object: "it is taken for itself", without previous idea or hypothesis, "not under any external conditions, laws, grounds."[23] We have to consider the object in itself with its determinations. Treated as such, it begins to reveal its contradictions, showing that it has "opposed determinations". Since it has opposed determinations, the contradictions, it transcends itself.

Thus, we take the object in its objective contradictions. "True dialectics leaves nothing whatever to its object."[24] This is a profound statement, inviting endless analysis. True dialectics must cover all the endless aspects possible, treating the object as it is. But treating the object as it is, is a highly complicated job: you treat it as it is, you leave nothing to your imagination, yet you imagine everything. You do not allow imagination to run away, but it must run only towards the object to be really dialectical. Aspects reveal themselves, and thus the object disintegrates as 'object'. By the time you grasp it, it has become something else. An object before comprehension and after are two quite different things.

Developing this dialectics further, Lenin observes that everything passes from one into another. Development is not simple growth or enlargement. Evolution has to be understood as arising and passing away, as mutual transition. In the course of this evolution, concepts and categories also evolve. Thinking is connected with being. There is a dialectics of concepts and a dialectics of cognition. The universal principle development should correspond to the universal principle of the unity of the world.[25]

The whole process of understanding/comprehension/cognition, Hegel puts as completing the half into one, and the lack of it as if the object "were deficient on one side only."[26] That is why he appears to state that cognition disintegrates the object.

Hegel makes some extraordinary explanation of motion and

reveals its inner source. According to Hegel, "...we say that the body is in one place and then it goes to another; because it moves it is no longer in the first, but yet not in the second: were it in either it would be at rest. If we say that it is between both, that is to say nothing at all, for were it between both, it would be in a place, and this presents the same difficulty. But movement means to be in this place and not to be in it; this is the continuity of space and time–and it is this which first makes motion possible."[27]

This is an amazing exposition of motion, and reminds one of the quantum motions, which are being discussed and debated by the scientists today.

Conversion of Dialectics into Motion

While developing Hegel's concept, Lenin criticizes the interpretation of motion wherein "movement is the presence of a body in a definite place at a given moment and in another place at another, subsequent moment."[28] Lenin criticizes Chernov's objection to the Hegelian explanation (in his *Philosophical Studies* of 1907). Chernov takes precisely the mechanical position in relation to motion, objected to by Hegel and Lenin: "At one place at one moment, at another at another moment." Lenin explains that this objection is incorrect. This is generally not understood.

Lenin objects to the objection on three counts:

"1) it describes the *result* of motion, but not motion *itself*; 2) it does not show, it does not contain in itself the *possibility* of motion; 3) it depicts motion as a sum, a concatenation of states of rest, that is to say, the (dialectical) contradiction is not removed by it, but only concealed ...."[29] This definition brings out and explains motion in its source and in all-sidedness. The contradiction is brought out and it is then resolved.

This is the most outstanding interpretation and explanation of motion. *It is not to be found anywhere else.* It particularly expresses itself, and fully, in the world of quantum mechanics. It is amazing that even when quantum mechanics had not come into being, Hegel and Lenin could develop a highly dialectical explanation of motion.

Lenin emphasizes, following Hegel, that motion means to be in one place and not to be at the same time. Hegel continues and makes one of the most striking statements in the history of philosophy: "The essence of space and time is motion".[30] How very close he is to the conclusions of quantum mechanics! Lenin further explains it thus: "Motion is the unity of continuity (of time and space) and discontinuity (of time and space). Motion is a contradiction, a unity of contradictions."[31]

That means the inner conflict shifts the being in time and space. But the motion itself is multidirectional. It is a conflict for and in space and time.

Motion is not a sum but a process. It is not a series of rest: this point, then the next, the next, and so on. Motion does not mean rest, it is not revealed when you kill it at one point and say it is here and now. It is a conflict, among others, between what is and what it is going to be.

Lenin says the second interpretation does not remove contradiction. He takes the help of Hegel here to explain: "What makes the difficulty is always thought alone, since it keeps apart the moments of an object which in their separation are really united." And Lenin exclaims: "Correct!"[32]

We see things in rest and understand them only in rest. For that purpose we divide the time into moments like a watch. And that is "the difficulty with thought"; the problem lives with thought alone.

The point is to overcome the contradiction inherent in the motion. This contradiction is at the same moment, at the same place. How is it resolved?

This question is not easy to answer. It is not generally faced, generally no effort is made to solve this problem, to provide answers to this crucial question, the very source of motion. It is the continuous transformation of opposites, of different aspects. It has been stated earlier that movement means to be and not to be in the same place and at the same time. That means one aspect, tendency, the opposite gives way to another, one is transformed into another, the present becomes past as it moves towards the future. The 'moment' is not something separate, distinct; it is a continuous existence. If this particular moment is magnified, we will find that it is not a moment, but a whole process with innumerable shades and transformations. It is all the time becoming. So, a moment reveals opposites, which takes the process forward.

Taking Hegel's explanation further, Lenin delves into the question deeper. Lenin says:

"We cannot imagine, express, measure, depict movement, without interrupting continuity, without simplifying, coarsening, dismembering, strangling that which is living." "The representation of movement by means of thought always...kills". Even sense–perception kills live movement and every concept.[33]

"And in that lies the *essence* of dialectics."[34] This essence is expressed by unity and identity of opposites.

So, part of the answer is provided here: movement, motion results when the opposites become identical, when unity and identity of opposites is achieved.

Lenin quotes Hegel on Heraclitus: "This harmony is precisely absolute Becoming, change, – not becoming other, now this and then an other. The essential thing is that each different thing, each particular, is different from another, not abstractly so from any other, but from its other. Each particular only is, insofar or its other is implicitly contained in its notion..."[35]

The most crucial part in the quote is the one dealing with the difference with "the other". The difference is within the essence itself, the other is a particular's other. The difference is within the particular or the self. It is this self which is changing, with transformation of 'this' into 'the other', into the opposite.

Hegel characterises Zeno's treatment of motion as objectively dialectical.[36]

Ultimately, to enter the essence of a thing is dialectical materialism, a conclusion implicit in Hegel.

Hegel and Lenin on laws, *sixteen elements* and determinations of dialectics

In this volume we find one of the rarest and most interesting of the treatments of dialectics by Hegel and Lenin. Dialectics has widely been misrepresented, misinterpreted and misunderstood. In Hegel, dialectics forms the very core, the source of motion of the ideas and of the world. Hegel is nothing if not dialectical. He is basically a thinker of motion, and only later of philosophy. It was Lenin who for the first time identified and analysed these elements of dialectics out of Hegel. ***Not even Marx did it.***

Lenin enumerates 16 elements of dialectics, which are extension of three *basic* elements of his.[37]

Usually, materialist dialectics is reduced to a skeleton of three laws, a few categories and some rigid, lifeless formulae.

But it is astonishing that all the works of philosophy, including by the Marxists, have overlooked the 16 (sixteen) elements of dialectics mentioned by Lenin. This is a great, astonishing work by Lenin.

We are bringing out a detailed exposition of these elements and aspects of dialectics here for the first time. This would dispel the impression that dialectics is *only its three laws* or the so-called Hegelian 'triad' (which in fact does not belong to Hegel).

Three determinations or elements of dialectics were first identified by Lenin, following Hegel:

1. The determination of the concept out of itself: i.e. the thing itself must be considered in its relations and its development.
2. The contradictory nature of the thing itself, the other of itself, the contradictory forces and tendencies and forces in each phenomenon.
3. The union of analysis and synthesis.[38]

Lenin goes on to develop these determinations or elements further, again following Hegel, as under:

Hegel and Lenin evolve *16 (sixteen) elements of dialectics* as under:

1. The objectivity of consideration (not examples, not divergences, but the Thing-in-itself).
2. The totality of the manifold relations of this thing to others.
3. The development of this thing, phenomenon, its own movement/life.
4. Internally contradictory tendencies and sides in the thing.
5. The thing (phenomenon, etc.) as the sum and unity of opposites.
6. The struggle and respectively unfolding of these opposites, contradictory strivings, etc.
7. The union of analysis and synthesis: the breakdown of separate parts and the totality, the summation of these parts.
8. The relations of each thing (phenomenon, etc.) are not only

manifold but general and universal. Each thing and phenomenon, process, etc. is connected with every other.

9. Not only the unity of opposites but transition of every determination, quality, feature, side, property into every other and into its opposite.
10. Endless discovery of new relations, etc.
11. The endless process of deepening of knowledge of the process/ thing etc.: from appearance to essence and from less profound to more profound essence.
12. From coexistence to causality and from one form of connection and reciprocal dependence to another, deeper, more general form.
13. The repetition at a higher stage of certain features, properties, etc. of the lower one.
14. Apparent return to the old (negation of negation).
15. Struggle of content and form. Throwing off of the form, transformation of the content.
16. Transition of quantity into quality.

These are extraordinary points. Credit for them goes first to Hegel, and then to Lenin. Nobody else has tried to dissect the highly conflicting mesh of dialectics operating in the world and in ideas. Lenin has not elaborated them further. We should not expect it here because he was only studying Hegel's works, and the comments came as a consequence.

The elements of dialectics need to be gone into detail. They need thorough analysis and study. So also many other aspects dealt with in Volume 38.

Several things stand out while carefully considering the 16 elements. We have to master the outlook and method of dialectics to the deepest extent possible. Dialectics is all about understanding the source of motion and motion itself as they operate, without our subjective imposition. This is a very difficult endeavour. Motion and its concept is a very complicated one. We are not used to grasping it properly, although movement, motion and change is our common, everyday experience. Everything, phenomenon or process is internally, inherently contradictory.

A process (thing, phenomenon) is the one that contradicts itself.

That is how it exists, and that is how it proceeds. It is always going beyond itself, and every part and aspect of it is doing the same thing, has this very tendency.

We are used to seeing the objects as they or the object as it is; the same applies to a process. Little do we realise that it is tensionised, it is constantly differing with itself: look at a river to understand it, somewhat.

This difference, the slightest one, is the source of motion. It is this difference that brings it in relation with other objects/processes. In fact, one thing is nothing but a part, on aspect of the totality. Endless inter-relations result.

The thing (process) is the sum and unity of opposites.

What are opposites, what is contradiction?

Anything that moves, does so against itself, away from and beyond itself. There is a tendency to remain as it is (and that is itself is in contradiction), and there is another, which endeavours to break out of it, to move forward. Differences are constantly emerging in the process, and that means inequalities and disequilibrium. A thing, or abstractly the being is moving constantly towards non-being. In fact, it is more accurate to say that a being is a non-being at the same time.

The point is, within a process a change starts at some time at some point. The thing is the thing, and yet its being non-thing has begun. The difference does not accord with the thing ('being') and therefore is its opposite. Any process consists of so many, endless, opposites, and in abstraction an opposite.

Dialectics is an active, living source, without which a thing cannot exist, and also cannot change. That is why, consciousness always carries contradiction of itself. Anything that is, is not also. Therefore, dialectics is multifaceted, multi-layered, multi-aspect.

To proceed, to live is to not to be. And therefore reality, taken as a whole, has to justify how and why it is, which also means how and why it is not.

The aspect, the thing is all the time relative. For it, all other aspects are the other. So, it is the other that is all the time being created (imaging) out of this.

Modern science proves that the being, anything, is a bundle of endless contradictions. There is constant conflict, not only between old and new, to be and not to be; there are contradictions of contradictions at various levels of motions. A living body or organism is perhaps the most complicated unity of contradictions, containing almost all the opposites of nature. Yet it exists; that is why it exists.

Mechanical materialism has taken a reductionist, mechanical attitude to opposites and contradictions. It takes a tangible one-against-one attitude, as if the opposite stands on the other side.

Here it should be clear that the 'opposite' is not necessarily against. It is a contradiction, not in a mechanical sense, but in a dialectical sense. The opposite (and different) tendencies get transformed, converted into one another. The very motion of the thing is through the other, the opposite. The differences, the opposites, the poles are constantly transformed into one another. They express through one another. This is mutual penetration and at the same time mutual exclusion of the opposites. The differences being multifaceted must include all, yet change in the course of notion.

Modern science, particularly the quantum field, expresses this motion and mutual transformation, and therefore dialectics, in the most open form. That shows that dialectics is being uncovered in an unprecedented way, *needing less and less philosophical speculation.*

At the quantum levels, mutual transformations are quite common, the very form of existence of matter. Particles and energies constantly and easily change levels, forms and configurations. So much so that even an empty space acts as a particle, and it becomes near–impossible even for the scientists to tell whether an empty space is 'empty' or space or particle: the aspects, determinations and differences are so endless that one must determine the frame of reference in order to determine the determinate. Even the concept of a particle, say an electron, is relativistic: it exists at one level but has no existence at another! Both at the same time! You cannot determine the velocity and place of a particle at the same time: they are relativistic and mutually exclusive concepts and realities.

We will discuss quantum philosophy elsewhere.

Considered objectively, the opposites and their struggle unfold themselves. What unfolds, is the contradictory strivings. These are very important, even crucial points. We must not allow one subjective observation or wish to impose itself on the contradictory nature of the thing. The contradictions should be allowed to unfold themselves, and we try to understand, comprehend them, reflect them as they are, as they unfold themselves.

The contradiction, the struggle expresses itself, comes out into the open in many ways and forms. It/they acquire more and more varied aspects. That is precisely what is dialectical movement, dialectical unfolding.

If the unfolding is not permitted, then the contradictions are sought to be covered up, veiled; that is what happened with the definition of motion given previously. The result was instead of dealing with motion itself, we dealt with the results of motion. And this is a more complicated example. This often takes place with simple day-to-day events and things and examples.

We often try to substitute our own (subjective, consciousness-made) contradictions for the objective ones. And the subjective contradictions are not necessarily dialectical ones, which ought to be imposed as the real ones; they are or they are rendered mechanical, as distinct from the real, dialectical ones.

Subjectivity separates contradictory, differing aspects (tendencies) into mechanical substitutes (here and there, black and white, etc.), or aspects or moments, etc. We break up a process or an object into its imaginary mechanical constituents and parts.

That is why the necessity of allowance for unfolding: only then the event is properly understood.

That is only how the "endless process of the discovery of new sides, relations, etc." (element number 10) can proceed. The revelation and unfolding of new sides is an endless, inexhaustive process. In fact, this is a struggle of opposites, of contradictions. Not one opposite but innumerable, endless ones, coalescing into polar opposites. A river has contradictory strivings, endless differences and opposites, exemplified by endless currents, pressures, temperatures, water drops, vapours, chemical composition and what not. It all must be the source of motion, must itself become motion. A slightest disturbance, a drop or increase in current at a corner can lead to series of differences, contradictions, opposites creating unending series of currents. Sometime somewhere it all must have originated from the cooling of the vapours, which must have had its own contradictions.

The internal development and contradictions are represented also by the constant transformations of processes and things into one another and by their interconnections, which also are a form and consequence of dialectics. The elements reflect the laws and categories of dialectics in all their richness.

Dialectics, Bipolarity and Multipolarity

The sixteen elements of dialectics constitute the infinite richness of contradictions, the very process of jettisoning being and acquiring the other of being, the contradictions of being as non-being.

Analysis and synthesis, the inevitable opposites accruing from the contradictory nature of processes and phenomena, help us reach the dialectical source. Contradictions and opposites are not two-sided; hardly ever so. They are not struggle between two opposites alone, two elements opposed to each other. To think so is to follow reductionism. Dialectics can never be reduced in aspects, trends and interconnections. On the contrary, it should contain as many conflicts and aspects thereof, as many trends and tendencies as possible. The result and purpose of dialectics is not to reduce and simplify motion, but to see it in all its complexities and endless, infinite changes, transformations and motions. It has to be realized that each aspect of dialectics has its own motion and dialectics. Motion itself is dialectics. We should have 'three-dimensional' rather than 'two-dimensional' picture. Bipolarity is an important constituent of reality, but it is not the whole; it is not even the only source of motion.

Motion constantly and continuously brings about changes in the role, place and inter-relationships of aspects and tendencies and strivings. Bipolarity only manages to cover up the rich multiplicity of dialectical reality.

Constant changes in aspects and differences causing an inability and near-impossibility to catch hold of place and time of dialectics and to grasp dialectics as a constant shift of and in space and time, a constant endeavour of the consciousness to grow out of its own time and space in order to encompass the space and time of that which exists, renders comprehension dialectical. For we have to realize that comprehension itself has its own limitations, making it difficult to catch hold of real motion and motions thereof. Consequently, our consciousness tries to break up something into many things, into constituents separated by space and time, which in reality is not so. Therefore to understand is 'to kill', to kill in order to understand: kill the motion, apply brakes, slow down, divide, 'analyse',—so that consciousness comprehends. This is a dialectical conflict between two types of motion. Historically superior motion (consciousness) is also historically inferior, because to grasp (catch hold of) motion, it has to break it up, and thus take recourse to 'analysis'; only then can synthesis be achieved, that is the completion of comprehension. Consciousness comes back, returns to its opposite, i.e. the matter, in doses ('quanta'!) in order to justify itself and thus to justify whatever exists, because whatever exists is reflected in consciousness, but in broken form, so that this and that does not as yet get reflected: They have 'to wait'!

Dialectics is multipolar; the resultant trend or the end result could be, and is, bipolar, though not always. Has the result been confused with the operation of the process itself? Why this impression that dialectics "means unity of opposites" and "struggle of opposites"? or only this? And, in contrast, why do Hegel and Lenin talk *also* of it?

This question needs to be discussed. Both Hegel and Lenin (and, of course, Marx too) have expressed dialectics as the unity of opposites, and their struggle. But a careful study of their works and of the treatment of dialectics therein shows that they talked of it in an entirely different meaning that has been imparted to them. Dialectics and motion for them expresses a conflict between 'is and is not', that too not as separate elements: that which is, is not, it exists but does not. A being is a continuous negation of being. To exist means to not to exist.

As we mentioned earlier, and we take that Hegel's exposition, developed further by Lenin, motion (movement) means "to be in this place and not to be in it".[39] It is this unity of opposites that Lenin dealt with in his "On the Question of Dialectics".

That is the richness of dialectics. The moments of motion cannot be separated, isolated from each other. The moment is the same, yet the moment is not! Herein lies the contradiction, which can only take place 'in unity, i.e. at the same moment, at the same place and in the same identity. This precisely is the identity of the opposites. You see a tree only because there are trees. So, when you see a tree, you commit a mistake, you mistake what is for what is not. There is no justification for registering a tree from the philosophical point of view; it is only a biological/physical act.

But it is possible to see a tree only as part of, only because of existence of trees. A tree can exist only as part of trees. And therefore in order to see the tree, you must see (and contemplate, create concept of) trees.

According to Hegel, dialectics is the result of contradictory determinations or opposite determinations. Besides appearing as contingent, in respect of particular object (world, motion, point, etc.) it has particular determination, e.g.: finite space and time, presence at this place, absolute negation of space (respectively). It has at the same time the equal necessity of the opposite determination, which means respectively infinite space and time, non-presence at that very place, and a relation to space.[40]

Dialectics in ancient world brought out contradiction and the nullity of the assertions made. This could be taken in an objective sense – the object which contradicts itself is held to cancel itself. This is how the Eleatic school concluded that the world, motion and the point were not true: thus they used dialectics chiefly against motion.[41]

"The conclusion drawn from such dialectics is contradiction and the nullity of the assertions made."[42] The result reached, that of subjective nullity may also relate, not to dialectics itself, but the cognition against which it is directed, as in the case of scepticism.

"The fundamental prejudice here is that the dialectic has *only a negative result.*" (Hegel in ibid., emphasis in the original)

Hegel's Exposition of Dialectics

Hegel presents an excellent exposition of dialectics saying it is not "The fault of an object, or of cognition, that they manifest themselves as dialectical by their nature and by an external connection..." "...Thus all opposites which are taken as fixed, such as for example, finite and infinite, or individual and universal, are contradictory not by virtue of some external connection, but rather are transitions in and for themselves..." Thus, it itself is its own other.[43] Supporting Hegel, Lenin says that the object manifests itself as dialectical, concepts are not immobile but by their nature in transition.[44] This should be taken as mutual transition.

The other is not an empty negative, "which is commonly taken as the result of dialectics".[45] It is the other of the first, the negative is the immediate. "It is thus determined as mediated – and altogether contains the determination of the first."[46] The first is thus essentially contained and preserved in the other. The positive is held fast in the negative.

Lenin comments: "This is very important for understanding dialectics." Negation is moment of connection, of development, retaining the positive.

Dialectics is the negation of the first proposition, transition of the first into the second, in connection of the two.

"The second can be made the predicate of the first"[47], for example, the finite is infinite, one is many, the individual is the universal..."[48]

The first term is the notion in itself, and therefore it is negative in itself, therefore its dialectical moment is the distinction implicitly contained within. The second term is distinction, i.e. it is the determinate entity.[49] So, the dialectical moment is the unity contained.

Lenin explains Hegel's concept further. In relation to the simple and original first, positive, assertions, the dialectical moment is the connection, transition, the difference. The demonstration of these is the scientific consideration. The second, negative assertion, the second dialectical moment demands demonstration of unity, i.e. of the connection of the negative and positive, of the presence of the positive in the negative. From assertion to negation, from negation to unity with the asserted – this is the living dialectics.

Hegel continues and makes some astounding formulations. It is not clear why Lenin criticizes them: is it because of a misreading of Hegel by Lenin?

Let us see.

Hegel states that if all the determinations, which fall under the second moment, do not of themselves appear as contradictory and dialectical, "this is a mere fault of thought", which does not confront its thoughts with one another.

So, if the contradictions and dialectics in the objective processes and negations are not reflected in ideas, it means the thought (this particular thought) is not dialectical. It is extremely well-put and is highly dialectically materialist. Hegel says that the 'materials' or sources of thought are already opposite determinations in one relation".[50] They are thus ready for thought process!

Hegel criticises formal thought for allowing contradictory content in front of it "to drop into the sphere of sensuous representation, into space and time, where the contradictory terms are held apart in spatial and temporal juxtaposition and thus come before consciousness **without mutual contact.**"[51]

This is extremely well-expressed, and needs to be understood. Hegel's criticism of formal thought is revealing. Contradictions are allowed to sink to the lower level of contact and sensuous perception. That we can also call 'experience.' What Hegel clearly says (we have mentioned this earlier too) is that sensuous perception (or experience, say direct experience), contradictory terms of space and of time are separated from each other and then understood, or this is done in the course of process of cognition. Contradictions are "held apart" – it really expresses the mechanics of mechanical comprehension.

Lenin makes a critical comment here. He says that the expression "come before consciousness without mutual contact" (the object) is the essence of anti-dialectics. His point is that idealism is shown here by referring to space and time (in connection with sensuous representation) to something lower than thought.

But is it not clear that Hegel is really referring to 'something lower...' Hegel says that it is this, lower, formal thought, which separates, pulls apart, hold apart, the dialectical points in time and space.

He seems to object to refer to time and space by sensuous contact to something lower than thought. But why he does so is not clear at all.

Furtheron, during the same discussion, Lenin does differentiate "in a certain sense" between sensuous representation and thought (why only in a 'certain' sense? Is not clear–AR).[52] He brilliantly theorises that the crux lies in the fact that thought must apprehend the whole representation in its movement. This could be done only if the thought is dialectical.[53]

"Is sensuous representation closer to reality than thought? Both yes and no."[54] Sensuous representation cannot reflect movement as a whole. He gives the example of light speed of 3 lakh km/second. This could be apprehended only by thought. Thought also reflects reality. Time is a form of being of objective reality. "Here in the concept of time (and not in the relation of sensuous representation to thought) is the idealism of Hegel."[55] How? This is not clear.

Continuing his treatment of dialectics, Hegel further criticises formal thought, for which "contradiction is unthinkable".[56] The reality is, on the contrary, that the thinking of contradiction is "the essential moment of Notion."[57]

Negation is the turning point of the movement of the Notion. It is negative self-relation, the internal source of all activity, vital and spiritual self-movement. There has to be the transcendence of the opposition between the Notion and Reality (i.e. concept and reality), their unity is the truth. The second negation, the negative of the negative is this transcendence of the contradiction; it is the innermost and most objective moment of life and spirit, which is the being.[58]

This is "objectivism to the highest degree".[59]

This negation of negation is the third term; it can also be taken as the fourth, counting two negations. According to Hegel, triplicity ('triad') of the dialectical method is its external and superficial side.[60]

Hegel savagely attacks formalism and idle play with dialectics.[61] The formalists, according to Hegel, *have seized and held fast to the empty framework of the triad.* It has been made of ill-repute by the shallow and barren modern "so-called philosophic construction, which consists simply in attaching the formal framework without concept and immanent determination."[62] They use it for all sorts of matter and for external arrangement.

The result of negation of negation, the third term is unity of contradictions, the self-mediating movement and activity.[63] The content of cognition already enters into the new premise, the assertion of the new unity. The method is extended into a system.[64]

The beginning of the whole analysis, the first premise, now appears indeterminate. The need arises to derive it: "this may seem equivalent to the demand for an infinite backward progress in proof and derivation" but on the other hand the new premise drives forward..."[65]

"Thus, cognition rolls forward from content to content."[66] Each subsequent determination is richer and more concrete. The result contains its own beginning. The development of the beginning makes it richer by a new determinateness. Notion preserves itself in its otherness, and the universal in the particular. Whole mass of the antecedent contents are raised to ever new levels. The dialectical progress loses nothing and leaves nothing behind "but carries with it all that it has acquired, enriching and concentrating itself upon itself..."[67] This is a kind of summing up of dialectics, according to Lenin.[68]

The richest is also the most concrete and subjective, according to Hegel. That which carries itself back into the simplest depth is also the most powerful and comprehensive. Thus, each step in the progress from the indeterminate beginning is also a rearward approach to it. So, the two processes appearing at first as different (the regressive confirmation of the beginning and its progressive further determination) coincide and are the same.[69]

The beginning is incomplete because it is beginning, but also incomplete in general as necessary, because truth is only the coming to itself through the negativity of immediacy.[70]

Hegel defines science as "a circle of circles":

"By reason of the nature of the method which has been demonstrated, science is seen to be a circle which returns upon itself, for mediation bends back its end into its beginning, simple ground. Further, this circle is a circle of circles...the various sciences...are fragments of this chain..."[71]

The significant definition concentrates the whole essence of science and its motion.

Hegel Approaches Dialectical and Historical Materialism

Lenin brilliantly develops Hegelian approaches to historical materialism, saves its traces and germs from Hegel's complex world of idealism, and shows how Hegel nearly *discovered* historical materialism, as also approached dialectical materialism, as a result of the logic and momentum of Hegelian dialectics itself.

Hegel makes very profound formulations on subjectivity and objectivity that bring him very near dialectical materialism. This is due to his dialectical approach to these and other concepts. According to him, man cannot comprehend nature in its totality and completeness, as a whole. He can only come eternally closer to it, and in the process create concepts, categories, etc.[72] "The realized Notion" is the object. This transition from the subject, from notion, to the object is to something definitive, independent and complete in itself. The world is the other being of the Idea. Subjectivity (Notion) and the object "*are the same* and *not the same...*" "It is wrong to regard subjectivity and objectivity as fixed and abstract antithesis. Both are wholly dialectical..."[73]

Objectivity has two-fold significance; it stands in opposition to the independent notion, but also is that which is in and for itself. Therefore, knowledge of truth is the cognition of the object "without the addition of any subjective reflection..."[74]

This is extraordinary; Hegel virtually states materialism. Criticizing Kant, Hegel says that one must always reflect upon all natural events according to the principle of natural mechanism; at the same time, one must investigate certain forms of nature. It is **the subjective that is the contingent**, which applies one or other maxim according to the situation.

Here onwards[75] begins a series of proposition wherein *Hegel almost establishes dialectical materialism.* Lenin makes brilliant interpretation of Hegel's formulations and discoveries. Hegel can be found to say that the laws of nature and external world can be divided into mechanical and chemical ones, and they are the bases of man's purposive activity.[76] Objectivity has two forms: nature (mechanical and chemical), and man's purposive activity. Human consciousness reflects the substance of nature. These two forms have a mutual relationship. Lenin notes and interprets Hegel's statement on techniques of chemical and mechanical nature, and puts it in direct and clear materialist form, saying that "MECHANICAL AND CHEMICAL TECHNIQUE serves human ends just because its character (essence) consists in its being determined by external conditions (the laws of nature)."[77]

Explaining Hegel's dialectical materialist tendency, Lenin brings out the fact that the laws of external world, of nature, are the basis of man's purposive activity. Man is confronted with the objective world, and mechanical causality appears as through external and hidden. Hegel puts it like this: "An objective world to which it relates itself still stands opposed to it. From this side, mechanical causality...still appears in this end-relation....but as subordinated to it and as transcended in and for itself."[78]

Law of 'external middle' and historical materialism:

According to Hegel the 'End' of man is connected with objectivity through *Means*. The 'means' play the same role here as that of the tools in Marxist historical materialism. The End is not reasonable in itself and is finite. Therefore, it has to be realized through the Means. Hegel calls Means "the external middle". The End manifests itself through means which is the external other of the End. To that extent the Means are higher than the End. Hegel gives the example of the plough which "is more honourable than those immediate enjoyments which are procured by it, and serve as Ends. *The instrument is preserved, while the immediate enjoyments pass away and are forgotten.*"[79]

Lenin says that there are "germs of historical materialism in Hegel", particularly in the following passage: "The means however is the external middle of the syllogism which is the realization of the End: in it therefore reasonableness manifests itself as such–as preserving itself in this external Other and precisely through this externality. To that extent the Means is higher than the finite Ends of the external usefulness: the plough is more honourable than those immediate enjoyments which are procured by it, and serves as Ends. The instrument is preserved, while the immediate enjoyments pass away and are forgotten. IN HIS TOOLS MAN POSSESSES POWER OVER EXTERNAL NATURE, ALTHOUGH AS REGARDS HIS ENDS, HE FREQUENTLY IS SUBJECTED TO IT."[80]

Lenin comments that in actual fact man's ends are engendered by the objective world. But it seems to mean as if his ends are taken from outside the world, and are independent of it. Therefore, Lenin characterizes Hegel's exposition as follows:

"Historical materialism as one of the applications and developments of the ideas of genius—seeds existing in embryo in Hegel."[81]

The seeds existing in Hegel are the ideas of genius, which when developed further results in historical materialism. Hegel endeavours to bring practice under the categories of logic. What he has extracted out of Hegel as materialist, he characterizes as "VERY PROFOUND, PURELY MATERIALISTIC CONTENT".[82] Lenin inverts Hegel's presentation. It is the practical activity that leads man's consciousness to the repetition of various logical figures endlessly. Hegel comes to "Idea" as the coincidence of the Notion and the object, as truth through practice, and thus moves from the subjective end to objective truth. Thus, Hegel comes very close to the idea that practice proves to be the criterion of truth.

Lenin comments that when Hegel endeavours to bring man's purposive activity under the categories of logic, saying that this activity is the syllogism, that the subject (man) plays the role of a "member" in the logical "figure" of the syllogism, etc., "THEN THAT IS NOT MERELY STRETCHING A POINT, A MERE GAME. THIS HAS A VERY PROFOUND, PURELY MATERIALISTIC CONTENT. It has to be inverted."[83] It is remarkable that Hegel comes to the "Idea" as the coincidence of the Notion and the object, as truth, through the practical, purposive activity of man. This is a very close approach to the view that the human being proves the correctness of his idea through practice.[84]

Hegel is constantly approaching dialectical materialism. It would be very interesting to study Lenin's comments on Hegel at this juncture. Lenin notes that it is noteworthy that the whole chapter on Absolute Idea in *Science of Logic* hardly says a word on God. It contains almost nothing that is specially ***idealism***, but has for its main subject the ***dialectical method.*** The sum-total, the last word and essence of Hegel's logic is the dialectical method–"this is extremely noteworthy. And one thing more: in this ***most idealistic*** of Hegel's works there is the ***least*** idealism and the ***most materialism.*** " 'Contradictory', but a fact!"[85]

To use the analytical method, to analyse the given concrete phenomenon, is to give the form of abstraction to its individual aspects and to bring into relief the 'genus' or force and law. The use of analytical or synthetical method *is not an arbitrary matter;* it depends on the form of the very objects to be cognized. Empiricists adopt the standpoint of analysis. But this turns things upside down: cognition, which wishes to take things as they are falls into contradiction with itself. "The chemist, for example, tortures a piece of flesh and discovers in it nitrogen, carbon, etc. But then these abstract substances have ceased to be flesh."[86]

The richer the object to be defined, the more numerous the aspects. Philosophy however must prove and derive everything, and limit itself to definitions.[87]

Hegel says, activity is a "contradiction": the purpose is real and not real, possible and not, etc. Disappearance of this contradiction, formally consists in activity abolishing the subjectivity of the purpose, and along with it the objectivity, the opposite. Both are finite. Not merely the one-sidedness of subjectivity is abolished but the subjectivity as a whole.[88]

Speaking of absolute idea, Hegel ridicules "declamation" over it, as if everything were revealed in it. The absolute idea is the universal, but the universal is not merely an abstract form to which the particular content stands contrasted as an other, but as the absolute form into which all determinations, the whole fullness of the content posited by it have retreated. "In this respect the absolute idea can be compared to an old man, who utters the same statements of religion as a child, but for whom they have the significance of his whole lifetime. Even if the child understands the religious content, it is for him still only something outside of which the whole of life and the whole of the world lie," "The interest lies in the whole movement..."[89]

The philosophical method is both analytical and synthetical, but not in the sense of mere juxtaposition or alternation. Philosophy holds both of them transcended in itself and *"in every one of its movements"*. So it is both analytical and synthetical simultaneously. Philosophy proceeds analytically insofar as it only accepts its object. The latter is allowed its own way, is looked upon. To this extent philosophy is passive. It is active to the extent that it is synthetic.[90]

Hegel says further:

"That however involves the effort to refrain from our own fancies and private opinions, which always seek to obtrude themselves..." "Thus the method is not an external form, but the soul and notion of the content..."[91]

Lenin mentions in capital and bold letters that Hegel *"almost completely approaches dialectical materialism"*, in the following statements:

"Aristotle and the more ancient philosophers took their start in natural philosophy from universal thought a priori and from this developed notion. This is one side. The other side is the necessary one that experience should be worked up into universality." In other words, the result which follows from the abstract idea "should coincide with the general conception to which experience and observation have led."[92]

This is a very important point that Hegel makes. The *a priori* in Aristotle is not sufficient, because it has no connection with experience and observation. The development from the particular to the general is the discovery of natural forces and laws. The "sense of nature" is more true than the other, the limited, abstract knowledge, without truth in itself.[93]

Hegel says further that "philosophy is dialectical, this dialectic is change; the idea, as abstract idea, is the inert and existent, but it is true insofar as it grasps itself as living; this is, that is, dialectical in itself and not contingent."[94]

Though Lenin does not make any comment on the passage, it needs particular attention. First, philosophy is dialectical; second, it is true only as far as it grasps itself. Thus, it transcends its inertness. Third, that is why, philosophy in itself is dialectical.

Put in opposition to scepticism and empiricism, the materialist dialectical content core of Hegel's thoughts comes to the fore. He says scepticism is "not doubt", which is the opposite of tranquility that is the result of scepticism.

Hegel goes into a detailed exposition of the living beings, various creatures and human beings, and into some of the natural sciences. According to Hegel they are quite valid against the dogmatism of common human understanding. Hegel expresses himself against the absolute, when the sceptics hold something determinate as the absolute, and thus "here we have the germ of dialectical materialism." Hegel also brings out dialectics as the 'destruction of itself'.[96]

Hegel and Lenin point out that Sextus Empiricus (second century AD) reveals the dialectics of the concept of a point. "A point has not dimensions? That means that it is outside space. It is the limit of space in space, a negation of space, and at the same time 'it touches space' – 'but at the same time it is also in itself something dialectical."[97]

In one of the most beautiful, *simplest and clearest examples of the dialectics* of notion and its materialist roots, Hegel (and Lenin) shows the individual to be the universal. The individual, the subject, "***is just as much not individual but universal***".[98] Lenin's emphasis) Besides, the understanding believes its reflection to be an external reflection which does not lie within the idea. It is an eternal creation i.e. dialectics. The "Idea" itself is the dialectic which continuously keeps differentiating out of itself. Hegel constantly talks of abstractions and relations outside idea.[99]

Dealing with life and inorganic matter, Hegel says that the question of life does not belong to logic as it is commonly imagined. Every science is applied logic "in apprehending its object in forms of thought and of the Notion."[100] The judgement of life consists in separation of itself as individual subject from the objective.[101] Inorganic nature is subdued by the living being: this is inorganic nature in itself, and life for itself.[102] We get pure materialism by inversion.

Hegel on Movement and Dialectics

How important and profound are the sixteen elements of dialectics mentioned earlier is clear from the study of Hegel and Lenin made so far, as also will be clear from the analyses to follow. The elements express the extreme flexibility, transitoriness and multiplicity of objects and relations.

In his *Science of Logic*, Hegel analyses the formulation that reason has its bounds. But he makes the profound discovery that the boundary is already surpassed by determining it, and this is not generally realised.[103] A stone does not think; "therefore its restrictedness is no bound *for it*. But the stone also has its bounds, for example, in oxidation, if it is a base capable of being oxydized."[104] This is the "evolution of the stone", comments Lenin.[105]

Everything ("human") passes beyond its bounds but *reason* cannot pass beyond its bounds. Every passage beyond is not emancipation. Despite his idealist limitations, Hegel displays an extraordinary materialist tendency in applying the category of necessity and freedom. If a magnet had consciousness, it would consider its turning to the north *as freely made*. Yet, Hegel says, then it would know all directions of space, and it would consider this one direction *as a boundary to its freedom*. This one is extremely dialectical,[106] and dialectical materialist at that!

Hegel presents the philosophical notions dialectically –

"It is the nature of the finite to pass beyond itself, to negate its negation and to become infinite ..." This is the dialectics of things themselves, of nature itself, of the course of events, the processes.[107]

It is *not the external power* that converts the finite into the infinite, but *its nature itself.*[108]

Hegel was a *master dialectician*. Hegel transforms lifeless concepts and ideas into those full of life and constant change, and expresses their inner, inherent dialectics. It is interesting to see what Lenin has to say on this. According to Lenin, "Hegel analyses concepts that usually appear to be dead and shows that there *is* movement in them."[109] Finite? That only means it is *moving* to an end. Something "means ***not that*** which is other".[110] Being in general means 'not-being'. There is all-sided universal flexibility of concepts in Hegel, a flexibility that approaches 'the identity of opposites'.[111]

The finite and the infinite are opposed to one another; the infinite begins beyond the finite. Yet they are inseparable, they are a unity. The unity of finite and infinite is not their external juxtaposition. They are not in an improper connection contrary to their determination, binding the entities as separate, opposed and independent, and therefore incompatible.

On the contrary, each in itself is this unity, "and is only in transcending itself". Finitude exists only as a passing beyond itself. "It thus contains infinity, which is its other..."[112] The finite itself is infinite.

Lenin comments that this should be "applied to atoms versus electrons"; in general it is the infiniteness of matter deep within.[113]

The infinite progress asserts more than mere comparison of the finite with the infinite; "in it is also posited the *connection* of terms which are also distinct"[114] the connection of all parts of infinite progress.

Therefore, the nature of speculative thought consists *solely* in seizing the opposed moments in their unity. The question as to how the infinite arrives at the finite is considered by some as the essence of philosophy. But according to Hegel it is the question of their connection. Being-for-self, i.e. infinite being, is the consummated finite (qualitative) Being. The 'One' is the old principle of the atom (i.e.

the indivisible) and the void. (cf. particles in quantum physics–AR).

"**The void is considered source of motion** not only in the sense that space is not filled but also contains the ground of becoming, the unrest of self-movement".[115]

"The ideality of Being-for-self as totality thus, first, passes into reality, and into the most fixed and abstract of all, as *One*."[116] The thought of the ideal passing into the real is profound and very important for history. It can be directed against vulgar materialism. The difference of the ideal from the material is also conditional. Hegel takes self-development of concepts in connection with the entire history.[117]

Hegel on Philosophy and Method

In a significant statement, Hegel said that philosophy cannot borrow its method from a subordinate science, such as mathematics. It is along the path of self-construction that philosophy becomes an objective science. The path of self-construction is the path of real cognition of movement. The movement of consciousness, like the development of all natural and spiritual life, rests on the nature of pure essentialities, which make up the content of logic; that means theory must be derived from the movement of natural and spiritual life.[118]

The concept of force in physics, and of polarity the things bounds up *inseparably* together, and the transition from force to polarity–this transition is higher relations of thought.[119]

To present the realm of thought in its philosophical aspect, that is, in its necessary development–this is the job of philosophy.[120] Nature in general is opposed, as physical, to the mental.

Hegel quotes Aristotle's significant words to the effect that it was only after nearly everything necessary was available that people began to trouble themselves about philosophy; the same applied to the leisure of the Egyptian priests and the beginning of mathematics.

Preoccupation with pure thought presupposes a long stretch already traversed by mind. In this kind of thought, those interests are "hushed which move the lives of peoples and individuals".[121] Hegel draws attention to thoughts of all natural and spiritual things: to bring into clear consciousness this logical character is our problem. Lenin clarifies and explains Hegel, saying, Logic is the science not of external forms of thought, but of laws of development of all material, natural and spiritual things, i.e. of the development of the entire concrete content of the world i.e. the sum-total of the history of knowledge of the world. Instinctive man, the savage, does not distinguish himself from nature. Conscious man does distinguish. Categories are stages of distinguishing, i.e. of cognizing the world, focal points in the web, which assist in cognizing and mastering it ("In this web, strong knots are formed now and then, which are foci and direction".[122]

Method is the consciousness of the form taken by "the inner spontaneous movement of its content." The given sphere of phenomena is moved forward by the content itself of this sphere, the dialectic, which the content has in itself: this is the dialectic of its own movement.[123]

"The negative is to an equal extent positive": negating is something definite, has a definite content, the inner contradictions lead to the replacement of the older content by a higher one. In the old logic there is no transition. Hegel puts forward two basic requirements: the *necessary* connection, the objective connection of all the aspects, tendencies, etc. of the given sphere of phenomena; the "immanent *emergence* of distinctions", the inner objective logic of evolution and of the struggle of the differences, the polarity.[124]

Hegel says, dialectics is generally regarded as an "external and negative" procedure, not belonging to the subject-matter."[125]

Lenin says: "I am in general trying to read Hegel materialistically: Hegel is materialism which has been stood on its head (according to Engels)–that is to say, I cast aside for the most part God, the Absolute, the Pure Idea etc".[126]

According to Hegel, it would not be difficult to demonstrate unity of being and nothing in every example*: 'neither in heaven nor on earth is there anything not containing both Being and Nothing".*[127] The objections presume the determinate being ("I have 100 thaler or not"). But that is not the question.

"A determinate or finite Being is such as refers itself to another; it is content which stands in a relation of necessity with other content or with the whole world. In view of the mutually determinant connection of the whole, metaphysics could make an assertion – which is really a tautology – that if the least grain of dust were destroyed, the whole universe must collapse."[128]

"What is first in science has had to show itself first, too, historically. (Hegel, ibid). It is said that darkness is the absence of light. But "as little is seen in pure light as in pure darkness..."[129] "There exists nothing that is not a mean condition between Being and Nothing."[130]

Lenin explaining the dialectics in Hegel, says, dialectics is the teaching which shows how opposites can be and begin to be identical, becoming transformed into one another, why our mind should grasp the opposites not as dead, rigid, but as living, conditional, mobile, becoming transformed into one another.[131]

Hegel on Quantity, Magnitude and Numbers

Commenting on Kant (and criticizing him), Hegel says that concreteness and discreteness, taken separately, do not constitute truth ("neither determination has truth"), but only their unity. This is true dialectics, according to Hegel.[132] "Discreteness, like continuity is a **moment** of quantity..."[133] (It could also be called separateness or dismemberment, etc.).

Quantum means quantity having determinateness or limit–in its complete determination, number. Amount and unit constitute the moments of number.[134]

This is a very profound statement. The quantitative determinateness break up the continuity of thoughts and render them *more and more arbitrary*. Numbering means break the process of thought or any process. Their representation as numbers is senseless and arbitrary.

"In the infinitesimal calculus a certain inexactitude (conscious) is ignored, nevertheless the result obtained is not approximate but absolutely exact!"[135] Hegel's answer is highly complicated and demands higher mathematics, as did Engels in *Auti-Duhring* on differential and integral calculus. Hegel presents a most detailed consideration of the differential and integral calculus, with questions from Newton, Leibnitz, Carnot, Lagrange, Euler etc. That showed how interesting Hegel found the "vanishing" of infinitely small magnitudes, this "intermediate between being and not-being". Lenin comments that the title of Carnot was characteristic: "Reflections on the Metaphysics of the Infinitesimal Calculus". He also comments that "without studying higher mathematics all this is incomprehensible".[136]

Quantum is limit external.[137] The ancients were aware of the connection by which a change appearing as merely quantitative turns into one which is qualitative. Quantum when taken as indifferent limit is that side from which "an existent being can be attacked and destroyed." "It is the cunning of the Notion to seize it from this side, where its quality does not appear to come into play."

"It is a great merit to become acquainted with the empirical numbers of nature (as the distances of the planets from one another), but an infinitely greater merit to cause the empirical quanta to disappear and raise them into a *universal form* of quantitative determinations, so that they have become moments of law or Measure. The merit of Galileo and Kepler was that "They *demonstrated* the laws they discovered by showing that the totality of details of perceptions corresponds to these laws."[138]

Hegel gives examples from chemistry, musical tones, water etc. Then he says: "It is said that there are no leaps in nature;" ordinary imagination thinks that *it* has conceived them. "But we saw that the changes of Being were in general not only a transition of one magnitude into another, but a transition from the qualitative into the quantitative, and conversely; a process of becoming other which breaks off graduality and is qualitatively other as against the preceding Existent Being. Water on being cooled" (Hegel gives an example) "*does not little by little* become hard, gradually reaching the consistency of ice after having passed through the consistency of the paste, *but is suddenly hard*; when it already has *quite attained freezing-point it may (if it stands still) be wholly liquid, and slight shake brings it into the condition of hardness*)"[139]

"The gradualness of arising is based upon the idea that that which arises is already...actually there, and is imperceptible only on account of its smallness; and the gradualness of vanishing is based on the idea that not-Being or the Other which is assuming its place equally is there, only is not yet noticeable; —there, not in the sense that the Other is contained in the Other which is there in itself, but that it is there as existence, only unnoticeable. This altogether cancels arising and passing away..."[140]

But countering such a superficial analysis, Hegel candidly explains that understanding of gradualness and qualitative change often falls into tautology; the change is seen as an external expression of gradualness and process, and the qualitative change is seen as an external transformation. Actually, the qualitative change is that of the something into the Other, into the opposite. Missing this point leads one to fall into an observation of quantitative change only.

This is an extraordinary explanation of the law of the change of quantity into quality by Hegel.

Doctrine of Essence

Lenin, in this chapter, deals with the theory of essence and its role in the development of theory of knowledge. He analyses Hegel's views on Essence and conversion of idealistic expressions into realistic ones through dialectics of the motion of the concepts. Lenin quotes Hegel from the latter's volume 4 as stating that "The truth of Being is Essence". It is the first sentence of "Essence as Reflection in Itself", a section in *Science of Logic.* This first sentence sounds "thoroughly idealistic and mystical", but immediately afterwards, a fresh wind, so to speak, begins to blow, says Lenin: "Being is the immediate. Knowledge seeks to understand that truth which being, *in and for itself,* is, and therefore does not halt" (Lenin emphasizes the words: "*does not halt* 'NB'," i.e. very important) at the immediate and its determinations but *penetrates* through it, assuming that *behind* (this one Hegel's italics) this Being there is something other than Being itself..."[141] "Does not halt" is important to grasp motion, as it reveals the inner dialectics of being.

Being is understood, is "penetrated" by understanding, which goes beyond and into it, thus revealing the continuous difference between what is and what is understood. This is transition and passage beyond what is. The movement of knowledge is not external to Being but is the movement of Being itself.

Criticism of idealism by Hegel: Hegel makes a very significant statement that "**modern idealism did not dare to regard cognition as a knowledge of the Thing-in-itself.**"[142] This is sharp criticism by Hegel of modern idealism and its superficiality. This is very significant as Hegel has been repeatedly accused of being hardly more than an idealist. He was no doubt an idealist, but that is not important; what is important is that he was a thorough dialectician. Idealism of Leibnitz, Kant or Fichte, according to Hegel, did not reach beyond "Being as determinateness", beyond this immediacy.[143] That means they did not go deeper. Besides, the objective idealism of Hegel almost touched materialism in the course of its criticism of idealism, particularly of subjective idealism.

"It is the immediacy of not-Being which constitutes semblance ("Semblance = the negative nature of Essence – Lenin); in Essence, Being is not-Being."[144] Thus, semblance is not–existent which exists. Essence contains semblance within itself, as infinite inte rnal movement."[145]

"Becoming in Essence – its reflective movement – is hence the movement from Nothing to Nothing and through Nothing back to itself..."[146] Lenin comments that this is a profound statement, and then explains: "Movements 'to nothing' occur in nature and in life. Only there are certainly none "from nothing". Always from something.[147]

Hegel emphasizes incorrectness of "law of identity (A = A). "If everything is self-identical, it is not distinguished: it contains no opposition and has no ground."[148]So, there must be difference, opposition, dialectics.

The principles of difference lead us to say things like "All things are different..." "A is also not A" etc.[149]

There is customary "tenderness" for nature, history, etc., leading one to wish that they did not contradict one another. But such people forget that there is no escape from it; the contradiction is merely planted elsewhere, into subjective or external reflection. Lenin terms "this irony" as "exquisite!"[150]

The result of the addition of plus and minus is nought, but "*the result of contradiction is not only nought.*" So, contradiction is not simple cancellation but a process, motion and growth. It is really very profound how Hegel uncovers contradiction and dialectics.

The resolved contradiction is precisely the Essence as the unity of Positive and Negative.

According to Hegel, even a slight reflective thought will show that if anything has just been determined as positive (posited, positedness), it straightway turns into negative. The positive especially means an objective entity, and the latter subjective, belonging only to the external reflection. Insufficient acquaintance leads us to a subjective error. Truth is positive. But as self-equality, knowledge takes up a negative attitude to this other and *penetrates the object,* transcends it, i.e. the negative. Consciousness is not always aware of this metamorphosis.[151]

Error is also positive, in the sense that it is "as an opinion affirming that which is not... But ignorance is indifference to truth and error."[152]

Law of the Excluded Middle

Hegel quotes a proposition of the law of the excluded middle: "Something is either A or not A; there is no third", and "*analyses*" it.[153] "Everything is a term of an opposition", – means everything has its positive and negative determination, and that is all right. But if it is taken as either this or that, it leads to nothing.[154]

"And then – Hegel says wittily – it is said that there is no third. **There is** a third in this thesis itself. A itself is the third, for A can be both +A and –A. 'The Something thus is itself the third term which was supposed to be excluded.'"[155] That means everything, every concrete something is in contradictory relation to every other thing" "it is itself and some other."[156]

Hegel says, ordinarily contradiction is removed, first of all from things (from the existent), and then it is asserted that there is nothing contradictory. Next, it is shifted into subjective reflection, but there it does not exist, because it is impossible to imagine contradiction. One should disregard the statement that contradiction does not exist. Hegel strongly emphasizes that "contradiction is the **root of all movement and vitality**"; "it is only insofar as it contains a contradiction that anything **moves and has impulse and activity.**"[157]

Lenin positively and approvingly notes these views of Hegel and includes them in his general analyses. He then quotes something very crucial and extraordinary from Hegel's *Science of Logic.* That reveals and explains the very dialectics of motion.

"***Something moves, not because it is here at one point of time and there at another, but because at one and the same point of time it is***

here and not here, and in this here both is and is not."[158] "Motion is *existent* contradiction itself."[159]

This is an extraordinary passage from Hegel. He here fully explains motion and its dialectics, its very meaning and essence. He says that old dialecticians definitely brought out the *contradiction in motion;* but that is not enough; what must be revealed is that motion itself is contradiction!

This aspect is extremely relevant in the context of the present-day ongoing quantum revolution, and very helpful in explaining subatomic inter-stellar motions, the motions of the waves and the particles and of their duality.

Similarly, internal self-movement is nothing else than the fact that something is in itself and is also negative of itself, in one and the same respect. "**Abstract** self-identity **has no vitality** but the fact that Positive in itself is negativity causes it to pass outside itself and **to change.** Something therefore is living only in so far as it contains contradiction..." "If an existent something cannot in its positive determination also encroach on its negative, cannot hold fast the one in the other and contains a contradiction within itself, then it is not living unity." It perishes in contradiction.[160]

Simplicity conceals–above and below, right and left, etc. contain contradiction in one term: that is above which is not below; 'above' is determined only as not being 'below', and is only insofar as there is a 'below'.

Thought does not become aware of contradiction. It keeps the two determinations external to each other, and have in imagination, in mind only these and not their transition.[161]

Hegel on Matter

There are several passages in Hegel, which show that he came very close to the discovery of scientific and dialectical materialism and even of historical materialism. In his works like the *Phenomenology of Mind* and *Science of Logic* there are passages difficult to separate from dialectical materialism and scientific world outlook. They are extra-ordinary works, which have been neglected by the philosophers and scholars or only superficially touched up.

Form is essential, essence is formed. Essence as formless identity of itself with itself becomes matter. The matter "is the real foundation or substraction of form." Something from every determination and form is matter. Matter is a pure abstract. (Matter cannot be seen or felt, etc. –what is seen or fell is a determinate matter that is unity of matter and form."[162] "Matter must be formed, and Form must materialize itself."[163] Activity of form and the movement of matter are the same.[164]

Hegel deals with material forms objectively and in motion. He emphasizes that "the world is nothing but Nature itself".[165] If nature is to be the world, then manifold determinations and interconnections are to added. Lenin comments here that even with defects and mysticism, Hegel's ideas are of a genius. Hegel finds out vital and all-sided interconnections of everything with everything, and these interconnections are reflected in human concepts equally flexible, mobile and interconnected. According to Lenin, the "Continuation of the work of Hegel and Marx must consist in the *dialectical* elaboration of the history of human thought, science and technique."[166]

Discovering or showing changing interconnections between processes and the objects is a hallmark of Hegelian dialectics coming very close to materialism. "The word "**moment**" is often used by Hegel in the sense of moment of *connection*, moment of concatenation."[167]

Lenin refers in this connection to Hegel's example of the river. The relation between the river and the drops is dialectical: the position of *every* drop could be considered, with its relation to all others; there are endless inter-relations, direction of movement, line of movement, etc. The sum total of the movements results in a totality of process. Concepts emerge as the *registration* of individual aspects of the movement, of individual drops (="things"), of individual "*streams*" etc. "This is approximately "the picture of the world according to Hegel's Logic", says Lenin.[168]

'Essence must appear ...'[169] and appearance/s must evolve dialectically; in fact both evolve dialectically. "The intro-reflected self-existent world stands opposed to the world of Appearance..."[170] Hegel criticises transcendental idealism for placing all *determinations in consciousness.* He says, critically, that from its point of view, it is upto the subject to see the leaves of a tree not as black but as green or the sun as round and not square. Further criticizing transcendental idealism, Hegel says that "the essential inadequacy" of this philosophy is "that it clings to the abstract Thing-in-itself as to an ultimate determination; it opposes reflection..."[171]

It is very significant that Hegel, despite his idealist limitations, goes to the very limits of objective idealism, and emphasizes the primacy of the reflection of the external world upon consciousness.

He then deals with the objective laws of reflection of appearance, which establish identity between the involved opposites. "This identity, the foundation of Appearance, which constitutes Law, is the peculiar moment of Appearance..." "Hence Law is not beyond Appearance, but is *immediately present* in it; the realm of Laws is the *quiescent* (Hegel's italics) reflection of the existing or appearing world..."

On this, Lenin comments that "This is a remarkably materialistic and remarkably appropriate (with the word "ruhige" or quiescent) determination. Law takes the quiescent—and therefore law, every law, is narrow, incomplete, approximate."[172] Further on, Lenin interprets Hegel as saying that law is the reflection of the essential in the movement of the universe.[173] Analysing Hegel's *Phenomenology of Mind*, Lenin says, according to Hegel, "The world in and for itself is identical with the world of appearances, but at the same time opposite to it. What is positive in the one negative in the other." The world of appearances and the world in itself are *moments* of man's knowledge of nature, deepening of knowledge.[174] "***Thus Law is Essential Relation***,"[175] "The term *world* expresses the formless totality of multifariousness..."[176] Lenin comments that the criterion of dialectics has accidentally slipped in into Hegel when he says that the conflict between the inner and outer is apparent ***in all natural, scientific, and, in general, intellectual development.***[177]

Knowledge of matter must be deepened to knowledge or concept od substance I order to find the causes of phenomena. At the same time, the actual cognition of the cause is the deepening of knowledge from the externality of phenomena to the substance. Examples from history of natural science and from the history of philosophy as also from the history of technique would help, as per Lenin, and this is what Hegel strives to do. Hegel deals in detail with causality and all-sidedness. Effect, in the opinion of Hegel, is the manifestation of cause. Hegel says, it is customary in history to talk of anecdotes as the causes of major events. But the reasons are far deeper and serious.[178] Lenin explains that Hegel subsumes history **completely** under causality and understands causality a thousand times better than most others.[179]

A stone in motion is cause; besides, it contains many other determinations such as colour, shape, etc. So cause has many determinations that do not enter into causal relations. Says Hegel, the cause in its extinction becomes again, and effect vanishes into cause but equally becomes again in it Each of them cancels itself out in its positing and posits itself in the cancellation. So it is not some external transition, but this becoming another is itself its own positing. Thus, as Lenin clarifies, It means movement of matter, of history, has to be grasped in its *inner* connection.[180]

Criticizing Kant, Hegel points out that the object is truly in and for itself only as it is in thought; it is appearance in ideation. Though admitting of the objectivity of the concepts, Kant leaves them sunjective. In Kant the exposition is truly incomplete. And then Hegel makes a leap in concept: "The Notion must not here be considered as an act of self-conscious understanding, or as subjective understanding: what we have to do with is the Notion in and for itself, which constitutes a STAGE AS WELL OF NATURE AS OF SPIRIT, LIFE, OR ORGANIC NATURE, IS THAT STAGE OF NATURE AT WHICH THE NOTION EMERGES." Lenin terms this transition as the eve of the transformation of objective idealism into materialism.[181]

Lenin here reminds that Engels had pointed out that the main point against Kant had already been made by Hegel, insofar as this was possible from an idealistic point of view. (Ibid) "From living perception to abstract thought, *and from this to practice*,—such is the dialectical path of the cognition of truth, of the cognition of objective reality. Kant disparages knowledge in order to make way for faith: Hegel exalts knowledge, asserting that knowledge is knowledge of God. The materialist exalts the knowledge of matter..." *Essentially*, Hegel is right as opposed to Kant. Thought proceeds from the concrete to the abstract – does not get *away* from the truth but comes closer to it. For example, this is true of all the abstraction of *matter*, of *value* etc., in short of *all* scientific concepts and abstractions.[182]

Lenin insists that one would have to return to Hegel for systematic analysis of current logic and criticism of theory of knowledge of Kant and others. Marx applied Hegel's dialectics in its rational form to political economy, he says.[183] Hegel says at one place[184] that "All things are a syllogism, a universal which is bound together with individuality through particularity..." Lenin comments that it is impossible deny the objectivity of notions, the objectivity of the universal in the individual and the particular. The formation of abstract notions includes idea and consciousness of the law-governed character of the objective connection of the world. Hegel is much more advanced than Kant in tracing the reflection of the movement of the objective world in the movement of notions. The simple form of value, the individual act of exchange of one commodity for another already includes *all* the major contradictions of capitalism; similarly, the simplest *generalization*, the first and simplest formation of the notions already denote ever deeper cognition of the *objective* connection of the world. This is the true significance of Hegel's *Logic.*[185]

Here Lenin criticizes the Marxists for their superficial approach to Kantianism and other trends. He reveals that the Marxists criticized Kantianism more in the manner of Feuerbach than of Hegel; in other words mechanically and not dialectically. Plekhanov merely rejects Kantianism but does not correct it, and is thus unable to deepen the dialectical materialist concepts, unable to show connections and transitions.[186]

And then Lenin makes a profound and revealing observation and criticism of the Marxist attitude to Hegel and his dialectical method. He says: "It is impossible completely to understand Marx's *Capital,* and especially its first chapter, without having thoroughly studied and understood the *whole* of Hegel's Logic. *Consequently, half a century later none of the Marxists understood Marx!!*"[187]

"Hegel actually *proved* that logical forms and laws are not an empty shell, but the *reflection* of the objective world. More correctly, he did not prove, but *made a brilliant guess.*"[188]

Hegel makes another brilliant statement, and a crucial one, this time on the nature of spirit. Let us see what he says: "Spirit, however, is only spirit through being mediated by Nature..." "It is Spirit that recognizes the logical Idea in Nature and so raises it to its essence..."

He is reaching the conclusion that spirit is the reflection of nature. Nature, as the immediate totality, unfolds itself in logical ideas and mind.[189] Lenin draws further conclusions from Hegel; logic is the science of cognition. It is the theory of knowledge, and knowledge is the reflection of nature in human mind. This reflection takes the path of series of abstractions, concepts, laws etc. here are three members, *really speaking:* nature, human cognition=human brain as the highest product of the same nature, and form of reflection in mind. "Man cannot comprehend=reflect=mirror nature *as a whole*, in its completeness its 'immediate totality,' he can only *eternally* come closer to this, creating abstractions, concepts, laws, a scientific picture of the world etc., etc."[190]

Hegel makes profound and clever[191] about laws of logic being reflection of the objective in the subjective consciousness of man. Thought, say Hegel, is not mere subjective and formal activity; in reality, "subjectivity is only a stage of development from Being and Essence..."[192] "It is wrong to regard subjectivity and objectivity as a fixed and abstract antithesis. Both are wholly dialectical..."[193] A really profound and materialistic statement from Hegel! He almost discovered dialectical materialism.

According to Lenin, *Encylopaedia* by Hegel contain "PERHAPS THE BEST EXPOSITION OF DIALECTICS."[194] The expression "idea" is used in the sense of a simple representation or objective truth. Says Hegel: "If *thoughts* are merely subjective and contingent they certainly have no further value; but in this they are not inferior to temporal and contingent *actualities...*"[195]

Hegel here makes certain points. The Idea or man's knowledge is the coincidence of notion and objectivity. Secondly, the Idea is the **relation** of the subjectivity (=man) which is for itself (=independent, as it were) to the objectivity which is *distinct* (from this Idea). Thirdly, subjectivity is the **impulse** to destroy the separation of idea from the object. Fourthly, cognition is the process of submersion of the mind in the inorganic nature to subordinate it to the power of the subject. Fifthly, in the Idea the Notion reaches freedom, and because of this the Idea contains also the *harshest opposition*; it eternally creates and eternally overcomes it, coinciding it with itself. Thus the contradiction between thought and object is eternally created and overcome.[196]

Thus there is the eternal process of contradiction in thoughts and their being reflective of nature in the eternal arising of the contradictions and their solution and passing out.

Lenin explains that "Hegel brilliantly *divined* the dialectics of things (phenomena, the world, *nature*) in the dialectics of concepts." The totality of all sides of phenomena, of reality and their all-sided relations, that is truth, that is the main content of logic, by which these concepts are shown as reflections of the objective reality. The dialectics of things produce dialectics of ideas.[197]

What constitutes dialectics? Lenin answers, following and explaining Hegel, that it is the mutual dependence of all notions, transition of notions into one another, the relativity of oppositions between notions, identity of opposites between the notions, etc. "Truth is first of all taken to mean that I *know* how something is. This is truth, however, only in reference to consciousness, or formal truth, bare correctness. Truth in deeper sense, on the contrary, consists in the identity between objectivity and the Notion..." Nothing can exist entirely devoid of identity between the notion and reality. "Everything deserving the name of philosophy has always been based on the consciousness of an absolute unity of that ***which the understanding accepts as valid only in its separation...***"[198]

The dialectics in Hegel is the simplest and clearest when he deals with notions and their material roots. Hegel points out that the understanding falls into the misunderstanding when it tackles Idea or the objective reality, that the external reflection is that of its own upon the outside,mand not vice-versa. Actually, the Idea (objective reality) itself is the dialectics for ever separating the self-identical from the differentiated, the subjective from the objective, the finite from the infinite—the the process of eternal creation and vitality.[199] There is the difference of movement and moment.[200]

Life=individual subject separates itself from the objective.[201] question of life does not belong to logic, but in the dealing of truth, life has to be dealt with. Every science must be absorbed in logic since its every form apprehends objects in forms of thought. Inorganic nature is subdued by the living being because it is in itself the same as life is for itself. Lenin comments: "Invert it=pure materialism. Excellent, profound, correct!!"[202]

Hegel on Practice in Theory of Knowledge

Lenin, explaining Hegel's dialectical approach, reveals his positions on the subject: The notion(=man) presupposes the otherness which is in itself (=nature independent of man). This notion is an impulse to realize itself, to give itself objectivity in the objective world through itself, and to realize itself. Practice stands opposed to the actual. The world does not satisfy man and man decides to change it. The good or the practice is a demand of the external actuality. "This Idea is **higher than the Idea of Cognition which has already been considered,** for it has not only the dignity of the universal but also of the **simply actual...**"[203] In other words, practice is higher than (theoretical) knowledge, for it has not only the dignity of universality, but also of the immediate actuality.[204]

The "objective world" pursues its own course, and man's practice, confronted by this objective world, encounters "obstacles in the realization: of the End."[205] Hegel says that the "Good" remains "An Ought" in and for itself. On the other hand, Being remains determined against it as a not-Being. So the good is subjective wish. "There are still **two worlds in opposition**: one a realm of *subjectivity* in the *pure* spaces of *transparent* thought, the other a realm of objectivity in the element of an externally manifold actuality, which is an unexplored realm of darkness."[206] Thus, there are two worlds opposed to each other, yet dialectically related with each other. In the words of Hegel, the actuality "***is present independently of subjective positing.***"[207]

Hegel is explained by Lenin in the course of discussion on Cognition. Cognition is confronted by that which is existing independently of the subjective wish. Man's will or practice itself blocks the attainment of his aims because it separates from cognition and does not recognize the external world as it is. Consequently, a unity of cognition and practice is essential.[208] For Hegel, practice is the logical syllogism, a figure of logic, "and that is true!" That is because practice has its other being in figures of logic through a thousand-million-time-practice, resulting stable prejudices of axiomatic character.[209]

The detailed study, which we have done above, helps us to analyse and understand the implications of the sixteen elements of dialectics.

These elements bring out the endless transformations, interconnections, mutual struggles and motions, leading to an explanation of the world. A mastery of the method of dialectics is essential to explain the rapid transformations going on in the world presently in all the fields. Hegelian dialectics, the method enunciated and evolved by Hegel, is a great guide. There is no better example of dialectics than in Hegel. He took it to highest and the most natural, spontaneous levels, as well as to the most scientific ones. To study Hegel is to wander about in the live world of changes, motions and transformations. The fact that, overall, he was an objective idealist philosopher, in no way diminishes the importance of his dialectical method. Also he almost discovered dialectical and historical materialism. The heights achieved by Hegel in this field are yet to be surpassed. Only Marx, Engels and Lenin could match him. Nobody else has been able to do this.

A study and mastery of the Hegelian dialectics is far more relevant today when science has entered quantum and relativity domains; it is most suited to an analysis of and delving into the motions of the quantum world.

With the discovery and use of 16 elements, the treatment of dialectics changes drastically. It becomes more real, lively, multifaceted, and contradictory in real sense of the term.

Crisis in Philosophy including in Marxist Philosophy

Drastic and fundamental changes have gripped the world in the last 4 to 5 decades, whose roots lie in the whole of the previous century. There are several constituents and causes of these changes. The biggest is the STR (scientific and technological revolution), of which the information and communication revolution (ICR) is the most important constituent. The STR has also come to be known as the new technological revolution.

The STR and the ICR have brought about fundamental changes in modern life. The means of production created in the wake of the industrial revolution have undergone changes and at the same time they are disappearing, being replaced by new means and equipment of production. The means of communication are acquiring greater importance. So much so that we can talk of a 'mode of information', rather than of mode of production. We will have occasion to talk of it in other places.

Max Planck's discoveries at the beginning of the 20th century began the era of quantum mechanics. Einstein's theories of special relativity (1905) and general relativity (1916), and many other discoveries and theories (e.g. Michelson-Morley experiment at the end of the 19th century), Heisenberg's uncertainty principle, Niels Bohr's running battle with Einstein on the concept of causation and reality in the quantum world, the discovery of the dialectical relationship of wave and particle nature of light and other radiations, the constancy of light speed vis-à-vis other processes, and so on overthrew the Cartesian and Newtonian concepts and world view, particularly at quantum levels and in space world.

This has brought about a drastic change at the way we look at the world. The hitherto-held concepts of space and time are now in question. Theory of causation has been severely questioned and re-examined. Succession and history of events have lost their uni-directional and unilinear nature. Nature of 'reality' and 'existence' need redefinition. Concepts of time and its direction have added new dimensions. Space-time continuum is being discussed anew.

Time has become an important factor today, as never before. In fact, it has become the most decisive factor of human existence and its consciousness.

Satellite communication has created growing layers of internet, websites and e-mail around the earth. This may be termed another form of 'consciousness', which a crucial role in our life, and which needs analysis and study for its nature and implications.

Fundamental changes are taking place in the world economy, society and politics. The nature of economy is changing fast. Post-industrial and post-modern society is being talked of. Politics, political balance of forces, national and international inter-relationships are changing rapidly.

The social composition of the Indian and international society is changing–every stratum, section and class is undergoing transformations; at the same time new strata are coming up. The nature of the working class is changing: old industries and classes are receding from the history.

Concepts of Finite and Infinite: Lenin on Atoms and Electrons

It is very interesting to see that Lenin, while trying to assimilate Hegelian dialectics, tried to apply it to the latest scientific discoveries of his time. He basically studied Hegel during the years of the First World War, and his 'Conspectus on Hegel' belong to that period. It is interesting to find that when everybody else was busy doing politics of the war, for or against, Lenin also used the period to do some serious study of philosophy and natural sciences, although he was no less involved in the 'politics of the war'.

He has in, in many places in this volume given thought to the questions related with atom and electrons. For example, he mentions atom while dealing with the relationship and dialectics of finite and infinite in Hegel's *Science of Logic.* Hegel states that the unity of finite and infinite is not an external juxtaposition nor a binding together of separate and mutually independent entities. "On the contrary, each in itself is this unity, and is so only in *transcending* itself..."[210] That means, finite is also infinite and infinite consists of endless finites, is the 'other' of finite.

Here Lenin makes a profound comment, that this is "To be applied to *atoms versus electrons.* In general the infiniteness of matter deep within..."[211] It is clear that with the 'split' of atom at the beginning of the century and discovery of electrons and other 'elementary particles', a debate began in the scientific and philosophic circles as to the meaning of the 'inexhaustibility' of atom. A large number of scientists wrote on the subject, such as Max Planck and later A.S. Eddington. Lenin also wrote his profound work on the philosophical meaning of the discovery, titled *Materialism and Empirio-criticism,* which installed him as one of the leading philosophers of the modern times. Lenin wanted to use the categories of finite and infinite to analyse the nature of atom and its inexhaustibility, as new particles began to be discovered within it. It should be noted that he mentions 'atom *versus* electrons', which means he considered them to be *opposites.*

There are several places in the volume where Lenin refers to electrons. For example, he mentions Epicurus as ascribing to the atoms a 'curvilinear' motion, and rightly criticizes Hegel for ignoring and misreading his (Epicurus's materialism. Here Lenin is reminded of the electrons[212]) and perhaps has in mind as to where to put the curvilinear motion of the electrons.

Lenin again mentions electrons in his Conspectus of the Philosophy of Leibnitz.[213] He brings in the electrons while referring to the innumerable multitude of the microscopic objects.

While making notes on Abel Rey's *Modern Philosophy*, Paris 1908,[214] Lenin notes the position and importance of electrons in philosophy.

For materialism matter is infinite, and the dialectical method of Hegel helps us to reach this conclusion. With the help of these categories, the levels of matter deep within can be covered.

Ideal and Real

Here both Hegel and Lenin bring out the relative nature of difference between the ideal and the material or the ideal and the real.

"The thought of ideal passing into the real is *profound*: very important for history. But also in the personal life of man it is clear that this contains much truth. Against vulgar materialism..." "The difference of the ideal from the material is also not unconditional, not inordinate."[215]

So the difference between ideal and material can be conditional, that means there can be subtle transitions *of one into another*. The very case of being conditional presupposed transitions of qualities.

Essence — Appearances

That which shows itself is essence in one of its determinations. Semblance is the showing of essence itself in itself. What is 'semblance'? It is the negative nature of Essence. It is 1) nothing, non-existent which exists 2) it is Being as moment. Essence contains semblance within as infinite internal movement. In this self-movement Essence is reflection, which is nothing but semblance. Semblance is that which shows itself, as the reflection of the essence in itself. Movement to nothing occurs in nature and in life. That which shows itself is essence in one of its determinations and aspects and moments, semblance is showing of essence itself.[216]

Essence goes through stages of reflections. One thing, one phenomenon, one process replaces or is replaced by another through a series of cause-effect phenomena. There is becoming and passing away. It is in such becoming and passing away that the Essence is *revealed.* The process continuously goes through identity—difference-contradiction.

Identity : A = A.

But if everything is A=A, there is no movement; therefore this crystallization, emergence of new, a difference as a result of dialectics, identity is transformed into non-identity leading to a conflict between identity and non-identity, establishing new identity. Identity=that which it is and equally non-identity.

Here we can safely conclude that it is through continuous appearance of non-identity, and equally continuous merger with identity that essence expresses itself. The problem arises as to whether essence expresses itself in identity or non-identity? Without non-identity the essence cannot express, 'appear'; but at the same time it cannot find full identity without merging with identity, i.e. non-identity dissolves into identity to give full expression (appearance) to the essence. Therefore, non-identity is identity in transition. It can be concluded: identity is always in transition.

According to Lenin, in Hegel, A (something) is the third, for A can be both +A and –A, and comments, "This is shrewd and correct. Every concrete thing, every concrete something, stands in multifarious and often contradictory relations to everything else, ergo, it is itself and some other."[217]

Here we find a profound expression of a *continuous contradictory unity of the world!* "Contradictory relation with everything else". Contradiction establishes a continuity, thus one being the other. Without this there is no unity in the world, and of the world. Everything is itself and the other *all the time*, undergoing transformation. This is very important. The thing is *not* one at one time, and another at another; it is one and the other *at the same time. Only this* is the concept of matter and of development. The very one thing is connected with, in unity with everything else, so that the one is the pretext for everything else, one presupposes the other, and vice versa. Otherwise *nothing will exist.* We look for one into another. And if this is not so then we are talking of nothing; at the most we are talking of *nonsense!*

"Movement and self-movement (this NB! Arbitrary (independent), spontaneous, ***internally necessary*** movement), "change", "movement and vitality", "the principle of all self-movement", "impulse" to "movement" and to "activity", the opposite to "dead being"—who would believe that this is the core of "Hegelianism", of abstract and abstrusen (ponderous, absurd?) Hegelianism?? *This core had to be discovered*, understood, rescued, laid bare, refined, which is precisely what Marx and Engels did.

"The idea of universal movement and change (1813 *Logic*) was conjectured before its application to life and society. In regard to society it was proclaimed earlier (1847) than it was demonstrated in application to man (1859)."[218]

(1) Ordinary imagination grasps difference and contradiction but not the ***transition*** from one to the other, *This however is the most important*".[219]

This method suits so well to the developing societies, where there are transitions galore. It is these transitions we have to grasp. In India we have to understand the transitions, without which nothing can be understood. Understanding transitions is understanding dialectics.

(2) It is not enough to grasp contradiction, enunciate it, bring things in relation to one another, and allow the "concept to show through the contradiction". It is also necessary to *express* the concept of things and their relations.

This is the difference between *intelligence and understanding*, according to Lenin.

(1) The task of reason, understanding, is to sharpen the difference of variety, the manifold of imagination, into *essential* difference, into *opposition*. Only when raised to the peak of contradictions, the manifold entities reach the level of that negativity which is the pulsating inherent self-movement.[220]

The manifold entities become active and lively in relation to one another only when raised to the *peak of contradiction*: "They acquire that negativity which is the *inherent pulsation of self-movement and vitality*".[221]

So there is self-movement in the entities through acquiring negativity: every process, aspect, thing must be negated to acquire motion.

Lenin here brings out the minutest difference and oppositions of the dialectical motion and the need for us to fully grasp those contradictions. Only then can we understand the source of manifold motion.

"Inherent pulsation" – Here Lenin achieves total objectivity when looking at moment. His concept of matter in movement is that of utter contradiction which is never lost sight of; nothing, in Lenin, is without this pulsation. This is in contrast with other philosophers and revolutionaries who tend to forget it.

"Continuation of the work of Hegel and Marx must consist in the dialectical elaboration of the history of human thought, science and technique".[222]

Continuation of the work of Hegel is the great task of the Marxists. It is clear that the Marxists must establish direct links with Hegelian dialectics and absorb it, thus enriching the movement of the concepts and ideas. Without Hegel, Marx and Lenin there can be no movement in our theory.

Dialectical Law

Dialectics of drops–methodology for Marxists:

"A river and the *drops* in this river. The position of *every* drop, its relation to the others; its connection with the others; the direction of its movement; its speed; the time of the movement – straight, curved, circular, etc. – upwards, downwards, the sum of the movement. Concepts, as registration of individual aspects of the movement, of individual drops (= "things"), of individual "*streams*", etc. There you have approximately the picture of the world according to Hegel's *Logic* – of course minus God and the Absolute."[223]

"The concept of law is *one* of the stages of the cognition by man of *unity* and connection, of the reciprocal dependence and totality of the world process".[224]

It is through law also that appearance appears and is cognized, and thus essence is cognized. "Law takes the quiescent – and therefore law, every law, is narrow, incomplete, approximate".[225]

Law reflects appearance. But law in appearance leads to the law in the essence, because essence has also a structure. The structure is in existence as reflected in law.

"Law is essential appearance"[226]

"*Law* and *essence* are concepts of the same kind (of the same order), or rather, of the same degree, expressing the deepening of man's knowledge of phenomena, the world, etc."[227]

"Law is the reflection of the essential in the movement of the universe."[228]

"Appearance is *richer* than law".[229]

It clearly means, appearance is taken as totality, while law as part.

The answer is given:

"The movement of the universe in appearances, in the essentiality of this movement, is law."[230]

Law is the reflection of the essential in movement of the universe. Without it the movement is the very essence of leap of any kind; it explains how the change takes place.

"The world in and for itself is identical with the world of Appearances, but at the same time it is opposite to it".

"What is positive in the one is negative in the other. What is evil in the world of Appearances is good in the world which is in and for itself".[231]

The shifting of the world in itself further and further *from* the world of appearance was not noted by Hegel.[232]

It means the deeper the essence the farther way it is from appearance. Appearance itself becomes richer, more meaningful.

"The beginning of everything can be regarded as inner – passive – and at the same time as outer.

"But what is interesting here is not that, but something else: Hegel's *criterion* of dialectics that has accidentally slipped in: '*in all natural, scientific and intellectual development*' here we have a *grain* of profound truth in the mystical integument of Hegelianism!"[233]

What is the essence of dialectical cognition, according to Hegel and according to Lenin? "The unfolding of the sum total of the moments of actuality".[234]

The totality of reality is made up of series and system of moments, i.e. points of fading out and emerging. They unfold, i.e. they develop and fade out: the process reflected in brain is the process of cognition.

Developing Hegel's idea, Lenin explains that the knowledge of matter must lead us to the knowledge of substance. This leads us to the cause. The very discovery of the cause leads us from externality of phenomena to the substance. Natural Science and philosophy are examples. Cause and effect are moments of universal reciprocal dependence, of universal connection, links in the chain of development of matter. Causality only fragmentarily and incompletely, and one-sidedly expresses the all-sidedness of inter-connection of the world.[235]

Why incompletely? Because causality is 'merely' links in the chain of development of matter, it is only a moment. Because it is expression of connection and transition but not of totality. "Hegel subsumes history *completely* under causality."[236] Causality only *a small particle* of universal inter-connection, and it is not subjective but real. Causality has to be grasped in its inner connection.

Thus Hegel's causality is not simply a simple cause – effect series, one giving rise to the other. Cause is also the effect, effect also cause. One becomes the other, evolves into the other. Effect is all the time there in cause, continuously evolving out of it. Cause becomes a new cause as a result of effect. Cause never ceases to be cause, and the effect is always there.

Hegel says:

"But the *movement* of the Determinate *Relation* of *Causality* has now resulted in this, that the cause is not merely extinguished in the effect, and with it the effect too (as happens in Formal Causality) – but the cause in its extinction, in the effect, becomes again; that effect vanishes into cause, but equally becomes again in it. Each of these determinations cancels itself in its positing and posits itself in its cancellation; what takes place is not an external transition of causality from one substratum to another, but this its becoming other is at the same time its own positing. Causality, then, presupposes or conditions itself."[237]

Causality, and cause and effect, each emerge as dialectical event, which repeatedly affirm themselves, and thus posit each time.

"Concepts are the highest product of the brain, the highest product of matter".[238]

The *highest* product: what are the lower and lowest products? Various levels of ideas *leading ultimately* to concept. Here Lenin develops the entire range of development of consciousness. This range is not easily to be found in Hegel who is preoccupied with the *Absolute* idea.

Reflection of philosophy—The very "absoluteness" of the other element (idea) prevents Hegel from finding out the range and from connecting it with a material substratum which nevertheless pops up again and again through Hegelian integument.

"In general the refutation of a philosophic system does not mean discarding it, but developing it further, not replacing it by another one-sided opposed system, but incorporating it into something more advanced".[239]

In order to develop a philosophy we have to constantly criticize it. Criticising is not destruction, should not be, but should be an attempt to develop its features. It is an example of *dialectical* movement of philosophy. We may state: Refutation = dialectical development.

Hegel himself comes on the eve of transformation of objective idealism into materialism. In his words, Notion here must not be considered as an act of self-conscious understanding. It, the Notion, is a "STAGE AS WELL OF NATURE, LIFE OR ORGANIC NATURE, AS OF SPIRIT. LIFE OR ORGANIC NATURE, IS THAT STAGE OF NATURE, AT WHICH THE NOTION EMERGES."[240] It is on these lines that Lenin commented that it is the eve of transformation of objective idealism into materialism.

Path of cognition. Kant emphasizes faith at the cost of knowledge. Hegel significantly thinks that abstract knowledge is not mere setting aside of sensuous material, but its transcendence which brings out the essential which does not lower the sensuous material. Hegel here already transcends his own philosophy by showing the change of one into the other. But he does not derive one from the other, does not establish their unity. Hegel puts knowledge into its own laws, which consequently is detached from matter and attached to the Absolute Idea.

Lenin breaches the barrier, thus creatively negating and developing Hegel.

Lenin extracts the cognitive process from Hegel's criticism of Kant. Thought proceeds from the concrete to the abstract; in this way it does not get away from truth but comes closer to it. The *abstraction* (of matter, of law, etc.) reflects nature more deeply, truly, and *completely*. "From living perception to abstract thought, *and from* this to practice-such is the dialectical path of the cognition of *truth*, of the cognition of objective reality. Kant disparages knowledge in order to make way for faith; Hegel exalts knowledge, asserting that knowledge is knowledge of God. The materialist exalts the knowledge of matter, of nature."[241]

Abstraction reflects nature more completely. Therefore generalities, concepts, abstractions, theoretical knowledge are all important because they take us to the essence of matter. From abstract thought to practice – means clearly that an abstract knowledge (provided it is true) leads to a better practice, is a better starting point for practice.

Knowledge is the knowledge of matter for a materialist.

Logic = theory of knowledge, in general.

Logical figures are most common relations of things.

The chief thing for Hegel is the discovery of *transitions.* Universal is individual and *vice-versa* under certain conditions:

(1) Inseparable *connections* of all concepts and judgements.

(2) *Transitions* from one into another.

(3) *Identity of opposites.*

"One would have to return to Hegel for a step by step analysis of any current logic and *theory of knowledge* of a Kant, etc."[242]

"Marx *applied* Hegel's dialectics in its rational form to political economy".[243]

* * *

Abstract notions and operations with them *already* include the consciousness of the law governed objective world. This idea firstly reflects the reflection of matter in consciousness; secondly, operation of laws of matter is reflected in operation of laws in ideas. Causality exists here. To deny the objectivity of notions of universal in particular and in the individual is impossible. Therefore, Hegel is much more profound than Kant etc. in tracing movement of objectivity of world reflected in notions. The simplest *generalization,* the first and simplest formation of *notions,* already denotes man's ever deepening of knowledge of *objective* connection of the world. Here is where one should look for the true meaning, significance and role of Hegel's *Logic.*

Plekhanov merely rejects Kantiainism, etc. from a vulgar-materialist view-point and not from the dialectical-materialist viewpoint. He does not correct them, as Hegel corrected Kant, deepening, generalizing and extending them, showing the transition and connection of each and every thought.

"Marxists criticized (at the beginning of the 20th century) the Kantians and Humists more in the manner of Feuerbach (and Bichner) than of Hegel."[244]

* * *

The simplest truth obtained in the simplest inductive way is always incomplete, for experience is *always* incomplete, unfinished.

There is relativity of all knowledge, and absolute content in each step forward in cognition.

"It is impossible completely to understand Marx's *Capital*, and especially its first chapter, without having thoroughly studied and understood the *whole* of Hegel's *Logic*. ***Consequently, half a century later none of the Marxists understood Marx!!***"[245]

"Hegel actually *proved* that logical forms and laws are not an empty shell, but the *reflection* of the objective world. More correctly, he did not prove, *but made a brilliant guess.*"[246]

* * *

Theory of Knowledge

"Nature, this immediate totality, unfolds itself in the Logical idea and Mind."[247] "Logic is the science of cognition. It is the theory of knowledge. Knowledge is the reflection of nature by man. But this is not a simple, not an immediate, not a complete reflection, but the process of a series of abstractions, the formation and development of concepts, laws, etc., (thought, science = "the logical idea") *embrace* conditionally, approximately, the universal law-governed character of eternally moving and developing nature. Here there are actually, objectively, *three* members:

(1) nature (2) human cognition=human *brain* (as the highest product of this same nature, and (3) the form of reflection of nature in human cognition, and this form consists precisely of concepts, laws, categories, etc. Man cannot comprehend =reflect=mirror nature *as a whole*, in its completeness, its 'immediate totality', he can only

eternally come closer to this, creating abstraction, concepts, laws, a scientific picture of the world, etc. etc."[248]

Lenin interprets Hegel's statement as: "The laws of logic are the reflections of the objective in the subjective consciousness of man."[249]

Lenin on Materialist Dialectics

Lenin, while dealing with the question of objectivity in Hegel's Science of Logic, further develops dialectical materialism by evolving (discovering, dealing with) the laws of nature, concept of practice and its relation with objective world. Lenin also *profoundly* opposes nature to man's activity.

Lenin divides the laws of external world, i.e. of nature into two categories: *mechanical* and *chemical.* Obviously with the epoch-making and revolutionary changes in natural sciences, this points needs further enrichment. Soviet scientists in particular made tremendous contribution in philosophical generalizations of modern natural sciences. For the purposive activity of man, not only mechanical and chemical laws form the bases, but also genetic, biological, nuclear, various levels of physical laws, etc. Modern scientific and technological revolution (STR) has unveiled and deepened human knowledge about various levels of forms of existence of matter and their transitions into one another, thus deepening the very concept of matter. A clear series can be traced from bare physical to chemical, biological etc. in our direction, to mechanical, atomic, nuclear, etc. in another, intricate arrangement of these very levels in the biological level of form of existence of matter, and so on. Transitions from non-living to living and *vice-versa* are clearer if more complicated. The Hegel-Lenin analysis of laws of transitions are in their profoundest in the modern natural scientific developments. The endless depth of matter is reflected in that of knowledge about it; levels of matter reveal various and endless levels of dialectics; destruction of each of them gives rise to a new set of dialectics. The biological, as never before, encompasses all the other natural forces, itself constantly rising.

The discoveries of dialectics of nature are coming in increasing interaction with equally, or more complicated social dialectics. Human practice is increasingly depending on the discovery and operations the various levels of dialectics. The social and the natural, the social and the biological increasingly form opposites: human practice contains both these opposites.

Lenin says man is *confronted* by the objective world. Therefore, nature appears as something external, and *secondary*, hidden. So, that which is external, is external to man and his practice. In this interaction man seems to be primary and the external as secondary. But man himself is the product of the external; his practice is the necessity of his existence.

Lenin distinguishes two forms of objective process: nature and purposive activity of man. In this way he creatively develops the Hegel-Marx concept of practice, more precisely the Marxist concept. The purposive activity itself is part of the objective world; but it is so in a special way. It is objective in relation to the consciousness, therefore is part of matter. The inter-section of the two forms of objective process produces consciousness, in the main. Consciousness is also produced by direct contact between brain and nature. But this is only after a certain stage of consciousness development based upon the activity with primitive first tools. Thus, fashioned consciousness is in a better position to reflect nature.

Practice and Cognition

Cognition finds itself faced by independent existence; Hegal uses the folloing words: "actuality that is present independently of subjective position."[250] "Actuality present independently of subjective opinions": This is Lenin's rewriting of the above mentioned from Hegel's *Science of Logic* and on it he comments: "This is pure materialism!"[251] Thus Lenin here and all through the Conspectus on Hegel tries not only to salvage, but also to develop materialism, dialectical materialism, out of Hegel.

Will [=practice] itself blocks the attainment of its end: Is it not in conformity with reality fully? Practice has strong subjective side. The end is fully objective. End is part of the material world, while practice is partially in the subjective world.

"Man's **will**, his practice, itself blocks the attainment of its end..."[252]

Here we find man's will=this practice.

It is will because it goes towards reality, thus showing transitional features; it is not yet reality or objectivity itself, yet "it separates itself from cognition" (Lenin says so further). So it is no more (will is no more) since it is the realm of the subjective. It is **practice.** Then what is practice? The content of practice in Lenin is obviously far more profound and richer than what is generally understood. He says it blocks the *attainment of its end.* This conflict arises because it does not recognise externality as it is. So practice (= his will) does not recognise the external world as it is. For practice, the external material world, the whole of objectivity or part of it, is not enough. Practice attains full form by changing the latter. Therefore, reality is not complete without practice having brought certain changes to it. Practice siding with objectivity and with subjectivity are two poles of the same thing. "What is necessary is the union of *cognition* and *practice*."[253] Now, here the contradiction is resolved, by uniting cognition (= theory?) and practice. But what is practice here? Clearly, it is the interaction with objectivity, also of objectivity with objectivity. Here, so to say, practice sides with reality because it changes the latter. Practice is the reality which must change reality. Therefore, it is that part of reality which is consciously changing. Is therefore practice torn between two pulls, two aspects? From Lenin's expression the affirmative is deducible: practice as part of cognition, practice as part of reality. It is practice which reflects, transmits reality on consciousness in form of cognitive process.

"For Hegel *action*, practice is a *logical* "*syllogism*", a figure of logic. And that is true!"[254] In what sense? Man's practice repeating "a thousand million times, becomes consolidated in man's consciousness by figures of logic."[255] Here again practice is related with logic.

Lenin explains and clarifies further that "precisely (and only) on account of this thousand-million-fold repetition, these figures have the stability of a prejudice, an axiomatic character."[256] Thus, there arises the first premise of the 'good end' or the subjective end versus actuality or the 'external actuality'. The second premise is that of the external means or instrument, followed by the third premise or conclusion. The third premise is that of "the coincidence of subjective and objective, the test of subjective ideas, the criterion of objective truth."[257]

These are great examples of how Lenin is constantly converting Hegel's ideas into those of dialectical materialism.

"The activity of man, who has constructed an objective picture of the world for himself, *changes* external actuality, abolishes its determinateness (= alters some sides or others, qualities of it), and thus removes from it the features of Semblance, externality and nullity, and makes it as being in and for itself (= objectively true)."[258] Practice means *externality*. Is it the complete merger of activity of man and objectivity?

Again there is something far more profound than what is generally understood: Says Lenin, repeating Hegel's words on the criterion of objectivity:

"The result of activity is the test of subjective cognition and the criterion of OBJECTIVITY WHICH TRULY IS."[259]

In the words of Hegel, cognition is reconstructed "***and united with the Practical Idea***"; the actuality found at a given time is 'the realized absolute end' and not as merely objective, as supposed to be by the cognition which is enquiring into the world. The objective world therefore has the inner ground and 'persistence' and is therefore the Notion, and this precisely is the Absolute Idea.[260] According to Hegel, "The Absolute Idea has turned out to be the identity of the Theoretical and the Practical Idea; each of these is by itself one-sided..."[261] Developing this idea, Lenin formulates that the unity of the theoretical idea '*and of practice*', and this unity '*precisely in the theory of knowledge*' is the 'Absolute Idea', which is 'the objectively true'.[262]

We may add here that the reality is echoed, through practice, in the ideas. Objectivity, so to say, is constantly echoed with practice as the tool, leading to ideas. *The idea is the echo of the world through practice.* We should not have a narrow idea of practice. Even looking at the tree itself is practice. Human beings do so in the course of certain movements, and the event is related with a whole history and present of the humans and of the society.

It not only proves the correctness of objectivity; it also proves that objective world and the objective truth exist. A constant echo from the reality is necessary to be in the latter, in its movement, motion. It is this echo, reflection that forms ultimately the theory.

But is not a given theory itself objectivity? In particular dialectical materialist theory? It is already established, fixed (through "a thousand million" times), it is so to say objectivity itself from which to proceed further.

Dialectics as Vanishing Moments of Motion

Hegel comments that being and non-being, their mutual sublation, are vanishing moments, and Lenin's comment on it is that "vanishing moments" = Being and not-Being. That is a magnificent definition of dialectics!!"[263]

Hegel is here analysing Gorgias in detail, and makes a very apt and interesting comment that **every** philosophy goes further than common sense! To adopt absolute realism, according to Hegel, is *bad idealism* because it thinks what is thought is always subjective, and thus not the existent, since through thought an existent is transformed into what is thought.[264]

This thing exists in *totality of manifold relations* with others. To consider it is to consider its innumerable connections, and in this way to consider other things. But this thing *is motion and constant change.* Its own movement has to be determined, its characteristics, which nothing will head us to the connections with others, changing connections and changes in other things. The development of this thing cannot be traced without analysing contradictory tendencies and sides in it. It may have two or more sides, two or more tendencies. All these sides and contradictions are internal, therefore constitute the thing, the phenomenon. Analysis and synthesis actually reveal the endless connections and inter-connections, it should reveal. Without it a quality is not revealed. In the course of the analysis and synthesis of all sides and contradictions of the thing, we reach the conclusion that it is the *sum total and unity of opposites.* This is a serious philosophical conclusion. And that is any thing and phenomenon is a unity of opposites and cannot be anything else; it is a sum of opposites, and nothing else. Otherwise the thing remains unexplained. The contradictions do not exist as they are thought to be as if in a two-dimensional picture. They unfold themselves, and this philosophical method in very important, particularly in the social field because that is so common and everyday and with which we are more deeply concerned. The very *unfolding is the struggle of opposites*, contradictory "stirrings". In this we wade through with the help of *analysis and synthesis*, that is we break down separate parts and bring them together in a unity. The relations of the thing is *general and universal*, it is not only unity but also transition of opposites, sides, aspects into one another giving rise to multifaceted development of a phenomenon. As a result there is endless process of *emergence and discovery of new sides and* relations. It is such a process that gives rise to the process of knowledge and the deepening of the process. It proceeds from appearance to essence to more profound essence. *Causality* as a form of connection emerges expressing reciprocal dependence on each other, the form constantly changing and establishing continuity. Cause expresses the point of departure, the connection, the very meaning of development. There *are repetitions in development* but at different levels, and never at the same level, the repetitions returning the process to the old. Forms are constantly thrown off by the developing content. There is constant transformation of quality into quality, quality into quantity.

Dialectics according to Hegel has opposite determinations. Determination has to be understood, determined in order to reach the sense of conflict. While dialectics has finite time, space, place etc., it has at the same time infinite determinations. Each of the two presuppose the other; dialectics of both of them prove the operation of dialectics. The contradiction occurs in double sense, objective and subjective. If object-subject contradiction is replaced by matter-consciousness contradiction, things will be more accurate. The object contradicts itself, the subjective is continuously defective; therefore, the subject contradicts itself.

Lenin characterises it as a very interesting, clear and important outline of dialectics.[265]

The opposites, e.g. mentioned above are "contradictory not by virtue of some external connection"[266] but as transitions, as transitions in and for themselves and therefore as internal connections. The opposites are not "connected" with each other, mechanically. They are the one and the other. They are in movement, transforming into one another, are both one and at the same time one becoming the other, etc. So Lenin comments: concepts by their nature = *transition.*[267]

One is negated by the other, the other is not the empty negative; it the negative of the first, determines the first, mediated. The first is essentially contained and preserved in the other. The positive is held fast in the negative.[268] Lenin remarks that negation is a moment of connection, moment of development, *retaining the positive*, "without any vacillations, without any *eclecticism*".[269]

Eclecticism is unable to measure up to negation; in fact, it is a denial of negation. Eclecticism does not understand dialectical movements and inter-connections, and observes reality in bits and pieces without establishing unity in the observations and thus in the world.

Hegel says, there is *transition* of the first into the second; therefore, there is connection of the first with the second. That which is itself contains itself, it is "potentially not yet developed, not yet unfolded,"[270] it is negative only in itself. It contains distinction implicitly, then there is distinction, which is a relation. The dialectical moment consists in positing the *unity* which is already developing within. Lenin comments that in relation to the simple and original 'first' positive assertion, the dialectical moment or the scientific consideration "demands demonstration of difference, connection, transition. Without that the simple positive assertion is incomplete, lifeless, dead". In the second assertion, which is a negative proposition, the 'dialectical moment' demands the demonstration of 'unity', that is, the connection of negative and positive, the presence of this positive in negative.[271]

"From assertion to negation – from negation to 'unity' with the asserted – without this, dialectics becomes empty negation, a game, a scepsis."[272]

Thus, the two sides are inseparable, one transiting into another.

[Stating that India is a bourgeois country, has a bourgeois state, etc. does not means anything, unless we are able to determine the characteristics, the movements and moments, difference, peculiarities, *transitions* in this. And then we have clarify: bourgeois to what extent?—AR]

If judgments and relations do not appear to be contradictory and dialectical, it is a mere fault of thought which does not confront thoughts with one another. Opposite determinations are clearly posited, according to Hegel.

But formal thought makes identity its law, and allows contradictory content to drop out. (An extension or derivation of Hegel although he had some other meaning also).

Thought Process

How does thought comprehend? Thought has to reflect the whole while in its movement.[273] But for that thought must be dialectical. "Is sensuous representation *closer* to reality than thought? Both yes and no." Sensuous representation cannot apprehend each and every movement e.g. light speed.[274] Also innumerable others. *It is only thought that can reflect such a movement.* So, thought goes deeper, behind, around the material phenomena.

Dialectics is the negative self-relation, internal form of activity, vital and spiritual self-movement.[275]

Second negation is the transcendence as the contradiction. It is the inner-most and the most objective moment of life.

The result of second negation is a "third" term, a new assertion, source of a new development; into it has already entered the 'content' of cognition "and the *method* is extended into a system".[276] The first promise becomes indeterminable, imperfect. If it becomes indeterminate and imperfect, the need arises to re-analyse, re-evaluate to prove again in a new light this assertion, etc. So, according to Hegel, it looks to us infinite *backward* progress. But Lenin explains that the new premise drives forward.

[We study again and again primitive communist society; we do it on the basis of our movement to advanced communism—AR].

"Thus, cognition rolls forward from content to content".[277] Each subsequent one is richer and more concrete. Each result has its own beginning which has new determinations. All that is acquired is carried forward, enriching the content.

"The richest is the most concrete and most *subjective*"[278] Richest and that which carries itself back into the simplest depth is also the most powerful and competitive.[279]

"In circle which is complete in itself but whose completion is like-wise a passing into another circle."[280] Science is a *circle of circles*: mediation bends back its end into its beginning. Various sciences are fragments of this chain.

This is Hegel's idea of transition from idea to Nature. By so doing he has come "within a hand's grasp of materialism."[281] Hegel comes near the transition of ideas into nature, which was really discovered by Marx and Engels, and by Lenin.

The main subject of Hegel here is *dialectical method.* "In this *most* idealistic of Hegel's works there is the *least* idealism and most *materialism.* 'Contradictory', but a fact"![282]

Meaning of Motion

If we say that movement is the presence of a body in a definite place at a given moment, and at another place at another, we only describe *the result of motion, but not motion itself.* It does not contain the possibility of *motion,* it depicts the states of *rest.*[283] In order *to be in motion* the body has *to be and not be at a given point at a given moment*; it *is and it is not* at the place. To be at a place is not to be. The rest is relative.

Why this problem? Why do we face problems in determining social movements and phenomena? Or any other? When we express something, *we strangle, it destroy it, kill it.* It is as if the still photograph has taken only a moment and stopped it; we look at it and think that it is moving. And herein is the dialectics. It is precisely such thinking that takes a 'bit' of dialectics out of motion. But we project it all over to be a general dialectics. And a photograph a time suffices for us (for a non-dialectical approach, for dogmatism, for doctrinairism, for formulation, etc.). "We cannot imagine, express, measure, depict movement, without interrupting continuity, without simplifying, coarsening, dismembering, strangling that which is living. The presentation of movement by means of thought always makes coarse, kills – and not only by means of thought, but also by sense – perception, and not only of movement, but *every* concept.

"And in that lies the *essence* of dialectics.

"And precisely *this essence* is expressed by the formula: the unity, identity of opposites."[284]

Here, with the help of a 'photograph' of dialectics, i.e. a moment of development, Lenin explains *the whole of dialectics.*

Thought interrupts continuity, kills motion (photograph = dismembering). If we take this as a guide then it follows that we must keep our thoughts flowing and changing. We must solve the dialectics of moment and of infinite. Contradiction is resolved only by the correspondence of thought with the flowing matter, otherwise it remains unresolved or only partially resolved. This is not only a philosophical question. This is a practical question, particularly in a slow moving developing, emergent society like India whose top has been posited with fast moving capitalist change – sucking in other parts, but still containing extremely slow moving ones. Here we are bound to be un-dialectical and sectarian-dogmatic unless we take in the whole of reality. We are all the time killing reality by implementing certain partial and dead, fossilized ideas and formulations. But what about the movement, motion of the developing Indian society?

Being and Consciousness

Each thing is different from other; not from any other but from *its* other. So, every other is its *own* other.

Lenin discovers "a very profound and correct, essentially materialist thought"[285] in Hegel who says that the Being is *followed* by consciousness. Hegel is repeatedly touching the materialist grounds at various points because his dialectical reasoning leads, and must lead, him to the points from where the ideas have arisen. Hegel is a sort of substratum for the rise of materialist thoughts which are generally clouded in idealism. "His logic cannot be applied in its given form, it cannot be *taken* as given. One must *separate out* from it the logical (epistemological) nuances...".[286] Lenin's entire treatment in the *Conspectus* is precisely an example of this and guidance to us as to how to approach other philosophies dialectically, not only philosophies but various other ideas: economic, political, etc.

Lenin's attitude is made clear by his approach to Hegel and his philosophy. In philosophy he has placed him at the same level as Marx. Like Marx, Lenin has drawn heavily from Hegel regarding dialectics and materialism. He says: "Intelligent idealism is closer to intelligent materialism than stupid materialism." "Dialectical idealism instead of metaphysical, undeveloped, dead, crude, rigid and stupid materialism."[287] Lenin fully respects intelligent, dialectical idealism. For Hegel materialism was not a philosophy, because philosophy is always a science of thought. But in the course of developing dialectics he came very close to dialectical materialism. Lenin discovers the interrelations and transformation of objective idealism and its transitions, partial or full, into materialism. He says, "Objective (and still more, absolute) idealism came *very close* to materialism by a zig-zag (and a somersault), even partially *became transformed into it.*"[288] Objective idealism is transformed partially into materialism, Hegel into Marx-Lenin.

We find a glimpse of mutual transformations of idealism and materialism into one another in Indian philosophy, mostly partial. This is one of the major problems and also method of solution of Indian philosophy. Indian philosophical schools find themselves originating as one and ending as another, they proceed at one point as one, as another at another point. The complex, multi-layered social structures force them to move in such zig-zag ways. Absence of a God facilitates such transitions because then one deals with logical or objective categories.

Movement of Cognition

The universal is contradictory. It is dead and incomplete, it is endless and developings, and therefore never fully encompassible; "but it alone is a *stage* towards, knowledge of the *concrete,* for we can never know the concrete completely."[289]

Towards the concrete: the concrete can never be known completely. Its conceptions, laws are infinite. They give it the completeness=dialectics of cognition. Process of cognition moves *away from* the object. In this way it reaches the content and abstraction, i.e. looks at its object *more profoundly*. "The movement of cognition *to* the object can always only proceed dialectically: to retreat in order to hit more surely. Converging and diverging lines: circles which touch one another, knotentpunkt (nodal point)= practice of mankind and human history."[290]

The contact point is the practice of the individual and of the mankind. These points are unity of contradictions between being and non-being, "the vanishing moments". The points of contact are that of technique and history. Cognition thus is a repeated return to the reality and repeated retreat from the reality; every such movement away *and* towards enriches its content.

It is interesting to note that Hegel firmly stood against "empty dialectics", which Lenin notes with particular emphasis. Says Hegel: "If this passing to and fro is performed with consciousness, it is empty dialectics, which does not unite the opposites and does not come to unity."[291]

Here Hegel gives a definition of dialectics, which really speaking, should be able to unite the opposites. A real dialectics which not only describes different or opposite aspects but also unite them and show their transition from one into another.

Hegel could not understand the dialectical transition from idea to matter and vice versa; it was Marx also discovered the transition. By tracing the origins of ideas from matter, Marx put Hegel right side up, and consequently the dialectics was operating in a different terrain, operating as material laws. This is part of Marxist revolution in philosophy. The transition from matter to idea is dialectical, that from sensation to thought, is also dialectical, Marx solved the problem as the unity of matter and idea.

This transition, and any other transitions are characterised by the leap. The gradualness is interrupted and matter and idea, being and non-being, etc. are to be found in inseparable unity.

Concepts reflect material reality in a dialectical way. Concepts do not exist free, but originate from material substratum, projecting its appearances, form, content, essence, laws and the operation of dialectics.

Determination of ideas, of subjectivity is from without, the determination from within is only the second step at the most, which only propels the further development of ideas, due to its own laws of development. The determination from within can itself act as the determination from without *for the reality*. But the determination from within is immediately or ultimately determined, reflects, the material reality. So, for the further determinations to arise, it is necessary for them to originate from matter, outside and independent of consciousness.

The result from "the abstract Idea should coincide with the general conception to which experience and observation have led."

Here Lenin remarks: "THIS ALMOST COMPLETELY APPROACHES HISTORICAL MATERIALISM."[292]

What does concept (cognition) reveal? Concept is present in a process, and its recognition is cognition. It is characteristic of Lenin to always present ideas in motion. Having assimilated and mastered Hegelian dialectics, Lenin cannot but present things in motion, also ideas, phenomena. Having done this he proceeds further to analyse various fields of knowledge, and of material reality. This "having done" is not so easy as one may take it to be; it expresses a leap and a transition. It represents the very process of penetration of dialectics of material reality from ideas, and then having turned Hegel right side up, Lenin once again proceeds from dialectical material reality to the realm of ideas including the realm of Hegelian ideas in dialectical motion reflecting *now* the material reality.[293]

"Such is the general course of all human cognition (of all science) in general", Lenin says. Such is also the course of history, political economy and natural science. Having assimilated dialectics from Hegel, Lenin sets before us the task of analysing various realities, which he says would be an "extraordinarily rewarding task". This is a huge task before the Marxists: application of Marxism (dialectics) in general, in separate branches of knowledge, of revealing dialectics in separate fields of reality and knowledge. Lenin thus sets to rest the controversy that dialectics, though applicable to society, is not applicable to nature. He states: to apply dialectics "in the history of separate sciences".

Lenin pointed out the need to study those fields, on the basis of which dialectics could be enriched and developed. For example, he points out that Greek philosophy, history of philosophy and of society in general, history of separate sciences, mental development of child, mental development of animals, psychology, physiology of sense organs, and so on needed to be studied: "These are the fields of knowledge from which theory of knowledge and dialectics should be built."[294]

Hegel and Lenin

What is the difference between the socio-economic backgrounds of these two giants of philosophers, enabling the latter to grasp dialectics in the reality, like Hegel?

Normally the relation between Marx and Hegel has been dealt with, but that between Hegel and Lenin has been ignored. Not that the two relations are any qualitatively different from each other, not that Lenin deviated from Marx in discovering Hegel, in discovering dialectics in Hegel, in recovering it from Hegel and sort of put it in the material substratum.

But it has to be noticed that Lenin established relations with Hegel of the same quality as those of Marx with Hegel in a *different historical epoch:* that of advanced capitalism and industrialism, and of new discoveries and developments in science and technology. Hegel was a predecessor of Marx, and died in 1830, while Lenin lived at the end of the 19th century and beginning of the 20th. Lenin was one of the handful in history, who studied and assimilated Hegel. This is extraordinary, given the fact of his short life and breadth of activities including revolution. There is no doubt that the assimilation of dialectics of Hegel helped Lenin to reveal the processes and the underlying dialectics the new epoch, both in sciences and in society in general. Therefore, in certain senses the Hegel-Lenin relationship is more up-to-date than the Hegel-Marx relationship.

Lenin understood the great importance of grasping dialectics by the revolutionaries, and even commented that so far 'we have understood *Capital* without mastering Hegel', and that is why 'we have not really understood *Capital*'! This is a rare comment, and speaks a lot about the need to study and master dialectical method, and not just mouth some formulas from time to time.

Following Hegel, Lenin develops categories of dialectics in the course of movement, in motion. First of all impressions, then something emerges, afterwards the determination of thing is the concept of quality and quantity emerge. After that, study and reflection direct thought to cognition of identity, difference, causality, etc. These moments move from subject to object, are tested in practice, and through this test to help us reach the truth.

The very first and most familiar is the sensation, and **in it** is the *quality.*

Though Marx did not leave behind a separate logic, he left it in the form of *Capital.* He applied to it dialectics to the full. He took everything valuable in Hegel and developed it further. In *Capital* Marx analyses the most simple, ordinary, mass, immediate 'Being': the *single commodity.* Testing by practice is to be found at *each* step.

Lenin brilliantly traces the continuous branching out of knowledge and its results in the development of various branches of knowledge which become part of social life. Primitive and modern idealism confuse between the universal and the particular. Drawing certain conclusions from a study of Aristotle, Lenin points out the difference between and dialectics of a material form and an idea of it. For example, tables, chairs and *ideas* of tables and chairs, world and Idea of world,..." etc.

"The dichotomy of human knowledge and the *possibility* of idealism (= religion) are *given* already **in the first, elementary** abstraction": " 'house' in general and particular house".[295]

Lenin explains that the approach of the mind to a particular thing, "the taking of a copy (=concept) of it *is not* a simple" act, a dead mirroring; it is split into two, it follows a zig-zag path. It "*includes in it* the possibility of the flight of fantasy from life." There is a possibility of transformation of the abstract idea into fantasy; even in the simplest generalization, for example, talking about 'table in general', there is a slight fantasy. "It would be stupid to deny the role of fantasy, even in the strictest science."[296]

NOTES

1. V.I. Lenin, *Collected Works (CW),* Progress Publishers, Moscow
2. Ibid., Volume 38, pp. 359-63.
3. Ibid., p. 359.
4. Ibid., p. 350.
5. Ibid., p. 349.
6. Ibid.
7. Ibid., p. 361.
8. Ibid., pp. 361-62, emphasis in the original.
9. Ibid., p. 362.
10. Lenin, *Selected Works,* Volume 3, pp. 542-43, 1971 edition, Progress Publishers, Moscow.
11. Ibid., p. 542.
12. Ibid.
13. Ibid., pp. 542-43.
14. Ibid., p. 543.
15. Ibid.

16. Ibid.
17. Ibid.
18. Lenin, *CW,* Vol. 38, p. 252.
19. Ibid., p. 253.
20. Ibid., p. 254.
21. Ibid., p. 255.
22. Ibid.
23. Ibid.
24. Ibid.
25. Ibid., pp. 255-56.
26. Ibid., p. 255.
27. Hegel, in ibid.
28. Ibid., p. 159.
29. Ibid., p. 259, emphasis in the original.
30. Hegel, in ibid., p. 257.
31. Lenin, in ibid., p. 258.
32. Ibid., p. 259.
33. Ibid., pp. 259-60.
34. Ibid., p. 260, emphasis in the original.
35. Ibid., p. 262, emphasis original.
36. Ibid., pp. 254, 256.
37. See, ibid., pp. 221-23.
38. Ibid., p. 221.
39. Ibid., p. 259.
40. Ibid., pp. 223-24.
41. Ibid., p. 224.
42. Hegel in ibid., p. 224.
43. Hegel, quoted in ibid., pp. 225.
44. Ibid.
45. Hegel, in Lenin, ibid., p. 226.
46. Ibid.
47. Lenin in ibid., p. 226,
48. Hegel in ibid., p. 226.
49. Ibid., p. 227.
50. Ibid.
51. Ibid., pp. 227-28.
52. Ibid., p. 228.
53. Ibid.
54. Ibid.
55. Lenin, in ibid., p. 228.

56. Ibid., p. 228.
57. Ibid.
58. Ibid., p. 229.
59. Lenin, Ibid., p. 229.
60. Ibid., p. 230.
61. Lenin, Ibid., p. 230.
62. Hegel, ibid.
63. Hegel, ibid.
64. Ibid., pp. 230-31.
65. Hegel, ibid., p. 231.
66. Hegel, ibid.
67. Hegel, in ibid.
68. Ibid.
69. Hegel, in ibid., p. 232.
70. Hegel, in ibid., p. 233.
71. Hegel, in ibid.
72. See, ibid., p. 182.
73. Hegel, with explanations by Lenin, ibid., pp. 183-84, emphasis in the original.
74. Hegel, in ibid., p. 185, emphasis added.
75. Ibid., pp. 186, 187, etc.
76. See, ibid., p. 188.
77. Ibid., p. 188, caps Lenin's.
78. Ibid., pp. 187-88.
79. Hegel, in ibid., p. 189, emphasis added.
80. Ibid., p. 189, caps in the original.
81. Ibid., p. 190.
82. Ibid., Lenin's caps.
83. Ibid., p. 190, caps Lenin's.
84. Ibid., p. 191.
85. Lenin, ibid., p. 234, emphasis in the original.
86. Ibid., p. 235.
87. Ibid., p. 236.
88. Ibid.
89. Hegel, in ibid., p. 237.
90. Hegel, ibid.
91. Hegel, in ibid., pp. 237-8.
92. Ibid., p. 296.
93. Ibid.

94. Ibid., p. 298.
95. Lenin on Hegel, ibid., p. 301.
96. Ibid.
97. Ibid., p. 301.
98. Ibid., p. 199.
99. See, Ibid., pp. 199-200.
100. Ibid., p. 201.
101. Hegel, Ibid., p. 202.
102. Ibid.
103. Ibid., p. 111.
104. Ibid.
105. Ibid.
106. Ibid.
107. Lenin on Hegel, ibid.
108. Ibid.
109. Ibid., p. 110, emphasis in the original, Lenin's.
110. Ibid., Lenin's emphasis.
111. See, Lenin's comments, p. 110.
112. Hegel, in ibid., p. 112.
113. Ibid.
114. Ibid., p. 112, *Hegel's italics.*
115. Lenin's explanation of self-movement in Hegel, ibid., p. 113, emphasis added.
116. Hegel, in ibid., p. 114, emphasis in the original.
117. Lenin, in ibid., p. 114.
118. Ibid., pp. 87-88.
119. Ibid., p. 89.
120. Ibid.
121. Hegel, in Ibid, 90.
122. Lenin on Hegel, ibid., p. 93.
123. Hegel, ibid., pp. 96-97.
124. Lenin on Hegel, ibid., p. 97.
125. Ibid.
126. Ibid., p. 104.
127. Hegel, ibid., p. 106.
128. Hegel, ibid.
129. Hegel, ibid., p. 107.
130. Hegel, ibid.
131. Ibid., p. 109.
132. Hegel, ibid., p. 46.

133. Hegel, ibid., p. 116.
134. Hegel, ibid., p. 117.
135. Lenin, ibid., p. 118.
136. Ibid.
137. Hegel, ibid., p. 121.
138. Hegel quoted on p. 122.
139. Ibid., pp. 123-24, emphasis added.
140. Hegel, ibid., pp. 124-25.
141. Ibid., p. 129, emphasis in the original.
142. Hegel, quoted in Vol. 38, p. 131; emphasis in the original.
143. Hegel, in ibid., p. 131.
144. Hegel, ibid., p. 132.
145. Hegel, ibid., p. 133.
146. Hegel, ibid.
147. Lenin, ibid.
148. Ibid., p. 135.
149. Hegel, ibid.
150. Ibid., p. 136.
151. Ibid., pp. 136-37.
152. Hegel, ibid., p. 137.
153. Hegel quoted in ibid, pp. 137-38, emphasis Lenin's.
154. Ibid., p. 138.
155. Lenin, Ibid., p. 138, emphasis in the original.
156. Lenin's comments, ibid., p. 138.
157. Hegel, ibid., p. 139, emphasis in the original.
158. Hegel quoted, ibid., p. 140, emphasis added.
159. Hegel 140, emphasis in the original.
160. Hegel, ibid., pp. 140-41, emphasis in the original.
161. Hegel, ibid., p. 142.
162. Hegel, ibid., pp. 144-45.
163. Hegel, ibid., p. 145.
164. Hegel, ibid.
165. Ibid., p. 146.
166. Ibid., pp. 146-47, emphasis in the original.
167. Ibid., p. 147, emphasis added.
168. Ibid., emphasis in the original.
169. Ibid., p. 148, emphasis in the original.
170. Ibid.
171. Ibid., p. 150.

172. Ibid., p. 151.
173. Ibid., p. 152.
174. Ibid., p. 153.
175. Ibid., emphasis Hegel's.
176. Ibid., emphasis Hegel's.
177. Ibid., emphasis both Hegel's and Lenin's.
178. Ibid., pp. 159-60.
179. Ibid., p. 160.
180. Ibid., p. 161, emphasis added.
181. Ibid., p. 169, emphasis and caps in the original; see also the previous pages, particularly pp. 167, 168.
182. Ibid., p. 171, emphasis in the original.
183. Ibid., p. 178.
184. See, ibid., p. 177.
185. Ibid., pp. 178-79.
186. See, ibid., p. 179.
187. Ibid., p. 180, the first two emphases Lenin's; emphasis on the last sentence mine – AR.
188. Lenin in ibid., emphasis in the original, p. 181.
189. See, ibid., p. 182.
190. Lenin in ibid., p. 182, emphasis in the original.
191. Lenin, ibid., p. 183.
192. Ibid.
193. Ibid., p. 184.
194. Ibid., p. 192, caps Lenin's.
195. Hegel in ibid., p. 193, emphasis in the original.
196. Ibid., pp. 194-95, emphasis in the original.
197. Ibid., emphasis in the original.
198. Ibid., p. 197, emphasis in the original.
199. Ibid., pp. 199-200.
200. Lenin, ibid., p. 200.
201. Ibid., p. 202.
202. Ibid.
203. Ibid., pp. 212-13.
204. Ibid., p. 213.
205. Ibid., p. 214.
206. Ibid., p. 215, emphasis in the original.
207. Ibid., emphasis in the original.
208. Ibid., p. 216.

209. See, ibid., p. 217.
210. Hegel, in Ibid., p. 112, emphasis in the original.
211. Lenin, ibid., emphasis added.
212. Ibid., p. 294.
213. Ibid., p. 381.
214. See, ibid., pp. 409, 433 etc.
215. Lenin, ibid., p. 114, emphasis Lenin's.
216. Lenin and Hegel, ibid., p. 133.
217. Lenin, ibid., p. 138.
218. Lenin, in ibid., p. 141; first emphasis in the original, the second one added. Lenin here is referring to Hegel's *Science of Logic*, 1812-13, Marx's *Manifesto*, 1847, and Darwin's *Origin of Species*, 1859[See, Note No. 53, Lenin *CW*, 38].
219. Lenin, ibid., p. 143, emphasis in the original.
220. See, Lenin, ibid., p. 143.
221. Lenin, ibid., emphasis Lenin's.
222. Lenin, ibid., pp. 146-47.
223. Lenin, ibid., p. 147, emphasis Lenin's.
224. Lenin, ibid., pp. 150-51, emphasis Lenin's.
225. Ibid.
226. Ibid., p. 152.
227. Ibid., emphasis Lenin's.
228. Ibid.
229. Ibid.
230. Ibid.
231. Ibid., p. 153.
232. Ibid.
233. Ibid., p. 155, emphasis Lenin's.
234. Lenin, also Hegel, ibid., pp. 157-58.
235. See, Lenin in ibid., p. 159.
236. Lenin, ibid., p. 160.
237. Hegel, in ibid., p. 161, emphasis in the original.
238. Lenin, ibid., p. 167.
239. Lenin, ibid., pp. 167-68.
240. Hegel, in ibid., p. 169, caps in the original.
241. Lenin, in ibid., p. 171, emphasis Lenin's.
242. Ibid., p. 177, emphasis in the original.
243. Ibid., emphasis in the original.
244. Lenin, in ibid., p. 179.
245. Lenin, in ibid., the emphasis on last sentence added; other emphases Lenin's.

246. Lenin, in ibid., emphasis in the original.
247. Hegel, in ibid., p. 182.
248. Lenin, in ibid., p. 182, emphasis Lenin's.
249. Lenin, in ibid., p. 183.
250. Hegal in ibid., p. 215, emph. in the original.
251. Lenin in ibid., p. 216.
252. Lenin, in ibid.
253. Lenin, in ibid.
254. Ibid., p. 217.
255. Lenin's comment on Hegel, in ibid.
256. Ibid.
257. Ibid.
258. Ibid., p. 218, emphasis in the original.
259. Ibid., p. 219, capital letters in the original.
260. Hegel, Lenin, ibid.
261. Lenin. Vol. 38, p. 219.
262. Ibid., emphasis in the original.
263. Lenin, ibid., p. 273.
264. Ibid.
265. Ibid.
266. Hegel, in ibid., p. 225.
267. Ibid., p. 225.
268. Hegel in ibid., on p. 226.
269. Ibid., p. 226, emphasis added.
270. Ibid., p. 227.
271. Lenin, ibid., p. 227.
272. Lenin, ibid.
273. Ibid., Lenin on p. 228.
274. Lenin's example, ibid.
275. Hegel and Lenin, ibid., 229.
276. Lenin in ibid., p. 231, emphasis in the original.
277. Hegel in ibid.
278. Lenin, ibid.
279. Hegel, ibid.
280. Hegel, ibid., p. 269.
281. Lenin, ibid., p. 234.
282. Lenin, ibid., p. 234, emphasis Lenin's.
283. Lenin, ibid., p. 259.
284. Lenin, ibid., pp. 259-60, emphasis Lenin's.

285. Ibid., p. 265.
286. Lenin, ibid., p. 266.
287. Lenin, ibid., p. 276; the second sentence in the original obviously has some printing mistakes; therefore, it has been reconstructed on the basis of the meaning of the first sentence. – AR
288. Lenin, ibid., p. 278, emphasis in the original.
289. Lenin, ibid., p. 279, emphasis Lenin's.
290. Lenin in ibid., pp. 279-80, emphasis in the original.
291. Ibid., p. 280.
292. Lenin on Hegel, ibid., p. 296, caps Lenin's, p. 296.
293. See, ibid., p. 318.
294. Lenin, 'Conspectus of Heraclitus', in ibid., pp. 352-53.
295. Lenin, 'Conspectus of Aristotle', in ibid., p. 372, emphasis in the original.
296. Lenin, in ibid., p. 372, emphasis in the original.

5

Hegelian Method: Unveiling Contradictions, Difference and Dialectics of Motion

A Study of Hegel's *Phenomenology of Mind* and *Phenomenology of Spirit*

Along with *Phenomenology of Spirit, The Phenomenology of Mind* by Hegel is among the most outstanding ones on disclosing the inner sources of motion, of the difference and the resultant contradictions of processes and the dialectics. Perhaps no other work unveils dialectics and its spontaneity and naturalness so well and so profoundly as these two works. Here we will have a brief glimpse of it.

Generally, Hegel was *very critical* of philosophy as such and in general current during his time. And this should be noted as very crucial, as it flies in the face of the claims that he was virtually a philosopher only. Hegel came out as a great philosopher as a consequence mainly of the criticism of Kant's subjective idealism. He criticized Kant for the "things-in-themselves", that is, the things that cannot be known. Hegel throughout his philosophy has shown that things can be known if we study and grasp the motion and dialectics of concepts. Besides, Kant and many others were also a fashion during Hegel's times. Hegel never liked to degrade knowledge and abstraction, and disliked the philosophical display that was quite common at that time. He also disliked and criticized a lot of trash and truisms written in the name of philosophy.

Hegel says in Para 1 of *Phenomenology of Mind* that in case of a philosophical work, it seemed not only superfluous, but in view of the nature of philosophy, even inappropriate and misleading to begin by explaining the end the author has in mind. This was not the way to expound philosophical truth.

Philosophy essentially is that element of universality which encloses the particular within it; therefore, the final result seems already expressed in this fact. Hegel says[1] that the systematic development of truth in *scientific form* can alone be the true shape in which truth exists. He had set before himself the task of bringing philosophy *nearer to the form of science*, "the goal where it can lay aside the name of *love* of knowledge and be *actual* knowledge. The inner necessity that knowledge should be science lies in its very nature and solely in the systematic exposition of philosophy itself. To raise philosophy to the level of *scientific system* would be the only true justification. *Truth and science* are the same things, and they exist in contradiction with the current spread of ideas and what goes as knowledge."[2] Here, particularly noteworthy are the underlined words.

The self-conscious mind has motion not only beyond the immediacy of observation but to the opposite extreme of insubstantial reflection of self into self and even beyond this too. It has not only lost the concrete life but is also conscious of this loss and also of the transitory nature of content.[3]

Time was when man had a heaven, decked and fitted out with endless wealth of thoughts and pictures. The significance of that lay in the thread of light that attached the human thought to the heaven; *instead of dwelling in the present as it is here and now,* the eye glanced over the present to the divine *to a present that lies beyond.* Mind's gaze had to be forcibly directed to the present on the earth and to the earthly and kept fixed there. *It took a long time to clear the vision* on the things earthly, through Experience. *Now everything is turned opposite*: man's mind is so deeply rooted in the earthly that we need a similar and strong power to rise above that level. His spirit shows such poverty of nature that it seems to long for the mere pitiful feeling of the divine in the abstract.[4]

Our epoch is a birth-time, a period of transition. The spirit of man has broken with the old order of things and with the old ways of thinking; humans have all the time carried for long the stream of progress ahead. Suddenly, there is *a break in the process* and a *qualitative* change. The sunrise in a flash and in a single stroke has brought to view the structure of the new world.[5]

But this new world is as little clear and generalized as a newly born child. *A general notion of the whole does not mean that the whole has been realised.* "In the same way, science, *the crowning glory* of the spiritual world, is not found complete in its initial stages." The whole has returned to itself, but to the resultant abstract notion of the whole.[6] Science too is yet to assume the whole, and is filled with details.[7] The Idea, which by itself is no doubt the truth, really never gets any further than just where it began, as long as it keeps repeating the same things.[8]

The living substance is that being which truly is subject or the truly realized and actual. The subject is pure and simple negativity, and just on that account *a process of splitting up what is simple and undifferentiated,* a process of setting factors in opposition. True reality is merely the process of reinstating self-identity, of reflecting into its own self in and from its other. It is the process of its own becoming, the circle which presupposes its end as its purpose, and has its end for its beginning.[9]

It may also be said that the object is simple and undifferentiated. *Through subject,* it is split up and differentiated into differences, factors of opposition, negation, true identity, and thus true reality is reinstated as the self-identity.

Under the sub-head 'The element of knowledge', Hegel says that a self having knowledge purely of itself in the absolute antithesis of itself is *the very soil where science flourishes,* and is the knowledge in universal form. The beginning of philosophy demands from consciousness that it should feel at home in this element. But the element attains its perfect meaning only through the process of gradually developing meaning. Mind as the medium of thinking is the immediacy and thus substantial nature in general.[10]

On the other hand, the individual has the right to demand that science will help to climb the ladder, whereby he can live with and in science. His right rests on absolute independence, he is the immediate certainty of self. Science has to become *external expression*, and become *objective* on its own.[11]

Nature of Mathematics and Reality

According to Hegel, the process of mathematical proof *does not belong to the object*; it is a function that takes place outside the matter in hand. Thus, the nature of a right-angled triangle does not break itself up into factors in the manner set forth in the mathematical construction which is required to prove the proposition expressing the relation of its parts. It is only at the end that we find the triangle reinstated; it was lost in the course of construction, and was present only in fragments.[12]

The entire process of producing the result is an affair of knowledge. In philosophical knowledge too, the way existence comes about is different from that whereby the essence or inner nature of the fact comes into being. But the philosophical knowledge contains both, while mathematical knowledge sets forth merely the way existence comes about, i.e. the way the nature of the fact gets to be in the sphere of knowledge as such. Philosophical knowledge unites the two processes in another way: the inward rising is a continuous transition into outwardness, as also a withdrawal into the inner essence. Through such a two-fold process, the whole comes into being.[13]

In mathematical knowledge, the insight required is an external function in relation to the subject-matter. The means, construction and proof contain true propositions but the content is false. The triangle is taken to pieces, and its parts are made into other figures. Thus the triangle gives rise to other figures. It is only at the end that we really regain the triangle with which we were concerned. It was lost sight of in the course of construction, and was present only in fragments. It is a negativity of content. The actual fact is thereby altered.[14]

The real defect of this kind of knowledge is that we do not have any necessity of construction: the necessity does not arise from the nature of theorem; it is imposed. The drawing different lines and figures are arbitrary. An external purpose controls the process.[15]

The process has poverty of purpose. Its purpose or principle is quantity. The process of knowledge proceeds on the surface, and is not a conceptual way of comprehending.

Real Knowledge

About the depth and nature of knowledge, Hegel says that what is 'familiarly known' is not properly known, just for the reason that it is'familiar'. It is the commonest form of self-deception; knowledge of this type never gets off from the point, never develops, so to say. Subject, object, God, nature, understanding etc. etc. are uncritically *presupposed.* They are taken as something fixed, valid, familiar, given points from which to start and to return to. "The process of knowing flits between these secure points", merely going along the surface.[16]

It is interesting to note that Hegel criticizes the common theory of 'God' as uncritical and superficial. Much of that which has been stated against Hegel on the question of God does not stand scrutiny.

That only means that the above-mentioned concepts must constantly move, must not be taken as fixed and for granted. Concepts are not fixed entities, they are in motion, constantly changing.

The analysis of an idea must do away with the character of familiarity. The idea has to be broken up into its constituent elements, which are its moments, which cause the idea. *The concrete fact is self-divided, is made to reveal self-motion, self-activity.* "The action of *separating the elements* is the exercise of the force of understanding, the most astonishing and greatest of all powers, or rather the absolute power."[17]

Understanding is transforming negativity into positivity, by asserting what *is* through negation, giving determinateness. What is objectively presented becomes a possession of pure self-consciousness. The manner of study in ancient times was distinct from that of the modern times. The former cultivated the natural mind. It philosophized almost everything, and universals were the rule.

In modern times, however, an individual finds *an abstract form readymade.* Inner meaning is sought out without *mediation.* The *universal is abridged,* which arises out of details. Today, the task consists in actualizing the universal, by the process of breaking down. But it becomes difficult to form a continuous whole. The reason is the following:

"Thought determinations get their substance and the element of their existence from the ego, the power of the negative, or pure reality."[19]

It means understanding negates, understanding consist in what is being understood. It is the ego which provides the continuous whole, the fixity of the concrete is negated, leading to the self-moving generalized concepts. In other words, today the concrete is common but the generalization and universalisation suffers. Knowledge and information is available in details.

Here Hegel reaches conclusions *similar to those of Engels* in the *Dialectics of Nature*, that is philosophy has gone into serious crisis because of developments of concrete sciences; in fact, philosophy has almost disappeared.

Nowadays, according to Hegel, the task before us is the very opposite. "It consists in actualizing the universal, and giving it spiritual vitality, by the process of breaking down and superceding fixed and determinate thoughts."[20]

In other words, thought becomes more concrete with the development of various sciences, which provide "spiritual vitality" to the new discoveries. This stage of thinking expresses the levels achieved by the natural and social sciences and by technology. He says clearly: "This movement of the spiritual entities constitutes the nature of scientific procedure in general."[21]

Hegel comes very near the description and analyses of sciences in the modern age. Modern thought is generalization as well as concretization based upon the latest scientific discoveries and studies.

This is a movement from philosophy to concrete conceptualization in each field of knowledge. In an extremely significant statement on the status and future of philosophy, Hegel says: "This preparatory stage thus ceases to consist of causal philosophical reflections, referring to objects here and there", "the road to science, by the very movement of the notion itself, will compass the entire objective world of conscious life in its rational necessity."[22]

"This movement of the spiritual entities constitutes the nature of scientific procedure in general. Looked at as the concatenation of their content, this movement is the necessitated development and expansion of that content into an organic systematic whole." "This preparatory stage thus ceases to consist of *casual philosophical reflections*... The road to science, by the very movement of the notion itself, *will compass the entire objective world of conscious life in its rational necessity.*"[23]

This is an extremely significant observation by Hegel, in which he assesses the growing importance of science and its replacement of philosophy.

"A systematic exposition like this constitutes the first part of science, because the positive existence of mind, *qua* primary and ultimate, is nothing but the immediate aspect of mind, the beginning; the beginning, but not yet its return to itself. The characteristic feature distinguishing this part of science [Phenomenology] from the others is the element of positive immediate existence. The mention of this distinction leads us to discuss certain established ideas that usually come to notice in this connection."[24]

Conscious life, or in Hegel's words "mind's immediate existence", has two aspects: "cognition and objectivity which is opposed to or negative of the subjective function of Knowing." Scientific statement of the course of this development is a science of the experience. "*Consciousness knows and comprehends nothing but what falls within its experience*; for what is found in experience is merely spiritual substance, and moreover object of its self." Thus it is "an object for its own self and in transcending this otherness." Thus experience is the process by which the abstract externalizes itself and then comes back to itself.[25]

Here, for Hegel, the object is a spiritual being, and yet it is almost like a material object, to which consciousness returns. Hegel makes significant statements about the objects being experienced, which lie outside as objective existence. He also makes important formulations about consciousness comprehending only that which lies within its experience.

"Mind is an object to itself just as it *is*"; the separation between knowing and truth is overcome.[26] Being is entirely mediated; it is a substantial content, directly in the possession of the ego, and it is notion. "With the attainment of this the *Phenomenology of Mind* concludes." Opposition between being and knowing ends. "The process by which they are developed into an organically connected whole is Logic or Speculative Philosophy."[27]

Truth and falsehood are commonly taken as totally isolated from each other, with completely fixed nature, without any inter-relationship. But the reality is, according to Hegel, "that truth is not like stamped coin that is issued from the mint and so can be taken up and used." To know something falsely reflects inadequacy of knowledge. "This very dissimilarity is the process of distinction in general, *the essential moment in knowing.*"[28]

A Study of Hegel's *Phenomenology of Spirit*

Hegel's *Phenomenology of Spirit*, as also several of his other books/ articles are extraordinary works of dialectics, which even today have not been equaled. Hegel is known as a philosopher and more particularly as an idealist one. In the process it has been overlooked that he is perhaps the greatest dialectician in history, who dealt primarily with motion and its source.

Here we will take up some threads of his treatment of motion, transformation and dialectics, and try to incorporate it in the general picture to understand it.

Here we will see how Hegel derives the particular and the general even in the simplest of examples.

If we ask, for example, the question: 'what is this?' Then it has many implications which unveil a whole world of dialectics.

The 'this' in the question has two-fold shape of its being: as 'Now' and 'Here". They reveal two dimensions: of time and space.

To the question: 'What is Now?' we may answer: Now is night. We may write this down on a piece of paper. Suppose we look at it later, say at noon, we find that it is preserved, but stale. We find that it professes to be night but is actually not so now. Thus, 'now' is preserved, yet *not* really preserved but generalized in the not-now. The night preserves itself as and even when it is not night. It also preserves its own now in the face of *another* now, which is day. It preserves itself in the day as *not-day*. The negative becomes general.[29]

"This self-preserving Now is, therefore, not immediate but mediated" because it is determined as permanent and self-preserving. Now through *non-preservation* of something else, which is day and night. Yet so determined, it still is now, unaffected by and indifferent to day or night. Night and day are as little its being and as much its not-being. So the being of now is as much constituted by its being day or night, and simultaneously not constituted by it at all. In fact being constituted by one is also not being constituted by it. This 'this as well as that' is a universal.[30]

We Utter What We Do Not Intend To

When we say 'this' or 'it is', we utter the universal. We do not of course intend it. What we want to say is this, particular, thing. But that is expressed through the universal. "But language, as we see, is the more truthful; in it, we ourselves directly refute what we *mean* to say. Language alone expresses the true content as the universal; therefore "it is just not possible for us to ever to say, or express in words, a sensuous being that we *mean*."[31]

The Other of 'This'

The same is true of the other form of This, that is with 'here'. Let us take an example: Here is the tree. If I move around, the tree vanishes and the truth disappears; it is converted into its opposite: 'No tree is here, but a house.' It is to be noted that 'here' *does not* vanish. On the contrary, it lives through the constant vanishing of various objects and is indifferent to those objects. Thus 'this' is mediated universality.[32] We do not constantly mean the universal, and it is constantly that the universal emerges.

Thus the relation between knowing and the object is reversed. At the beginning, the object was supposed to be the essential element in the sense-perception ('sense-certainty'). Now it becomes unessential element. "The object, which was supposed to be the essential element in sense-certainty, is now an unessential element; for the universal which the object has come to be is no longer what the object was supposed essentially to be for sense-certainty." On the contrary, the certainty now resides in the opposite element, that is, in the knowing, which initially was the unessential element. The object now becomes 'my' object, it is 'I' who knows it.[33]

Immediacy and Universality of 'I'

I see the tree here and now; but another fellow sees house, instead of tree, here and now. The immediate disappears and the universal persists. Even in asserting that 'here' is not a tree, the 'here' is asserted even without realizing and intending. The truths are authenticated, but one vanishes into another.[34]

What does not vanish is the 'I' as the universal, whose seeing is not a seeing of a tree or a house but just seeing, which is mediated by negation, and which exists through negation. I do indeed mean a single 'I' but it emerges as a general I. In the case of 'this', I am saying all the 'thises'. Similarly in the case of 'I', I am saying all 'I's.[35]

For me, this 'I', here means the tree, for another 'I' here means house. If I do not want to lose my object I will not turn round.

If we go away from a particular now or here, stand at a distance or stand afterwards, we will lose it. Therefore, we must enter the same point of time and space, point them out to ourselves and thus make ourselves into the same 'I'. Then that immediacy is constituted in the following way.[36]

"The Now is pointed to, *this* Now." The 'Now' disappears in the act of pointing out itself. "The Now that *is*, is another Now than the one pointed to, and we see that the Now is just this: to be no more just when it is."[37] The Now that is pointed to us is Now that has been, and this is its truth; it has not the truth of *being*. But what essentially has been is in fact not an essence that *is*; *it is not*; it was with being that we were concerned.[38]

In this pointing out, there takes place the following movement:

1. The 'Now' is pointed out, but it is pointed as something that has been; thus the first truth is set aside.
2. Now the second truth is asserted, and it is set aside.
3. But what has been, is not; the second truth is set aside as the negation of negation. This results in the return to the first truth, that the 'Now' is. The 'Now' and the pointing out of the 'Now' are so constituted that they contain a movement, the different moments. "A *This* is posited; but it is rather an *other* that is posited, or the This is superseded: and this *otherness*, or the setting aside of the first, is itself *in turn set aside*, and so has returned into the first."[39] The first, reflected into itself, is not the immediate, not the one to begin with. On the contrary, it is something that is reflected into itself; in its otherness it remains what it is, that is Now with a plurality of Nows. The Now emerges as the universal.[40]

The 'here' also similarly turns to be a series of several 'heres'.

NOTES

1. Hegal, *Phenomenology of Mind,* Para 5.
2. Ibid., Para 5, emphasis added.
3. Ibid., Para 7.
4. Ibid., Para 8, emphasis added.
5. Ibid., Para 11.
6. Ibid., Para 12, emphasis added.
7. Ibid., Para 13.
8. Ibid., Para 15.
9. Ibid., Para 18.
10. Ibid., Para 26.
11. Ibid.
12. Ibid., Para 42.
13. Ibid.
14. Ibid., Para 43.
15. Ibid., Para 44.
16. Ibid., Para 31, emphasis added.
17. Ibid., Para 32, emphasis added.
18. Ibid., Para 33.
19. Ibid.
20. Ibid.
21. Ibid., Para 34.
22. Ibid.
23. Ibid., emphasis added.
24. Ibid., Para 35.
25. Ibid., emphasis added.
26. Ibid., Para 37, emphasis in the original.
27. Ibid.
28. Ibid., Para 39, emphasis added.
29. See, Hegel, *Phenomenology of Spirit,* Para 95-96.
30. See, ibid., Para 96.
31. Ibid., Para 97, emphasis in the original.
32. Ibid., Para 98.
33. Ibid., Para 100.
34. Ibid., Para 101.
35. Ibid., Para 102.
36. See, ibid., Para 105
37. Ibid., Para 106, emphasis in the original.
38. Ibid., emphasis in the original.
39. Para 107, emphasis in the original
40. See, ibid., Para 107.

6

Time and Philosophy

Without time there is no life. It is with time that we measure events, and it is around the clocks that our lives revolve. As soon as we talk of time we relate it with some instrument of measurement of time or calendar and diary and so on. Dividing time and our life according to it has become our habit, almost a feature of the human existence, almost impossible to part with. It has even become part of our philosophy and worldview. That is why, we find it difficult, excruciatingly painful, to think of any other concept of time, out of tune with out historical habit, particularly in the aftermath of the scientific, technological and quantum revolution. Today, as never before, it has become difficult and complicated to deal with the flow of time, with the past, present and future.

'Settled' questions have resurfaced: Does time *flow*? Can we measure it? Has it become independent of matter, space, reality and existence? These and other questions are bothering us, including the scientists. While we are in search of a coherent picture of the world, it is 'crumbling' around us. Without a standard time-directed picture, how can we understand the world? Do we have to deal with 'so many' times in the universe instead of one time? How is it possible? Then what happens to our concept of time or to anything practical and philosophical?

Time gives a sense of stability and change. We are used to continuous flux of time in description and observation; in fact, life itself is a continuous flux of time.

To understand something *we make time stand still*, long enough to be counted, measured and pondered over.[1] The idea of constancy and absoluteness of the physical things is part of human existence and foundation of the scientific development. Flow of social and individual lives has been recorded by stopping it on the fixed blocks of the calendar and time piece.

Essence of Time

The essence of time is that *it does not stand still;* the very concept of time is motion and its dialectics. Therefore, it has to be made to stand still. There are several methods in the sciences for it. In fact, one of the major methods and even nature of the various sciences is to make time stand still for various durations in order to grasp the physical reality in the particular field of study. When we use words we actually put time in it.[2] By putting time into words and concepts, we arrest it; concept is arrested time. Every concept and word has a long history. They reflect the flow of time and at the same time make it stand still. Time is dynamic while words are static. Jacques quotes Hegel as saying "words murder time".[3]

When do words do not murder time?! That is a very important and at the same time a curious question, curious from the classical point of view. That happens when words are able to cover time and/or time becomes too fast. It is normally very difficult for the words to cover time, particularly in the course of the electronics revolution. The concepts should be very flexible to win over time. Dialectics tries to achieve precisely that. It tries to go into the motion of the word and the concept. Hegel and Marx tried precisely that, and succeeded to a great extent. They went to the very limits of their era, and even beyond, to free the word from the limits of time and space to release the inherent motion and its dialectics. Hegelian philosophy and the incorporation of dialectics within the material world and within the words derived from the material world freed the concepts from the constraints of history and bindings of the present. It has to be realized that all the words and concepts have been derived from *a slowdown* of history and social development. Without such a slowing, history *cannot be created* and *society cannot exist* and move.

The great merit of Hegel and Marx was that they were able to show the word as representing the coordinates of time and space. The concept was shown to be receptacle of space and time in motion, a reflection, of the actual coordinates and indices of motion outside.

Time in Social and Natural Sciences

We partly discussed the question of social time, its origin and evolution. Without unifying the multiple manifestations of time into one system, we cannot have delineate our place and proper orientation in the world.[4] This is not given us beforetime; it evolves with social development (motion), and becomes part of our consciousness. In other words, the human beings have to overcome time and gain mastery over space in order to really become conscious beings.

Does multiple time in itself exist? This a philosophical as well as practical question. What is the meaning of time in the inanimate nature? : physical time, astronomical time, times of the plant and animal kingdom, and so on? The questions related with the past, present and future are very complicated.

In physical reality, the difference between the various kinds of time are not always clear, and tend to get obliterated. Gurvitch mentions various times as under. Macro-physical time does not correspond to the micro-physical time. While in the former, it is easier to identify time and its divisions, in the latter relativity and quick changes appear as the chief component.

Einstein demonstrated that in physics there are as many times as there are frames of reference. The speed of movement depends on the choice of the frame of reference by the observer. Thus, the time of micro-world does not correspond to the time of macro-world; similarly with various other fields of physics and physical reality.[5] You carry your own earthly time into the fast aeroplanes and rockets and behave as per normal times.

Social Time

Social time is complex phenomenon, needing a detailed treatment. Its interaction with sub-atomic time has become complicated and difficult because electronics has become the main means of communication. Society has so far been working out time with naturally occurring forces and processes moving in orderly and successive manner. But the intervention of electronically mediated communication has upset the order.

One of the main features of time in social development is its slowed down long duration, where the past is projected into the present and the future. This is the most continuous of the social times. The ecological time has the past as a remote one, yet it is projected in the present and the future, is more quantitative. The rural settings and groups like the kinships and the peasants actualize this time, and are a store-house of the times that are past.

On the other hand, time with the working class and its movement and aspirations is more in advance of itself. It is more qualitative, and the future becomes the present. The proletariat lives more in the future and is driven by it, towards an ideal. It is the time of discontinuity, contingency, quality, mass activity, communion in revolt, and confronts competitive capitalism of the present.

History studies the linear succession of the past, with almost no present. Sociology studies generally the present. So there is a historical time and a sociological time. History as science applies more continuous method than sociology. The total social phenomena are placed by sociology in a reconstituted time according to the criteria of the present society. From the methodological point of view sociology is much more discontinuous than history, as it emphasizes the discontinuity of various manifestations of time according to the groups. History on the other hand tries to fill in the gaps and ruptures and throws up bridges. History tries to re-establish the continuity of time.

There is a paradox of continuity in the science of history which studies the historical reality inclining towards discontinuity, and of discontinuity in sociology which studies a more continuous social reality than that of history. One of the reasons of this paradox is the ambiguity of historical time.

According to Gurvitch, the historical time is already a completed, elapsed time. The sociological time is in the process of happening. Historians constantly rewrite history. They do so according to the criteria of the present society. Historical time is rendered more alive and ideological. There is a forecasting of the past and this forecast is projected into the future. Multiple interpretations of the continuity of historical times are employed.

History seeks to establish continuity of different times. There is sought to be shown a continuity of events, leading to the reinforcing of the cause and effect relationship.

From Slowdown to Acceleration or Speed Up of Time

The social motion and thus time has speeded up throughout its history. Technology and science help the process, ultimately reaching the point of electronics revolution. This will constitute a very important point for our discussions later on. The medieval period became more and more time conscious. Later this consciousness spreads increasingly with the speed up and spread of the industrial society.

We may take the examples from England to make certain points, because it is the country of industrial revolution. Many of the points and examples are applicable to other countries too. Beginning in the 14th century, church clocks and public or square clocks began to be erected in most of the towns and cities and markets of England. Till the 15th century, the sundial was the main device to indicate time. Later clock towers in the main square/s of the towns became the distinguishing mark, including in India. These clock towers and squares are still in existence in many towns today.

The peasants were guided more by task orientation than by clock orientation. In this task orientation, a number of fixed points in time were woven, like meals, etc., and the use was made of devices like stick stuck in the ground or simply by the position of the sun.[6] There were cases of clocks being used not just to keep time but to tune it to the needs of the owner, e.g. his meal time or change in it. In such cases the clock was used more as a bell rather as time keeper.

In the medieval period, the week was not a common unit of time amongst the peasants and many other sections of the village. It was the rhythm of work and life that dictated routine like the months, seasons, religious festivals etc. The organization of the day, week and year in the rural areas was more rhythmic than measured. Thus, there were islands of time as measured by sundials and clocks, which were not segments of continuous time. So, there was an uneven quality to time. Punctuality was almost unknown. It was dependent on the reference to the events. Concepts of past and future were blurred. "There would be a general use of the present indicative tense.'[7] History was almost unknown and projections of the future were almost absent, and generally talks were about the present and the past. The future was imagined in the form of the past. The aim of daily life was simple reproduction. Pre-capitalist society was characterized by a general lack of time consciousness. [8]

Yet there were islands of more exact time-keeping in the medieval period, represented by the monasteries and towns.

In the medieval village the 'time of the merchant' was already beginning to triumph over the 'time of the church'. They, between themselves, gradually divided the religious and civic duties and ceremonies.

Till the 1650s there were very few household clocks in England, people generally relying on public bells and clocks. Bells were rung at fixed times, as also used to happen in the Indian towns and villages. But many people used to be out of the earshot and eye-sights of the bells and clocks. Starting in 1658 household clocks began to spread quickly in England. By 1680 the English clock and watch-making industry became very important, reaching its peak in 1796. Pocket watches also began to pick up with improvements in spiral balance-spring. By 1750 clocks and watches had become quite common in England. But they mostly were owned by the rich.

Thus from 1550 to 1750 the consciousness of time spread far and wide, which laid the basis for *the capitalist time*. The Reformation was the first blow to the pre-capitalist time. The secular made increasing inroads into the sacred. The process speeded up with the dissolution of the monasteries. Spread of schooling in the rural areas broke the bonds of the traditional time constraints and established regular time tables and routines. Between 1800 and 1850 the clocks and watches became common among all the classes of the society. People in general and the workers, owners, etc. began to work according to clocks from morning to evening, keep work-time and leisure and so on. Time began to be clearly divided and marked up as part and parcel of individual and social life.

Here onwards, so to say, people fast became *enwrapped* within the workings of time, so much so that they looked upon it as something independent, and over and above them, controlling their past, present and future. They became almost slaves of time. Time was now perceived as an objective force, detached from human experience and people had to rush to manage and keep pace with time. Time-keeping became more exact, and personal, family and social events became guided by divisions of time/clocks. Concept of time wasting or not wasting it came into currency.

With the growth of industrial production, production and labour time became step by step divided and identified by necessary, surplus and other kinds of time. Use and exchange values and their reflection/estimation by means of time and clocks became the ruling cultural-economic phenomena. Workers' time was recasted and reorganized into their own and that of their owners, personal as well as social, and so on. The owner-capitalist began to measure profits by reducing or increasing and regulating time of workers, production and labour. Discipline, particularly time discipline, was needed to integrate humans and machine. Human activity was synchronized with the movement of the machine. Human consciousness was similarly geared to new concept of time, not only in the production but also in society, the world and the universe. Concepts like 'time-work', 'time is money', value of time', etc. came into vogue. Mechanical time as reflected in the motion of wheels, gears, shafts, machines and so on became the guiding principle not only of individual and social viewpoint but also of philosophy itself. Mechanical materialist and idealist philosophies and repetitive concepts of motion became current.

Emergence of Industrial/Capitalist Time in Transport

Coordination of time-keeping developed with the growth of newer modes of transport such as stage coaches, steamers, buses and railways. It was in 1784 that stage coach was set up for mail, and later for passengers. This led to greater synchronization of time between different towns, e.g. between Bristol and London. It led to a change of the work-time of the postal employees. The rural areas were still enwrapped in their own local times, and it took a lot of time and developments to bring them out of this time-pool and to standardize them. Initially, there were differences between timings of watches in different towns, which gradually got standardized.

The inauguration of regular railway services in Britain in 1825 increased the speeds of rail travel, and thus the synchronization of

British towns to one time became imperative. At first there were various and differing timings of the modes of transport including of the railways. But gradually they coordinated their timings and uniform time came into being. After the railways started to carry the Royal Mail in 1838, keeping of strict time and synchronization became urgent. The difference between 'east' and 'west' *began to disappear.*

Birth of telegraph and related companies further necessitated, as well as complicated, the solution of the problem of synchronization.

The railway passengers faced peculiar problems. Each railway station kept, for example, both the London time as well as the local or particular station time. Thus the passengers were forced to keep account of *two* times. For example, in 1841 the London time was 4 minutes earlier than Reading time or 8 minutes earlier than Chippenham time.

So many of the rail travelers of those days carried especially made watches with two dials, one for the local time, the other for the place he was going to.

Rapid increase in railway mileage, increase in volume of rail traffic and excursion and other kinds of railway facilities necessitated uniformity of timings. It was suggested in 1847 that the whole of Britain keep one time: 'let the bells chime together' at one o'clock all over, instead of them chiming in waves from east to west! The Great Western Railway kept London time, which was 23 seconds different from Greenwich time. The railways and the post offices coordinated and decided to switch to the Greenwich time on December 1, 1847. The railway guides 1848 onwards began to show more and more stations on Greenwich time.

The clocks began to be adjusted all over England in towns and villages in the subsequent years according to London or Greenwich time, and the confusions gradually began to be cleared.

Some interesting developments took place in the course of the change, for example, in the west of England. Though other towns followed the change, Exeter resisted for quite some time, leading to problems. The Exeter station was opened on May 1, 1844. Its railway time was 14 minutes later than that of London, according to the time table (or Devonshire Directory) of 1850. Accordingly, for public convenience, a new dial was affixed at the St John's Church in 1845.

Clocks were provided in the city showing both Greenwich and local times.

In 1850, Exeter was 14 minutes and 12 seconds slower behind Greenwich. A meeting was held in 1851 in the town council. An interesting problem was presented in the course of the debates. That was about a young lady coming of age: according to the church clock she was already of age, but according to the Cathedral clock she was not! The court had decided that the Cathedral clock governed other clocks. The majority was for the change but the Dean refused to change the Cathedral clock.

In August 1852 the telegraph finally reached the Exeter railway station. It increased the pressure to change the clock, and the Dean finally agreed in November 1852 to adjust the timing.

By 1855, 98 per cent of the public clocks were synchronized with the Greenwich Mean Time (GMT). From August 2, 1880 all the activities in Great Britain followed the GMT.

Time in Different Philosophies

Different philosophies look at time in different ways. For the great Greek philosopher Parmenides, things are; Being *is* and will remain so. For Heraclitus everything is changing, transforming and flowing, nothing is still. Opposite becomes opposite, and thus there is Becoming all the time, which is the sole reality. For Parmenides, Being can never lead to becoming. On the other hand, for Heraclitus, Becoming can never lead to Being.

Democritus and Leucippus created atoms as the world building materials, located in space. This was the starting point of science.

Time and Grasp of World

To understand the events and things in world, human beings make them *standstill* long enough to be grasped and be counted and measured. The idea of relatively permanent or even absolute nature of physical things became the foundation of science, mathematics and thought in general. Thus arose the Euclidean system of axioms and theorems.

Early techniques for stopping time like recording it on notches on a stick or on fixed blocks of space in a calendar evolved gradually.

In contrast to the space orientation, time orientation is much more difficult to deal with. It is not available to the senses in the same way and so easily as space reflection. Space can be studied much more easily because it can be made to stand still, but time cannot be: for example and object can be put in a fixed position. That also, in a sense, involves fixing time, but is a far more complicated matter.

The flux of time makes it difficult to describe. To put time into words is to make things stand still. Time is dynamic and words are static: words pin things down; they ruin time by pinning it down. Consequently, there is a major difference between words and things and words and time. The problem of space was brought with the concept of atoms as bounded space and unchanging solidity. With the passing of time, the problem of space became increasingly problem-ridden.

Time in the Quantum World and Outer Space

Today, we are faced with a fresh problem, and as a consequence, our thought-process and worldview are in deep crisis. It is not a crisis of collapse or destruction; rather it is a point where we have entered a stage of development or new world. We have begun working with the instruments qualitatively different from those used so far in history. We are using software as our logical guide. This science and the consequent technology pose fresh problems for our existing concept/s of time.

Time has been speeded up as never before. We no more Live in a world guided by a slowdown of time, space and events. The events were already being speeded up with social development and progressively higher levels of productive and communicative forces. We have entered a new stage where these concepts acquire new meanings.

Quantum physics reveals that the discontinuous radiations of electrons and other particles are time resistant to quantitative measurements. Time and energy are combined in time-energy packets (quanta). Theorists talk of many times in micro-physics and in the outer space or the inter-stellar spaces. Until now, the physicist's time had appeared to be unique and absolute because he was placed on a particular experimental plane. Relativity has produced temporal pluralism, because there are many times for relativity, as time is a relative concept. In the opposite aspect of relativity, that of the waves, the concept of time still has continuity, as in electro-magnetic waves. But that breaks down as soon as waves are broken into quanta. Continuity suffers heavily. The durations are discontinuous. They do not have the properties of chain reaction.[9]

This only means that we are coming to the concept of multiple time, but at a higher level. The absolute time is dissociated into 'own' time for each process, and it is the conversion of one into another that gives us the relation between different times. Time is too fast for the event to be 'framed' or be frozen in a limit.

A second is a period too long in the quantum world. We have to deal with micro-seconds and almost infinite parts thereof. Time loses its meaning, almost detaching itself from the 'events'.

In the natural sciences, the relation between past, present and future differ with the area of study or the subject or the field. For example, the observation of stars conveys a sense of the present, and we think, and we have been actually been thinking so throughout the human history, that what we observe is the star as it is now, just like a tree or a stone. But in reality what we observe is the past or very remote past of the star, which may at that point of observation be thousands of years or even thousands of light years old (away). *The present is yet to come and will never come!* So the present of the human star is actually the past, or remote past, of the star. The future is absent here. The past of the space *has merged* with our biological and social present.

The human body, brain and mind in particular, carry *widely divergent* times and their interrelations in a complicated combination or combinations, which keep changing and shifting. An important and crucial component is the psychic time.

The time of thermodynamics does not correspond to the time of mechanics nor to the time of macro-physics. The time of the intensity of thermal processes raises the problems of their extinction, and thus is more related with the future and the present than with the past. It is more qualitative than the time of mechanics.

The time of astronomy is essentially a hypothetical time, which cannot be reduced to any of the times in physics. It is tied to the quasi-infinite distance of light, where the present is obliterated, and only the past and the future remain.

The time of chemistry is different; the present is projected in the past and future, and accentuates the transition from discontinuity to continuity and vice versa.

The biological time is a complex of times; evolution is interrupted by discontinuities. The qualitative asserts itself. One should differentiate between the real time in the vegetable and the animal kingdoms and time as constructed by biology as a science. There is biological time, physiological time in the human body, as well as time as reality and as constructed by physiology and anthropology.

Human time is a complex of times, as well as it contains dialectics of biological and social times.

Atomic Configuration of World and Motion

The atomic model is a *useful abstraction* for philosophy: it is a reality for day to day use as well as a non-reality and an abstraction for philosophy. The concept of atom and particle helps us *explain* the world or reality. Therefore, it is a *conceptual tool.*

The atomic model helps us with a certain sense of certainty, reliability and confidence that 'everything is in order' (!) and fine. We count on the tangible, on what is big and small, which provide us a reliable basis for observation and study. In that case we are sure that we know the world or can know it.

The introduction of acceleration of motion complicated matters. Galileo studied velocity and acceleration, which was made possible by inventions of pendulum and new types of clocks. That was in the 14th century and later. Uncertainty began to creep into what was established as certain. It was difficult, for example, to understand increase or decrease in rate of motion and calculate and understand the world accordingly. It was becoming difficult to understand without stopping the object. Acceleration cannot be stopped and seen.

This aspect of social development has increasingly been a problem for human thought.

Another interesting kind of time is represented by 'Quentin's watch', with its time of 'trip mechanism'. Here we measure time by *stopping it!* This is unprecedented. This precisely is the principle of the stop watches.

It was this intermittently stopped clock time that was incorporated into Galileo's inertia of physical bodies and Newton's mechanics.[10]

Atomic World and Time

Emergence of relativity and quantum physics create fresh problems: One would expect that the mechanical time would be replaced by flux time. But this does not happen. The atomic world of objects is three-dimensional. In this world, time enters as the fourth dimension as in a Cartesian world of three spatial coordinates. But here time is a more important dimension because of very high velocities. Consequently, the three other dimensions of space more and more get modified and even partially lost because of time. So, our view and worldview are distorted because of drastic changes in the 'objects' and their relationships with time. At these speeds, the three spatial dimensions find it difficult to keep themselves together, at least 'in the shape' that we are used to. The speed of light and other phenomena like those of the quantum world leave behind the problems related with 'death of time' from our point of view.

The phenomena of waves, particles and fields complicate the questions of time and space in the sphere of electromagnetic fields and their motions, and in the outer space in general. It is also difficult to clearly apply the concept of time to the wave-particle duality and particle conversions. Several problems arise when we try to relate the problems of being and becoming to particle-related and space-related realities. At first sight Being appears to be closely associated with the world of atomic clock time, while Becoming is associated with the flux time of the force-field. Yet it is all not so easy and simple, particularly in view of the wave-particle duality.

In philosophy the two types of time are often associated with the subjective and the objective worlds. The flux time of past, present and future is related to the psychological processes and with the subjective world, while the clock time of orderly manner is related with the physical and objective world. Grunbaum[11] for example quotes authors to say that 'now' is the temporal mode experiencing 'ago'. An indeterminate universe makes it difficult to define an objective 'now'.

The 'now' involves peculiarities of consciousness. The transient nature of the 'now' has meaning in the context of the conscious beings, and not inanimate nature. Recording of events by inanimate apparatuses does not have the same significance. The meaning of 'now' on the conscious brain has the features of brain traces and a succession of states of awareness. But they do not explain the temporal features or nature of many events. Succession of states of awareness and the awareness of succession are two things. Flux of time includes awareness of the succession of the 'nows'.

The 'now' and the 'here' have been so profoundly analysed by Hegel in his *Phenomenology of Spirit*, which we have dealt with elsewhere.

NOTES

1. See, Elliot Jaques, "Enigma of Time", in, J. Hassard, Ed., *The Sociology of Time*, Macmillan, London, 1990, p. 27.
2. See, Elliot Jaques, ibid.
3. Ibid.
4. See Georges Gurvitch, "The Problem of Time", in J. Hassard, ibid., p. 38.
5. Based on Georges Gurvitch, in, ibid., p. 41.
6. Based on Nigel Thrift, "The Making of a Capitalist Time Consciousness", in J. Hassard, ibid., p. 107.
7. Thrift, in ibid., p. 108.
8. Based on Thrift, ibid.
9. Based on Gurvitch, in, ibid., p. 41.
10. Elliot Jaques, in J. Hassard, ibid., p. 28.
11. Jaques, in, J. Hassard, ibid., p. 31.

7

Quantum Revolution, Speed Up of Time, and Crisis in Philosophy

Quantum Revolution Speeds Up Thought

The quantum revolution in physics of the 20th century has completely transformed the nature not only of physics and science in general, but also of philosophy and our worldview. So much so that we are now talking of a *quantum philosophy* in a quantum world.

The quantum revolution and related development in atomic processes, discoveries of momentary particles, wave/particle duality, radiations and their nature, relativity, studies and discoveries in the vast spaces etc. have all speeded up our thought processes because of the very high motions discovered both inside and outside the atom. We stand on the verge of new thought based upon very fast concepts and realities. We are living in an age of speed up of ideas.

Quantum revolution began in the early 19th century with the discovery of 'quantum' (plural 'quanta') principally by Max Planck, and with theories and discoveries in the field of relativity, linked inseparably with the name of Albert Einstein.

Quantum revolution and relativity, and other developments in natural sciences, *have fundamentally changed our worldview.* They have upset the Newtonian/Cartesian worldviews, developed just before and particularly during the industrial age. They have changed the way we look at the world, at reality, matter, space and time, motion of particles, cause-effect phenomena, the subject-object relationship, at the relationships of position and motion, wave-particle contradictions, the nature of idea and consciousness, and so on.

These developments have led to an unprecedented speed up of time/s, imparting increasingly transitory nature to the concepts and to thought and philosophy in general. Philosophy itself is under threat, getting toppled in one area after another, underlining a need for new world outlook.

This is because the movements of the sub-atomic particles and of electromagnetic and other waves cannot be explained with the Newtonian, classical laws of mechanics. Classical mechanics collapses in the world of waves and particles, for example in the world of light and electrons, though are still applicable to everyday motions of tangible objects. Besides, the 'world', universe, 'reality' that emerged in the industrial age can no more be with the philosophy created as a result and during the industrial age.

We badly need a new world outlook, consisting of fresh concepts, both philosophical and non-philosophical. Philosophy itself is in a serious crisis.

Quantum phenomena and relativity (special and general) are ever adding novel aspects to the nature of dialectics of matter and idea. The structure of atom has been fundamentally questioned. The nature of matter and motion and their relationship with space and time has undergone radical changes. The particles and waves are revealing ever-new features.

Quantum philosophy is fast superceding all other forms of thought, philosophy and world outlook.

Quantum revolution is perhaps ***the most fundamental and spectacular revolution*** in the history of science, thought and philosophy. Its implications are so deep that we have begun to assess them properly only now. They are yet to reveal themselves fully. They are bringing about drastic changes in the very depths and appearances of the society by becoming new productive and communicative forces, particularly through the STR (scientific and technological revolution) and ICR (information and communication revolution).

Concepts, theories and hypotheses in science and philosophy are rapidly becoming obsolete. This concept or that, and the technologies, already become old by the time we grasp them. Many of the developments are absolutely shocking and beyond belief. Classical concepts are quickly being overcome and replaced by the new ones.

It is this scientific revolution, which is becoming a productive force, causing deep-going changes in the society, thought and practice.

Quantum Revolution

'**Quantum**' (plural 'quanta') means a certain quantity, 'packet' of, say, energy. The concept of quantum was first advanced by a great scientist Max Planck in 1900. He had to resort to the concept of 'quantum' because he had to solve a certain problem in a peculiar way. Planck, as also Einstein, came to the conclusion on the basis of certain experiments, observations and conceptualization that light transmits energy to matter in bundles or quanta. Its size is E=hv, where v is the frequency of light wave, and h the universal constant. The constant was later known as Planck's constant.[1]

Let us not have the idea that Planck made some elaborate experiments and then 'found' that the quanta were there! No. He used the concept for certain mathematical solutions; only by so doing could he solve the problem at hand. Today, that very quantum has become a common 'thing' of the quantum processes.

What was the problem? Let us first be clear about what we are talking. We are using the words 'classical' and 'quantum'. We are normally living in a classical world, that visibly and non-visibly surrounds us. We use rocks, spheres, logs of wood, iron bars and balls and so on and so forth. Suppose we hit a ball with bat or one sphere with another. The harder we hit the faster will the ball go. To hit harder, we use more body force or energy. We burn a log of wood, and the more we heat, warmer will it be for our body, and greater light will be there. There is more fire when more wood is added. But it is not like that in quantum processes. Then there are molecules which unite to form certain compounds, and there are atoms which unite to form molecules. So, this in very brief is what we call the classical world. It has its own laws, known as the classical laws, with which we commonly work and which are generally known. All our thoughts, philosophy and worldview are based more or less on this world.

But things are different in the quantum world. The laws of the classical world do not apply there. And this is the problem. Not only this; what is true and applicable in the classical world is no more so in the quantum world. And it is this problem that has led to a crisis in science, thought and philosophy.

In our everyday experience, and in the classical physics and mechanics, energy and force are emitted and applied continuously and 'in bulk', so to say. We hit an object with big or bigger force. We burn wood and other things in bulk to get more energy, etc.

But when we work with electrical particles, electromagnetic waves and such other processes, things are quite different, so different that they are unimaginable. This is what Max Planck across. And he was so shocked and surprised that he developed and discovered 'the quantum' in the process.

He ***had to*** develop the concept of 'quantum', had to ***discover*** 'the quantum'.

You can hit one ball with another, one rock piece with a bigger or smaller piece, and they will remain the same until a point. After that they may break up or may not. You can go on adding more and more wood and oil to increase the fire.

But you cannot do this with a charged particle, radiation, light and electromagnetic waves. For example, if you 'hit' one particle with another, they will convert into a new particle or waves or charges and so on. You cannot go on adding particle upon particle! You cannot 'pick up' a particle and 'throw' it against another! You cannot go on adding waves after waves (!) and create a big 'fire'. A wave will immediately convert into another, and all your plans will disappear into particles and waves! You cannot 'heat' anything or 'throw' anything in that world known as the 'quantum' world. It is a different one where these actions simply cannot take place.

Max Planck's discovery led to the following situation. Light sources and emit light in quanta or packets of fixed energy. Similarly, light and other radiations travel or exchange energy in fixed quanta. Even the electromagnetic fields and waves can be reduced to or converted into or interpreted as movement of 'quanta'. For example, waves have wavelengths. Each wavelength itself is a quantum, that is, has a measurable energy pack.

This changes the situation regarding the reality completely. A new particle or 'atom' (not the correct word, though) thus found. Light moves as particle. These particles are different from 'our' atoms, the atoms we know, which are complicated structures. The new, quantum, particles are extremely temporary and transitory packets of energy, but very effective and crucial to the new world. These quanta are extremely minute, less than minuscule. They disappear as soon as they appear.

Thus, at this level and speeds, all the exchanges and existences are converted immediately into the 'particles' known as quanta. They have very high speeds. Light has a velocity of 3 lakh (3 hundred thousand) kms per second. Many other particles have a life of a millionth part of a second.

The discovery of quantum also explained the nature of atom. Within the atom, for example, the electrons move along fixed orbits. When they change their orbits they either release particle/waves/energy or absorb it. So, the structure and fixity or otherwise of the atom is explained. The particle within the atom move at an extremely high speed. Their conversions take place through absorption or release of the quanta.

With this we enter the world of quantum conversions where the laws of the classical world are not applicable. In this world, our observation and worldview is also qualitatively different.

Max Planck Grapples with Quantum

Max Planck came across the quanta when he was studying what is known as the 'blackbody radiation'. The blackbody absorbs heat or light fully. Blackbody radiation is electromagnetic radiation within a body which is in thermodynamic equilibrium with its surroundings. If such a body is heated to a certain temperature, it emits radiation. The radiation at each wavelength can be measured. The radiation shifts to the shorter wavelengths with the rise in temperature. But classical physics could not explain the mode of radiation at shorter wavelength.[2] It was supposed that the radiation would be highest at the shortest wavelength, so much so that it would not be possible to measure it. At that time, the electromagnetic waves were considered in the manner of water waves or waves produced by wires (say of musical instruments). Suppose you sit near the water waves. If they increase in motion and intensity, you are hit. But that does not happen with radiation waves etc. You are not hit; in fact, you do not feel the change at all!

Computations and mathematical calculations too were done accordingly in the above case. In was presumed that high frequency would lead to high levels of energy radiation, as happens in ultraviolet radiation, which was called "ultraviolet destruction" or "catastrophe". It was presumed that with continued increase in intensity, as you move towards ultraviolet side of spectrum, everything would reach a state of high energy, and would ultimately turn into violet, ultraviolet, x-ray radiation and so on.

But this did not happen, *and it led to the birth of quantum science or quantum mechanics.*

Different laws tried to explain radiations from different wavelengths. Raleigh-Jeans' law was applicable to the blackbody radiation only at long wavelengths (very low frequencies), while Wilhelm Wien's law was applicable only at short wavelengths (high frequencies). Wien's law broke down at infra-red region of the spectrum. The problem was disturbing the scientists since the end of the 19th century itself. Attempts were made to combine them to explain the continuous black body radiation.[3] But they failed. They failed because they tried to explain using the classical *wave* model.

Marx Planck, on the other hand, decided to divide the radiation into 'packets', and suddenly everything fell in right place and could be explained!

It was an *amazing discovery, and it led to a qualitative transformation of classical physics into quantum physics.* The classical science and viewpoint was unable to explain the new discovery. Suddenly a new field opened up, where the classical laws and concepts were not applicable. New explanations were given and new concepts emerged fast, leading to an entirely new science as well as to a new outlook. Quantum and relativity demanded novel solutions and formulations because they were faced with a new world of reality.

According to Planck, the electric oscillators within the atom receive or emit energy in a definite amount, known as quanta.

In this context another important experiment needs mention. It is known as the photoelectric experiment, by Einstein in 1905. The experiment and results are very simple. When light is radiated on a metal plate, some electrons are liberated from the plate. Each electron will have the **same** amount of energy (E=hv) *irrespective* of the intensity of light, at a particular frequency of light. Thus, even at weak light, the energy gain will be the same, though fever electrons will be dislodged. Energy is transferred from light to the electron.

So, what is the problem?

What is the significance of Planck's theory of quantum? And of Einstein's photoelectric effect?

The facts obtained in these experiments cannot be explained with the help of classical theory of light. In both the experiments/ observations, **energy of the electrons should keep rising with the increase in the intensity of light.**[4] This does not happen.

Steelmakers have been aware that if a piece of iron or black body turns cherry-red around the temperature of 1300 degrees Celsius, coloured objects have an intensive colour, black bodies don't have any.

Classical physicists assumed that like everything else in the world, a black body should obey Newton's laws. But they don't as we saw above. The scientists kept coming to the conclusion that the black bodies should glow bright blue at all temperatures.[5]

Then what really happens? What exactly is this all puzzle business?

When an iron piece is heated, or any other black body radiation takes place in any other way, the classical scientists and scholars assumed that it would go on absorbing energy in increasing intensity. Therefore, But in fact, it does not happen. And Max Planck tried to find an answer. The conclusion he came to was that the black body on being heated **does not follow the classical, Newtonian laws.** Its energy does not rise to 'dizzying heights'.

While making calculations, Planck could follow classical formulae only slightly, to an extent; after a certain point he had to assume that the light (or electromagnetic) waves did not come out *continuously* as stream of energy. The light was emitted in separate, discrete packets.

What does that mean? It meant only one thing: However much light is there, however intense light is emitted, it consists of a series of quanta, each with a definite, fixed amount of energy, so that the energy released from the black body never passes beyond a certain level (for a frequency of light). If there is more energy, it is distributed over greater number of quanta (or lesser in the opposite case).

This discovery changed the nature of the natural sciences, particularly physics. At the same time, it affected the *philosophical concepts of the world* seriously, as also the worldview. The structure, constituents and the laws of 'reality', the 'world' got changed completely, as we shall see later.

Concept of reality: What is the concept of reality, matter, world in classical thought and physics? Stone, apple, trees, earth, etc. etc. are made of matter, real matter.

Then there is the concept of fields–electric, magnetic, electromagnetic, gravitational etc., common to our use and experience too. There is distribution of force in the field (e.g. magnetic).

For classical physicists light is like a wave in electromagnetic ocean. How do the waves behave? If there are ripples while you are sitting at the sea shore or river bank, you feel pleasant, even cosy. But if they keep on increasing in intensity until they become strong, giant forceful waves, you are thrown back forcefully, even getting injured in the process. *This does not happen with light waves. In fact, it is exactly opposite.*

Study of photoelectric effect (1905) showed that for light of a given frequency, the energy of photoelectrons remains constant; it does not increase, even while the intensity of light increases, but these quanta are of fixed size. The number of quanta increases in direct proportion to the intensity of light. It is also shown that for varying frequency of light, no photoelectrons are emitted until the frequency exceeds a certain limit.

These facts could not be explained by the classical theory of light, and even contradicted the latter. Light is short electromagnetic waves. Normally, an increase in the intensity of light should mean an increase of the oscillating electric and magnetic forces propagating through space.

Electrons are ejected from the metal by the action of electric force. Therefore, it was assumed that their energy should increase with the increase in light intensity. But this does not happen. On the contrary, the energy of the electrons remains constant.[6]

How do we solve this problem? It was Einstein who solved it, thus further providing solidity to the quantum theory. He used Planck's idea of light quanta. Einstein assumed that they existed as independent energy packages flying through space. A single incident light quantum collided with the conductivity electron with electric current in the metal. As a result of the collision, the light quantum vanished, transferring its energy to the latter.[7]

If the frequency of the incident light is kept constant, the energy content of each quantum remains the same. If the intensity of light is increased, more electrons are ejected, but with *same energy* as before.[8]

Newtonian Atom to Quantum Atom

Light not only travels through space as quanta but also releases or absorbs energy in quanta. This discovery drastically changed the concept of the structure of atom. J.J. Thompson visualised atom as the unity of positively and negatively charged particles: as negatively charged particles embedded in positively charged substance distributed uniformly in the entire body of the atom. In this model of atom, it was possible to calculate equilibrium distribution of electrons. It was assumed that vibration frequencies would coincide with the observed line spectra of various elements.

But this was not so. The experimental results were negative. The theoretically calculated spectra of Thompson model did not accord with the observed spectra of the chemical elements.

This and many other aspects underlined the need to bring about drastic and fundamental changes in the classical model of atom.

Niels Bohr argued that light should not be treated as continuously propagating waves. It should be imparted properties of emission and absorption of discreet packages. Since the electromagnetic energy of light is quantized, it was possible and reasonable to assume addition and substraction of energy. Niels Bohr, in his attempt to solve the problem of light emission and absorption of atoms, introduced the idea of discrete quantum states of atomic electrons.[9]

In fact, when an excited atom emits light quantum with a particular energy, its mechanical energy must also decrease by same amount. Thus, the atom has different energy levels. They may, for example, be represented by the energy levels of the electron/s.

Quantum Epistemology

Problems of ontology and epistemology in classical physics and quantum mechanics are quite different. That is why the transition from one to the other presents us with problems. *What is given and proved in classical philosophy is undone in the quantum world.*

In classical physics in particular and the classical world in general, there was no serious problems with objects, objectivity and ontology. In classical physics, particles and fields have an existence independent of the observer. In broader view, everything, the world, exists independent of the observer and of the consciousness.

From epistemological point of view, it was taken for granted that "the observing apparatus" obeyed "the same objective laws as the observed system."[10]

So, "out there" was something fixed and given, even if moving and evolving, fixed in its laws of motion, orderly, successive, obeying its own regulations. The subject, in particular the consciousness part of it, reflecting the other, the 'out there', followed the same laws of objectivity, now only in reflection. So, the subject, consciousness and reflection did not affect the objectivity, the reality, the reflection did not basically or in any way alter the latter. The "out there" was there only to be grasped and reflected by the "in here" (in the brain and consciousness).

Epistemology goes into crisis, when we make **transition** from the orderly tangible world to the quantum world. The classical approaches to ontology and epistemology are *no longer* applicable in quantum mechanics. Regarding ontology, a basic question regarding the validity of reality arises, which is taken as given in the tangible world. Reality and existence are clouded.

The quantum reality consisting of electrons, photons and so on, behaves sometimes as waves and other times as particles. In fact, scientific thought has gone through, at one time, through 'wave-phase' and as 'particle-phase' at another, both as real as anything! Both can be proved and disproved.

What does it mean, epistemologically? Is the world made of waves or of particles or of both? Suppose we assume the world is made of both. Then why both the features do not reveal themselves simultaneously?

There is something wrong somewhere. There is something missing in and about the reality, the existence, the "out there".

In the classical situation, a particle is a particle. *It just exists*, it is measurable, its radius, circumference, etc. can be known. It has a position, it has motion and movement and a velocity that can be calculated and measured. It simply exists 'there'.

All we have to do is to approach 'it' with appropriate sophisticated instruments, and theories, just catch hold of it, carry out our experiments and reach certain conclusions. We will come out with particular results, which are then fixed for all the times as it is with the movements of the bodies/planets and moons in the solar system. All this we have been doing so far in our experiments.

Similarly, with the waves (classical waves). Here are water waves, sound waves, music and so on, which can be known, measured, even seen in many cases, etc. They exist, we can state that with certainty. One can measure the waves, the wavelength, the direction of their propagation etc.

But what about the quantum waves? They produce interference patterns on screens. In other words, photons and electrons behave as waves, rather ***we find*** them ***behaving*** as waves.

So, the inherent question is whether they are really particles and waves, or we find them ***behaving*** as such?! This is the crucial difference between the classical and quantum realities.

Do the waves exist exactly or nearly so, before we observe them, touch them? Or does our observation (use of 'instruments', etc.) bring about changes in them?

A photon can display both wave-like and particle-like properties. Photons in certain experiments produce diffraction and interference patterns, showing their wave-like nature. On the other hand, photons knock electrons out of metals, thus displaying their particulate nature.

In classical situation, a wave is a wave; we simply observe or discover it to be so. We simply have to approach it and describe its outlines, nature and properties.

But the quantum state is quite different. We are not sure, absolutely sure, whether particles and waves are 'out there', existing and waiting for us to approach them and measure them! Something happens in between, some change, modification or interaction (with, say, the instrument), between pre-observation and observation. We 'observe' with the help of certain instruments, or also, increasingly, with hypotheses, predictions, probable course and direction and nature of events. We cannot study and measure them even in the manner we study the molecules and the atoms thereof.

They are such fleeting and transitory events, so fast, and changing so quickly, that it is next to impossible to 'catch them'. We may observe the motions but not the thing itself. The question remains to be answered as to *the motion of what*?! By the time we approach them, they are gone, disappeared! They are more likely to be quanta, about which we have just talked or waves moving at near light speeds. Obviously, they cannot be caught hold of.

How do we ***know*** what existed before observation? It is not like observing a tree/s, rocks or bacterium/bacteria, amoeba etc. The more we enter the quantum world, the more we are unsure, because we keep modifying the observed.

The microscope (of whatever variety), the equipment, the cyclotrons, etc. are all made up of the tangibles; yet, and that is more important, they are made of particles. The metals and such other materials consist of molecules, atoms and their particles.

Do these atoms and particles disturb the observed entities? Obviously they do, the information that reaches us is *a reaction between the observer and the observed.*

There is an intrinsic fuzziness in the micro-world. That is manifested when attempts are made to measure position and momentum of particles, of a particle. In contrast to the measurements in the classical world, of tangible bodies, ***either the position or the momentum*** of the particle can be measured, not both. A particle can follow a well-defined path only when it has a definite position at each instant–and a motion. But a quantum cannot have both. You can either determine the position or the momentum of the particle, not both.

In this context, Thomas Young's famous 'two-slit experiment' is very revealing, as also interesting. In this experiment, a beam of particles is emitted on two screens, one behind the other. The first screen has two apertures, while the second one has none.

After passing through the two apertures of the first screen, the light (photons) or electrons or whatever, create images of a series of interfering patterns, as if waves have hit the second screen. An image of holes is created. Waves from one hole interfere with the wave images from the second hole.

Thus, the *wave-like* nature of the photons or electrons is demonstrated.

Now suppose, the intensity of the beam is reduced so much that only as single particles of light travel to the screen. We block one of the apertures, and thus only one aperture is left open. Each particle can be recorded. The interference pattern disappears. They leave behind marks of specks, a sign of particles. Each arrives on the screen at a definite point. Other particles leave their own specks elsewhere. Any single photon or electron or particle does not make a pattern; it makes only a single spot. The effect seems random at first, but soon a pattern emerges, when a large number of particles pass through. The particles 'coordinate' in such a way to build up the pattern in a 'probabilistic' fashion.

Here the behaviour of the particles change dramatically. Interference pattern disappears. Interference happens only when both the apertures are open simultaneously.[11]

Now, suppose, we keep *both the slits open and only one particle is left to pass through.* What will happen? Which of the slits will it pass through? The result will be clear from the pattern it makes on the back screen. It should, of course, leave a mark of speck because it is the lone particle and can pass through one of the two slits.

The result is extraordinary and most unexpected! ***It reveals an interference pattern on the screen!*** As if more than one particle has passed through. And here only one particle has remained, and it has passed through **both the slits simultaneously!**

So, one particle has passed through two slits at the same time! That is possible only if the particle behaves as waves ***at that moment,*** the moment when it is left alone and both the apertures are open.

So, we reach a very interesting stage *in the history of scientific investigations.* We reach a stage in our scientific, and, by implication, philosophical studies and interpretation, where ready-made concepts so far used in the tangible world become increasingly inapplicable and the way opened for a redefinition of reality.

First of all, it all means that both the particle and wave exist simultaneously; to the extent that they are ***the same,*** these seeming opposites having an identity.

Why this problem? Because we are dealing with forces at quantum level, having extremely unstable and rapidly changing aspects.

Niels Bohr called these aspects complementary. According to this theory, one can choose to measure the position of a particle, and in that case the momentum is uncertain. Or, one can measure momentum, to the exclusion of the position. Bohr argued that we would never meet a situation where they conflict with each other.[12]

In fact, Bohr's argument resolves the contradictions; of course, it resolves it without recognising the contradiction. Why this contradiction? This problem hardly exists in the classical world. But as we enter into and proceed onwards into the quantum world, the problem, the contradiction arises, not just between particle and wave, position and momentum, but also between others. We reach philosophical contradictions about reality.

What exactly is a point? This is not only a physical, whether classical or quantum, problem but also a philosophical/conceptual problem. The particle may be speeding along 5000 (five thousand) miles a second, or even more, much more.

So, what is a 'point' here? And, what is the point of asking 'what is a point'? At such speeds, the position, the point exists simply for $1/5000^{th}$ of a second, or even less! So, the 'point' quickly passes, too quickly for any stability.

The world of stability, of the tangibles is constituted of so many, in fact, endless instabilities, uncertainties, too many transformations too quickly to determine what actually they are, what is their 'position'.

That is why Heisenberg adds uncertainty to observation and the observed in form of the 'uncertainty principle'. As you enter the quantum world, you meet series of uncertainties, changes and motions too rapid. These magnitudes of possible deviations have to be added to observation so as to reach fairly a accurate picture.

The electrons and other particles have been identified as clouds of particles or of paths of motion. Each particle, thus, is full of fuzzy, wavy and cloudy realities. Therefore, *each particle is less a particle* if we examine it further.

A particle is not a particle in the sense that it has a number of orbits ('particles') orbiting it. It is particle at a certain level, in a certain manner, ***for a certain purpose,*** say the chemical or biological one. A certain amount, quantity, of *indeterminacy* is to be added to determine it. For, if a particle is a cloud, it is particle from certain distance and to one extent, and fuzziness of cloud from another distance and to another extent. It is particle to the extent that it is not, it is non-particle to the extent that it is cloud.

Suppose we observe an electron under microscope (or whatever latest apparatus is available) to determine its position. For that, it should be *illuminated.* It should also scatter the light so that it reaches our eyes or the computer etc. In the least, it can scatter one quantum. But, in the process, the electron (or whatever particle) is disturbed; there is interaction between the quantum and the electron, as we saw in the photoelectric effect; it is shifted, 'kicked around', changed and so on. This disturbs its momentum. To minimize this, a quantum of smaller energy should be used, in other words, light of long wave-length. But that will *reduce* the accuracy of the microscope. ***The longer the wave, the longer the diffraction images.*** That will need great many quanta to outline the diffraction image. But one scattered quantum can *only stimulate one atom in our retina,* leading to an uncertainty in our determination of position of the electron proportional to the size of the diffraction image.[12]

An interesting epistemological point emerges here, among many others. Observation of an electron, a particle, involves stimulation of one atom in the retina of our eye. Is it observation? How do we define and interpret this phenomenon or redefine it? We will return to this point sometime in the course of our discussion.

Here there is a great dilemma. We can improve the determination of the position with the help of light of a shorter wavelength, but that gives the electron a greater hit, adversely affecting the determination of the momentum.[13]

Quantum Theory, Particle and Worldview

The first quantum-mechanical theories on electron in mid-1920s did not take into account the effect of velocity of light, and were therefore non-relativistic. Dirac first introduced a relativistic theory of electron in 1927. He hypothesized that *in vacuo*, all the negative energy states are occupied by electronsn but the resulting distribution is unobservable for reasons not relevant here. Removal of an electron from negative energy state would result in an observable 'hole' in vacuum, which would behave like a normal positive-energy particle.[14]

Thus, there is *a radical alteration* of our view of the vacuum itself. In the pre-quantum stage of our knowledge (and philosophy), "it was pure and simple empty space containing nothing at all." But the quantum view takes the opposite view: no vacuum is allowed here! The empty vacuum is a sea of infinite variety of particle and waves etc. This reality has important consequences for *the structure of the world.*[15]

A.S. Eddington[16] puts the secret of mystery of this world, and of our ignorance of it, succinctly and concisely, in form of 'a little thing'. The nature has 'successfully' (!) hidden her fundamental secrets from us. The fundamental conception of physics and of the greater world has so far been limited, superficial, comparatively speaking, and meets with a transition that demands a transition in our world view as well as in our method.

Let us follow something very crucial to the new worldview. ***Erg*** is the unit of energy and ***second*** is the unit of time.

Here is something very interesting. In our daily life, we often divide energy by time. Motorcycle, car etc. drivers divide kilometers by liters of fuel to get mileage or kilometerage. Horse power or kilowatts are divided by the number of hours of consumption. But in the micro-world, if the energy content of a particular space is described as so many ergs, the corresponding content of the region in space-time would be in so many *erg-seconds.*

Thus, rather than divide energy by some category, we multiply it, say with time. This quantity is in the fourth dimension, having been multiplied by a duration. That is how action is described.

'h' is a constant found in various action in nature. It is very very small, and is the result of the multiplication of ergs and seconds. It consists 27 zeros after the decimal point followed by 655.[17] Another way of writing it is $6.55.10^{-27}$ erg-seconds. This energy or 'h' is continuously turning up during reactions and actions.

Action has two ingredients: energy and time. Therefore, in nature, we should look for a definite quality of energy with which is associated a definite period of time. We should try to locate energy which has a definite and discoverable period of time. Light waves are its example. The waves have a time unit i.e. the period of their vibration.

The yellow light from sodium (Na) consists of 510 billion vibrations per second. An amount of $3.4.10^{-12}$ ergs during a time lapse of $1.9.10^{-15}$ seconds is to be found during emission. If we multiply them, we obtain the 'h' of 6.55×10^{-27} erg-seconds. We may take any source of light, e.g. hydrogen, calcium or any other atom. The quantities of energy and time may differ but the product will be the same number of erg-seconds. This also applies to x-rays, gamma rays and other forms of radiation. It also applies to light absorbed by an atom as well as to light emitted.[19]

So, absorption as well as emission is discontinuous, in packets. Thus, 'h' is a quantity of action, ***also known as quantum.***

Whereas there are more than a hundred kinds of atoms, there is only one *quantum of action.* Both the red light and the blue light contain the same number of erg-seconds. The difference between these two, for example, kinds of light is that in space and time, the ergs and seconds may differ, but the result of their multiplication is the same. The apparent difference is only relative to a frame of space and time, **but does not concern the absolute size of action.**

The red light changes to blue light in Doppler's effect. The energy of the waves is different, but the quantum is the same. By radiation emission and absorption, energy is transferred, but only as a whole quantum at each step. It was this definiteness of thermo-dynamical equilibrium, which first led Max Planck on to the track of the quantum.

The paradox of the quantum is that it is indivisible, yet it does not hang together. In the course of the motion of electron, the energy is continuous, ***and no 'h' can be found. But as soon as energy dissipates through space, i.e. as light waves, 'h' appears.*** The atom of action has no coherence in space; its unity overleaps space.[19]

How does this unity appear in a world of space and time? Here a philosophical problem presents itself. The quantum appears as indivisible, yet as a divisable entity. It is the ultimate 'packet' of energy, yet this packet varies. The energy packets constitute the material forms, which contain, emit, quanta of varying sizes, quantities. The hitherto-existing world has been dissociated into limited and limitless quanta, constituting the quantum world. The dialectics of the quantum world is the rapid, almost uncatchable transformations of energies and their mutual exchanges.

Dialectics at quantum level is turning out to be quite a different proportion. In fact, it clarifies itself at that level. It would have taken eternity, if quantum were not discovered, to understand, and even really 'see', dialectics. In the tangible world, we have to dissemble and assemble several components of dialectics and motion. Motion is more orderly, one stage succeeding the other, the aspects more or less clearly demarcating themselves.

The problem is that dialectics cannot be tangible. The intangible has to be discovered in the tangible; the tangible has to be traced to the intangible. One is the opposite of the other, the intangible expressing itself as numerous tangibles.

Motion is the form of existence; at the quantum levels, motion is transformed into, separates out as an independent entity. It is not motion of matter, it is motion itself. We usually fail to assimilate the motion as reality, something existing as absolute. The absolute and the infinite should lose their absoluteness and infinity in order to be identified as existence. That is the dialectic, the problematic of cognition.

The transformations at the atomic, subatomic and quantum levels are so rapid that it is the motion and time that are the determining factors of events, which themselves happen at near-light speeds.

Therefore, it is wrong to suggest that the laws and categories of dialectics remain in tact at the quantum. They cannot. Dialectics not only remains but even becomes clearer. Laws and categories cannot remain intact at those speeds. It is 'pure' speed, motion as such. Time separates out. Dialectics is revealed.

Dialectics and the dialectical method is enriched at the quantum level. This method has to enrich itself on the basis of the discoveries of the quantum world. The dialectical method in the dialectical materialism of Marx travels a long way ahead.

Wave-particle Duality (Dialectics)

The dialectical method *permeates the whole transition* from classical theory to the quantum theory. One of its major points of enquiry is the wave-particle duality, an area full of conflicts, contradictions and transitions.

What is light wave or particle or/and both? The quantum theory has moved along interesting zig-zags in the course of solution of this problem. Similarly with other relations. To begin with, light may be said to be an entity with wave property: it spreads out all-round from the point of origin. But these waves are not waves of our common experience, e.g. water-waves like. In the Newtonian physics itself, both the corpuscular and wave natures of light were recognised. That physics and the world view emanating from it had its own concepts of particles and waves, and they proved to be limited in the view of the subsequent development of quantum theory.

The discovery of quantum broke down the waves into an assemblage of precise waves, exactly calculable as to length, height, frequency, energy packets and so on. This is something that brings a wave into the zone of energy packet, that is, a particle. A wave is convertible or translatable into a system of elements that together are energy levels. A wave is made up of 'packets' or quanta. So, a wavelength and height actually is an energy unit, a quantum.

So, energy packets or quanta take the form of a precise, succession, of wave lengths.

Some have described it as a "wavicle".[20] this almost brings us back to Newton's theory of light as a mixture of the corpuscular and wave theory.

But it is both a return and no-return: a return at a higher level. *That which we consider as wave includes particle, and conversely a particle also includes a wave or waves.*

Thus it happens that there are no pure waves or pure particles. Suppose, then is a definite 'particle': a point, a speck or an atom or particle. Let us begin to reduce it. Can we reach the 'smallest' particle? We can never quite reach the ideal classical particle: there is no such a thing as a classical ideal, ultimate particle. A particle can exist only upto a limit in space and time. Beyond that it becomes fuzzy. Not really. It reverts back to wave or waves.

Waves of what? **Not of** particles or a particle. We are used to think of a particle as a dot that moves, propagates in straight line, for example, as a bullet straightens, the point goes. That is the Cartesian or Newtonian, mechanical worldview. The dialectics of the tangibles become mechanical in the view of the quantum motions.

The particle is reducible to the non-particulate. The smaller the particle the shorter its existence. It is then reducible to the quanta of varying energies and existence in time. Time emerges as an increasingly important factor. As we approach the tiniest, we approach the shortest possible existence. It converts into motion, with its characteristics wavelengths, frequencies and so on. In other words, it converts at once into waves. Therefore, if you try to locate a particle beyond a certain point, it appears as a wave! One has to perform one type of experiment to determine a particle, another to identify a wave.

Can we look at the electron in the same way as we look at the moon? At the quantum levels, the exact position cannot be associated with the exact momentum: **there is no such thing in nature.**[21] To see an electron in an atom, no ordinary light will do. That will do in case of the moon! The ordinary light has greater wavelength than that of the atom, and therefore overshoots it. Short wavelength radiation, such as x-rays, is needed. A quantum of x-ray may or may not hit the electron. If not hit, we may not see it, if it is hit, it may be knocked out. Longer wavelengths may not define the electron, the shorter ones may knock it off. Therefore, 'seeing' or observation is a complicated matter as we descend deeper down in the quantum world.

The theory of knowledge applies to the moon, but it is extremely complicated, involved when applied to an electron.

According to Davies and Brown[22], the coexistence of wave and particle properties leads to some surprising results about nature. They discuss the experiments on polarized light and the two-slit equipment.

It is really not the coexistence of wave and particle functions; it is really their *unity and identity in their opposition.* This law of dialectics is nowhere else so open, so clear and so easily in operation. In our daily life, it is common knowledge that a body, say a sphere or a ball, follows a well-defined path, has a direction, a velocity and momentum, and at the same time a particular point or several particular places.

We know when and where the ball makes a shot and where it goes. We take these laws for granted.

But this is not so in the quantum world. Photon or electron or any such particle or quantum does not move along a definite, well-defined path. We can define a point of departure or a point of arrival, but not the trajectory. Each particular point has several alternative routes of movement. The motion of the quanta is random, producing fuzziness.

The point here is that the classical concepts of motion are not applicable in the quantum world.

Let us, for the sake of argument, suppose, that photons or electrons do move along straight and definite lines *from* one point *to* another, as our common sense and laws of classical science would suggest.

So, what is the particle of electron or proton like in motion? Do they move like a ball? Obviously not. Then? These particles are not something tangible, with a clear-cut structure, consisting of this and that. Then, what is a 'particle' we are talking about? Obviously, we will tend to say that such and such a particle or the particles contain energy. This is a common expression, reflecting the reality: it is so minute that **it is not possible for it to remain a particle.** The moment a 'particle' moves, it is converted into and spreads as waves. So it may travel anywhere and not as particle. It is not 'a particle moves from here to there'. No. No such particle moves; it is only converted into action, energy and wave motions. The idea of 'a' 'particle' moving from 'here to there' is inapplicable in the quantum world. In fact, there are no 'here' and 'there' in the quantum 'terrain', and therefore there is no 'now and 'then'. The moment you talk of now and then, here and there, they immediately become a continuous infinity, an infinite moment!

This is a truly Hegelian world, the reality described by theory of quantum.

According to the quantum view, radiation or photons etc. move in packets of energy. It is this 'packet' that flits through the space momentarily because certain energy conversion has taken place. It is the action, the event, that swishes past in a flash!

This particle has the properties of both wave and particle. Therefore, the term 'particle' becomes more and more a working hypothesis. It increasingly breaks up, dissociates into 'constituents', which are un-particle like. It is better to say, the particle and the waves dissipate constantly.

There is no straight line in the quantum world; in fact, *there is no line at all!*

The Copenhagen View of Reality

According to the Copenhagen view of reality, an atom or an electron cannot be said to 'exist' on its own, at least in the common and classical sense of term.[23] What is an electron? Or any such particle? To talk about it, it must exist out there, independently, objectively. We have discussed this above. Niels Bohr's arguments and philosophy reduces the electron etc. to an abstract state, and dissolves its concreteness. More so with the photon.

The quantum reality of the microworld is inextricably *entangled* with the organization of the macroworld.[24]

What is 'a photon'? It is a philosophical abstraction to *negate* the classical world. The same applies to the 'quantum', which was invented in order to explain certain phenomena. A hypothesis to explain a hypothetical notion. The moment you try to catch a photon, it is converted into waves, which is another name for energy conversions. *Tangible world disturbs the intangible one.*

Observation and generalization of the observed world is a complicated and contradictory process. While generally speaking, we can observe what we observe only upto a certain level, after which we are not really observing what we 'observe'; so after that level 'observation' becomes problematic. Observation becomes an *interaction* between the observer and the observed.

Observation is always an interaction: When we look at the tree or the stone, light or surveys reflect from the objects onto our eyes and retina, and proceed to create an image in or on our brain. The whole process, particularly the processes that are unleashed in the brain, are a complex of complicated biological, chemical, physical, and even electrical and electronic processes.

In the course of our observation, even in simple observation, many endless interactive processes are going between our body, brain and mind on the one hand, and the objects outside. We need not go into their details as they are irrelevant to our present discussion.

The point is that in the course of observation *at this level,* we do not affect or influence the object, certainly not fundamentally. No change is brought about in the things that we see; if at all, there are may be changes at the atomic and subatomic constituents of the object, about which we do not know and which do not matter as they do not affect the object as a whole. May be, in future, with further development of quantum sciences, something will be known about the process at those levels.

But it is different with the observation of the processes of and at atomic, subatomic and quantum levels, phenomena and processes, of the subatomic 'objects'. The observations at this level are more in the nature of interactions, resultants, inferences, conclusions, implications, hypotheses, probabilities, working hypotheses and assumptions to fill in the gaps so as to complete the picture or the calculations. It is not like observing a tree or a stone: we stand in front and 'see'. It is not even like seeing bacteria, etc. under the microscope: we magnify the object hundreds or thousands or ten thousands of times, and observe the bacterium swimming and moving about in all its 'royal splendour'!

Classical Approach to Observation

To observe at the quantum level is basically to affect it, to interact with the 'object'. Therefore, we do not really know what 'object' was *before* observation, as we know about a ball or a rock. Then we see the result of this interaction, and then draw certain conclusion about the observed object, more about the *probabilities* connected with the object. Therefore, it becomes more and more difficult to talk about the object **as such**, existing independently, 'out there'. We begin the process of observation by assuming that 'something' exists 'there', or *should* exist. We are habituated to *such a way of thinking*, observing, understanding, drawing conclusions, etc. The human beings are habituated to this kind of observation since very origins. This 'classical approach' has been in operation for thousands of years.

We have given the example of observation of electron etc. under light or x-rays. What we saw was an interaction and its result.

At the micro-world level, our target/object is elusive, and becomes ever more so. We enter an entirely different world where we affect whatever is there, whatever is happening there, in the course of our observation.

It is through adjustment that we observe and get a 'feel' of the nature of the object. And in the course of observation we adjust and reorganize ourselves and the structure of our thought and consciousness.

An atom or particle has to be 'lighted' to be seen, that means some sort of radiation has to be directed to it. A microscopic observation of it involves an exchange of energy. This energy may shift the position of the particle, as we have seen.

When we throw torchlight on some object, say, a plant or chair, it is lighted and we see it. Two things an important here. One is that we *know* that the plant or the chair is there, whether we throw light or not, we are 'confident' about their existence. The other is that the stream of light does not bring about any change or any seemingly important change in the object; so, we don't have to add or subtract anything from what is observed, we don't have to make any other kind of adjustment or assumption. Plant is plant, rock or chair is rock or chair, and torch is in our hand. We switch on and off the light, without bringing about any change in the object of study.

But in the observation of the micro- or the quantum world, we have to make adjustments of various kinds regarding the lighted 'object' and also in our calculations of light thrown upon the object. We can't say that the particular object is there and we just throw light and 'locate' it. Actually it is through a series of complicated calculations of the numbers and factors that we reach conclusions about the nature, place, velocity, particulate or wave nature of the object, etc. We even have to discuss whether that object is there at all or not. The particle may not be seen at one or two attempts; why? And what is the meaning of 'seeing'? And when at last seen, we ask how and why, again? That takes us into complicated calculations, which do not matter here – they involve wavelength and so forth. Somehow we have to conclude that we have just something passing, and start wondering what it was?

Among the many problems, for example, may be that the incident radiation or light may displace the particle; by how much? So, one has to add the displacement to understand the nature and position of the particle.

Interaction of Apparatus and Particle: Problem of 'Reality'

There is another serious problem in the context of observation in the quantum world. This problem is both practical as well as epistemological/philosophical. That is related with the *instruments* of observation. The instruments belong to the classical world and follow classical rules. *It is with these instruments of classical nature and functions that we observe the quantum phenomena.* The interaction between the two creates unforeseen and unexpected results.

Do we observe what we observe? Can we really observe quantum phenomena with classical means? Are our 'observations' made this way dependable at all? These and several other questions force themselves in the course of practical and philosophical comprehension, and we cannot ignore them.

Now here arises the 'paradox of measurement', the paradox flowing out into the general reality, raising a question mark on the existing concept of reality itself. "The apparatus is itself made of atoms, and so subject to the rules of quantum behaviours. In practice we do not notice any quantum effects in microscopic devices because such effects are so small."[25]

This is a profound reflection of the reality of the interaction of the mechanical/classical reality and the quantum 'reality' (i.e. reality with reservations).

'The measuring apparatus is itself made of atoms': This is the greatest reality as well as problem of the modern times; *it destabilizes and shifts the observer towards a postmodern position,* and produces the greatest unreality as we transit towards the post-classical. Quantum observation puts a question mark over our status as observer. Are we observer or part of the observed or is the whole exercise *a complex of observer and the observed*? And so on. Object-subject relationship is *re-opened* in its entirety.

According to Rudolf Peierls[26] the concepts of observation and reality are very complicated at the quantum levels. He objects to the use of the words 'real' and reality', without qualifications. He says apparatus or instrument cannot replace the human observer because then we have to interpret the instrument in a quantum way, and the instrument is not a quantum phenomenon. The effects made by the particle or wave or whatever are 'recorded' needing innumerable further interpretations. With human observation, something called the 'collapse of the wave function' comes into play. There is no clear assumptions about a quantum wave or electron particle or wave until we really observe; and when we observe, the wave function collapses, that is the waves that were produced suddenly convert into something else.

Many others like John Bell, Alain Aspect, John Wheeler, Basil Hailey, David Bohm, David Deutsch and others have clarified several complicated aspects these and related questions.

We are trying to uncover the reality of the quantum world with the help of the measuring etc. apparatuses, which are tangible, easy realities for the biological eyes. But the apparatus is inadequate because it is governed by classical rules and concepts. So, we are measuring a quantum state with the help of non-quantum state. In the first place, therefore, the results are undependable. Because, how do we take into account the interaction of the two states and their results? What we see on the screen is not the process/object as such, but the result of the interaction between the two states.

Besides, any impact the particles would make on the apparatus or any large tangible body is likely to be lost *within the system* or without. So, unlike the classical experiments, instruments are not totally reliable in the quantum field.

Secondly, the apparatus itself is made of atoms etc., and so, at that level, behaves *in a quantum fashion*. Naturally, the particles, the quantum worlds, of the two sides, the apparatus and the field it is looking at (or we looking at the field through the apparatus), interact and interact in the fashion of quantum forces (particles). In this way, the quantum forces within the arms of the apparatus constitute a system *independent* of the tangible, classical world of the apparatus. Consequently, we are not sure of the results and their interpretations.

Thus, even if we use apparatus, conduct experiments (with its help), it remains *outside* the quantum world, as just a reflector, and a poor reflector at that, needing a series of adjustments, additions, deductions, approximations, probabilities, constants and so on. One of the main reasons needing adjustments is the very nature of the classical apparatus.

In fact, it is the unity of the quantum world in the apparatus and outside it in the atom, that present us with 'reality', or unreality, of existence.

It is not the apparatus that measures the particles; it is the particles (and waves) that measure the particles (and waves); the results have to be magnified in order to be seen as waves, specks, particles, spots, lines, etc., i.e. we see the results of interactions.

That is why, von Neumann opined that the measuring apparatus itself has to be subjected to an act of measurement in order to understand what actually it has measured or what are its results. But it then leads to *a series of measuring apparatuses*, each measuring the other *ad infinitum.*[27]

The unity of particles prompts us to a situation where we measure *a particle with a particle*, or a wave, or both and so on. How can we measure a particle with a particle (or wave)? Is it possible? Logically, and epistemologically in particular, one particle is not distinct from another. They constitute part of a system. In order to measure, we must have a means (apparatus) i.e. a subject, outside which there should be an object (the particle). After all, we take a slide or a scale or a weighing machine (or just nothing but our eyes) and measure a pebble, a stone or a ball ('see it'). And we draw away, and things remain 'the same' as before (almost).

But this does not happen with the particles. They form a unity. The subject i.e. the particle that measures, unites (they unite) with the object of measurement. But the divide disappears into *a new unity.* It is this unity which provides ideas on particles and motions and energies, and so on.

What is an electron? (or any other particle) – this question crops up again and again. It is not being answered satisfactorily. With the development of quantum knowledge, electron increasingly becomes a convenient tool to explain this or that process. According to the Copenhagen Interpretation and the dominant views in quantum mechanics, 'atom' is simply a convenient way of dealing with a set of mathematical relations connecting different observations.

The concept that the reality of the world can be grasped through observation does not apply exactly as such to the quantum world. We modify or change quantum reality in the course of observation. We cannot treat this world in a commonsense way. Many of the mathematical concepts assume a spurious air of reality, which is also true of classical physics. For example, the concept of energy. It is a purely abstract quantity. It is often used to short-cut complex calculations. Its use has become so common that many think it to be a tangible entity. Energy is really a set of mathematical relationships connecting together various observations. "What Bohr's philosophy suggests is that words like electron, photon or atom should regarded ... as useful models that consolidate in our imaginations" what actually is a set of mathematical observations.[29]

Atom or electron or any such particle cannot 'exist' in full, commonsense notion. Bohr's philosophy reduces the quantum entities to abstract concepts, which have nothing to do with reality or existence.

Niels Bohr's theory, combined with Heisenberg's 'uncertainty principle', has created new concepts to explain the quantum process. Electron has been treated as and found to be a 'cloud' by Bohr. The moment we try to determine the limits and structure of electrons (and other particles), we begin to encounter difficulties.

What is there inside the electron? Can we determine its internal structure? According to Bohr, electron, supposed to be particle at one level, turns out to be a cloud of indeterminate waves at another. A complete break with classical physics comes with the realization that all the particles, including the electron, are a combination of particles and waves.[30]

And that is where and how we get involved in insoluble contradictions. Wave aspects are insignificant at macro, everyday levels. The wave nature and wave function become increasingly apparent and crucial as we pass through to the micro levels.

We stand at apparently insoluble contradiction of the macro- and micro-worlds.

Epistemology of 'Electron': Is There a 'Structure' of Electron? Presence in Absence and *vice versa* of 'Particle'

Is electron a wave or a particle? And in what way? What are its philosophical implications? We have raised the questions earlier.

De Broglie thought of waves as being associated with particles.[31] But experiments went much ahead. The experiment was conducted on diffraction of a beam of electrons from a crystal. The gaps between the regularly spaced atoms in the crystal provided just enough space to diffract high frequency (small wavelength) electron waves. Electrons, with their small mass and corresponding (small) momentum, make the most 'wavelike' particles known. The electrons are diffracted by crystal lattices just as if they are a form of wave.

J.J. Thomson got the Nobel Prize in 1906 for treating electrons as particles; his son George Thomson got the Nobel for proving electrons waves in 1937! Both are correct: *electrons are both!*

The full quantum theory is that all the particles and all the waves are both wave and particle at the same time: it establishes wave/particle duality.

Electron/s is/are in motion around nucleus. Is it a particle that is in motion? *We can say so only with reservation.* The motion can be *quantized*: whether the motion in orbits or out as free particles. In other words, motion has to be converted into particles. So, a particle ('quantum') is a quantity, a measure of motion. Electron, i.e. a particle and its motion is convertible into quanta i.e. particles.

But since, we are out to measure motion, the motion substitutes for particle; in other words the particle is converted into motion. But this does not make sense because before conversion the particle cannot be without motion. The particle itself is motion: motion has to be particularised. The moment motion is quantized, particle emerges as a measure of motion. Motion is a measured measure, a conversion made necessary by the ultra-high speeds.

In other words, *the particle is converted into its opposite*, the wave; particle into motion of particles/waves. It is identity of opposites, as the particle becomes wave, and wave particle. *The moment we try to understand either particle or wave, the one becomes the other.*

When an electron assumes characteristics of wave and wavelength, what does it contain? Here, wavelength is the secret; it contains certain amount of energy, which is a precise measurement. Thus, waves, wavelengths and other related characteristics have certain peculiar features: they are not particles, yet they are particle-like.

Electrons do not have circumference and other precise limits of a sphere or a particle. Obviously, we are talking of two different kinds of preciseness and particulate nature. There are several motions, orbits and transformations 'inside' an electron.

Thus, it gives an impression of 'cloud'. That is impreciseness, a wave characteristic. Therefore, the sphereness of an electron can be determined only approximately.

Once the electron waves out, it moves at a great velocity, producing electro-magnetic and other kinds of waves. A particle is waves in orbit; a particle is waves over infinite distances. Particles and waves are indistinguishable.

'Standing' wave and electron (particle): Experiments show that the electron is just a knot in the electromagnetic field, with no solid surface or internal structure. If one scatters more and more energetic particles off it, one finds high electric field strength. Electron is a pure point-particle with no internal structure, and the quantum electro-dynamics (QED) confirms it.[33]

Thus, it is clear that the 'structure' of the electron and other 'particles' is nowhere near the solid spheres and other objects that we meet with in our day-to-day lives. This picture of the electron completely changes our view of the world.

How are the 'electrons' and the 'particles' formed? This is a very interesting phenomenon having great bearing on our worldview.

The following figure will explain things in a simple, though simplified, manner.[34]

There are dynamic waves of space resonance out in the vast spaces. The resonance is composed of a spherical incoming wave or IN wave, and an outgoing wave or the OUT wave. One diverges fron the centre, the other converges on it. The spce is full of the motion of such waves, and there chances that the wave two waves combine at certain point in a fraction of time to form a very momentary '*standing wave*'. Its peculiarity is that it has a finite amplitude at the centre (that is the distance between high points of the two opposite waves, in a simple explanation; see the accompanying figure).

This standing wave is the structure of the electron. (Ibid) The outward and the inward waves provide communication with other forms of matter in the universe. The spin of the electron is the result of the reversal of the IN and OUT waves.

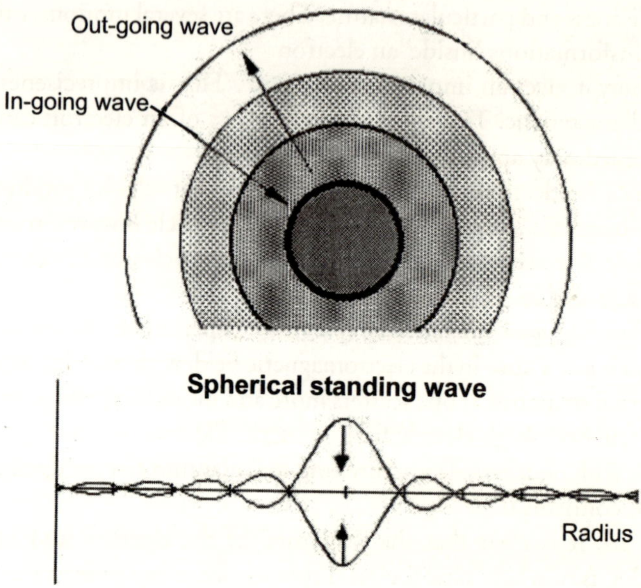

Figure 1. The Dynamic Waves of a Space Resonance. The resonance is composed of a spherical IN wave which converges to the centre and an OUT wave which diverges from the centre. Their separate amplitudes are infinite at the centres. When combined, the two waves form a *standing* wave which has a finite amplitude at the center. The standing wave is the structure of the electron. The inward and outward waves provide communication with other matter of the universe. Spin of the electron is a result of the reversal of the IN wave at the centre to become the OUT wave.

(*Source*: Ibid)

"The most extraordinary conclusion of the space resonance electron structure is that the laws of physics and the structure of matter ultimately depend upon the properties of space determined by the matter itself. Matter in the universe is inter-dependent."[35] Every 'particle', such as that has been described above, communicates its quantum-wave state with every other particle and waves and with the wave/particle dualities appearing and vanishing in the space. Energy exchange and the related laws are properties of the entire material world.

Two worlds within our universe: Thus we are faced with two real, yet parallel, 'worlds' partaking in the physical behavior of matter. One world is our familiar 3D type, governed by "the natural laws and observed by us using our five senses and their extensions as laboratory instruments. Its attributes are familiar material objects, events, and forces between objects, plus the related energy exchanges which enable us to observe the objects and form mental images of them. This world can be termed the World of Energy-exchange since energy-exchange is the unique attribute which allows us to observe this world."[36]

The other world is that of the wave/particle duality and of the 'Scalar Waves', which forms the structure of the particles, electron, protons, and neutrons composing the material objects and the space of energy-exchange. "These waves in space are unseen by us. We only know of their existence when an energy (frequency) exchange occurs to stimulate our senses. Nevertheless this unseen scalar wave world is basic and determines the real action in both worlds. The waves obey the rules of superposition and interference..."[37]

"The behavior of the particles (space resonances) in their interactions is largely due to their oscillating scalar waves which reveal their behavior to us via the rules of quantum mechanics and relativity. These waves (inward and outward) fulfil the requirements of matter inter-dependence..."[38]

"One role of the scalar waves is inter-particle information exchange of their quantum states." This is unseen in our world and we are making scientific discoveries regarding them. Information must be exchanged between the partners of a future energy exchange.

"Another role of the waves is as a universal cosmic clock...The clock is the fixed frequency of the IN and OUT waves pervading the universe."[39]

It is because such peculiarities that the 'electron' can be in two places at once; in fact, it can be located everywhere in space and time simultaneously. This is because of its wave function. The moment we try to put in a hurdle or screen or whatever, its 'wave function' collapses, and the electron is found in one place only at that moment as a particle.

Thus, *the 'electron' can be and cannot be in two places at once!*

A crisis for philosophy!

So, we are faced with a full play and display of the Hegelian dialectics! Hegel, for one, would have been jumping with joy!

This duality, as well as the impreciseness of the particulate nature has put microscopic physics in a severe crisis. When we apply the existing quantum theory to the electrodynamics of elementary particles, contradictions in theory come to the fore. The so-called 'elementary' particles include electrons, protons and such others. The problem is related with infinite values for various physical properties, such as mass, energy, charge of electrons, etc. The current theory is applied to the distances that are infinitely small. At the same time, particles such as electrons occupy no space at all, and therefore are mathematical points.[40] *Thus, a major characteristic of particle is lost.*

At this point, the concept of space triggers a series of questions and discussions. What is 'space'? What do we mean when we say electron occupies no space at all? Obviously, space has certain classical connotation in our mind. That begins to disappear as we enter the quantum world. An 'elementary' particle does not 'occupy' space; it is space itself; it is part and parcel of it, one of its functions. And this space is infinite, not finite. Thus, we are forced to conclude that the particle is infinite, and therefore it is no particle at all. We may even say that *the particle is a function of space.*

The electron/particle is expressed as a momentary flash of space; it loses its objectivity and independence because we become part of the observed and the observer.

Even after many years of active search throughout the world, no clear-cut basis has been found for the assumption that electron occupies a finite space. It has been suggested that infinites may come from inadequate techniques, but improved techniques have not led to favourable results.[41]

With the framework of the present theory, many calculations can be made, which do not depend on the assumed size of the particle. The calculations show that they do not depend on what happens at distances shorter than the Compton wavelength of electron ($3x10^{-11}$ cm). This kind of experiment is insensitive to the domain of very short distances.[42]

Experiments with particles of very high energy (100 million electron volts or more) produce extraordinary results. The socalled 'elementary' particles, e.g. protons and neutrons can now transform into each other. Besides, many new particles are discovered: positron, neutrino, about 10 different kinds of mesons, new particles called hyperons, etc. No limits to the emergence of new particles have been found. Most of these new particles are unstable, and they transform into each other. They can decay into electrons, etc., can be 'created' in energetic collisions with nuclei, etc. These new properties of matter assume importance only within a distance, between the particles, of 10^{-13} cm or less. That is why, no indication of new properties are to be found in experiments at atomic levels.[43]

This leads to a question mark on the theory that the universe is made of elementary particles.[44] In the domain of very high energy, the 'elementary' particles are sufficiently disturbed to reveal their inner structure. There are strong reasons to believe that there is a connection between the structure of 'elementary' particle and their infinities. If the particle has a structure, that implies its occupying certain space. In that case uncertainties and infinities are not possible.[45]

Philosophy of 'Electron' (of 'particle')

Electron was the first "elementary particle" to be discovered: by Joseph J. Thomson in 1897. Attempts since have been made to split it, to know its inner structure or particles constituting it. Energies a hundred billion times greater than those hold the atom together have been found, but electron has remained as it is.

To know the particle's nature, one can see the effect of individual electrons at low-beam intensity. The dots on the phosphor screen do not now shine but sparkle as each new electron excites a clump of phosphors. At very low brightness, one can watch the arrival of single electrons striking the TV screen. They are tangible evidence for the electron's particle nature.

How small are they? Physicists use another electron to determine electron's size. Two electron beams are accelerated, and then bent with magnets to make them meet head on. Electrons are surrounded, each, with their own electric field; so *they don't have actually to touch each other* to interact. Physicists hope to measure that size by pushing them closer until deviations from pure-field scattering take place, which indicates that they are touching each other.[46]

The present-day accelerators can probe distances even upto 10^{-16} cm. This is thousand times smaller than the diameter of a proton. But even at the minuscule distances, electrons show nothing but pure-field scattering. If the electron has a size, at all, it is smaller than it is possible, at present, to measure. According to some physicists, electron is a *point-particle*, i.e. *its size is zero*! In other words, it is a mathematical point. The same is true of other particles, e.g. quacks, leptons, gluons, etc.

"Electron is an example of quantum stuff which possesses both wave and particle properties."[47]

The diameter of electron particle may be zero, yet we "see" these electron particles. "Evidence for electron's particle nature is clear and indisputable".[48]

To find about wave nature of electron, a small circular iris is inserted between the electron emitter and screen. The electron beam goes through the hole, and the hole is made smaller and smaller, to squeeze down on the electron beam. At first, the beam itself gets smaller as shown by the spot on the screen. But beyond a certain point the spot, instead of getting smaller, begins to get larger. As the size of the iris decreases, the image on the phosphor screen expands until it ceases to be a spot. It becomes a series of bright and dark rings resembling an archery target. Further narrowing of the hole results in the uniform glow on the screen.[49]

These are the typical wave features. The notion that the electron also possessed wave features was proposed by Louis de Broglie in 1924. He predicted momentum/wavelength relation. The electron diffraction experiments showed a simple connection between momentum, a particle property, and wavelength/frequency, a wave property.

Not only does the electron possess both wave and particle properties, these properties also coexist and convert into each other.

As one turns down the brightness in the above experiment, the number of electrons hitting the screen decreases. Finally only one electron per minute hits the screen. After days, one can see thousands of dots i.e. electron impacts, but they are not scattered at random; they form the Airy pattern, i.e. *a spread-out diffraction pattern.*

Electrons behave like waves, however much their number is reduced. The quon dilution experiment shows that the electron appears as a particle on the screen, but *in between, during the travel from the source to the screen, it transits as a wave.* Whenever it is being observed, it becomes a particle, but in between, away from observation, the same particle spreads out like a wave over large areas of space.[50]

What we see is correct: a particle. Our observation and experiment is correct; all the evidence shows that the electron is a particle. *Yet it would be totally wrong to conclude that* it is a particle or a particle alone. In the quantum, it is dangerous to conclude anything on "seeing", on experiment! In fact, you should conclude the exact opposite! To observe or experiment in quantum is to work out one reality to *the exclusion* of the other, exactly opposite, reality; in fact the opposite is being all the time proved through the identity of opposites, through the conversion of one pole of reality into another, the opposite pole. True Hegelian dialectics is in operation at high and very high speeds, not imagined by Hegel, Lenin and other dialecticians themselves. The wave/particle duality (and many other pairs) are the very epitome of identity and exclusiveness of opposites.

The measured electron is different from unmeasured electron. We really do not know what is an unobserved electron or particle like. One observation shows particle-like nature of the observed 'object', and another shows it to be wavelike. Quantum facts give us two descriptions, not just one, each one separately inadequate, and both together contradictory as well as complementary. Observation divides as well as unites the observed phenomenon. Contradictions are united through exclusion. The two sides are united in the act of contradictory observation.

What is an unobserved particle? It is *the absence* of interaction with the observer/apparatus. It is like touching water surface to see the waves.

In classical physics, the attributes of a thing/process are measurable. But the situation is qualitatively different with a quantum situation. One can precisely measure one of the quantum attributes/functions/qualities. But while so doing one is, to the same extent, imprecise in other attributes. These attributes seem to be joined together, at least during the act of measurement.

Studies show that the quantum attributes come in pairs. They are called conjugate attributes. Suppose A and B are conjugate attributes. If one measures A with precision, B has to be imprecise, and vice-versa. The product of the precisions of the two measurements can never be less than a certain constant K. For a perfect quantum measurement, the product of two conjugate variances equals K. If one attribute is known with perfect precision, all knowledge of its conjugate attribute is lost or is not known at all.[51] Thus, *half of a particle's attributes are always hidden.*[52] The most important conjugate attributes of a quantum particle are its position and momentum. (Ibid)

This position, where the mutual measurement precision is restricted, is known as Heisenberg's uncertainty principle. According to it, if the position is measured accurately, an accurate knowledge of momentum has to be sacrificed. Therefore, we are unable to resolve wave/particle and other dualities.

According to Airy's formula, the smaller the hole, the more the beam diffracts as it goes through. This means, for a small hole, the beam acquires a large spread in sidewise momentum because of the position measurement. The spread in momentum can be calculated. The mutual spreads in precision of these two conjugate attributes is equal to Planck's constant.

Airy's experiment shows a world whose attributes come in pairs jointly resisting closer examination, preventing us from preparing a non-observer picture of reality. It is a world that is wave-like when unobserved, and particle-like when observed.[53]

The particles may behave like waves, the waves like particles. Most physicists treat the wave as a device to make calculations, not as a real wave somewhere out in the space.

This wave or wave function (represented by the 23rd Greek letter 'psi') differs from the ordinary waves in one very important attribute. ***It carries no energy.*** For an ordinary wave, the square of its amplitude shows its energy. For the quantum wave, the square of its amplitude, at location x, re***presents probability, not energy.*** It is a probability that a particle or a packet of energy at a point ('localized packet') will be observed if the detector is placed at the point. Thus, *since the quantum wave carries no energy, it is not detected, quantum waves can never be seen, only quantum particles can be seen.*

The shape and nature of waves can be inferred after many particles have appeared.

The quantum theory does not 'describe' 'reality' or 'particle' or 'entities'; it represents them. In the course of description, the entity is replaced with a proxy wave. The square of this wave at any location gives the probability that the particle aspect will manifest itself. This is the position attribute.

We have written some words above in quotation marks, because the concept of reality, particle, etc. in the quantum world is questionable.

The quantum theory began with only three particles: electron, proton and photon. But today there are more than a hundred major particles. Their major dynamic attributes are position, momentum and spin orientation.

Dynamic nature is an important attribute. For example, position attribute keeps track of a particle's position. Position identifies the location or whereabouts of the point. The secret of how quantum theory works is in its combination of waveforms with attributes. Quantum theory associates each dynamic attribute with a particular wave.

In classical theory, there was no limit on the value of various attributes. But in the quantum world, the attributes, qualities and features *are quantized.* Spin and other attributes are quantized, i.e. they have certain values, not others. They are digitized.

Quantum theory represents attributes as waveforms. According to HUP or Heisenberg uncertainty principle, every attribute A possesses a conjugate attribute V. The spectral area code leads directly to the HUP. Conjugate attributes correspond exactly to conjugate waveforms families via waveform-attribute connection. If a quantum beam for measurement of attribute A gives a narrow attribute spectrum, it must give a broad attribute spectrum for the measurement of its conjugate attribute V.

HUP follows solely from waveform-attribute connection; it has nothing to do with disturbance by measurement. "Both Heisenberg and Bohr warned against interpreting the HUP in terms of a measurement disturbance.[54]

Even the best apparatuses can't measure both position and momentums of a particle. Heisenberg himself used the example of electron to make his point. Seeing it involves bouncing photons off it/them into our eyes. Electron is so small that we have to use electromagnetic waves with a short wavelength in order to see it. This gamma radiation is of high energy level, and it may knock the electron out of the atom altogether. The very action of bouncing off may change the position and momentums of the electron.[55]

But the uncertainty principle is not just about impossibility of measuring both position and momentum of electron or any other particle. It tells us that according to the fundamental equation of quantum mechanics, there is no such thing as an electron that possesses both a precise momentum and a precise position.[56] As Heisenberg said, we cannot know the present in all its details. This is where quantum theory cuts free from the determinacy of classical ideas.[57] In a Newtonian world, it would be possible to predict the course of development and the future if we knew the position and momentum of each particle. But in the quantum world, we cannot know the position and momentum of even **one** particle. Therefore, a perfect prediction cannot be made.

The history of the uncertainty principle has developed in a peculiar way. Uncertainty relations have been developed from the fundamental equations of quantum physics/mechanics. But quite often, explanations begin with the uncertainty principle. In that case, one cannot work out the basic quantum relations.

Therefore, 'uncertainty' has to be put in a proper perspective.

What is in Motion?

What is it that is in motion as waves and particle? When we say the electron moves within the atom, is in motion, what does it mean? When the electron moves within and moves out, what does move? An electron moves in too small a space in too short a duration to really exist as a particle or as particle only. Such 'particles' must assume a continuous path, a continuity. So much so that it would be increasingly difficult to identify a point, a 'particle'. The path describes a wavelike pattern, which is subject to precise calculations.

Electron moves out in form of waves, e.g. electromagnetic waves. So, radiation of particles create waves (as waves; give the impression of waves, etc.). So, when we say it is particle, what we say in fact is that there is a pattern of wave, because the 'particle' does not remain a point. Therefore, 'particle' is nothing but an attempt to freeze the motion of the waves.

Yet, waves are identifiable by a fixed energy for fixed time. They are unlike water-waves or such other waves. They are not waves of some other material, e.g. 'waves of water', etc. *They are waves themselves,* independent, sovereign, to the extent of being abstract. Of what? The question remains to be answered or has been answered unsatisfactorily.

A wave consists of a series of packets of energy in a certain time-limit, i.e. in form of 'work done'. Therefore, its identification is in the form of and through 'packets' or 'quanta' or 'particles' of 'work done', 'action', 'event', etc.

This is a fundamental difference with the classical, mechanical and Cartesian world.

As we have already seen, an electron itself is 'fuzzy' in nature: it has an endless series of waves or motions, and therefore it has no borders or limits. The implication of this is that the electron moves means energy moves. What is energy? Nothing except work done; ***it is not motion of something, but the motion itself. Matter dissolves itself,*** dissociates itself, translates into energy or work-done. Matter *absolutises* itself as energy (motion; that involve certain timeframe, a receding one), as motion.

The nucleus of the atom is one lakh times smaller than the atom. In terms of volume the atom is a thousand million (10^{15}) times bigger that the nucleus. Is this matter ***or*** motion?

De Broglie realized that the electrons were not the "well-behaved", "good" particles. They occupied distinct energy levels inside atoms, and ***only existed "in orbits"*** defined by whole numbers. Such numbers were integers, and the only phenomena involving integers in physics were interference and normal vibrations. Thus, the electrons were not simply particles; they have to be assigned periodicity also. In fact, the electrons and other particles are numbers, representing certain energy levels *for* a certain time limit.

In the sub-atomic world of quantum laws, language and description have to be different from those in (applied to) the classical world. Energy in the quantum world is not transmitted continuously but discreetly. At this level, the electromagnetic force between two charged particles takes place (or is understood) in terms of exchange of photons. ***The photons are the quanta of electromagnetic field.*** When electrons approach each other, they are influenced by such fields and forces, causing deviation in the particles. These disturbances are transmitted *in form of photons*.

Therefore, when we talk of interaction between charged particles, we cannot talk in the same terms as applied to the processes operating between the sun and the earth. Tangible objects interact without disturbing their basic nature; the intangibles interact by completely transforming each other. These interactions can be envisaged only as an exchange of discrete particles like photons and such other events.

Nature of Particle

According to Richard Feynman, the 'really' quantum scientist, who operates entirely ***within*** this domain, the basic element of quantum theory was the double-slit experiment, because it was a phenomenon which was impossible, ***absolutely*** impossible, to explain in any classical way.[58] Among the peculiarities was that ***one*** particle passes through two holes simultaneously to produce wave interference pattern.

Among the most significant tools of quantum analysis is that of the 'attribute'. Quantum nature has its own peculiar way of representing physical attributes.

The position, momentum and such other aspects of particles (as well as waves) are to be considered a result of space and time coordinates and dynamism of waves. Particle, in contrast to the classical view (and reality), is not something given; it is a function, a consequence of rapid processes at a certain time and in space. We come across, identify a particle simply because it is an ***event,*** rather than a fixed, definable object. These events are constantly happening in a world of waves, wave formation and motions that *momentarily* create particles. Therefore, to say that the world is *made up of* elementary particles is to ***kill*** motion, the transformations, to limit and pre-determine the constant coming into being and going away.

Classical physics places no limits on the values of an object and its properties and processes. On the other hand, quantum world has several attributes quantized, and thus puts no limits on their immediate infinity. This infinity is only momentarily mediated by introducing time as mode of infinity and absolutisation. This produces peculiar opposites, where even the *uncertainties are quantized*. Indeterminacy, uncertainty, and fuzziness are released and expressed in precise quanta. Infinity is expressed as and through an instant and the instant (quantum) becomes and infinity by shedding time. Time is engulfed and overcome and matter thus is converted into motion of precise packets, whose identification depends on our nature of approach. Experiment interferes with truth, which comes out, expresses beyond and independent of the observing instrument. Motion is absolute and the instrument is redundant. It is because of conversion of matter into motion. Uncertainty and indeterminacy lie in the determination of the intangible, which cannot be determined and which can be determined through indetermination in their minutest determinations, so small that they lie beyond the zone of any determination. . In this conversion, motion (dialectics) emerges as a pure reality in Hegelian abstraction process. Abstraction no more remains a mystery: it is something which 'happens'. In fact, abstraction happens more often than reality. Only, the concepts of the tangible world are to be negated in order to grasp and live within the quantum world; a combination and transitions of the real and the unreal.

Quantum motion is the abstraction of the abstract in its most abstract form. As us earthlings, we have to 'go back in time' to far ahead in the space and within the atom. It is really not going back in time; it is unfreezing the frozen time. Once you calculate time, it is frozen; with quantum it leaps out into and as spread out space. Going back or forward has then no meaning because a particle and wave is *constituted by both going ahead and going back!* Our earthly forward *is* constituted of numerous 'back and forth' that keep happening, a wonder for us planetary beings, who are by comparison are the products of almost no happening. For something to happen, time must first be jettisoned and space turned inside out. A planet is the congealing of the instant conversions, and therefore, is absolutisation of an instant. For the quantum conversion a moment of conversions in micro-seconds is equal to the millions of years that the planet spends. If the planet earth is made to move at light speed it will cover its 4 billion years in just second!

How does quantum theory *describe* a physical attribute? This is a great epistemological question. The answer is that it does not describe it or them; it represents them.

Let us take wave/particle duality here. It is the wave-like distribution of the field that determines particle-like manifestations. How to understand the particle-like properties of bosonic field e.g. photons or bosons with mass?[59] Initially, the field is distributed throughout the space. Energy is swept in from the entire field and concentrated into the form of atoms. Energy is absorbed by the atom/s. Thus, field manifests itself in particle-like way, *as if* the field was composed of photons!. It is the wave-like distribution that determines discrete manifestations.[60] Photons have never been observed directly but only through ***their manifestations*** in particulate matter.

This is one manifestation, as well as explanation, of the wave/particle duality. In case of field view, there are no particles, only dynamic states with particle-like features in overall behaviour.

The fact that we do not observe photons directly is of great epistemological significance. They are manifested in particulate matter attributed to them. These manifestations all can be explained; therefore there is no need to further assume a 'bullet-like' photon or a sphere of photon to account for what is observed.[61]

We need not even assume the existence of a particle: the interactions with light or waves etc. create various manifestations, sufficient to account for 'particle-like' behaviour. 'Particle-like behaviour' of what ? – that is not important at all! Because a particular particulate particle, like the ball or sphere or even sand-particle, is not needed here at the quantum level, the level of motion. It is not the level of matter but of motion. The point, besides, is that a 'particle' can't exist at all at that motion at that level! It is wrong, epistemologically and philosophically, to constantly try to congeal space and time into particles. Does 'particle' have a 'role' at this level? None at all. Particle is deprived of being a particle and becomes packet/s of energy existing like non-existence: for billionth part of a second, and to that extent they are just 'particle-like', nothing more; they are also 'wave-like' with wavelengths and such other attributes, which again are very temporary and transitory. So, both waves and particles are transitory, constantly changing from one into another, one being the other, both being one and the same, yet direct opposites of each other. This is dialectics at its purest.

Philosophy, therefore, collapses here; and dialectics is absolutised. We are in relationship with motion, not matter.

In our quest for matter, we are ride the wings of motion and dialectics, revealing itself in all its splendour.

It is not possible to make an ontological interpretation of the field in which there would be a well-defined particle trajectory; such a field collapses.

How then can we explain, ask Bohm and Hiley[62], gamma-ray passing through a gas not only leaving behind a trail of ionized particles and observable development in time suggesting a bullet-like object, i.e. a photon, striking one atom after the other? They answer that this bullet-like object itself is never observed. "All that can be observed are the manifestations of the field in particulate matter."[63] This is done, for example, by ionizing gas atoms or producing photoelectric effect etc. "So it *cannot be concluded* that experiments have proved the existence of 'particles' of light."[64]

Bohm and Hiley propose a different interpretation. The electromagnetic field undergoes an inelastic scattering involving definite quanta of field energy. The scattering is brought about by the absorption of a quantum of energy swept up into the atom and by the re-emission of a quantum of slightly lower energy.

Matter becomes so saturated with the material that it transgresses itself into space and time, which assume an independent existence. It is inside out. Matter is so materialized that it leaves behind tangible material forms. Matter had space, time and motion as its attributes, as its forms of existence. Now it is the other way round: space, time and motion have matter as one of their attributes, appearing and disappearing, depending on nature of motion. For the first time, we come across space, time and motion in their independent existence.

Bohm and Hiley say[65] that, after defining velocity, it may be taken as determining the guiding relation for a particle.

One of the problems is related with the way we look at the 'world'. Our view is limited and/or partially hidden by the world of ordinary, large-scale classically describable experience. This experience of this world limits our full and proper description of the quantum world and processes. The quantum properties are manifested in this world and generally interpreted as such. Are we really grasping the quantum realities? : that is a big question. Measurements an done that favour the natural, not the quantum, processes.

In order for the particle to be a particle, it must remain stationary, which is hardly possible in the quantum world. How do two distant, 'non-local' particles connect with each other? Through their spin. Experiments suggest a change in the spin of one particle 'causing' a change in that of the other. How is it possible?

The signal of the spin (or whatever) must be carried at light–speed. So, the 'caused' spin takes place one second later. Till that time, what happens or what is happening to the other particle 3 lakh kms away? Is it existing or not? In what state? And so on.

One affects the other one second later and we come to know of the whole process say, two seconds later. But what guarantee is there that it is this particle, and not that, which is affecting or getting affected? Does one affect the other as a particle, as a wave or both? After all, particles exist even for micro-seconds and even less. So, within that second, what has affected what? It is just as well possible that the other particle have at the same time begun affecting the first one, or even earlier. It is just possible that the first particle is carrying the effects of the second one back, an example of the time moving back!

NOTES

1. David Bohm, *Causality and Chance in Modern Physics*, Routledge, 2008, p. 70.
2. John Gribbin, *In Search of Shroedinger's Cat*, Wadland Woodhouse, London, 1984, p. 36.
3. See, John Gribbin, ibid; Manjit Kumar, *Quantum: Einstein, Bohr and the Great Debate about the Nature of Reality*, Hachette India, 2009, p. 47.
4. George Gamow, *Thirty Years that Shook Physics*, Dover Publications Inc., New York, 1985, p. 25.
5. Nick Herbert, *Quantum Reality: Beyond the New Physics*, Doubleday, 1987, p. 34.
6. See, Gamow, op cit., p. 25.
7. Gamow, ibid.
8. Ibid., p. 26.
9. Ibid., p. 40.

10. D. Bohm and B.J. Hiley, *The Undivided Universe*, Routledge, 2008, p. 13.
11. Based on P. C.W. Davies and J.R. Brown, *The Ghost of the Atom,* Canto, Cambridge University Press, 1993, pp. 5-10.
12. See, A.S. Eddington, *The Nature of the Physical World,* The Gifford Lectures, 1927, MacMillan and Cambridge, New York, 1929, pp. 224-25.
13. Ibid., p. 224.
14. Based on Jagjit Singh, *Space Time Waltz,* Publication & Information Directorate, New Delhi and Wiley Eastern Ltd, New Delhi, 1995, p. 80.
15. Partly based on Jagjit Singh, ibid., p. 82.
16. A.S. Eddington, *op.cit.,* p. 179, etc.
17. Ibid.
18. Ibid., pp. 183-84.
19. Ibid., p. 185.
20. Ibid., p. 201.
21. Ibid., p. 225.
22. Davies and Brown, *The Ghost in the Atom,* p. 5.
23. Ibid., p. 24.
24. Ibid., p. 12.
25. Ibid., p. 27.
26. Ibid., Interview of Peierls, p. 70 onwards.
27. Ibid., p. 28.
28. Ibid., p. 25.
29. Ibid., pp. 25-26.
30. John Gribbin, *In Search of Schrödinger's Cat,* p. 91.
31. Ibid., p. 89.
32. See, ibid., pp. 89-90.
33. Dr. Sten Odenwald, www.astronomycafe.net, "The simplest particle electron: its structure".
34. The description is based on internet version of the reprint of "Beyond the Point Particle : A Wave Structure for the Electron", reprinted from *Galilean Electrodynamics* 6, No. 5, October 1995, pp. 83-91, updated May 15, 1998, Technotran Press, Manhattan Beach, California; available on www.quantummatter.com/articles.
35. Ibid.
36. Ibid.
37. Ibid.
38. Ibid.

39. Ibid.
40. See, David Bohm, *Causality and Chance*...etc. p. 121.
41. Bohm, ibid., p. 122.
42. Ibid.
43. Ibid., p. 123.
44. Ibid.
45. Ibid.
46. Based on Nick Herbert, *Quantum Reality*...etc., pp. 60-61.
47. Ibid., p. 61.
48. Ibid.
49. Ibid., pp. 61-62.
50. Ibid., pp. 65-66.
51. See, ibid., pp. 67-68.
52. Ibid., p. 68.
53. Based on Herbert, ibid., pp. 68-69.
54. Ibid., p. 110.
55. Gribbin, op. cit., pp. 156-57.
56. Ibid., p. 157.
57. Ibid.
58. Ibid., p. 164.
59. See, Bohn and Hiley, *The Undivided Universe*, p. 230.
60. Ibid., p. 231.
61. Ibid., p. 231.
62. Ibid., p. 259.
63. Ibid.
64. Ibid., emphasis added.
65. Ibid., p. 272.

8

Philosophy of Quantum Particle

Why do we need 'particle'? To what extent does it exist, and does not exist? In the course of human history we have reached a point where the particle, the basis of existence and of tangible forms, itself is dissolving, and is opening a whole new world of processes and 'realities'. What is the epistemology of particle and particle of epistemology? It is very interesting to find that the 'particle' emerges in our recent debates almost as *a philosophical category.* This is a revolution in philosophy and worldview: even while creating philosophy, the 'particle' takes the opposite path and disappears as and into quantum particle as not-particle, as into that which really is not! Philosophy is dissolved into quantum philosophy, which is really not the philosophy created by the hitherto existing human thought but its dissociation into 'constituent' aspects/processes/conversions such as time, space, matter, energy, measure, etc.

A Discussion on Philosophy of 'Electron'

Particles exist because e we want them to exist; otherwise, for us, the world cannot exist and be understood. We are forced to hang on to it, we are habituated to it. Therefore, for us, understanding the world means at least to grasp the particles, which form and structure the world. For us human beings, the world *cannot* be created without the *building blocks.* They in the course of development of science become our mental blocs!

But in the present reality, the more we try to catch hold of the particles, the more they dissolve. *That is the crisis of thought process.*

The more we try to study the particle, the more it resolves itself into time, space, waves and other phenomena.

After all, what is time? It is an interval between two events related with each other. But motion is to be and not to be at the same time, and therefore is an attempt to overcome time. Time therefore turns out to be a mechanical measure of motion; overcoming time brings us preciseness of dialectics. Time can be questioned increasingly as we enter the world of temporary particles with decreasing span of life. The signals are transmitted in quanta of energy i.e. both as waves and particles. It is difficult to assume that *the other particle is 'waiting' for the signal to reach it. And this is a crucial clue to the resolution of the problem of particle, to its understanding.* More on it later.

If time is an interval between two events and points, then what is the interval constituted of? And what is the point constituted of? Is the point without time? If not, how is time constituted in the point event? And is the interval without event and structure? We have created too many classical and mechanical barriers to the understanding of the world.

How do we measure time lapse and material structure between two points? By the time signal travels from one event/particle to another, the latter has changed. Is it the same particle? It is the time interval that imparts the particle its particulate nature, by riding the wave of the waves. If there were no time interval, there would not be particle, which in this case becomes a mode, vehicle and method grasp of the reality, which becomes questionable as it is resolved into the solubles. Therefore time and its attributes in fact become mode of existence of consciousness. Time can have particle as its attribute, its mode of existence, crucial increasingly for consciousness rather for material reality, which is being resolved into attributes not attributable to it but to the non-existence. Time congeals into particle and space/ waves.

Therefore, matter is convertible instantly into non-matter, which becomes the form of existence of matter. What we grasp is the constant dissolution of forms of matter, and that how the world proceeds. Consciousness proceeds by dissolving the laws of the material world and thus by identifying with it. That is how it is justified as proceed deeper into the quantum universe.

We, the individuals, the society and history, have assumed till date that there are more than one particle constituting the world, 'waiting' for all other particles to constitute and deconstitute the objects constantly, as if they are planets and satellites of a solar system! We as the history of human consciousness have created a mental jam. With the passing of history, and therefore of the higher positioning of consciousness, we need the 'particle' to interpret existence, without which we ourselves cannot simply exist. Here again the methodological problem of time lag interferes. Human development results in further reductions in time and space till time becomes primary or even independent and the particles (events) become secondary, to the point that they disappear, at least notionally. And space absolutises itself to infinity and independence.

Can there be more than one particle at the same time? History of society and philosophy teaches and reveals that this is precisely so: without so many particles the world cannot be created. This question, therefore, appears as a strange one. Yet this very human genius leads to a point where an *assumption* of particle/s becomes more important than their real existence. We reach a point in our development where the point itself may become an infinity, as is happening with the ongoing STR. Without realizing that, we cannot make the quantum jump in consciousness. By the time we as history have assumed the tangible and the particle as the basis of creation, the particle itself has disappeared, and becomes convertible into waves, thus undermining our age-old assumption. For the individual and the society, they become increasingly momentary and hypothetical. At light speeds, one loses contact with the reality; even one particle proves to be enough to discharge the functions of millions.

Then what is time in such a situation, and what is particle (event)? A new relationship between particle, time and space emerges. Particle is turning out to be a loss and dissipation of time. Time then becomes the measure of the loss of the particle. The rapidity of time shows the minuscule and fleeting nature of particle.

We need time to measure this point and that, to differentiate between the two, to measure the point itself, the very particle of existence. But time is when the point is and is not. Time is more accurately when it is not. Time represents identity of this and that, of being and non-being. But more accurately it is an identity that is all the time becoming non-identity, and at that point time loses its importance and meaning. It is motion and dialectics, and that means to be and not to be at the same time: Something is, happens, at a point, yet not at that point. That point is the point of event, the event itself. Dialectics is to show that one is at the same point *and* not at that point at the same time. It is *not* moving from one point to another. Dialectics also means to prove that the particle is not any more, and that consciousness has overcome it and lost it, throwing itself into a crisis. A crisis is nothing but a jump in the state of consciousness and therefore of the world. Crisis is the culmination of dialectics and a beginning of new dialectics simultaneously.

It is a constant self-transcendence, more a feature of our consciousness. The particle is all the time non-particle; in fact it 'exists' more as non-existence, more as *non-particle,* which is the pure form of motion. It is easy for the particle to not to be, but much more difficult for the consciousness to follow this path because all through its history, it has followed the track of the particles and its structures. Therefore, consciousness has to deconstruct and dissociate itself.

It turns out therefore that we use the term 'particle' more as something to hang upon, to hang upon our past, our history, to explain things. We are habituated to explaining and not exploring at non-explanable levels. For explaining is based upon history and matter, a distorted form of matter, and we do it on that basis. The particle is particle for us but a non-particle for itself. We 'need' the particle all the time; we are in dire need of it. But the more we hang on to it, the more it becomes elusive, tending to disappear and dissolve into something else, creating *epistemological crisis* for us.

The particle was a hurdle that we crossed by constituting the *quantum* particle. The particle constituted an era; the quantum constitutes an infinity yet to be explored. We finites need to be part of an infinite reality, so unreal that the particle has no limits, it is unbounded, bounded by an unbounded space.

It is a critical juncture; so much so that the quantum scientists deny the very existence of the particle. We tend to deny the quantum its reality because of the realness of our consciousness. We are yet to define and identify the quantum because we are bound by the 'particle'.

This reductionist act is profound and deep, full of its own negation as it converts into waves as soon as it is grasped. We try to locate the particle with so many additions and probabilities. With the shift of reality to time and motion, which are inter-related, matter has to be located, constituted, in motion and as motion. What has so far been constituted *in* motion is now being constituted *as* motion.

When matter is located in motion and time, its constituents lose their limits and determinations. It is now a question of abstracting matter out of non-matter, that is out of its constituents as its characteristics, and of essentialising concept out of the concept. Matter loses its materiality and emerges out in and as its *attributes*. So, matter resolves itself into attributes that constitutes matter but now it is attributes which are independent of matter that the humanity had so far been aware of. Humanity stands at crossraods of its consciousness: the consciousness is now being fashioned by non-matter-like attributes more amenable to consciousness, though very much material in the sense of their independent existence.

Matter must now be redefined as the dissociation into constituents, each of which forms independent universes, together or separately. For example, it is the space now that creates point particles and tangibility, which no more exist than non-existence. *We are in conflict with 'matter'.* Consciousness has now to resolve itself into motions of *events* which need to be grasped in order *to materialize* ourselves. These motions create new realities when touched or approached, and therefore the task of the consciousness stands redefined.

Quantum world is a world of *constant* transformations, which is the only constant, from the point of view of the worldview. It is less and less of a worldview and more and more of a 'motion-view'. The point is that we try to quantify and identify the nature of the transformations. *And here lies the problem.* Our worldview being limited, we must identify and transform, that is kill, the motion. The transformations are expected to be into fitting something fixed, pointed, particulate, tangible. Understanding, comprehension means killing the motion, 'catching' time. If they are in motion, they are beyond grasp, beyond comprehension.

Thinking is gripped by crisis. Therefore, it must now redefine itself.

It has been more comfortable with the fixed things or slow-moving processes, less with fast motions and high-energy conversions. How to comprehend something that is in motion, particularly in extreme motion? If it is in simple motion, it can be categorised into categories, laws, directions, orderly change, stages, structures, successions, etc.

But if thing is in extreme motion, all these structural barriers fall away. Thought is set for high speed motions, which only means not to see the tangibles.

That is why we increasingly have to resort to 'temporary particles' of very brief life, and to energies, which are nothing but the measure of motion. These particles are temporary and extremely transient conceptualizations of motions, a kind of reference points for breath-taking transformations unveiling before us.

What is external world (of physics and in general) from the point of view of the 'electron' and of the quantum transformations? That question is yet to be answered. Eddington[1] is quite succinct, lucid and profound in saying that the external world has been formulated as an answer to particular problems in human experience. Atoms and electrons answer, meet, many problems.

We really do not know what is electron, as also other particles. Yet a whole world is created out of them, prompting us to give them a status of 'elementary' or basic particles, which really do not exist. "No familiar conceptions can be woven round the electron; it belongs to the waiting list".[2] We contemplate electrons moving round within the atoms, certain numbers in this orbit and that. We differentiate between oxygen and nitrogen by identifying 8 circulating electrons in the former and seven in the latter. Whole parts of world are created out of such a differentiation and mutual interaction. Compounds, organic compounds and biological entities are created through higher (more complicated) levels of interactions.

Yet, at the quantum levels, there is uncertainty, Schroedinger's Cat, collapse of waves, disappearance of particles into the fuzzy world of waves, passing through of one particle through two slits *simultaneously* creating waves, complementarity, and so on, creating a whole world of momentary existences. The existences are so momentary that they can almost be not existing at all! And yet they create the whole tangible world!

It is a world which exists in and through extremely momentary events, additions and possibilities, our job being (via epistemology) to try to catch them or to approximate to them.

This is because we deal with certain numbers; it is these numbers, the quantities that bring about changes in qualities, which are what make the world. The numbers represent relations; the shorter the time and higher the motions, greater the conversions into numbers.

In the words of Eddington[3], we see the atoms with girdles of circulating electrons darting, colliding, rebounding. Electrons torn hurry away a hundred times faster; they curve round the atoms and their periphery just so and speed away, some of them getting caught elsewhere. X-rays collide with atoms and toss electrons into higher orbits or toss them out. The electrons then may fall back. (A movement ahead in time or backwards?). And behind it all, the quantum 'h' regulates each change with a mathematical precision.

Reality, Experience and Quantum World: 'Particle'/Electron as Concept

We are making a transition from one reality to another today. We have so far been habituated to observe and explain things which are tangible, observable and with certain size and shape etc. We are habituated for example to see and think in terms of rocks and spheres, balls and so on. Even our traditional 'particles', so essential for some of the philosophies, have been of a similar nature.

Consequently, we try to explain the new particles and other scientific and physical phenomena in the same way as we experience spheres and balls or rocks. We cannot imagine that new particles at the sub-atomic and quantum levels are qualitatively different, and the ways and methods of the tangible world cannot be applied to them. We have so far experienced the external world as it exists around us, and continue to so experience it.

But now we are confronted with a rapidly emerging new world, that of the quantum and sub-atomic particles and processes, And we are finding it difficult, almost impossible, to experience, know and grasp it. What do the two words that confront us – 'external' and 'experience', as also, by implication, 'reality' – mean in this context? What do we 'experience' in the quantum world? Do we experience at all?! If we say, as we have already stated, that it is a world of numbers, mathematical formulae and calculations and numerical adjustments, then *can we experience numbers*?! And exceedingly fleeting moments? What about them? And if they are all numbers, are they under the category of 'existence'? Do we experience the waves?

It appears that in order to experience them, they must attain at least some level/extent of tangibility. Or through our calculations and generalizations, we transform them into some tangibles to comprehend them.

The waves, the particles and the energy transformations are obviously not part of our experience, they cannot be! As we go out into the space or deep into the atom, we lose what we call experience, of something out there, outside, objective, 'real'. They lose their meaning, existence and reality.

The numbers and transformations are about the energy changes and particle conversions. How can we experience, for example, 6.55 X 10^{-27} erg-seconds, i.e. 'h', a quantum of action? To get full idea of this number let it write out to see how very small it is: h= .000000000000000000000000655 erg-seconds!

This 'atom' or quantum of action exists only for this much of time, a minuscule part of 'reality'. So, what is reality? Here we become part of the processes that proceed in ways we don't know. Having become part of the processes, we indulge in a series of calculations, probabilities, additions, constants (and variables), and only then reach certain numbers and figures. Every quantum and wavelength and wave must contain certain energy for certain amount of time. So, we must first calculate this 'reality' or whatever, and then only reach conclusions and assumptions. These calculations and conclusions are reached in certain conditions only, not in others. So they exist, they do not exist!

In order to 'make' them exist, we should undertake only certain type of calculations. The sun exists, the moon exists, the planets etc. exist; but the particle *does not exist*; it has to be *made to exist*, only then we 'experience' them. The particle is no more than a fleeting expression, at variance with the nature of our consciousness. The sun and the moon, the rock, can exist but not the particle or the wave because they are forms of motion. We try to make them acquire existence in order to experience them. The 'we' loses its meaning as we deal with unnatural and unusual forces because we must first enter into a system with them. That constitutes a unity between the experiencing and the experienced. The relationship between the two is extraordinary, unprecedented, inter-penetrative and incompatible. To understand/ comprehend, we have to go through a series of conversions and transformations ourselves. Every meaning, every 'entity' has to be translated into something else before it makes some sense. So this 'reality' is trans-sense, beyond senses, really and literally.

This other world is that of too much speed. Our notions are slowed down. Therefore, consciousness cannot grasp motion and time in their pure form or state.

So, what is reality, existence like at non-classical, quantum speeds? The tangible reality existed before the human consciousness; the human beings, came into existence. But they needed no separate efforts to make them exist. We do 'know' about the sun and the moon. They did exist, as they were and exist as they are.

But there is no past or future for the waves and the particles. They simply appear and disappear. Time cannot be quantised for them as succession. Quantum carries a speck of time because we need to comprehend it and the processes in the quantum world. But the quantum really *does not need time*. It eases out of 'existence' the moment we try to catch it even while it 'comes into' existence. Time loses its moorings as the event is itself a non-event, all the time constituting its opposite, which dissolves unto and into itself. Time itself becomes non-time. Time and particle are mutually exclusive, while the wave eases out into an infinity. Quantum in itself does not need time because it has no history. Between two events is constituted time as no more than a relationship.

The waves and particles are not carriers of time, solidity and succession. They are 'within' comprehension when we look for them, and that is when they appear as 'specks'. In that sense they are 'beyond'; they are formed by comprehension. So, they can go backwards as easily in time as forwards; it does not make a difference. Their time is not carried as history, which does not exist; it only comes alive when motion is caught hold of. In fact their time is killed: it simply disappears. Time is not past nor is it present; it is only towards future. Therefore we divide what 'is there', not what *was* there. There is only becoming, no being. How can we divide what was not there at all?! It is only the conversions that constitute the world, and when non-time and non-histories congeal, they form the times and histories of the concrete; time succession comes into being.

Did electrons exist earlier? We do not know for sure. No doubt the transformations did exist. But when we try to observe, we come in contact with them and change them, leading to certain events.

Can we talk of the past for the waves and the particles? No, because they did not exist. A 'particular' particle did not exist. They do not exist as present; they can exist only as future. The particle did exist, that is as a concept, because a particle never exists, and it is only by making them exist can we find a reference point for the event moving to the future. And that is why there is no past for them. A particle has no particularity; it only has a generality, which transcends time. Only as such can it exist, as a negation of existence. It is the negation of all that is, and therefore it is the generalization and abstraction of all that is not, constantly.

It is only in this way that we 'look' at the stars.

Our body is made of waves and particles, but they must slow down in order to crystallize the body and the brain, which in turn reflect the world. But the reflection is limited and motion unlimited. They constitute two poles, united in the process of exclusion.

In the Cartesian/Newtonian worldview, we stand opposed to the system of things/objects/processes, observe and study them, penetrate them, unveil their dialectics and laws of motion and existence, and thus try to resolve the contradiction between the subject and the object as far as possible. We are observers, who analyse, dissociate the observed. In the unreal quantum world, the difference between the observer and the observed is dissolved progressively. It is the observer who is first dissociated in consonance with the quantized reality with non-real features. The quantized reality is the reality which is dissociated into the unreal generalities and absolutisations.

There is a clear-cut relation between the subject and the object in the existing world, particularly between consciousness and the reality outside, but it is not so in the unreal or the trans-real world of waves and particles. Consequently, that is a reality standing opposed to reality.

Then there have been the Kantian, Hegelian and other views, where the subject is partially or fully the part of the object, the reality. Marxism developed the most complete subject-object relationship with the inputs from the above-mentioned and other systems. It discovered and evolved dialectics out of the objectivity and universalised it as self-sustaining source of motion.

The Subject in Classical and Quantum Realities

We have discussed some aspects of the classical world and have delineated the outlines of the classical subject. But things are different with the quantum subject and his/her worldview. The quantum world leads to a rearrangement of the subject/object relationship. The nature of the reality or of what is being observed is qualitatively different from the one in the tangible world. Consequently, the nature of the observer/subject too undergoes a drastic transformation. The observer/subject is no more opposed to the observed/object, but is immersed in the latter in a dialectical relationship of opposition leading to identity of the opposites. Perhaps such an identity was never achieved before. The pole of subject reaches out to that of the object and becomes one with it. It is only through such an identity and obliteration of reality that the reality is really understood. The observer continuously interferes with and modifies the reality, is part of it. This way the subject looks at itself by transcending itself and denying itself, and this process needs a whole history. And that is the problem. So, it is no more the question of 'out there'; it is very much that of 'in here'. What we observe is the continuous action and reaction due to our presence and reaction. To observe means to interact. In fact, at the level of brain and the consciousness, there is an identity between the subject and the object. We at increasing and deeper levels become one with the observed world.

What we try to observe crosses/passes through us (the microworld outside is one with the one inside us!): our eyes and bodies. So, subject-object relation becomes interpenetrative and inter-connected. What is the 'object', the 'objective world' like? The answer is a continuous modification of what we see or are supposed to see.

Crisis of Atomism

What are we supposed to see, what do we see? Not exactly the thing that exists. We do not know as to what really exists, in what form. What does it mean? ***It is not mysticism.*** There is no mystery. What we see is the result of a continuous interaction between ourselves, apparatuses and the observed. And the observed is an unknown quantity and quality. We observe by placing ourselves *in* a certain space and time, we do not observe the space and time of the observed. (We do it later.) We begin by placing ourselves in certain coordinates, which gradually lose their identity. We lose our time and our space, and come increasingly across different spaces and times and their relationships. We have first to resolve the problems of space and time of the observed. Then we set ourselves in the new coordinates; in other words we redefine and reorientate our position, our thought process *as well as our philosophical positions.*

We transform what we observe into a system of waves, particles, space and time, *each with their own system of space and time.* We change their histories. We observe wave and particle, not from outside, but progressively from inside, with and within them. Without that we cannot 'observe'. We modify, therefore, while we observe, and thus observe the modified, increasingly. Particle and wave jettison matter, become momentary and infinite, and create a new system of space and time, where the events occur in microseconds. Therefore, observance is a momentary creation, a conversion of the reality into non-reality, opposed to it, *so that it becomes observable.* At such levels and motions, it is the unreality that is observable, not the reality, it is the unreality that is really constituted of motion, space and time. Reality loses all the attributes of existence, loses right to 'exist'.

But that which is observable is not really what is observed; it is not what is intended. We always, for example intend and 'want' to see a particle but never observe that particular particle, only an interaction, ***any*** particle, not the particle; the 'the particle' only becomes a generalization of the intention and tool that we apply, providing us the resultant data with a series of adjustments and natural 'constants' to reach approximations of what would roughly be an event's 'existence' and nature. Observation therefore is conversion; only then something can be observed. To observe is to get converted. Therefore, it is a negation of observation; observation is actually non-observation. It is done only through a series of elimination and conversions of the qualities that supposedly should have been there but are absent. In the course of observation, space and time are not only modified but also alienated from matter and inverted as the dominating factor over matter itself. Consciousness floats on the momentary particles and infinite waves, which are more a creation of observation than real. Consciousness is split into real and unreal, and it is more at home with the former, but more identified with the latter. The former is reflected, the latter inferred. Consciousness is split between wave and particle.

Naturally, we in classical, Cartesian way try to approach the wave and the particle to find out as to 'what they are', 'what are they made of', etc., which is absurd. And that is the mistake we commit!

How do we observe atom/particle/wave? The observing apparatus ***interacts*** with atom/particle/wave through particle exchange and waves. The atom is changed in the course of this interaction in a way that cannot be predicted, controlled, described or even conceived of.[4] Thus, each different apparatus and parts/regions thereof create different kind of atoms and particles. Even this way of putting things is ***too definitive***, devoid of motion and therefore faulty, because we assume that atom/particle has definite properties, even when not observed. These properties are changed by interaction with the measuring apparatus. "But in the usual interpretation of the quantum theory, *an atom has no properties at all when it is not observed.*"[5]

Why this repeated fall into atomism? This is because of "an instinctive belief that beneath all the changes of our sensible world there must be something permanent unchanging."[6]

Nature of Particles and 'Events' at Very Short Distances

When one applies quantum theory to the electrodynamics of "elementary" particles such as electrons, protons, etc. internal inconsistencies arise in theory. These inconsistencies are connected with the prediction of infinite values for values for various physical properties e.g. mass and charge of the electron. These infinities arise from the extrapolation of the current theory to distances that are infinitely small. Among the things that make such an extrapolation necessary is the assumption that the socalled "elementary" particles such as electrons are only mathematical points, that is, they occupy *no space at all.*[7]

The particles are certain energy packets/units of certain magnitude for certain seconds; there is no space, no length, breadth, height etc. of what we designate as the 'particles'. They don't have space, and exist for certain microseconds only. Then, what do 'exist'?! A unit of action for a certain time.

As Bertrand Russell expresses it lucidly, an atom at a certain moment is a certain occurrence or event, creating 'disturbances' in the surrounding medium, and this we in our commonsense would term 'causation'. Waves pass outwards and inwards, and create an event, which we would prefer to call a 'particle'. Our series of hypotheses is supposed to create a point, and thus give shape to 'matter'.

The world which theory of relativity presents to us is not that of 'things in motion' but that of 'events'; particles are more like strings of connected events, "like the successive notes of a song". "It is *events* that are the stuff of relativity physics."[9]

Thus the electrons do not occupy any finite region of space, contrary to popular impression, even among scientists..

Within the present theory, those results can be calculated that do not depend critically on the assumed size of the particle. Tomanaga, Schwinger and Feynman measured magnetic momentum of the electron. The quantum calculations throw minimal light on the problem of infinities; that is one of the most important manifestations of crisis in physics.[10]

These calculations show that the theories do not depend significantly on what happens at distances shorter than the Compton wavelength of electron i.e. 3×10^{-11} cm. Failure of current theories should become important at around 10^{-13} cm.

Existence/reality become non-existence/non-reality at quantum/ sub-quantum levels/distances!

Experiments with particles of very high energy e.g. 100 million electron volts or more lead to a bewildering array of new phenomena, and there is no adequate explanation existing. The so-called 'elementary' particles, e.g. protons and neutrons can transform into one another. Positrons, neutrons, various mesons, hyperons etc. have been discovered and there is no limit to this process of discovery. Most of these particles are unstable, quickly decaying into several others. They can all be 'created' in collisions of other particles with nuclei.[11]

These new properties become important only when the particles approach within a distance of the order of 10^{-13} cm of each other.[12]

Certain Processes at Sub-quantum Levels

1. Processes with very high energy and very high frequency are faster than the processes at the lower levels. 'Creation' of meson, for example, is taken as a well defined process at the sub-quantum mechanical level. In this process, *field* energy is *concentrated* in certain regions of space in discreet amounts; the 'destruction' of the particle is just the reverse process: energy disperses and takes another form. The current quantum theory discusses the creation and destruction (or dispersal?) of the particle as merely their 'popping' in and out in the space.[13]
2. The treatment of the Dirac quantum leads to a situation where *different kinds of fields may be described as different modes of vibration of a field.*[14]

The 'Other End' of 'Reality'

Thus, we are gradually getting certain clues about the nature of the processes, 'events' and 'matter' at the quantum and sub-quantum levels of the world. We are, in the course of our investigations, shifting towards the other ends of the spectrum, which actually resulted in the course of a 'slowdown' in the emergence of particles, tangible materials and clearly visible events and objects.

The clues provide us with some steps to the solution of the problem of nature of particles and waves. *The vibrations in the space create waves and their temporary expressions are the particles.*

In this manner, we are reaching the 'other end' of the problem of 'reality'. It would be interesting to begin from that end!

The introduction of the concept of field involves a fundamental modification of the concept of matter and space. Field implies that even when space contains no bodies, it could still be a site of constant changes and variations. In fact it was the electromagnetic waves or the field that led to the discovery of the quantum, as the field is composed of the packets or particles of energy. The fields can be shown to carry energy, momentum, angular momentum etc., thus simulating some of the properties of moving bodies, particularly at light speed. Einstein even suggested special kinds of field having motions of the type in which there would be pulse-like concentrations of fields, sticking together, acting exactly like moving bodies; even particles like electrons and protons may consist of such modes of motion. Thus the concept of matter has been expanded to include notion of the field[15], and that is very important, even crucial.

The hypothesis at the end of 19th century that field exists in its own right was *a new addition to the concept of matter.*

So, it was a *transition from the concept of motions of bodies through space to motions of the space itself.*

For many physicists and philosophers, nature could be reduced to the motions of a few bodies or few kinds of fields (e.g. Einstein) or both. The fields being continuous, required non-countable infinity of variables for their mathematical expressions. This also helps the mechanistic view that everything in the universe can be reduced to a few basic kinds of entities never changing qualitatively.[16]

Historically the mechanistic philosophy assumed that the basic units of the universe were the ultimate and indivisible atoms.

The purely quantitative laws governing the motions of these atoms were, consequently, regarded as the laws from which everything followed.

Physics later discovered that atoms were not the fundamental units, and were composed of electrons, protons and so on. So, the atom was divisible. The laws of atomic and above levels were then, not applicable to these subatomic levels. Laws governing atoms were *not applicable everywhere* in the universe. The laws of the microscopic and subatomic levels had to be *different*, as the subsequent development of quantum physics has shown.

The molecular and atomic motions are determined and transformed by high degrees of temperatures and the mean kinetic energies. But as soon as it is discovered that the atom is constituted of electrons etc., those factors cease to play a decisive role. Sub-particles can assume autonomous and independent existence under different set of laws, with this autonomy itself redefined, with probability, indeterminacy and transitoriness of the nature coming to the fore increasingly.

Throughout the classical period (of physics, etc.) it was determinism, mechanistic or dialectical, materialism that dominated. It was assumed that though the details would change, the basic theory and philosophy would remain the same.

Relativity and quantum mechanism drastically changed all this. Determinism was closely interlocked with causation. But these two theories uncoupled causation from the worldview. The quantum theory was the first example in physics of an essentially statistical theory. The quantum theory did not start from the laws of the objects, transiting from there to the statistical considerations of those laws, which is the case in classical mechanics. From the very beginning, the quantum theory took the form of laws with statistical predictions. The question of the laws of the individual system was not even raised. The Heisenberg indeterminacy led the physicists to conclude that no precise causal laws could ever be found for the individual systems. Causality was renounced in the atomic domain. According to some[17], causality could still operate at sub-quantum levels and in some quantum processes, if the limitations of indeterminacy are shown.

Classical theory was characterised by the assumption that the bodies of matter moved constantly and exchanged energy *continuously* with the electromagnetic waves, such as light. But Planck and Einstein showed that matter exchanged energy with light, and light transmitted energy to matter in form of "quanta" (bundles) of the size of E=hv. (V= frequency of light x universal constant).

An electromagnetic wave can be produced when a charged particle such as electron moves through space with oscillatory motion, and this disturbs the electric and magnetic fields. In case of electrons, this motion can create light waves, radio waves and other types of electromagnetic waves. Light-waves and fields will act on charged particles imparting them an oscillatory motion, with an energy proportional to the intensity of the light-wave.

The experiments on photoelectric effect contradicted the predictions of classical theory. The energy gained did not depend continuously on intensity of radiation, so that with weaker light less energy should be gained. The experiment suggested that light consists of small discreet particles of energy, so that when one of the particles strikes an electron, it transfers the discrete energy E=hv. Weak light–wave has few such particles, and an intense wave many. This suggestion was clearly made by Planck in his black-body radiation study.

Wave and Particle

The evidence of light as discrete particles came in conflict with experiments on interference, which demands that light appear in *continuous* wave motion. Thus light displays both wave-like and particle-like properties or 'behaviour'. Light is a unity of wave and particle. This is further confirmed in a more profound way by the experiments conducted by Young and later by Vavilov.[18] They are famously known as the 'two-slit experiments'. In the experiments, at the end, only one light particle passes through both the slits, producing a wave-like interference pattern. This proves that even a single light quantum (particle or packet) is itself wave-like. This is a great example of unity and interpenetration of opposites (opposite poles) and their constant conflict, their conversion into one another while at the same time being mutually exclusive. In fact, exclusion takes place through mutual conversion and interpenetration. When one talks of a particle, one actually is talking of a packet of waves, as Niels Bohr has shown![19] And when one treats light as waves, the waves break up into particles (quanta)!

According to classical theory, a moving charged particle like the electron should lose energy by radiating electro-magnetic waves. The rate should be proportional to the square of the acceleration of the electron. The particle or the electron moving in a curved orbit is accelerated towards the centre of the atom. Thus, it should reach the centre in a small fraction of a second. But in reality this does not happen. What happens is that the electron stops radiating when it reaches the normal radius of the atom, and remains there as long as it is not disturbed. The size of this orbit is of the order of 10^{-8} cm.[20] There are a number of fixed orbits with respective energy levels. These orbits are not continuous spiral ones; this point should be particularly noted. The electrons jump from one energy level to another, staying there till disturbed; thus the orbits and the jumps are ***quantized***, and that is how they do not fall into the nucleus of atom. The frequencies of the light emitted correspond with the particular orbit/s.

The individual quantum shows particulate qualities also because "in a beam containing a small number of quanta *there are statistical fluctuations in the time and place of liberation of an electron which are just those that would come from a beam of particles distributed in space in a highly irregular or 'random way'*", something expected if particles were emitted by a source with chaotic molecular motion.[21]

So, one set of experiments suggested light as waves, while another showed light as particles.

Bohr suggested that *as electrons moved around the nucleus, they should emit electromagnetic waves of the same frequency as that of the rotation.*

The frequency was found to be of the order of 10^{15} cycles per second, the same as that of light. Thus, it is light was emitted. Electrons follow disparate orbits.

Bohr presented convincing evidence for the idea that the energy of electrons and all forms of energy also came in discrete packets. A basic "atomicity" of energy was established.

Electron often behaves like a system of waves when it was expected to be a particle. A particular phenomenon is the shower of electrons bouncing off a metal plate. They do not bounce off like spheres or balls. They produce a diffraction pattern, a result of wavelike behaviour. When electrons are shot through a tiny aperture, they spread laterally, producing diffraction pattern.[22]

This does not prove and mean that an electron actually consists of waves. It raises the question whether system of waves provides better picture of the electron than as the 'hard' particle. The picture of a hard particle as the constituent of the world *disappears*. Our concept of the world changes. This particle, the one of the micro-world, actually transforms into waves, energy, motions and such other phenomena; a particle is therefore constituted of non-particulate properties and feature such as the waves, time-energy combinations and so on. The particle has *no* inbuilt constituent structure *at all*, in contrast to that of the tangible reality. So *the query as to what is inside a particle is rendered irrelevant and superfluous.*

Waves provide a picture which has never failed to predict electron behaviour. On the other hand, the particle-picture of the electron has failed on numerous occasions. Yet, it is the waves and the wave-dominated space that provide certain explanation of the 'particle-like' events.

New wave mechanics shows that a moving electron or proton ought to behave like a system of waves of quite definite wavelength. This depends on the mass of the moving particle and its speed of motion, but on nothing else.

If we want to understand the fundamental nature of the physical universe, it is to these small-scale phenomena that we must pay attention to. They reflect nature of things at this stage.

The waves which represent on electron in the wave-mechanics may be probability waves, whose intensity at any point measures the *probability* of the electron being at that particular point.[23] The wave-intensity measures the probability that a single diffracted electron would hit, say, a plate at a particular spot.

This view enables the electrons to preserve their identity. If the electron waves were true material waves, the waves would be dispersed by the experiment. Any encounter with matter would 'break up' electrons, that is convert them into waves. This renders the 'electron' as no more than a concept: they do not have a permanent structure. Actually it is the shower of electrons rather than the individual electron that is diffracted. The individual electrons move as particles, retaining their identity in the midst of the mass of electrons, which is nothing but waves. It is a conflict of the individual with the mass. It is in the background of and in contrast to the mass that we preserve the concept of the particle.

The particles have been resolved into a system of waves, as in case of light. In many circumstances the behaviour of the electron is found to be too complex for it to be considered a particle. Louis de Broglie, Schrödinger and others tried to interpret the behaviour of a particle as that of a group of waves. Consequently, they founded a branch of mathematical physics known as wave-mechanics.

The bouncing of a tennis ball off the hard tennis court surface is well-known. We can understand a lot of things about mechanical motions through this act. We can retrieve the tennis ball as it is after it has bounced off. But that is not the case with the electron and such other particles. We cannot use this example to understand the processes in the quantum world. And here lies the secret to the new world. *If we replace a tennis ball with an electron,* the motion of the electron coming off a surface would be like that of a system of waves!

Heisenberg's "uncertainty principle" makes it impossible to say: electron is here at this spot now, moving with such and such speed. According to Paul Dirac, when an observation is made on any atomic system, the result in general will not be determinate. In other words, if the experiment is repeated several times, different results may be obtained.

Can you catch hold of the same particle again?! 'No' is the obvious answer.

Heisenberg and Bohr suggested that these waves are merely symbolic representation of our knowledge in the context of state and position of the electron. We hardly think of waves as being located in space and time. *They are mere visualizations of a mathematical formula of wavelike but wholly abstract nature.*[24]

According to Bohr the minutest phenomena of nature do not admit of representation in space-time framework at all. The four-dimensional continuum of theory relativity is adequate only for some phenomena, including the largescale ones and radiation in free space; other phenomena can only be represented by going outside the continuum.

Electron and other particles do not have a finite and bounded size or limit beyond certain limits. In fact, shape and size are not the main problem for us in our subjective quest of the quantum world. It is the 'jerks' to be met in the universe while moving about that creates problems. The nature moves in certain jerks or 'deviations', and it is to this that we have to adjust. Planck's constant or unit, known as 'h', helps us cover these jerks by measuring and incorporating them in the calculations.[25]

The essential fact is that *all* the pictures which now science draws of nature are *mathematical* ones.

Mathematics and statistics are both real and unreal. They are relationships between phenomena and processes. Numbers like 2 or 4 or 1 or 7 and so on do not 'exist'; they are not objective reality in themselves. They are subjective arbitrariness. Yet they represent certain relations that compares and contrasts various processes or events.

The event of the electron has to be interpreted in considerably similar way. One has to go deeper to unveil the underlying layers of processes.

Earlier, the propagation of waves and transmission of energy were independent. According to Osborne Reynolds's paper of 1877[26], an instance can be given of a simple case of no energy transmission, namely a row of disconnected pendulums, all alike; by starting the pendulums oscillating, one after the other regularly, we can get a wave-form advancing with a speed exactly proportional to be wavelength. Here, the frequency is definite: the time of period of the pendulum oscillation, but the wavelength is optional, so the velocity is optional too. The energy in the oscillation is not transmitted. The velocity of transmission of energy is zero. The medium surrounding the pendulums takes no part in the action. The energy remains steadfast as regards locomotion.

If some electric connection between the pendulums is introduced, that will act as a medium uniting them. Now energy begins to flow. Energy belongs to a group of waves and travels with it.

Electrical and other energies travel in groups. Wireless telegraphy is one instance of group waves.

The history of wave theory originated in the studies of quantum theory and properties of light. The 20th century studies established a connection between the wave and the point electron. Waves of light of suitable frequency could eject an electron with an energy corresponding to the frequency. The electron as a result is tossed up or tossed out (of the atom). Conversely, when an electron fell back into the atom; it emitted waves of particular frequency, which it must get rid of to settle down into the orbit.

This is *photoelectricity*.

De Broglie suggested unification of the two inter-related phenomena: particle and wave. Therefore, light is both a particle and wave. We are using the word 'phenomenon' for the particle, and that only is appropriate here. A quantum of light is like a particle, yet light is composed of waves. Similarly, electron too is both a particle and wave. Electron is nothing but motion, and therefore a phenomenon. Electron could be a group wave. It may also be a travelling electron, with which group of waves is associated; their frequency or rate of vibration depending on the energy of travel. De Broglie connected frequency and energy, that is the length of waves with the momentum of the particle.

These and other developments gradually erased the difference between particle and wave. One deals with something that is neither, yet has the properties of both. The name 'wavicle' has been suggested. The constitution of electron is by no means simple. The electron behaves like a particle at a long distance from the nucleus, in the outer orbit. But when it is nearer the nucleus, and therefore is traveling at high speeds, it does not seem to be located at one point at all, but spreads out over the orbit like a succession of stationary waves.[27] The difference between wave and particle is one of degree than of quality or kind.

"A group wave of certain frequency may appeal to us as if it were a moving particle of given energy."[28] Matter may be consisting of particles; that also may mean it is made of group waves. The stormy or perturbed areas of the group waves were found to move about under precisely the same laws that govern the motion of particles in ordinary mechanics. The frequency of waves (rate of vibration) appears as the energy of equivalent particle. Eddington sums up Schrödinger's theory in this connection thus:

"The equations for the motion of a wave group with given frequency and potential frequency are the same as the classical equation of motion of a particle with the corresponding energy and potential energy."[29]

Bohr postulated that the continuous range of orbits permitted by classical theory was in reality *not possible*; the electron could follow only certain discrete or quantized orbits. If the electron could jump from the outer to the inner orbit (lower one), it would radiate the *full* energy difference between the two orbits. *So only discrete frequencies of light would be emitted.*[30]

Thus Bohr resolved the problem in a *qualitative* way. He then proceeded to derive a quantitative rule. This permitted him *to calculate the allowed energy levels* and the corresponding frequencies of light. This quantitative rule permitted frequencies of high precision.

Thus, according to Bohr, not only does energy of light but also of electron come in discrete packets or quanta. The discontinuity and thus a basic 'atomicity' in all the forms of energy and in general was established.

It has not been explained why the energy is atomic in nature. The atomicity is *postulated.* It was not explained as to how a quantum was emitted and absorbed, in the course of which electron jumped from one state to another.

According to de Broglie, just as light waves were particle-like, the atomic particles were wave-like. Classical waves consisted of discrete *frequencies.* He postulated that there existed a new kind of wave connected with atom. It will have discrete frequencies of oscillation. If we connect energy of the wave to its frequency (E=hv), then *discrete frequencies* will imply *discrete energies.* De Broglie then connected the waves with momentum of the electron. When the wavelength was evaluated for an electron of a particular momentum in experimental condition, it was found to be of the order of atomic dimensions. Experiments with light showed that a wave-like character manifested itself only when these waves met with obstacles not too much larger than a wavelength in size. Otherwise *it goes in practically a straight line as if it were a particle.*

Thus, on the large scales, de Broglie's waves would not show themselves clearly, and the electron would act as a classical particle. But at the atomic level, the wave connected with the electron would produce new effects. One of the effects would be discrete frequencies of vibration due to confinement of waves within the atom. De Broglie was able to calculate both the frequencies and the corresponding energies of the discrete possible modes of vibration of these waves. The Bohr energy levels were explicable in terms of an assumed wave, *provided that one also* assumed that the energy of *this wave was related to its frequency by the Einstein relation E=hv.*[31]

"Experiments by Davisson and Germer on the scattering of electrons from metallic crystals disclosed a statistical pattern of strong and weak scattering very similar to the fringes obtained by passing a beam of light quanta through a set of slits."[32] It was suggested that here the waves were manifesting themselves; the atoms in the crystal were playing the role of the slits in the interference experiments. Thus the conjecture that electrons possessed wavelike properties was confirmed. Later it was proved that all the particles had wave-like properties.[33]

Schrödinger obtained a partial differential equation for the waves, determining their future motions. Now precise calculation of energy levels in a wide variety of atomic levels could be made. He also showed how the waves moved in transition from one energy level to another.

A paradoxical situation arose when a limitation of wave theory was discovered.[34] Schrödinger proposed that the electron should be thought of as a continuous distribution of charge. Thus, the waves of de Broglie and Schrödinger *were to be interpreted as waves of electric charge.* Schrödinger's equation leads to the conclusion that the total amount of charge would remain constant, no matter how it flowed from place to place.[35]

But interpretation worked only as long as the Schrödinger wave remained within the atom.[36] In free space, the wave must spread out rapidly over all space without limit. On the other hand, electron is actually found within a small region of space! Its charge therefore is not equal to Schrödinger values.

Here Max Born proposed a solution. He applied the concept of *probability*. He conceptualized that wave intensity represented not actual charge density of the electron, but rather *the probability density*, that the electron as a small localized particle, shall be found at a certain place. Thus the wave amplitude spread out all over space does not contradict appearance of electron at a certain place.[37]

[In this way, quantum physics reached the point of a strange combination of determinate and statistical aspects, leading to complicated causal relations. Among the problems was the motions of the individual electrons, light quanta etc. It was thought that to explain these events, one would have to go to some deeper levels (cf. Brownian motion). Those levels would have the same relation to the atomic levels as would atomic levels would have with the Brownian motion.]

Thus, the fact that the wave amplitude for a free electron spreads out over all space is no longer in contradiction with the appearance of the electron at a certain point. The total probability of the particle to be found somewhere in space remains equal to unity.[38] It is possible to calculate *the probabilities of transitions* between the two states, the two energy levels.[39]

Thus, the quantum theory gives statistical predictions of subatomic behaviour; any attempt to go beyond that is met with by uncertainty principle, which yields *probabilities.* A particle can be anywhere until we 'meet' it or measure it; obviously our attempt to examine it to a considerable extent determines its quantities and qualities.[40]

Thus, energy is not something abstract; in general it appears to have certain atomicity. This could be in form of light quanta and in form of discrete energy levels. All the manifestations of matter and energy appear to have aspects both of wave and particle. The numerical value (E) of energy in the particle-like manifestations is related to frequency v; in the wavelike manifestations by Einstein relation E=hv. Similarly, the numerical value of momentum in the particle-like manifestation is related to the wavelength. The basic laws of atomic physics appear to be statistical in form. Only a probability of a certain *function*: wave or particle, can be predicted.

This leads to the contradictions in the act and the process of observation at quantum level.

This has to do with particulate and wave nature of light. We observe, for example, electron with the help of light (using a microscope). Light comes in form of quanta or discreet packets. At least one quantum is needed to observe the particle (the electron). And this quantum will surely create certain minimum disturbance in the electron. To minimize this difficulty, we may use electromagnetic waves of low frequency, which would give us smaller quantum.

Light not only act like a particle but also like a wave. A light wave scattered from a definite point does not form a definite image point; instead it forms a small poorly defined image region proportional in size to the wavelength. At low frequency, the wavelength will be big. Consequently, the image in the microscope will be so poor that it will be difficult to locate the electron.

Thus, two problems arise in the course of the above observation. Due to *the particulate nature of light,* the momentum of the particle is disturbed. This disturbance is unpredictable and uncontrollable. *According to the quantum theory,. there is no way of knowing the precise angle with which the light quantum is scattered.* Thus results an uncertainty in the momentum transfer to the electron.

This is one aspect of the uncertainty principle.

The other aspect of the principle, and the other difficulty, arises from the wave nature of light. The result is that we cannot avoid uncertainty in the position of the electron, due to the absence of a sharp image. It leads to the indeterminacy relations of Heisenberg.[41]

The accurate determination the position of the electron requires the use of light of short wavelength. This involves transfer of a large but unpredictable and uncontrollable momentum to the electron. On the other hand, an accurate determination of the momentum requires light quanta of very low momentum, and therefore long wavelength.[42]

Can one use means other than interaction with light quanta to observe the electron? A beam of electrons can be substituted for the beam of light quanta. But the situation does not change essentially. *All* energy comes in quanta, and *all* matter has the properties of both wave and particle. Therefore, the indeterminacy principle will continue to operate.

Heisenberg considers indeterminacy as one of the basic laws of nature, to which all other laws will have to correspond. It would have an absolute and final validity, which will continue indefinitely. The future developments in physics will be in the direction of less and less precise determination of the behaviour of particles and 'things' and processes.[43] For example, Heisenberg even proposed that for the distances shorter than the 'fundamental length' of the order of 10^{-13} cm, *even the properties of time and space would cease to 'exist'* (to be definable).[44]

A Discussion on Electron, 'Particle' and Existence

It is apparent from the above discussion that any attempt to locate particle beyond a certain limit, leads to complexities, problems and uncertainties. *Our traditional, existing concept of the particle is shattered.* We are accustomed to delimit, determine a well-defined object as the object of our analysis. A particle, a sphere, a tangible, solid unit is almost always, and basically, the very basis of our observation, interpretation and worldview. It has been *the very basis of philosophy* and of generalization almost since the beginning of knowledge. Even without realising, it is the unit not only of analysis, but also of knowledge in general. Knowledge and the process of cognition have to have a base, and that base is the particle (or sphere and other tangibles), and also the wave. But wave comes later. Wave comes in generally in the course of treatment of motion and flow. Yet, today, it too is an important unit of investigation(and therefore, by implication, a 'particle' of its own kind!).

The history of cognition is that of its development around and within the particle and other tangibles. Therefore, it is a concentrated development. In order to cognise, we need a certain basis, a firm surface, a terrain of certainty, of confidence, and an infallible one at that. Only then can we cognise the objective, material world. In the ancient Indian philosophy it was provided by the particles seen in the sun-rays filtering through the slits in the window. In the Greek philosophy, atomism constituted a powerful trend in Democritus, Leucippus and Epicurus. Particles subsequently have played a crucial role in the history of human thought and life.

We have always cognised, 'looked at' the *objective* world, and that world has always existed outside us, outside our consciousness. To analyse and understand is to grasp what existed outside. What exists inside is, has always been, a mystery. Yet, materialism, in particular dialectical materialism, resolved the contradiction between idea and matter, and between inner and outer selves, showing them to be in a dialectical and conflicting unity.

Particle and the concept of particle has always carried us into that which is the other of ourselves. And 'our' 'selves' have been the opposite, mutually excluded, of the other 'self'.

Human consciousness has been endlessly identifying and penetrating the particle (and the wave). The particle at first was a *philosophical deduction* from the observed world. The industrial revolution imparted it the necessary concreteness. The particle was discovered as the basis of chemical, physical, biological reactions, interactions and structures, at least in most cases.

Science and philosophy in the 19th century in particular, as also in the 20th century have been on the lookout for the ultimate constituent particles of matter, the 'builders' of matter and the world. The process of investigation began in the ancient Greek, Indian and other philosophies, and the quest continues today.

This has left its own impact on the nature of our thought (structure and aims) and the thought-process (path of movement of thought). The whole human consciousness has so evolved as to look for the 'building blocks' of reality, particularly under the impact of the industrial revolution and in the industrial age.

Thought always looks for (thinks of) the ultimate, whether in materialism or idealism. The particle has always acted as the guiding star for the evolution of our consciousness.

Consequently, thought in its process of evolution is considerably distorted and misled. It has always been assumed that we are approaching reality, knowledge, from the position of non-reality or partial reality, and non-knowledge; the assumption has dominated all the thought. Consequently, it has acted as a presumption, assumption and pre-determination, particularly the last one. Our thoughts are predetermined, and hence limited subjectively, negating objectivity, which must be endless and infinite, which is not to the liking of the 'victorious march' of thought (consciousness).

The particle is always the limit, like the 'concept', in philosophy, and in all the thoughts. This quest imparts a meaning to the process of thought, gives it is validity.

Atom was one of the greatest discoveries of the human thought, the science, technology, of philosophy. In fact, it has been so since the very beginning of philosophy. At last during the 18th, 19th and 20th centuries, the building blocks of matter were discovered (Dalton, etc. onwards) and concretised (Rutherford and so on). The entire edifice of chemistry and physics was built up on this basis, and so also of philosophy, particularly of the materialist kind. The configuration and structure of atom were decided upon, atom because fixed and finalised as the ultimate unit of matter.

And then it became *unfixed* in the beginning of the 20th century. The atom was divided after the discovery of protons, electrons and nucleus, etc. The developments gave rise to controversies. Philosophers, scientists, physicists and others were seriously exercised over related issues in the wake of Michelson-Morley experiments, discovery of Planck's quantum, Einstein's relativity and so on. Planck, Eddington, Ernst Mach, Bohr and many others were involved in the discussions and debates on the nature of atom and of matter itself, definition of reality, causation, wave-particle duality, subject/object relationship, inexhaustibility of atom, disappearance or persistence of matter and what not! Among the most interesting books that came out one by a philosopher, who is more popularly known as a revolutionary leader: V.I. Lenin, who wrote an extraordinary book titled *Materialism and Empirio-criticism* in 1909. He contradicted the thesis about the 'disappearance' of matter in the wake of the split in the atom, and showed the inexhaustible nature of matter. It is amazing to see Lenin finding time to go through most of the possible literature in physics and philosophy to defend his viewpoint, despite being such an active political being. The work brought out the theorist and philosopher in Lenin. It is without doubt one of the most extraordinary books written on philosophical implications of new scientific discoveries. There can be differences of opinion.

Then there were the famous 'Solvay' congresses of the scientists of the world, beginning in 1927 and held on several occasions subsequently. They were marked by sharp debates not only on the interpretations of the physical and scientific discoveries, particularly in the field of quantum mechanics and relativity, but also on their philosophical implications. Philosophy and its categories more and more became the subject of debates among scientists and others.

The 'opening up', the division of atom led to the discovery of a series of particles and waves, of a whole world inside it (the atom), to gradual expansion of that world to a sort of parallel, new reality (world), quite different from what hitherto existed. Yet, this new world was gradually related with the existing world at new levels, giving rise to new interpretations, new realities, questioning the very concept of 'reality'. New interlinks were, and are being, established between the world, inside and outside the atom. There are certain common constituents and denominators in the two worlds.

'Opening Up' of the Atom

Opening up of the atom meant the breaking down of the 'last frontier' of reality. And that meant the breakdown of all the existing concepts, theories and philosophies. So much was discovered, and is being discovered, within the atom that it has ceased to exist by opening up a new universe itself. And thus it created problems for thought, science and philosophy.

At the same time, the infinite stretches of the outer spaces are being explored and ever new discoveries are being made, changing our thoughts in novel ways.

The solid, dependable terrain for thought process and philosophy has got disturbed and disrupted. The *atom has become a problem,* instead of being a solution; it was something taken for granted; but no more. So much has been discovered within it that it cannot exist, cannot be real, and has ceased to exist. It has been dissolved in new realities, particles, waves and processes. The atom, consequently, exists only as a concept, not as a concept of reality but from the unreality of that reality, as a shell; it is made to exist, recreated and brought to life as a tool to explain certain things, Dalton has been put upside down. The atom exists now only as a working concept, as a series and receptacle of statistical numbers. So we move on from a real, tangible atom to the statistical, conceptual atom. Concept is detached from the real, from tangible reality. It becomes a medium of explanation.

The greater the number of particles discovered within the atom, greater the confusion about the nature of particle/s. Elementary particles have lost their position as the 'building blocks', which themselves have become divisible.

This divisibility and the progressive 'miniaturisation' (!) were bound to give rise to the questions about the very nature and reality of the particle. Can such a particle exist at all?

A particle can be a particle, can exist as a particle, only upto a certain limit. After that it ceases to be anything definite, a particle. Beyond the minutest limits, the dimensions of the classical world gradually fall away. Length, breadth, height, radius, and other dimensions cease to have any meaning. The 'minute' itself becomes a relative term. One can't measure beyond a certain limit; *the concept of measurement itself becomes questionable* beyond this point. One can't point out the point. We continue to work with the old concepts of time, space, dimensions, measurement etc. But how can 'something' exist *at all* at extremely minute levels? Can a thing be a 'thing' at such exceedingly minute scales of time and space?

When x-rays or light falls upon the electron/s, they do not do so on a solid, particular, tangible 'surface'; what falls is also not solid or tangible. We expect solid particle/waves of one type, particularly the particles would 'hit' one type, particularly the particles would 'hit' or replace another particle or set of particles. In reality, this 'hitting' does not take place *at all*, at least the way we understand it. A series of other, unexpected kinds of changes take place, which open up entirely novel fields of knowledge, generally covered by the quantum science and *quantum philosophy*.

The minutest 'particles' exist for the shortest possible time unit. Is it possible for something to exist at that border of time with any sense of existence? Can we term existence for millionth or billionth of a second an 'existence'? We should redefine existence. Is it possible for 'something' to exist within the dimensions of, say 10^{-10} or 10^{-12} cm and so on, and that too for tolerably 'decent' period? What is the meaning of reality and existence at such dimensions and for such short, fleeting moments (or endless divisions of a 'moment')?

So nothing exists for any tolerably 'decent' period at such levels, nothing can. Reality stands *revised*.

We began with clear-cut time and space dimensions of matter and even particles (spheres). We end up, so to say, by seeking particles *in space and time*, that is, independent of space and time! We are forced to. For us, the particle must exist, but it does not exist with space and time.

In the course of our analysis of and journey into the particle, we go beyond it and into the world of rapid transformations of energy, waves, time and space. The analysis of the particle leads us to temporariness, to rapid transitions in the time dimensions, to the discovery of new 'particles' known as of various energies and time; and to the very spatial dimensions themselves.

Space consists of rapid energy transformations and transmissions calculable for particular time periods; all of them again have 'atomicity', i.e. they are quantized. So, in the course of the analysis of the particle (say electron), we come upon energy transformations in certain fixed time units, and these energies and time units themselves, in turn are discrete.

It is being found that the particle is more and more **a function** of space. In the endless world of *motions* there could be a particle-like concentration of these functions, partially or fully, anytime, anywhere, giving full freedom to uncertainty and probability.

A chance concentration of qualities, more particularly a slowdown of time at a particular place, gives rise to particles. Particles are not permanent, solid structures. Instead, they are particular concentration and constellation of dimensions and qualities at a certain point. Here, it is space which **functions** as particle.

So particle does not exist in space and time. It is the space which expresses itself *as 'particles' of exceedingly fleeting moments*. Therefore, the questions like what is particle or electron are rendered meaningless. The particle just appears as a 'shooting star' and disappears. The 'particle' ceases to play it has so far played; it is now just a momentary byproduct of the greater spatial processes.

Thus, particle proves to be nothing but a quality, a function of space. Now it is found out that space is nothing but energy in general. This energy has a certain atomicity and a discreet nature, a wave nature at the same time, and considerable statistical form.

Question of the Negated Atom/Particle

Now, the particles and waves, and space, acquire statistical manifestations. 'What is a particle?'–the question should be asked afresh here, and one of the answers is that it is a statistical manifestation. Of what? Of relations, energy transformations, existence of energy for a speck of time, penetration into deeper levels, etc.

This is a very important point–that of the statistical and mathematical relations, manifestations and forms. From that point of view, atom is nothing but an statistical/mathematical relation. What is, for example, 2+2 (two plus two) or 2x2 (to into two)? Nothing?! It does not really exist! Yet it very much exists. Two plus two or two into two do not exist 'out there'! Yet they represent and reflect profound relations between certain aspects, functions of reality.

Here, thought is liberated from the confines of particle, from the limits of the concept. The concept has reached its limits, after having discharged its functions, and has spread out into transcendence through self-transcendence. Concept has been the greatest achievement of philosophy. Concept also is the greatest impediment to philosophy. ***Society and consciousness have just come out into the open in vast***

endless spaces, where humanity and thought are about to begin fresh journey into a fresh new world.

The particle had bound our thought within limits, giving us, all the time, a misleading satisfaction of constant discoveries. Those discoveries must be undone at this level; those very discoveries were our bindings chains because they hovered round within a closed atom, and the world was created upon those atoms. The particle recedes as we proceed toward and within it. It must become smaller and smaller, if we are to explain it. But it cannot be fully explained, unless it recedes, and recedes completely, into its opposite; ***it must spread out into the infinity***. The infinite is made up of quanta of energy. Each wave is only a wave-packet, energy/ time packets.

We proceed from 'atom' to 'endless' atom, which is a world of infinite energy.

As Bertrand Russell said, in the world of immediate data nothing is permanent; even the objects, which we regard as permanent, become data, when we do not see them.[45] This needs to be elaborated; it is a very important point in defining reality and in philosophical experience.

Beyond the particle, the experience, the tangible, the world is made up of what? We began our journey with atom. It *was* a dialectical concept. Now the concept of atom has become transformed into a mechanical one. Argued *from the other end*, the concept of atom becomes to be almost an absurd one!

Subject and object become one with quanta, on way to resolve the conflict of "reality'.

"The belief in indestructible 'things' very early took the form of atomism."[46] That is the problem with atomism, as we here already stated. It is fixed, roots for the fixed, the immutable, the 'basic', etc. The world is discovered as dialectics and in dialectics. Ever new aspects and levels are discovered. But this motion-based investigation is done *on the basis of* the immutable 'atoms' and 'particles'. To maintain matter, first atom and then the particle are sought to be preserved. *The dialectical is transformed into the mechanical.* One can't analyse change and motion with the help of the immutable 'particle'. That which was the vehicle for dialectics becomes a vehicle for non-dialectical mechanics.

The discovery of quanta in 1900 began a new process of philosophical generalisation. It particularised experience, yet it was a particularisation that led to the dissolution of the particle. The 'particle' quantum dissolved the particle. The particles or quanta replaced the historically established atoms and particles by energy/time packets. These packets exist only for the sake of carrying energy and come into being only at the moment and then disappear. They are the basis of energy conversions, radiations and exchange of energy: they are units of motion. They virtually have no existence, no structure, shape and size, no limits as such. The transformations are quantized. *We enter a relativistic quantum world.*

This is a very important point, this entry into the relativistic world. Our observation and philosophical generalisation becomes relativistic. So far, our observations were from 'outside' the objects. In other words, it was 'objective', 'real', 'material'. But as we observe, the observer itself gets absorbed into the observed and his/her observations relate space and time and frame of reference. The final step in the beginning of that linkage is the discovery of quanta and relativity. The quantum itself is a relativistic concept.

It means much. To observe means to change! That is because we begin to observe, not from the outside or by situating ourselves at the edge, but by entering the real, objective world. The linkages are established by the quanta. We become part of the quanta as we observe. Now the observer and observation enters as serious, active element of the reality, of the observation process.

'Quantized' observation cannot be done in isolation, from 'outside'. The quantum unites the outside and the inside in a continuous whole, thus beginning the dissolution of the division between the subject and the object, gradually bringing them together, reducing their difference and distance, merging them. *Quantum is something common between the two.*

Consequently, observation is something affecting the observed as well as the observer. In essence, observation is an exchange of and between particles, as also a continuity of waves. It is this exchange that effaces the difference between them. The observed particle is disturbed, changed, even *created* in the course of observation. Observation is thus not simply a process of reflection of light images on our retina, and of other kinds of reflection. It is not as in the tangible world.

Entering the depth of matter, we meet with a world of particles and waves and motions pure and simple. It is the motion at its purest and best, isolated from other attributes of matter.

In order to observe a particle (motion) or particles (motions), we have to disturb them. It/they *cannot produce simple images.* The light thrown upon the particle (motion) produces certain deviation or disturbance, which is then fixed; these disturbances can be calculated. They are separate field of science. So *to observe is to disturb*, and to observe a particular aspect is to disturb *in a particular way*, to a particular extent, and for a particular purpose.

It has to be clearly realized that motion itself is quantized, is particularized.

Light falling upon the particle (quantum, that is, motion which can be quantised), is itself quantized. Light is motion, it is also particle (quantum). And that can be calculated. So, to observe is to calculate, estimate, create statistical images and calculations. No retina is involved, no other biological organs and senses, except pure brain power, and calculations and inferences, *and consciousness* ; not even scientific apparatusus are involved: most of the processes are beyond the instruments. And where there are instruments, they interfere with the quantum processes/events.

How do you know that the electron exists, or for that matter any other particle and sub-particle? And how do you know that a wave esists? By making 'it' react with the incident particle/wave. Only then can we infer that it exists in such and such conditions to such and such extent. For example, it was found that "the fastest electron" emitted by a body exposed to x-rays possesses precisely the same velocity as the fastest electron in the cathode beam that produces the x- rays.[47]

So, the subject and the object, the observer and the observed interact; it is not a simple reflection of one on the other. It is the interaction that helps us reach certain conclusions. The interactions create certain 'realities', which *may not be the realities in the absence of such an interaction.* The particle is a particle only for certain purposes and at certain levels (e.g. chemical reactions), and not at other ones; its independent existence, therefore, is in question.

Philosophy, Quantum Theory and 'Lighted' Knowledge

As we have seen, in the usual sense the world is not affected by the manner of our looking at it. It is out there, governed by its own laws, in motion in a deterministic manner.

But the world beyond the tangible one, the one of the micro-'reality', including of the quantum variety, *is* affected, and affected deeply, *by our observation, with and without instruments*. This is the fundamental difference when we transit from one world to the other. The nature of the object is definitely *affected*, and so also our worldview. The quantum theories are nothing but an attempt to account for and explain these effects, changes and resultant facts.

So, observation is change. The subject increasingly becomes part and parcel of the object. In other words, to observe and to understand means to explain the extent of this unity, its effects, merger, and the changes in the direction and nature of motion/s. To estimate the observed means to observe the observer too. The conscious being brings about a change in the sense that it forms one aspect or pole of unity. There is greater and greater identification of the polar opposition, literally speaking.

Why is it so? Because we meet a world of rapid motions.

So, the point, essentially, is whether we (our thought, consciousness, etc.) can comprehend high speeds. Our consciousness essentially has evolved in the course of slow speeds, slow motions and gradual evolution of material forms, as we have discussed particularly in the chapter on slowdown of motion. The ***whole of the conscious being*** is the result of slow-down. Never in the history of consciousness had it to confront high speeds; neither has it met with the micro-objects/processes. These speeds really remain outside its domain. They have hardly played a part in the consciousness-formation, or none at all. Any acceleration or *speed up of events* beyond a certain point needs statistical, mathematical, philosophical and other kinds of interventions, as also sophisticated instruments, in order to bring reality within comprehensive limits; comprehension not only that of matter, but also of space and time. Thus, here is the problem of the transition from classical to quantum reality, as also of philosophical generalisation of this transition.

At high and very high speeds, matter loses its material aspects and qualities. It more and more becomes 'energy', which better reflects the transformations at high motions. At those speeds and these shorter and shorter times, matter step by step loses its existing qualities and features. And this is the source of ***philosophical crisis***. The new reality is characterised by preciseness in certain aspects, and also by series of uncertainties, indeterminacy, and such other aspects.

The momentary nature of existence is the greatest problem of this giant step forward in comprehension of the world. This comprehension meets with a situation, which is complicated in the sense that it defies all the existing laws.

For, to comprehend is to follow the laws discovered, which act as guiding points for the process of cognition. These laws have been upset, chiefly because of high speeds. At those speeds, the laws just disintegrate. Yet new laws appear, but those laws are very temporary.

At this point, comprehension itself appears as comprehended. It is the consciousness about itself, in the sense that the particles and waves, of the object and the subject, unite and identify with each other. Comprehension is also one about the extent to which it disturbs/ modifies reality. Comprehension is the study of interaction between the subject and the object, with their traditional alignment disturbed. The relationship and the cognitive process reaches qualitatively new levels. Cognition is not only penetrating matter, but changing it while and in order to comprehend it and changing itself.

We are entering the domain of instability and rapid changes, and it is that domain we are to comprehend, not the thing as it is. The 'thing', as it is, is 'incomprehensible', not in the sense of agnosticism, but as it is in constant high-speed transformation, it is constantly ***quitting itself all the time***. Therefore, it is motion that is to be grasped. That grasping is ungrasping of everything else, of the history itself, history of particle, philosophy and consciousness. Matter does not only *have* motion, it is **converted** into motion (instant transformation endlessly). It leaves nothing that is a thing. We are more and more faced with discovering/dealing with motion and dialectics in matter. **We are having to discover motion as matter, rather than matter as and in motion.** Much more, it is to discover, to come face to face with, motion and dialectics in their purer and more abstract form. Motion and matter enter into new synthesis.

Energy is the precise manifestation of motion and conversions. Time is reduced to nothingness in the world of energy. The constants, the deviations, the uncertainties, the indeterminacies, constant additions and reductions, and simultaneously the great preciseness, point to the continued motions that come in contact with the process of cognition. We are bound to disturb these processes.

Lighted Knowledge: A Restricted Knowledge

Our existing knowledge/consciousness is based on a very narrow patch of lighted reality. Whatever we know emanates from a limited band of ***visible*** world, which is less than four percent of reality. Even our philosophical abstractions are grounded upon the 'world' as we have 'seen'. The instruments and apparatuses that we have developed in the course of the social development are also mostly based upon light and its seven wavelengths. It is only now that our instruments, tools and means have begun moving towards areas and wavelengths away from light. It is only now that we are entering the 'dark recesses' of reality/universe/atom. The non-lighted part of the world or the universe constitutes is more than 96 percent of that which exists. So, all our theories and concepts and notions have too narrow a base. No wonder, today we are rapidly having to revise all that.

It is interesting to note have that the light that lighted the reality for us for thousands of years, more particularly during the industrial age, itself now is quantised, 'lighting up' energy conversions. In a great unraveling of mystery, light is broken up into quanta, which interact with other quanta and energies.

So, reality is lighted up in a different way: it is quantum to quantum. The phenomenon changes all the existing concepts.

Our existing knowledge is based upon the information brought us by the reflected light. That is the essence of cognition, of cognition at least. Generalizations and speculations follow later. But lighting up is a continuous process. Without light, no concepts could be formed. Even the notions of space and time, of tangible things, are based on light. But there is a *total transformation* when it comes to the ***space and time of light!***

The Objectifier and The 'Third Factor'

What happens when light itself is reduced to waves and particles, and is transformed into space and time? What happens when the particle is turned into non-particle, into infinite space and time? The **objectifier** itself becomes dissociated, dissembled and transformed into space and time. This time ***it does not illumine something!*** For illumination, we need interaction.

Does it mean, here, that the light acts as a ***'third factor'***? Let us, for the present, suppose so: light must light up the object, and *create conditions for objectivity*. Light *simultaneously creates the subject/ subjectivity* (action on eyes, retina, optic nerve, brain, sensations, ideas and so on). Thus, *it also creates conditions for subjectivity*. Consequently, *two poles are created*, and they must reflect each other, particularly the active side (consciousness) must reflect the passive side (matter or object).

Thus, if there is darkness, there is no knowledge, consciousness. It is another matter that now we are penetrating darkness and reflecting it. But that is possible only after experience of dissociation of light, on the basis of the concepts born in and due to light. There can be no concept-creation in darkness; concepts about darkness are based on experiences in light. Hence the contradiction between the two.

But now the concept must be created in darkness by analysing (penetrating) it.

So, the 'third factor', which is also a material reality, particularly in relation to consciousness and subjectivity, has a special role of lighting up the reality for our experience and cognition. ***The third factor now must light up the light, the objectifier.*** This is a 'triad' in certain sense, but *not really*. It exists independently, but its only job is to 'light up'. But now it can light up only as quanta. Only then consciousness can form, and cognition can proceed. Light has a peculiar, special role to play here, it lights matter to enable the concept of 'matter' to emerge. Otherwise, we would be in complete dark, literally. Brain receives reflected matter, and consciousness (subjectivity) is the result of reflected, seemingly non-reflected, and un-reflected parts of reality (matter).

Consciousness is the function of brain. Therefore, it can 'look' at dark spaces too. But, for this, lighted spaces are essential. Light creates light about darkness, about the unseen, the unseeable.

So, what is the function of light? It causes the contradiction between subject and object, matter and consciousness, and acts as the site of the solution of this contradiction. It the process it itself is dissociated in quanta and stretched out into infinity through waves. A wavelength is both a microscopic speck and limit of the limit, and at the same time it is infinite, the bundle of contradictions: the moment we try to catch the contradiction, it has already travelled millions of kilometres!

The duality is resolved at 3 lakh (3 00 000) kms per second!

This is the reason why almost all our knowledge pertains to the lighted part of the world. Very little is known about the dark areas. What happens when we enter the particulate and quantum levels?

In the course of cognition, we enter (consciousness enters) deeper levels of matter. Cognition, subject-object, consciousness-matter relations become complex. Do we still need light to 'see', to conceptualise, to cognise? It is interesting to note that we still very much need light. Microscopes of increasing magnification need light. Other equipment too.

It is, at the same time, also interesting to note that this light increasingly breaks up, dissociates into waves and particles, which become the new terrain of cognition. History of observation at this level has been that of transitions of light and radiations into waves and particles. So, light lights up reality in a different way. It breaks it up into quanta, giving rise to quantum interactions and quantum reality, which is in fact the result of these interactions.

We thus enter into a different world, a world, which for us is a break up of the existing reality. Hence the need to redefine this different world, the different reality, or no 'reality' at all.

The new reality is the conversion of the material particles into energy x time particles, an expression of extreme motions. Light reflects (lights up) this reality, not by getting reflected as it is, but by *interacting* with it; it is a world of interactions, quick changes and momentary existences; it is not a world of fixed and tangible successions of tangible objects; it is not the world of things and objects. Matter is reduced to distances where event cannot take place, at least as of now. A qualitative change has taken place. Fixed existences, the existence, the thing or things, tangibility is not the order. They have simply disappeared as mere superficial appearances or end results of something deeper, of deep processes of interactions and transformation.

What we have been seeing, dealing with, throughout our i.e. human, history has been the end results, confirming that knowledge begins from the end results, from the past, as in case of our observation of stars, the product of thousands and millions of years reaching us as the given

Matter (particle, thing) breaks up into energy packets, radiation, quanta, and to see it, we need a different function of light (and such other radiations).

Light continues to discharge its function of enabling observation, but now it is interactive with the object, and we have to calculate the results of the interaction in order to reach certain results of our observation i.e. of interaction between the incident light and the object. Therefore, *observation is interaction.*

The position of the observer is also unique. The apparatus and the human eye and brain are made up of the same particles, and therefore *the subject also is interactive with the object.* The particles of the apparatus interact with the observed particles, and therefore it is the interaction that the apparatus and the observation catch hold of.

Thus, here we have s system of the object, the subject and the illuminating source that constitute the reality, *a constantly interacting reality.* The dividing lines between them are dwindling. The formation of idea and consciousness takes place increasingly as part and parcel of existence. Consciousness becomes more dispersed in the objectivity; it is not outside the object and objectivity but increasingly part of them. Subject and subjectivity more and more move towards unity and identity with object and objectivity. Subjectivity argues as to the nature of knowledge obtained because it is not as such but the nature of light that illumes and drives consciousness. With the entry into the quantum world and the outer spaces, light is hardly required; it is now the dark/darker areas that light our knowledge. Knowledge is about that which is not visible light but only waves, particles, energy conversions, etc. Reality acquires similarities with the inner-most processes in the brain, and vice-versa.

There are two major ways in which we obtain our knowledge without light. One is to look at the wavelengths beyond the visible light with the help of new instruments. We use wavelengths on both sides of light, and the various radiations. We also look into the growing depths of the 'atom'. Second, we have dissociated light and other radiations into wave/particle duality. This is a 'dark' world, needing no light to 'light up' the 'objects'. We have begun to look into and construct a whole universe made up of the socalled 'dark' matter, black holes, particles, waves, gravitational and other fields, and so on. The unlighted world has its own structures and processes, *and it is for the first time that we are really looking into and inside the universe.*

So, ***we are entering 'the 96 per cent' part of the reality for the first time in human history.*** Consciousness is on the verge of fundamental and qualitative transformation. It is **the first time** that we are consciously making a bid for 'total knowledge', for the 'hundred per cent'!

Reality acquires similarities with the innermost processes in the brain, and vice-versa: this similarity is a problem because it does away with differences and creates differences in similarities. These differences can only result due to high speeds. There are the speeds that unite the various aspects and elements of cognition discussed earlier. Their qualitatively different natures, which posed a problem for the history of consciousness and philosophy, are resolved or are sought to be resolved though identity and inversion, i.e. movement/conversion of matter into space and time. Matter moves but jettisons space and time, losing its own identity in the process, acquiring a new identity as specks or moments on the vastness of spreading out space and time.

When we are talking of space and time here out of matter, what do we mean? The vast spread, sheets and congregations as well as thin dispersals of space are endless, interminable energy conversions into so many 'events' that we are unable to catch them. They are no more the 'matter' from which we began our journey. They are more happenings/events through extraordinary dialectics and motion in which no material forms can exist. Time is but local slowdowns here and there, coming out form of planets and nebulae. Time is also an event measurement, yet time is unable to measure them. Therefore, it loses its succession.

Time is now only the moment of expression in the infinite spaces. These spaces are curved, turned, concentrated and dispersed, bent and so on. But, still they do not constitute the property of a three-dimensional reality. It has come out of that reality. To investigate matter is first to convert it into space and time. Space and time only consist of conversions, no results of conversions, no histories, no stability. History here has to end as history of matter and move as multi-directional processes in form of specks of energy conversions, new beginnings, new 'histories', both micro and macro, going back and forth, made of extremely fleeting existences. ***Electrons move backwards in time the moment they move forward and vice-versa;*** the same with most of the other particles and waves. It all depends on where we are placed and what is our frame of reference.

Matter can exist only when the energy x time conversions and wave propagations rise towards and to the surface, the 'surface' of 'calm reality', of which we are the part and from which we have sprung forth, imparting stability as slow-down of conversions. It is only when the conversions/processes slowdown that 'we' emerge to look upon the light reality, majestic in its lighted expanses!

Stability is the conversion of conversions into something. This stability, this *ceasing* (relatively speaking; actually an extraordinary slowdown) of motions gives rise to the tangible nature of existence. Time congeals here. Space becomes part of our selves and existence becomes three-dimensional. Its fourth dimension, time, is so slow that it becomes the measure and the indicator. Motion is the disruptor, the tearing asunder of source of cognition, and dialectics is the source of this motion. Motion at first cannot be cognised as motion. It must be turned into its opposite to be part of our consciousness. Only then we enter, first the process of motion and then the world of motions, through dialectics of several orders. Consciousness falls into itself at high motions, and therefore is detached from itself and from reality. Philosophy comes into conflict with motion, and therefore with time. Particle indicates the very limit of philosophy, beyond which its (latter's) subject-matter must change. *Time is antithetical to matter*, for it drives away speculation, stability and the concepts, the whole host of them.

History, Philosophy, Particle and Beyond it into Conversions

The question of relationship of space and time with philosophy has never been clear and never been comfortable. Today, philosophy has once more been thrown into an uncomfortable position.

What should philosophy, and thought in general, base itself upon? Suppose, as we have discussed at one place earlier, 'atom' is our object of investigation and at the same time the goal we hope 'finally' to reach. But as we approach it, it disintegrates or begins to convert into cloud of waves or simply dissociates or moves back! In other words, it is inapproachable. It also reverses back in time.

How does philosophy construct the world then? The concept of construction as well as of the 'atom' or the particle itself undergoes crisis.

Thus, there is alround philosophical and thought related crisis. Philosophy itself is *in deepest of crisis* ever.

The methodological problem is that we must approach something all the time. Philosophy disintegrates as it approaches the particle/wave duality, and is surrounded by a world obtaining inside the particle. We are surrounded by electromagnetic and other waves. The question is, the *problem* is, that the particle is the wave, the wave is particle, and therefore it is a world of contradictory *conversions.*

The conversions are rapid, instant, and contradictory. That leaves no space (possibility) for history. History is the basis for philosophy, because the latter must have time for speculation, and space for succession, for basing itself.

The present-day accelerators probe distances as small as $\mathbf{10^{-16}}$ **cm,** which is *a thousand times smaller* than proton's diameter. At these distances, electrons display pure-field scattering. If the electron has any size at all, it is smaller than it is possible to measure at all!

So, what does philosophy 'philosophize' about at such tiny distances and time: a time that does not exist, and space that is elusive. Yet, such a mathematical point becomes converted into infinite waves, which become one with space, with dots momentarily display themselves as constitution of that which does not exist! Because to exist means to momentarily slowdown time.

Conversions are particular *forms of transcendence.* At these distances and in those moments, reality becomes both momentary and infinite.

We become part of it, and only then can we philosophise. To philosophise is not about something alone, but in something. Motions continually overcome us and ***prevent us from building up anything.*** Therefore, to philosophise is to do so about motions and conversions. The particle has turned out to be a bundle of time and its immediate negation. The notion of the particle, and of everything, *prevents* it to be itself. Therefore, it is wrong to think of a particle except as its disintegration, conversion and infinite spread. A particle can only be thought of, not as present, but only as a future. And that which is not is yet to be because it is already gone. Among such processes, we (consciousness) are all the time yet to be; when it should be, it is already past.

It is as good as to consider the whole existence as one particle. To think is to immerse oneself. Cognition can only take place with full identification with that which cannot be cognised, because that we cognise transforms into cognition-in-motion.

So, we are all the time catching hold of the ***past and future.*** Events have crossed, and we interfere and create new events. The result can only be a past. They are transmitted, no doubt, at light speed, but the light speed only brings out the events or their results of microseconds. It is not a question of what is taking place, it is a question what *has* (*already*) taken place, and that amounts to ***millions of years in micro seconds.***

Dialectics of Dialectics and Philosophy

When we try to grasp a particle, or mathematical point synonym with a cloud of waves, we are grasping already that which has been left behind, a vacuum, an exact replica of what was there! What else can happen at the infinite division of a second at dozens of decimal points of space. To talk of the mathematical point is talk *of the past*, and thus of the history, *that history which is not.* It makes, creates, leaves behind history by not making history at all, because it does not exist in any time and space for any length of time and space to really claim history. For history is succession of events, but there neither succession, nor events, only the event of non-event. And therefore further movements have only so many possibilities and possible and real conversions. Motion kills history, freeing itself as pure dialectics.

It does leave us histories in form of probabilities of events, with present merging totally with the future. It is about this history that we are forced to philosophize.

Dialectics and philosophy stand in direct opposition to each other. They both part ways and merge with each other. Philosophy is elevated both as the non-philosophical and as absolute philosophy: it is to philosophise about something which now occurs as nothing, transiting into something through pure motion, because we have been so dialectical that it is impossible for something to be something and exist. This is purest reason at thins level of cognition.

Philosophy has for the first time to station itself upon attributes of matter such as time and space, and not matter as such.

So, what is the world made of? The answer to it now, at this stage of development of science, technology and knowledge becomes less certain. A transition is made from certainty to uncertainty, in relative terms. World is made of certain things and process, which get deconstructed and dissociated as we proceed further into the deeper levels of matter. What we know for certainty, for well-defined laws, particles and waves, are at deeper levels unmade, become inapplicable. A world of rapid conversions, motions and transformations lies inside the deeper layers of relative calm, fixed structures, slow motions.

Therefore, philosophy makes a transition to dialectics. Motions go beyond the control and limits of matter and concepts.

The world consists increasingly of rapid motions, conversions, waves, temporary particles, time, space, etc. It is a world dominated by relativity. It is a world, in which nothing is fixed. Therefore, we cannot say that it is made of this or that, of anything or things fixed in nature. It would be wrong to look at this world from the vantage point of our world. We face or enter a world where our fixed concepts are more and more losing their meaning or are totally inapplicable.

It is a world wherein the observer is part and parcel of the processes. Therefore, we understand it through that which transcends the immediate, through generalisations and mathematical relationships. It is a world of uncertainties.

It will take a long, long time for us to come out of the classical world. We and our subjectivity have been formed and have evolved in a classical and natural world. It will take a long time to merge with and assimilate the new reality, if that word is still valid. It is the first time that we are really entering the world of abstracts; these abstracts discharge the functions of generalising and transcending motions. The subject looks at, grasps the world in a different way: as momentariness, as motions, as becoming something else all the time. It is momentary only from the point of the classical disunity and imbalance between the object and the subject. In fact, every moment is infinite in itself, has its own infinite time direction, uniting at certain points to come up with material structures.

Hegelian motion and being come alive in this world. It is the world of becoming and absorption of the future in the process. Mind constructs abstract and mathematical constructs to grasp and assimilate the continued radiation, which is an extension of time and space.

At this level what idea grasps is numbers, relations, and time and space. We are dealing with the spread and momentariness of matter. We deal with time, a world made up of time and timelessness, wherein mind becomes a receptacle for infinity because of the separation of time out of reality. *We cannot escape this conclusion.* It is a conclusion that is inconclusive. Mind's receptacle is limited because of its history, but it is unlimited because it enters *new history, a history which is non-historical.* Development is taking place in all possible directions and without directions, independent of time with endless kinds of time in and with limitless space. We meet with the reversion of history, rather of historicity, when we jettison the world as it existed. And therefore, we cannot talk of history in the outer spaces. The outer space is full of conflicting histories. The old, existing world is an opposite world, a world at the other pole, which *contains* contradictions and evolves with and due to them. The new world releases contradictions, lets them play with motions, and they contribute to and cause the world.

The cognitive process of the subject, of the self, **unites and identifies** more and more with the world of motions and its results. That is the commonness between the two. Mind and being begin to identify, having created a history of contradictions. World turns into a mental creation, *not in the sense of mental product*, but in the sense of **derivations** of interactions and generalisations. A mind grasping three lakh kms and one second encompasses a whole history in a moment and therefore congeals past, present and future. The problem with brain and its idea/s is the past. In that sense, for the first time, in reality, millions of years have been compressed into a second and parts thereof. Having compressed time, massive spaces are released/covered. It is the first time that the mind is released of limitations and becomes infinite. It identifies itself with the ethereal processes of the world of time and space.

To grasp this new world, the tangible, material limits have to be jettisoned. This almost certainly will be misunderstood in many ways. The point is that the earthly limits put a limit on our understanding, and therefore it has to go out of these limits. That is why the limits of history have to be done away with. History is limitation in both time and space.

To do away with time and space is to unite and identify with them. Matter has always been *the limit* of knowledge, the unknown mysterious factor, which has always been finite. Therefore, infinity has been the domain mainly of philosophy.

Now, philosophy faces endless new problems, including that of its identity. It has to redefine and re-invent itself. Human beings since ages have been trying to find meaning of reality and existence, being and non-being, matter and spirit, subject-object relation, of idea and consciousness, of motion and dialectics, transcendence, meaning of self, and so on and so forth.

There is no independent existence of matter because all matter is converted into energy and radiation; yet this existence is totally independent, our brain and consciousness being just a speck of congealed matter. The distances in the space are too vast and time taken to measure (cover) them too big (too small) to allow them conversion into matter and consciousness. It is all history, which is under constant demolition. **None** exist as existence; they all *exist* as *non-existence, converting all the time.* Motion exists as conversion from one into another; one is the other. We can't even identify, say 'one' and 'another', 'something', 'this', 'that' and so on. They simply do not exist out in spatial infinity, being dissolved in an instant and in the instant. Being is absolutised as non-being. Non-being does not mean non-existence. It simply means overcoming of all the momentary existences into a moment, which simply exists for us human beings, because it then absolutises itself for us. It is absolutised as space and time, which are derivatives of the world for the world of our consciousness. *The world needs all the time to be converted, translated, into another world for and through our consciousness.*

Spirit, the consciousness must move rather than catch hold, and thus encompass as and in the moment of concept (idea, a 'particle' of consciousness), the entire reality, too unreal for us. Our mental tools are *too inadequate* for the vastness of space and the moment of time.

Why this contradiction? *Because the space is too unlimited for the too limited a consciousness.* Our ideas and concepts lie in and upon time and space of a very limited nature. Our time and space is limited by idea and matter. Can we philosophize about the great conversions of nebulae and galaxies that reach us today, when consciousness has become too conscious of its limitless limits? The galaxies and stars exploding all the time are not stars and galaxies we were familiar with; *for they never exploded till now!* Till now, we simply looked at the stars. For them to explode, a whole phase of social development, leaps of science and technology, and new consciousness was needed. Consequently, the present of the stars has become the past, and the growth and development of consciousness enables us (it) to cover longer distances in shorter time; thus, we uncover the past by dissociating the star/s into waves, particles, time and space, and in that way we dissect philosophy itself. The more we move towards stars and nebulae as they had appeared to us earlier, the more we dissect them and the more they disappear into dualities. This is the conflict of consciousness.

This characteristic, among others, is due to light. Our consciousness has always been lighted. Light and philosophy/ worldview has always been inter-related. While light has caused stable conceptualization, its dissociation into dualities destabilizes concepts and conceptualization. With the dissociation and break up of light philosophy disappears. A new worldview appears that emanates from and sinks into the space and time conversions.

Stability is light, and light is stability. A star is fixed in space, unchanging, ever-existing. Hence the 'fixed' nature of our consciousness. Such a star does not bring us consciousness of distance (space) and of timelessness of time, its infinity, the temporariness of existence. Gazing stars fixes time and space. This idea of space and time is just opposite in the conditions of the planet earth. In reality, the star is not fixed at all; it is the hot-bed of mind-boggling transformations, a boiling pot of matter and energy. That is why we have to unfix our consciousness in order to and in the course of our approach to the star.

Light reveals a certain falsity about itself that springs from our social base. Our observation of light is social, and therefore as if through a prism. It takes really a long time to reveal the object in scientific manner, clearing layers of misconceptions and upside down images. It is a disjoint in our observation, and when light reveals itself, it breaks up into space and time, packets and waves and energy transfers. The lighted object is really distanced from us when it is revealed that light travels at 3 lakh km/sec. These kilometres and seconds bring home the vastness of space and the remoteness of the observed. *The object breaks up.* The object had been created out of a mis-observation, through ignoring space and time. We attributed wrong space and wrong time to the star. It is now destabilised, when we are really approaching it, revealing its real vastness and the giant transformations taking place on and inside its surface. It is dissociated into infinities and endless momentary events.

Light consists of the unlighted and the unlighting. It radiates all sorts of radiations; in fact light is but ***the best expression of the dark.***

When we are talking of the lighted and unlighted parts of the world, we are first talking of the visible and non-visible parts of light waves or spectrum. It is the seven wavelengths or colours that light up the material reality. The rest are also wavelengths and radiation, but they do not light up. The non-visible wavelengths make transition to the visible and act as the source of idea. The non-visible part is unable to light up, and therefore is useless as far as our primary knowledge at the initial stages are concerned. Certain levels of social development must take place before non-visible light participates in idea-formation. Thus, the non-visible light has till now virtually *no role in the social development.* Most of the social development has taken place in the visible light and with reference to it. This is a negative side of social development, being revealed now.

At this point, the wave nature of light becomes clear. Only certain waves are suitable for us as *social beings* as well as biological beings. It is a particular level of energy pack and 'work done' by them that help create new consciousness. Thus, radiation and different parts of its spectrum become involved in social evolution at varying stages. We are in the midst of shifting from the social to the universal.

Visible light is unlimited in possibilities of social, biological, and other kinds of evolution. Yet, it acts as a great **limiting factor** in the growth of our ideas, thought and consciousness. The way the visible and non-visible parts of spectrum play a role in the formation of consciousness are quite contradictory and opposed. They are opposites in the treatment of almost every category. The radiation as light first creates our consciousness of matter, and the same light through the invisible past demolishes that very consciousness (concept). The consciousness reaches new levels of negation.

Light provides us with the solidity and tangibility of the world. The same light demolishes it as quantum and as non-visibility. *Non-visible light poses a challenge for our existing concepts and for our existing society.* Our visible concepts have been shown to be flawed, and in comparison with the rest of the world (1. outside the earth conditions, 2. in the atomic and outer spaces), upside down. Our concepts about space, time and matter have turned out to be flawed.

We stand at the turn of a new social development so that we can comprehend the new world.

NOTES

1. A.S. Eddington *The Nature of the Physical World,* The Gifford Lectures, 1927, MacMillan and Cambridge, New York, 1929, p. 286.
2. Ibid., p. 290.
3. Ibid.
4. David Bohm, *Causality and Chance in Modern Physics*, Routledge, 2008, p. 92.
5. Ibid., emphasis in the original.
6. Bertrand Russell, *Our Knowledge of the External World,* Routledge, 2006, p. 110.
7. Based on Bohm, *Causality*...etc. p. 121.
8. Bertrand Russell, *ABC of Relativity*, Routledge, 2007, p. 144.
9. Ibid, p. 150, emphasis in the original.

10. See Bohm, *Causality...* etc. 122.
11. Ibid., pp. 122-23.
12. Ibid., p. 123.
13. See, ibid., p. 125.
14. Ibid.
15. Ibid., pp. 43-45.
16. Ibid., pp. 46-47.
17. Ibid., p. 69.
18. Partly based on Bohm, ibid., p. 72.
19. See, ibid., p. 73.
20. Based on Bohm, pp. 73-74.
21. See, ibid., p. 73, emphasis in the original.
22. Sir James Jeans, *The Mysterious Universe*, Pelican Books, 1938, p. 57.
23. Ibid., p. 148.
24. Ibid., 149-50.
25. Based on ibid., p. 41.
26. See, Sir Oliver Lodge, *Beyond Physics*, 1930, pp. 118-19, etc.
27. Lodge, ibid., p. 126.
28. Ibid., p. 126.
29. Ibid., p. 128.
30. David Bohm, *op.cit.*, pp. 74-75.
31. Bohm, pp. 76-77.
32. Ibid., p. 77.
33. Ibid., p. 77.
34. Ibid., p. 77.
35. Ibid., pp. 77-78.
36. Ibid., p. 78.
37. Ibid., p. 78.
38. Ibid., p. 78.
39. Ibid., p. 78, emphasis added.
40. Based on Lee Smolin, *The Trouble with Physics*, Allen Lane, 2006, p. 6.
41. Based on Bohm, *Causality...* etc., pp. 81-83.
42. Ibid., p. 83.
43. Ibid., pp. 83-84.
44. Ibid., p. 84, footnote.
45. Bertrand Russell, *Our Knowledge of the External World,* p. 109.
46. Ibid., p. 110.
47. Bruce R. Wheaton, *The Tiger and the Shark: Empirical Roots of Wave–Particle Dualism,* Cambridge University Press, 1991, p. 265.

9

Quantum World and Concept of Matter

What is matter in a world of the most rapid changes? In such a world, it is near impossible to lay hands on anything, identify 'objects' and processes, keep track of the events, their direction and nature, their histories, and generally to understand what is going, except through extremely involved calculations and deductions about 'what exists out there'. That is the world of exceedingly rapid transformations, where nothing is stationary even for a micro-second; every'thing' is momentary, even fleeting, almost just a 'pop out' in a vast ocean of dark space, a space or spaces that are bent, curved, twisted and what not.

There is an epistemological error in the posing of the problem/ question: 'what exists out there?' or 'what is reality?' or 'what is particle?' etc. as far as quantum world is concerned. Such questions regarding 'what' presuppose certain picture or notion of reality formed over centuries and millennia. As we have come to know by now, nothing really can *exist* 'out there' because it is not a world of stability, tangibility and things, and therefore of 'existence'. It does not mean that there 'nothing' there, but the word 'exists' or 'reality' has to have many qualifications and riders. These qualifications go on increasing as we go deeper into matter. The deeper and farther we go into matter, the lesser the words like 'existence' etc. applicable. Nothing remains there as it is; there is nothing which can be *described as being there*, which we have to catch and comprehend. It really becomes almost impossible 'describe' at that level. Existence and reality can only be very broad and general concepts; only the concepts of abstract nature can cover what exists out there. But they too break up as soon as thought tries to approach the 'concrete' reality.

Actually, thought is habituated to contemplate concrete things; it cannot exist without concreteness. The historical development of thought and thought process has been such that it cannot do without a reality which must be seen and shown. The entire philosophy, thought and theories are based and developed upon things that can be shown or seen. Eyes and sight have had a major role in the development of consciousness. Other sense organs too have contributed significantly to the process of cognition. Besides, as we know too well, tools, implements and equipment have a decisive role in the evolution of consciousness.

But this consciousness has a limited nature, in a certain sense. It is unable to encompass motion to any considerable degree. The minuteness and motion are in direct contrast to the human consciousness. Actually human consciousness can either contemplate abstractly or concretely. It cannot comprehend or assimilate abstractness having passed through concreteness. Science, having taken the human consciousness on a tour of the concrete reality and its various forms, makes it nearly impossible for the consciousness to generalize on the basis of endless concrete realities. Consciousness can encompass motion in its abstract form and abstractedly, but it is very difficult for it to deal with the concrete abstractions, with the real infinite forms that transit from the concrete to the abstract, from the tangible to the intangible.

As a result, human consciousness has entered *a period of crisis*, where it is next to impossible to build the world on the basis of intangibility. The past and present and history of the evolution of thought become *a hurdle* to assimilation of reality that is not reality as 'it should be', a reality that has lost its concreteness and tangibility. The concepts are destroyed or broken up, and new concepts cannot be formed and made stable on new basis that easily.

Consider this. The wavelengths of red light vary between 610 and 700 nanometres (nm). An nm is one billionth of a metre. The red light of 700 nm has a frequency of 430 trillion oscillations per second. At the other end of the spectrum, violet light ranges from

400 to 450 nm, with the shorter wavelength having a frequency of 750 trillion oscillations per second.[1]

So, what is the 'reality' at these speeds and scales? What is it like? What exists and how? You try to catch the moment and the waves have already traveled 3 lakh kms after a second, some 400 or 700 trillion oscillations have already gone out of your grasp, if at all they were in your grasp! So, what you measure or grasp is not some particular thing or tangible 'matter' but motion, the sweep of conversions and change; and increasingly so. In the microworld, a second covers a massive change or changes, a whole world of it own kind. Of what kind, we do not yet know. Can we imagine travel *from* one particle *to* another? It is *impossible*, because firstly, the concept of one point to another is a classical philosophical and physical one; secondly, there do not exist 'this' point and 'that and that one', etc. or 'a particle'. They come into being and disappear in no time before you think. The two points or the particles do not exist really; they non-exist and disappear instantly and constantly. In the sub-atomic and quantum world, *the particle does not exist*; this has to be understood. It comes into being *as a condition* of the motion and existence of the wave. It is only an expression, an assertion in the reverse that the wave does exist *in so far as* the particle does not. A particular particle, electron or photon, can never be seen again; we can never again come across the same particle, wave, etc.

The particle has always been a philosophical and conceptual *tag*, with whose help we try to cover and explain certain phenomena for a time. The event disappears, the concept remains, which is as unsure of itself as the particle itself. The concept hangs on to the particle like the very dear life which is about to go out of itself! World is not, really speaking, made up of the particles; it is non-made of the particles. This continuous unmaking of the 'particle' is what makes, constitutes the world. Unmaking is really the making. That which goes away instantly constitutes the world, the universe. The particle is simply a way into that world where particle does not exist, being a constant non-being. It is the future that constitutes the present, which therefore is empty because the future is the reality, the existence. Therefore the *reality is the world of constant futurisation*, the rise of which creates the concepts. This world cannot live in the present because the present is the death of it. The dialectics of this motion does not allow it.

So we must all the time deal with what is to be and not with what is; even then the whole reality cannot be comprehended. It is because it is a reality that is unlike reality. 'What is to be' constitutes the reality and consciousness and its making.

What are these waves made of, the waves of say light? Quantum science says they are made of erg-seconds, that is, the result of multiplication of certain energy in certain amount of time. We have already dealt with it elsewhere. They are packets or quanta of some kind of energy, in common human understanding. That is how the quantum world is made. Very quick changes in the shortest possible time, not even 'split second', much less than that.

So the world is made of what exactly? Of particles, waves, both, something tangible or non-tangible or only motions and so on? It is obvious that as we enter the world inside the atom or go out into the vast spaces, it is not the same that we have been familiar with so far in our history and the present. It is also obvious that the rules, laws, methods of observations, laws of existence and reality etc., all that we have been familiar with are no more applicable or less and less so. This 'reality' almost coincides with non-reality, a non-reality of what we have so far been used to.

We cannot hope to proceed even a little unless we are able to answer as to what constitutes matter and material 'objects' out there. Physicists and scientists have shown that there exists wave/particle duality in the microworld. This is a dialectical unity of what exists as the contradictory transformations, or rather what non-exists. Yes, it will be better to use the word 'transformations' to describe the processes in that world. It is a 'flip/flap' world, as if oscillating all the time.

What is particle, for example? We will remind that we have talked elsewhere about spheres or balls, or of dust particles when we think and talk of even the minutest 'particles'. And we are used to think of water or sound waves. A tennis ball and such other things are very convenient because they have clear-cut limits, length, shape and size, etc. It is in similar vein that we try to think of particles. In fact, the atoms of chemical reactions are more in tune with this kind of description.

But then enter the quantum and everything collapses! Simply disappears!

Scientists have found that beyond a certain limit, the electron cannot be measured. It begins to elude attempts to measure its speed or size or position or structure. Great scientists like Niels Bohr, Max Born, Heisenberg, Wolfgang Pauli and many other outstanding ones faced these and related problems. As a result they had to take recourse to several theories as to the nature of quantum particles and waves. We need not go into those complexities, at least now, except sometimes mentioning them.

When they really tried to catch hold of the particle, it simply disappeared. Some of them found, as they approached the electron, that it was looking like a cloud. Of what? Of waves. The nearer you approached, the greater the number of waves and fuzziness. It was as if the particle was oscillating like a string. That is because the electron was in a state of energy conversions. When it gives up one state for another, it releases gains some energy or particle. So conversions lead to gain or loss of energy.

The atom is as porous as the solar system itself.[2] *This tells us volumes about the concept of matter.* Reality is made of particles/waves or empty spaces? What is its significance? If all the empty spaces in the human body were filled in with the particles like electron and proton etc. in the body itself, the human being would be reduced to a speck just visible with a magnifying glass![3]

What is the meaning of the energy? The energy radiated during the discontinuous emission from sodium atom is found to be 3.4×10^{-12} ergs. It has a distinctive period of 1.9×10^{-15} seconds. On multiplication we obtain 6.55×10^{-27} erg-seconds[4], as we have seen . That is the universal quantity *h*. Take any source of light, e.g. hydrogen, calcium or any other atom; the amount of energy and the time period would be different but their multiplication will produce the same number! It is a constant. We have discussed it earlier.

How does it affect our observation? Suppose light has emanated from somewhere and reached an observer, a person standing at some point on the earth surface 8 years later. Light enters his eyes, hits his retina. How? The light has already covered billions of miles. Yet when it enters the retina, it does so very precisely: *it must enter as a single quantum of action h*, that is 6.55×10^{-27} erg-seconds, *not more, not less.*[4]

This event tells us a lot of things. We will not go into everything. But we have seen the interaction between the human eye and the quantum particle. It is because of such an interaction that we are able to 'see'. This is another material process, in which a classical system and a quantum system are involved. That itself is a field of investigation, and there are lots of interpretations of such interactions.

Classical and Quantum States

Suppose there are two balls, white and black, kept in boxes. If we knew their colour, we can tell about the white one after seeing the black ball. There is no doubt or ambiguity about it. So even if we are not looking at the white or the black ball, we are sure about the particular color or whatever other characteristic. The experimenter or the observer simply infers one from the other.

This is a 'classical' viewpoint. But in the quantum state, the things are different. Suppose two particles, electron and positron, are produced by the decay of a single particle, which does not have a spin. These two move directly outwards in opposite directions Each of them has half a spin, and must add up to zero. There is a surprising implication here. When we measure the spin of the electron in one direction we choose, the positron must spin in the opposite direction! The two particles could even be light years away![5]

Wave-particle Duality: Best Example of Dialectics of Nature

We keep talking about particle and wave, without giving much thought to the implications. While dealing with particle e.g. electron and its behaviour, we often reach, unconsciously and imperceptibly, a point where we begin to speak of waves, and vice-versa. In fact, the history of modern science and physics in particular is full of the controversies around whether matter is constituted of waves or of particles. Scientists have received acclaims and prizes, including the Nobel Prize for discovering one or the other of them. Yet at some point of time it has been found that matter is both at the same time.

We have seen that light can behave as particle at one time and as a wave at another; so also an electron. More, any radiation, light or electron or any other is **both** wave and particle **at the same time.** The best example of this duality and dialectical existence is the famous and fundamental experiment known as Young's experiment, also known as two-slit experiment, described elsewhere.

A single particle behaves as waves when confronted with two slits and as a particle when faced with one slit! *Thus one particle passes through two slits simultaneously!* The experiment reflects the very nature of the quantum world.

The point is that the wave, particle, wavelength, energy, conversion, exchange, etc. exist *as one another*. Every wavelength is a unit in itself, and thus acts as a quantum. A particular length and amplitude of the wave can be measured as fixed. It leads to the discovery of the constant 'h', which is fixed for all the elements, with the energy and time varying. The radiations *resolve* themselves into fixed quanta. The spatial continuity, i.e. the wave is resolved into temporal discontinuity i.e. the quantum.

Louis de Broglie reinterpreted a study published in 1919 by Marcel Brillouin, who wished to show how an electron moving along a continuous periodic orbit could be explained by discontinuous quantum laws. Brillouin was following a hypothesis by Vito Volterra that under certain circumstances, a 'hereditary' field is established by a moving particle. According to Brillouin a particle moved through a medium with a velocity greater than that of the waves in the medium. He had in mind the quasi-periodic motion of an electron constrained by the Coulomb force of the atomic nucleus to remain within a certain space. It was imagined that a spherical wave arose from the electron at the start of its periodic motion. At the end of the period, the electron must still lie within the sphere to which the wave has expanded. The particle moves faster than the wave and does not simply leave the wave behind. Under these special circumstances, the particle catches up at regular intervals with the waves it produces in moving through the medium.[6]

Consequently, an electron circling a nucleus creates a series of imaginary points trailing in its wake. From each of these points a spherical wave, emitted when the electron was there, would catch up with the electron at the same instant as all the rest. The hereditary field thus established embodies one possible past history of the particle.[7] When de Broglie presented his fusion of particle and wave, he did it not for the light quantum but for a particle of matter. For example, if we consider a particle moving past two observers with uniform velocity, one observer watches for the quantum-wave effects of the moving point, the other notices only the relativistic effects of the point oscillator. De Broglie suggested that the first observer is seeing not the wave effects of the particle itself but rather than those of an associated plane wave travelling in the same direction as the particle.[8] A stationary observer will measure a lower frequency than a moving one when a particle travels with certain velocity.[9]

Nature of Electron

An electron is being created all the time in the universe, when two or more waves meet together, *creating an amplitude*, resulting in a 'standing wave', which we have discussed in the earlier chapters. This can happen both when the waves go out and come into, for example, the atom or meet outside. Waves of what? Of energy.

That means, what is created temporarily and accidentally is taken by us as permanent, stable, though with changes and motion; yet we want it to be repetitive, for we want the 'world' to be stable, evolving but stable, subject to our easy interpretations. This is the contradiction of thought, the limitation of the brain, more particularly of ideas/concepts. Since we exist, the idea or the concept too must exist, which only means, for us, no change or little if at all, even while we do want to say that world changes. Therefore, the change should be within our 'control'; otherwise it, the world, goes out of our history, and thus becomes non-history and incomprehensible. Unless something exists, how can we explain, *understand*? Thus thought sets a limit to the unlimitedness so that it can understand. Comprehension must have a human limit, the limitless limit, because we are limited in every way but we do not want our thoughts to be so. Yet we want them to be limited to concepts so that we exist! We always try to conceptualize, that is, to set limits; reality and existence also prove to be such pre-conditions. They are transformed into concepts, thus limited to our will.

Now this reality undergoes crucial and fundamental changes. What had been stable so far is now rendered unstable. The basic building blocks of the world, the tangible and solid foundations are now found to be highly unstable and intangible. We cannot escape this new reality. It is not the reality of tennis balls or rocks or even of solid atoms. We have reached a stage of knowledge where there are no basic or building blocks *any more*. The solidity and particularity lose their nature into momentary and temporary processes. We cannot identify or label anything. We can label groups of even micro-organisms, we can identify genes and its constituents. But we cannot really 'identify' electrons, quanta, particles or waves. That stage is past.

The contradiction and the resultant cognitive break is that an extremely unstable reality becomes a 'building block' or basis for the expression of highly stable material reality! This is an unprecedented development leading to *a progressive and revolutionary crisis in human thought.* The particle is no more there as we proceed further in our quest of nature. Particle can no more be taken as the basis and as one of the constituents of nature. It and other 'constituents' become unstable as the representations of pure motion. As we have seen, we enter the world of rapid motions of processes which are hardly 'in existence' for fleeting micro-seconds. We can identify 'objects' even and measure their properties even at the chemical and biological levels but not at the universal level. Thus it is motion that 'constitutes' the electron as a highly transitory alignment of waves. The particle is the result of the combination of waves of energy; at least that is how it is expressed.

Now, the point is that our concept of the material reality and matter has to change drastically. The concepts of time, space, reality etc., have all to change. What we are meeting with are temporary results of rapid processes.

We cannot say that the world is made of this particular thing and that, in succession and with fixed laws. The basis of cognition of the world now has to be the transformations or motion itself, and the associated space and time realities/concepts.

The theory of quantum helped to divide the waves of light, etc. so that it, the latter, did not 'gobble up' the energy of the universe, or 'the ultraviolet catastrophe' did not take place. Photons, in this process, were 'created', discovered. While not losing its wave character, light could be divided into little parcels with a definite quantity. The parcel has the nature of a wavelength. Light of long wavelength is made up of small parcels and vice-versa. The amount of energy contained in each parcel is inversely proportional to the wavelength. The energy of the photon can be calculated from its wavelength and vice-versa.[10] "It appears that the seventeenth century, which regarded light as mere particles, and the nineteenth century, which regarded it mere waves, were both wrong, or, if we prefer, both right. Light, and indeed radiation of all kinds, is both particles and waves at the same time."[11] In one type of experiment, radiation falls on single electrons and behaves like a shower of discrete particles; in another type, radiation falls on solid crystal and behaves like a succession of waves. The same radiation can simulate both particles and waves at the same time: now behaving like particles, now like waves.[12]

What is space in relation to the particles, and in general? The traditional concept has been that it is the background for events; each object and thing and process occupies certain space, thus constituting and becoming event and creating events through self-motion.

But things change when looked at from the opposite end. Events become a quality of space, its simple expression. *Space is all the time being converted into energy packets, electrons and particles* and so on, waves and harmony and disharmony, etc. *The particles do not constitute but are constituted.* They are simple and extremely transitory **events** in space, a temporary conversion into non-space. Thus the particles are the results of deeper processes, which need to be discovered.

Changes in modern physics have been too rapid. We are used to think of electrons (and particles) as definite dimensions moving through the space. But can we talk of particular particles moving through? They convert into other events while moving rapidly in the inter-stellar spaces. But with space broken up into waves and quanta, and because of wave-dynamics, a particle becomes wave, and this picture collapses. It also collapses with the emergence of quantum particles.

Because of the wave dynamics, a particle may be regarded as waves. They act like group waves, and often the border-line between them is blurred. Their energy appears concentrated individually. As a result, when a wave encounters an obstacle, it acts like a projectile, which may hit or miss, and which in fact absorbs or emits a certain quantity of energy or none at all. The distinction between matter and radiation is blurred.[13] So, they are not like the usual projectiles; they are instantly converted into other forms of energy.

The 20th century experiments have revealed astonishing relations between waves and particles. Waves of light of suitable frequency ejected electron with an energy corresponding to the frequency. Similarly, when an electron falls back into an atom, it emits waves of frequency of energy which the electron had to spare, which it must get rid of to settle down.[14]

This is very interesting and important point, reflecting the peculiar form of existence in the quantum world. The electron or the particle *has to spare* an amount of energy or has to absorb it to reach a certain state. So there is a continuous interchange and interpenetration of forms of motion to exist or to quit existence. The particle thus created or de-created is a concentration or disintegration of energy, which itself can be explained in terms of quanta and waves. Through such exchanges, the particles and waves express their dual nature. The energy itself is certain motion in certain time lapse, a measure of motion.

It was de Broglie who unified particle and wave, showing they are the same; they are identity of opposites. A quantum of light is a particle, yet light is composed of waves.

Similarly, the question should be raised whether the electron itself is a wave of some kind or a group wave. Are group waves associated with a traveling electron, their frequency (rate of vibration) being dependent upon the energy of travel? G.P. Thompson fired electrons of known energy on a photographic plate. He found the point of impact surrounded by diffraction or interference rings, representing radiation of a corresponding frequency. De Broglie connected frequency and energy, that is the length of waves with the momentum of the particle.

The difference between a wave and a particle is *disappearing*. We are now dealing with something which is neither, and yet is both at the same time. Some have termed it as the 'wavicle'.[15]

The constitution of the electron is not so simple, as one would expect. In the outer orbits of the atom, which is a very long way from the nucleus, an electron *behaves like a little sphere*. It revolves round the centre of force under the astronomical laws. But as it nears the centre, *it begins to lose its particle-like behaviour*. It travels at high speeds and is subject to stiff control. It does not appear to be located at any point at all, but *spreads all over* the orbit like a succession of waves.

For stability, a whole number of pulsations must cover a closed curve. The succession of orbits are composed of such waves. The difference between a wave and a particle *is one of degree rather than of type.*[16] A group wave of certain frequency may appear to us *as if* it were a particle of a given energy.

Particle, Wave and Basic Questions of Philosophy

Why should we talk of a 'crisis' in philosophy and of philosophy being in crisis? Do we need to change our philosophy and the worldview? Let us examine a point and answer it. We have a certain worldview. So far, we have been able to explain the world with this view. But can we do so now? We have been able to see the world; but can we now 'see' the world with the existing epistemological tools? As we try to do so, we increasingly come in conflict with greater number of unusual 'events', etc. Can we explain the quantum world with their help? It becomes clear that the existing worldview as well as philosophy *is largely inadequate and ill-equipped* to explain the qualitatively new world we are entering. We have already explained many facets that we are unable to explain.

We are talking about crisis in philosophy and in thought itself because almost none of the concepts are able to explain the new developments and discoveries. And the discoveries are coming by the minute!

So we are reaching a point where we are forced to have fresh look at the problem of *the nature of matter*. There is no doubt that matter exists and exists objectively. After all, what we are analysing, and what we investigated so far is the material world existing outside our brain and consciousness. It is also undeniable that brain/consciousness emerged later, and matter has been in existence since ever, before and after our consciousness. So there is no question of the world being *created* by our consciousness.

Having said this, we find that these statements are now becoming more and more inadequate, and there have emerged gaps that need to be explained. The stability and tangibility of matter is gone, replaced by ever rapid motions. It is a situation increasingly where our brain and consciousness relates, not with matter as such, but with the motion of matter. We deal more with images and results of the interactions of different processes, the nature of which is not always clear. It is as if motion has been detached from matter! As soon as we try to observe a process, we change it, and what we see is the result, not the object as such, as we have mentioned elsewhere. This is different from our direct subject/object relationship existing so far. There is a certain change in the relation between matter and consciousness, subject and object. It is more a relation between motion and consciousness, and that also means a relation between time and consciousness. The constituents of the concept of matter and of matter itself are dissociating. The process is both a continuation of the old relation of matter and idea (consciousness), and at the same time a new abstraction where the relationship is *extended* to include the relationship between motion and idea, space and idea, time and idea, independent of matter-idea relation! We cannot escape this conclusion; we have to reach it and face it. **There is a fundamental transition here, significant for human thought and future history.** And it is very crucial for consciousness. *For consciousness is not able to keep track of the philosophical abstractions because of the growing motions, which are going beyond the confines of simple reflection, beyond the relation between matter and idea.*

This means many things. The relationship between matter and idea is changing in its dimensions. Consciousness is no more a simple reflection of matter. It is a reflection of the changing interrelations between matter, space, time and motion. Our concept of matter itself has to undergo drastic changes.

We become aware of matter, not through matter itself, but through its motion. Now onwards, our entry into matter is not direct but through motion, as well as through space and time. In the process, matter breaks into endless constituents, each in motion a very high speeds. In fact, we hardly come to know of matter, we come to know of motions and energy becoming an infinity going beyond time. We stay afloat not in the world of matter but in the curled up spaces and twisted times, with energy as the 'basic constituent'. This is a drastic change that the concepts of matter and idea are undergoing. When we reach deeper world of matter and material realities, like the particle and wave, we do not simply get hold of its, matter's or particle's structure. That is what we had expected, and that is what we were aiming at. But we enter the world of the most unexpected. We do not come across any structures whatsoever, even of particle, except initially; we come across the demolition of the structure of atom and particle and waves, and thus of matter itself, matter as we had so far understood. Does this mean that 'matter' and its concept are demolished? Does matter get demolished? The question will naturally arise. And the answer is a clear no. Matter does not get demolished, nor does it disappear. Yet, its concept changes, aspects or projections get constantly transformed, so that matter does not appear to be matter; it even resembles idea so much! The particles and waves in our brain and instrument are entering into inter-action with the quantum processes. If not interpreted correctly, it creates grounds for idealism. It is an easy path to idealist diversion, and religious and mystic superstition, which of course are unable to explain the world at all. That speaks volumes for the significance of new discoveries of science and for their misinterpretations, because *philosophy is lost.* It is philosophy whose structure is getting transformed. Philosophical idealism is an attempt to deny matter its existence, and mechanical materialism is an attempt to stick to the concept of matter *as it is*, as a direct, mechanical, reflecting opposite to idea, mechanically.

Idea is the reflection of matter, so says, correctly, the existing materialism. But this statement is inadequate now. Idea no more reflects matter as such; it reflects motion, time and space. They are attributes of matter. *But they exist independently and objectively in the quantum world, and it is matter that, on occasions, becomes their attribute.* Our consciousness has been so fashioned that we find it difficult to visualize motion and time as independent entities. But they appear independent *relatively.*

Particles were analysed for their structure and peculiarities, but after a certain point, they were found to be having no structures, they are no more than attributes of something that was supposed to be their attribute, e.g. space. It is the accidental and innumerable expression of the energy changes going on in space that produces particles at certain level. Such concentrations are only manifestations of a much deeper and larger reality, in which many of the attributes of reality are questioned. One is forced to go into the concept of reality. Obviously, the concepts of the tangible, visible world are reversed in the world beyond the tangible.

Does idea reflect 'reality'? Which reality? As we have been arguing, we need to redefine reality. It is not simply 'out there'; it interacts with the observer. We have seen that 'seeing' is interacting, to the extent of modifying the reality or the process we observe.

Are we dealing with matter or its reflections, images and calculations or calculated possibilities? We enter the world of probabilities and possibilities, where the reality is reconstructed with the help of the tangibles to impart it a nature of reality understandable to us. We create a concept and the next moment give it up to explain something new. It is the world of uncertainties, wonderful certainties. It is too fast to be certain; we add factors *to slow it down* within the range of our brain and the consciousness limited by it. It is a new material world, which is non-material in many senses; the processes of the brain, and consciousness try to compete with the unnatural processes.

Undoubtedly we are dealing increasingly with reflections, both in our social life as well as in our explorations of the atomic as well as astronomical worlds. We have dealt with the first kind elsewhere in detail. It is clear that today the society is transforming tangible objects and processes into their images in order to understand them and work with them. This happens, for example, in factories, offices and institutions, etc. The earth is rapidly being surrounded by images, and we will soon be wondering whether the world is constituted of objects or images thereof. We are no doubt increasingly living in a world of images. It is through the manoeuvring of the images that we now manoeuvre material forms.

As for the sub-atomic world and the world beyond the earth constituted of the endless interstellar spaces, particularly the dark world, we know almost nothing except of minuscule portions. And whatever we know is not direct and definite. The knowing is through so many deductions, calculations, inferences, adding numerous x factors and so on. That world is made of suppositions, and of images, as is evident from the discussions going on about the particle and waves and so on. We are not sure of what the known world is made of. They are all speculations and mathematical calculations. All our experiments are relative. As we enter the quantum world, we conduct more 'thought experiments' than the real ones, simply because it is not possible to conduct the real experiments. One of the basic reasons for this is that the moment we 'touch' the object (if that word is applicable here), it undergoes a change or changes. The degree and the nature of change have to be calculated with certain approximations, so that we very roughly know the nature of reality we are dealing with. The observations and their results are based on the velocities of the observer and the observed and so many other things. Cause and effect relationship is disrupted. An event appears to have taken place earlier for one observer, while for another it appears to have happened later.

So, how to account for such a world? How do we explain it? It does exist, but how? It is obvious that lot of it is made of suppositions. We are faced with epistemological problems of the comprehension of the world. To what extent are we part of existence and to what extent do we transform or affect it in the course of our comprehension of it? What then is reality and realism?

Normally, in the course of our comprehension of the world, we do not change it. When we say 'world', here it simply means the world, the world of objects on the earth and elsewhere, particularly of everyday life. We do not affect the reality, existence and the world simply by looking at it. That is how the relationship of the subject and the object came into being. We take it for granted that world remains as it is before and after observation. So we 'know' what is what. The world is unchanging, so to speak, or predictably so, and we are aware of and confident about them. Thus we have already 'philosophized' about it, about existence and reality, we have generalized and abstracted essence of existence, we have analysed them and reached certain conclusions.

But that does not happen when we enter the quantum world. Did the particles, waves, energies, electro-magnetic waves and so on exist as we saw or deduced them or did they or do they exist differently? Something must be existing, surely. But what? So it is a question partly of interpreting reality and partly of creating it for observation. How do we interpret something that we do not know, and in all probability cannot know as it is. Then what do we come to know? One thing is clear. What we do come to know is the result of the interaction between ourselves and the reality we do not know for sure, but which transform in the course of comprehension. So comprehending is transforming.

'Standing Waves' and Dissolution of the Particle

Let us 'philosophise' and 'quantise' about another phenomenon, or about something that we can imagine realistically. The particle is formed of what is called *the 'standing waves'*, consisting of the incoming and outgoing waves and their symmetry at the amplitudes. They have been mentioned and discussed about in the previous two chapters. Here we only deal with certain 'philosophical' questions. These waves are very important and crucial for our discussions; they move at light speeds or near light speeds. Therefore the particle exists only for that fraction, a second or part thereof. And then disappears. We can imagine two things here. The image of this particle can be 'seen' 3 lakh kms away after one second. Secondly, the particle itself can be 'transmittted' to distances. The waves forming it travel further and form fresh particles elsewhere in no time. So, it is not the particle as such that moves; it is reconstituted, deconstituted and/or carried by the waves, forming it afresh elsewhere. Waves carry the 'information' and 'events' in the spaces.

Let us take light, for example, for quantum description. Light is there, for sure. There is sunlight all-round, even if we do not look at it. This is a material reality, no doubt. But things begin to change and become complicated as soon as we begin to study and analyse light itself. It is composed of invisible waves and particles, with seven different wavelengths; it is composed of photons or quanta. Now, if we try to identify the quantum of light, it changes; so also the waves. *The sunlight does not change, but its particles defy precise observation.* So it becomes very difficult for us to identify a particle. It really turns out to be a wave. If it is true, we say that the particle is composed of waves or energy. Actually, it is not 'composed' of them. The 'particle' is a **measure**, the quantum is a certain calculation about energy. It is *not given*, as is the sunlight. It has to be calculated and then deduced or supposed. So, inside the sunlight, we enter a whole different world of 'uncertainties' and relationships. Thus the sunlight is composed of 'relationships' and conversions! Obviously, they are not objects and fixed entities.

It is the level of reality where reality is not real but transformed and consequenced. It is the perfect example of the interpenetration of the subject and the object. We cannot philosophise in the sense that we do not know the nature of generalizations of 'reality'. Yet, we have largely to philosophise and speculate about the nature of events/processes/'reality', and this leads us to abstractions. New physics and related sciences inevitably lead to the consideration of the philosophical questions. Without generalizations about certain epistemological and philosophical problems, one cannot proceed forward. For example, the concept and definition of reality is in question, and rightly so, and we are yet to know what it is.

It is also clear, and interesting too, that the subject and the object get integrated and identified as we proceed into the quantum world. Our brain and the related processes work at the sub-atomic levels, and the instruments that we use are also made of the atomic and sub-atomic materials, ultimately speaking. Therefore, somewhere, the observer and the observed get identified, being made of similar processes. Epistemology and the act of observation are faced with an unprecedented situation, never before met with in the history of consciousness. An identification is taking place in the world of comprehension, and consciousness is getting identified with actual processes going on. Consciousness is being dissociated into the constituents of the objective reality, thus affecting the latter seriously and philosophically.

A stage is reaching where consciousness itself needs redefinition, and not just reality and objectivity.

Now let us discuss the problems using some examples. Wave function represents the *probability* of finding the particle at a given point. That only means we reach the particle, not directly, but via the probability that it will arise momentarily and disappear. The situation is unprecedented in the history of comprehension. There is also an added dimension to be considered and that is of the very nature of particle, which needs constant redefinition and readjustment. What we receive in our consciousness is a picture of existence that is expressing itself as non-existence, and we are forced hard to fix up the bounds of reality. The reality exists in its probabilities and possibilities, and not in its finalities and concepts, which are hard to form.

And therefore the problem presents itself as to *whether the quantum particles are objects at all!* Because the more we enter this world, the more we wait for the 'events' to happen. Consciousness constantly falls behind the 'events', leaving us the function of generalizing alone. It is a probabilistic generalization about a probabilistic world. Nowhere does this world exist except as a philosophical and scientific necessity, because world has always been in existence. It is a transition from the world to the world, where consciousness is trying hard to unite the two. Even Einstein was forced to say that he would like to know what electron is like!

It is the standing wave that constitutes the electron. That means the amplitudes of the 'incoming' and the 'outgoing' waves must coincide to form an electron. These waves and their amplitudes are infinite, and it is only when they meet to converge that the event termed by us as 'particle' happens. And we have termed it particle for our own convenience

This is an absolutely temporary, fleeting event, a chance event, an event that is at the same time absolute and momentary. Its absoluteness lies in being a 'particle' and temporariness in disappearing as soon as it comes into existence. Such are the events that give rise to the finite and tangible world that we live in and see. These are the events, absolutely chance and temporary ones, that produce a continuous world we live in. As we go up from the depths, they create the visible world outside. It is the outward and the inward waves that provide communication with the matter of the universe. They provide the linkages between the different worlds we are talking about.

So what is our relationship with this world, with matter now? There obviously occurs a change. We are no more in direct relationship with matter and material forms, but with the results of collisions of two motions, ours and that of the quantum. We have to redefine this relationship. It is a relation which has evolved in the depths of the material world, but where this world dissociates itself into different motions and times, and where reflection is no more straight, direct and simple. In the ordinary world, we are linked together by and through the various material forms and their evolution. But here in a different world we are talking about, we are linked together by time, space and motion. It is motion that unites the world and gives rise to events. *They defy the usual concept of matter.* They not only contribute to the consciousness-formation, but consciousness itself forms them/it, so to say, in order to understand them.

In the words of John Taylor, you can't take a particular electron, at a particular place, and say I am now measuring its momentum![17]

We are very near an epistemological problem where we are compelled to question the existence of electron and particle as particle. We come to the conclusion that a particle does not really 'exist'; it is not a given. It is we who *want it* to exist, as we have tried to picturise earlier. Since we think that we are measuring the world material, and that it will be easier if the particle really did exist, we are vexed not to really 'find' it! Therefore existence and finding become epistemological prerequisites or preconditions of comprehension. So, the question is what exactly, what is it, that we are expecting of the world?! Do we want it to bend to our will? Electron and other particles are too momentary to exist; therefore, in the world of events they refuse to become a reality, to exist. You can't find particle in a particular place, and you can't find particle at all! It is a *vanishing act* on our behalf to 'locate' it because nothing is located in the world of non-locations. It is a world of constant non-being and non-locations, and therefore of future, and nothing can exist in future, only in the present.

Therefore, our act of measuring, of comprehending the particle is in direct contradiction to the nature of the world. Why should one try to understand that which is not? Comprehension has a selfish motive in trying to grasp that which is out of grasp, which only appears because the chance events come in conflict the necessity of consciousness, which imposes itself on the being as the all-encompassing dominating being, to which all the beings must submit. Little does consciousness realize that the given necessity of idea is only so insofar as it is consciousness reaching its limits where it must realize that it has to be realized differently, that is through the non-being. The problem with consciousness is that it is a formed consciousness, and therefore its concepts are inadequate and ill-equipped to deal with the dissolution of reality into non-reality.

Consciousness therefore stands in opposition to itself in the very act of comprehension. The very act of comprehension makes reality disappear! And that is because the idea has set itself wrong tasks. The process of observation makes the object want not to be observed. Observation is an act of negation of consciousness. Observation is in fact an act of the dissolution of consciousness along with that which is considered material. Consciousness/observation is anti-consciousness, a reversal and bending back of idea upon itself, because that way it can unite with the material that is not material. The very act of observation has either to be given up or to be united with the observed, in which case the two form a system in which what was being observed can no longer be observed, as it is rendered changed into that which is not objectively existing there as reality, but here as unreality of the subjective of reflection of the subject-like object in a higher unity of the subject and the object.

We as consciousness begin to follow an opposite path of creating that which was not there, and of comprehending resultant interactions, wherein comprehension proceeds through non-comprehension. Our projection into the world, our efforts, mechanical, childish and naively scientific, only scares away the real into the non-real! We can only proceed into a world of the transformed, resulting from the change of what could have been to what probably is. The world refuses to exist unless consciousness recedes into the series of transformations, bringing 'things' to the level of consciousness. But by so doing, the reality is dissolving into a transformed consciousness of the comprehension of non-comprehension. We therefore can differentiate increasingly and in greater numbers all that cannot be 'idealised', that which we thought material but has turned out to be eluding into the transformed reality beyond and into our consciousness. It is the interacted transformation that enters our consciousness and highlights, i.e. dissolves all that appeared to be within grasp. Consciousness finds its level in the non-realised. It itself asserts its subatomic level, yet in the course of it, it stumbles upon comprehended reality.

Only the results of a conflict with reality helps to create the world, and what follows is a series of comprehended and thus transformed world; it is therefore an unreal reality.

So here we are observing a completely different world. We are really observing it by interacting with it. Observation means interaction with the object, which renders the concept of the object and objectivity changed. And it also changes the nature of the observer/subject. We inevitably reach the conclusion that at the level of the waves and particles, there is no subject/object relationship of the existing kind. This relation now needs a *third factor* in form of calculations of the extent of displacements we have caused in the course of observations. We find it difficult, and it becomes increasingly unreal, to consider something as a thing or a particle. It is now *only a working hypothesis.* We have to change our entire concepts about time, space and motion to grasp what is what and what is going on. Waves and particles are to be met with, not as they are but as transformed in the course of observation. A particle is only the briefest of existence, and that too from the point of view of the assumption of particle. It is this briefest existence that we try to catch.

Observation is in contradiction with motion. Motion is not the source of unfolding of the material processes alone but of the transformation, continuously, of the observer.

So what exactly are we trying to find and describe through quantum and other theories? This much is clear that we have to change our posing of the question, which is now inadequate as we proceed further. It is a serious jam, a crucial intersection and turning point in our investigation of the nature, and of the nature of reality, object and matter. Many epistemological hurdles are raised here, but we have to set them aside, if we have to proceed further.

As we have pointed out, we describe the interaction with reality, which can be measured or gauged through the extent of interaction. We have at this stage to describe reality as nothing but interaction. We are forced to conclude that we cannot know the 'reality' without such an interaction, and mind is for the first time finding its real unity with its constituents. We do not observe even a simple star we think we are observing. The mind and brain are too complex, as everybody will agree. But the point is that it is also constituted of the portions that has something *in common* with the quantum world. Therefore, at this level the brain must function differently. It cannot be a simple reflector; it has never been. But today, it is more complex. The mind and brain inevitably interact with the processes, which now are not really or fully outside them, but are part and parcel of them. Brain is becoming part of the subatomic/quantum processes. They are also not outside the instrument that we use, but find a common level in them. Where does it all take us? It forces us to conclude that at this level the brain and the instruments are really constituted of the very processes that we are trying to investigate. It is a unified reality that can only be understood in terms of a unified system of the object and the subject, which were a product of the Cartesian world as also of philosophy, their mutual merger and disappearance, and appearance as unified process.

By resolving the world into waves and particles, we are really dissolving the dividing line between the subject and the object, as also between matter and idea. Only by presupposing that we are entering where we can only exist as we are not, can we investigate the world so that we can properly interact with that world?

That world has too much of a motion to exist as existence. It is no doubt there, but as we approach it, it appears to be dissolving and changing its nature. Philosophy resolved the problem by developing the concept of matter, which encompasses all the reality and existence. But that is not enough. It is a concept of the world that exists outside our consciousness. But the concrete sciences study each field of the concrete reality. So the reality has to be concrete in order to understand that matter is concrete. We must 'know' that matter is concrete.

So far, matter existed outside our consciousness, and continues to do so. As we approach the inner recesses of matter, it increasingly identifies with the production process of consciousness, and with the functions of brain. The processes of the quantum world increasingly take on the features of the processes within the brain. The quantum processes within the brain and matter become similar. Therefore, it becomes more and more difficult to talk of 'outside the consciousness', more precisely of 'outside the brain'. The activities or the events in the quantum world affect brain, and the brain processes affect processes outside. So, we can't understand the world outside without affecting that world. Brain and matter outside establish an interface, a unity, a complex of the subject and the object.

The subject is the conscious being. Considered from this point of view, the subject undergoes changes, even at times disappears. The body of the subject, as it is, already part of the material reality. But the brain has certain peculiarities, which makes it part of the quantum reality. It crosses and intersects time and space. Its function of reflection, that is, consciousness as the result of it, shifts more and more to the waves and particles rather than to 'matter'.

That divides brain into *two levels* of function/reflection. Its relatively tangible part unites with or veers round to the tangible physical world. Its more intangible and quantum-like part veers round to the quantum world. Consequently, comprehension becomes a two level process. The brain and consciousness are split in two contradictory parts/spheres (of reflection and the way of reflection) as they enter the world of particles, wave and energy.

The brain increasingly becomes part of the world of particles and waves. Therefore comprehension moves in the world of, and is the result of, the particles and waves. In fact, the process of formation of consciousness is nearer to the motions of waves and particles and events. Such a brain, when it tries to understand the quantum, *only manages to change it!* And it is only through such a change that brain understands that world. What is the guarantee that the particle and the wave in our brain do not disturb or modify the waves and the particles outside? *There is no guarantee.* What then is the 'real reality'? That is a highly complex practical, philosophical as well as epistemological question.

Cognition of Motion/Matter

One is forced to conclude that the study of matter at the quantum level is actually a study of motion itself. It is almost futile to ask: motion of what? Does it mean that there can be motion *per se*? Obviously not. But that hardly matters as the matter loses its tangibility. The motions are of the 'objects' that are extremely fleeting and transitory. Therefore, *the existing concept of matter does not help us here, even though it is correct.* But being correct does not help us to understand the world where motions rule and determine 'things'. Even if matter exists independently of our consciousness, and it does so, it does not answer the crucial and central questions about the quantum world and its nature and the philosophical relationships in it.

There is a certain shift in the spectrum of problem presentation ('the problematique'). Now we relate ourselves *not so much with matter as such but with motion/s.* Too rapid transformations render the question of matter immaterial. After all, matter at these speeds is motion only.

Matter and events are better understood as energy transformations and energy exchanges between 'particles', etc.

Therefore, it appears that the fixed concepts of matter and philosophy actually *prevent* us from really reaching out to the core of the problem. These concepts are more used by us as a tag or help, something to hang upon. We want to see that which is not there, which obviously cannot be there, yet we want it/them to be there and find ourselves helpless in their absence!

For example, let us ask ourselves: 'what happens when two particles collide?' Now, there is an epistemological problem in the framing of the question. It presupposes *existence* of particle, assumes that matter exists as particles or must exist as particles. Why should, in the first place, particles exist at all, and why should they collide at all? It also presupposes particles of fixed and given qualities, which 'hit' each other and then produce something. All this makes no sense as far as the quantum world is concerned. It is alright in our world for two objects to collide with each other! Quite natural! But not so out there! The particles, etc. are also taken as something given, *even when* we do not observe. This is an imposition of one's subjective will upon the 'reality', about which we do not know virtually anything! Such questions also presuppose a particular type of answer, making our investigation easier. The question flows directly from our entire history, social as well as scientific. *It is a wrong poser.* We are used to posing such questions in an 'earthly' fashion.

Our concept of *motion and dialectics* is mechanical, leisurely, orderly, successive, machine-like, repetitive. It is a divided concept, with each division separate and independent, fixed, compartmentalised, each standing separate from and opposed to each other. It at once becomes clear that we divide objects and their motion and change into compartments, each separating and uniting whenever we want. This is absolute subjectivism. While trying to understand motion, we first separate it from matter, then add time and space and look and behold! The recipe of 'matter' is ready, so delectable and useful! Yes, it is usefulness that has destroyed or dialectical flexibility. What we do is to first catch hold of matter and material forms, and then (*this is important!*) try to determine its motion, the various forms of motion. Then we divide motion into laws, categories, aspects, leisurely change of one into another, etc.

This is a mechanical approach in the name of 'dialectical' method, which in fact is turned into pure mechanical treatment, with words and concepts devoid of new content with the passing of time, ultimately emptied of any living content (devoid of motion).

The word 'dialectical' and 'scientific' are repeated endlessly without caring for their fresh contents, and are turned into insipid words capable of nothing.

The history of philosophy has been such that it first developed the concept of matter, then of motion and then of matter in motion, generally speaking. Therefore these concepts have evolved separately in our consciousness. And then we have *joined them together*.

After joining them together, we have generally been thinking in terms of 'matter in motion', as if saying 'matter' is not enough. Historically this is justified, but philosophically and thought-wise it is not justified as it is not synthesized properly, and that is why there are gaps in human thought. There still is the split, the disjunction. Motion for us has to be of 'something'. This reflects a particularly low and backward level of thought and consciousness. Motion is still to become a part and parcel of our consciousness: we continue to kill motion in concepts.

That is why, every time we seek to find out motion/change/ *within,* 'inside', a particular form, material or ideal, as if it were a 'receptacle' of motion. Here is the great historical error, a split in consciousness and thought: we want to *break down* motion into its moments, into concrete changes. Can and should motion be broken down? That is why we find it difficult to talk of motion alone, as given. We are used to the *successive* moments, that is, the thing is here at one moment and there the next. But it is really not so. 'Here' and 'there' are the same moment.

We deal with the particle, and things at once become different and clearer but far more complicated. A particle moves, at least we expect it to so move as to enable us to comprehend it. And here lies the epistemological problem. A particle must 'move' according to our conception. But we have found that a particle is momentary and also has a wave nature. Therefore, it itself is motion. Then what moves? *The question does away with the particle itself.* The wave moves differently. What really moves if it is the question of the moving waves?

The motion of the wave becomes one continuum. The particle is converted in the course of its motion. Particle is also converted into other particles in the course of motion and our observation.

So it is the continual conversions (motions) we are dealing with, in the course of which we can't identify a 'thing', can't stabilize it, because it has no stable existence, almost to the point of non-existence. In fact, as we have said, it is through particular things that we try to identify motion. For motion, something should exist for a certain period of time. Here again we come across epistemological barrier, a barrier that has roots in history, and therefore *this history must go.* Only then we can comprehend, or at least way can be cleared for comprehension. Comprehending is to be fully identified with motion. It is into motion that our consciousness should be converted. Can there be motions alone? To the extent that 'matter' in its material form disappears? That is one of the new epistemological posers that we have to answer. Human comprehension stands on the verge of a great transformation, revolution and qualitative leap. It has to convert as per the nature of motion, rather than according to matter/material forms. It, consciousness, has to convert into motion in order to comprehend motion. It has to go beyond matter into the depths of it and reach out to and identify itself with motion. Motion becomes more and more all-pervading, with matter its characteristic feature rather than vice versa. The identification of consciousness with motion is not an easy job. Consciousness has to be conversant with the motions to the extent of converting itself into motions. That involves jettisoning the material forms.

Sir James Jeans[18] is quite right when he says that all the pictures that science now draws of nature are mathematical pictures. The wave mechanics for example penetrates deeper into secrets of nature than any other system. The outstanding achievement of the modern science from philosophical point of view is the general recognition that we are not yet in contact with the ultimate reality, or even with the reality as such. We think that we are in touch with 'reality', but as the science progresses we find that we really are farther and farther from it because 'reality', we find, is quite different from what we expected.

Philosophy and materialism started their journey confidently with the surface of reality and began to go deeper into the inner realms.

We in fact began with superficial observations, thought that we are discovering this and that, and we really did to an extent, we drew up and discovered laws, including those of motion, and built up a system of thought and of objective sciences.

But as enter the realm of matter, all this appears 'fictional', so to say, immature, superficial. The development of our thought so far still reflects a kind of immaturity and narrow, limited nature. The laws and the observations made meticulously over the centuries are suddenly collapsing. Almost all the observations of the physical world are turning out to be mathematical observations. The events and processes are reducible *to numbers.* This world consists of numbers and additions to those numbers in order to approximate to the reality and its interpretations.

With the dissection of the atom, we come to the conclusion that the atom really does not exist. In fact it must not exist if we are to proceed further in our investigations. Similarly the particles also should not exist, and in certain senses the waves must dissociate themselves into the constituent waves further and into energy packets and actions. We move from the tangible to the intangible.

Indeed, our earth is such a minuscule existence, and we the intelligent being virtually the only ones in the universe, as far as we know, that our knowledge appears, on surface, as a massive body and as infinite, authentic and all-encompassing. But actually it is *accidental* and limited, even *minuscule*, and therefore *opposite to what really exists all over.* Ours is a composed knowledge, emanating from the solid and tangible, well-ordered earth. But the universe and the reality 'out there' is not composed that way. *It is composed in an opposite manner.* Therefore, our rules now appear increasingly to be accidental, and world is not at all composed according to them. The rules and the laws must increasingly be amended and transformed as we proceed further. If we are accidental and a chance, then what is the necessity, rule and general? ***This is a crucial question for human thought.***

The other world, that which exists just outside the tangible one like that of our earth, consists of momentary events and existences. The particles hardly exist. For example, photon has no rest mass; therefore it must always be in motion with the velocity of light. Consider, for example, the muons and the mesons. The muons have a mean lifetime of 2.2×10^{-6}, while the mesons (pions) have lifetime of 1.9×10^{-16} seconds and 2.5×10^{-3} seconds.

There are existences of even shorter durations. The source of muons is disintegration of pi-mesons. They are also the product of the disintegration of the K-mesons or the 'strange' mesons. The muons can convert into electrons.

Short Existence and Dialectics

How do we really look at the world of motions, if we say so? For the first time, motion has become primary and matter secondary. Motions become absolute, and matter becomes their forms of existence. Is this conclusion correct? *Is it not jettisoning the concept of matter altogether? No, it is not.*

What happens to the concept of matter then? That is not really important here, in this context, where everything resolves into motions of the highest order. Obviously they are motions of matter, but continuously and very rapidly, repeatedly jettisoning the material forms, so much so that we are unable to really catch them as matter; we can only catch them as motions: we can only comprehend speeds and conversions. We can't talk much about the structure of whatever has been created; we can only talk of what was left behind and what is going to be.

Let us discuss this problem through a simple, almost a crude example, a mental experiment. Let us take the example of a bulb or a lamp. Let us say, the bulb stands ten or twenty feet away. It makes no difference because speed of the light coming from it is 3 lakh kms per second (300, 000 km/sec). Every second we are being lighted, we can see the light, the room and the objects in it are reflected with this light. We can see everything clearly.

Now one photon must cover 3 lakh kilometres *every* second. So just one photon can move the whole of the bulb, even the ten feet to us, even the room, *several times* every second. That means, just ***one photon or particle*** is enough to light the small bulb or lamp, whose diameter, length and breadth are minuscule compared to the 3 lakh kms! And what guarantee is there that there is only one photon and not numerous?! Because it simply does not make any difference: whether there is one or several photons! Even to light the whole room!

One photon is enough to move hundreds of thousands of time to light up the lamp!

So we find a conflict of matter and motion here. Which is more important: material form or motion? In fact motion here replaces matter, almost, though not fully. This is the importance of motion. Conversions and motions become important, material forms are continuously being jettisoned as unimportant, as the hurdles in the path of motions.

It is this dialectics that is source of existence and conversions.

What are the chief differences between the classical and the quantum worlds? The following. In the classical world, the system has a definite value for the property being measured even before the measurement is actually made. But in the quantum system we do not know the definite value of the property, and whether there is any at all. The attempt to measure it leads it to change its state. So what we actually see is the changed state of the quantum system. The value one obtains for the system is the result of the measurements themselves.

In the classical system, the instrument or the apparatus does not affect the system.

When we use thermometer to measure the temperature, for example, of water, we assume, and it is true, that water has certain temperature *even before* the measurement is made. That is in no way disturbed before or after. We simply insert the thermometer and take the temperature. This act does not disturb the system in any way.

Thus in the classical physics the physical properties are attributes of the system existing on their own.

In the quantum system we cannot talk of definite values of the properties. Certain values are obtained *after* measurements are made under certain circumstances. If we change the experiment or the apparatus or the aim itself of the experiment or observation, results would be different. We can in ordinary world talk of a particular spherical object with certain properties. But we cannot do so in the quantum world; we cannot talk of a particular 'object', that is, of a particular electron or photon. We can only talk of the property obtained at a certain juncture in the course of observations in the course of collisions with innumerable particles. Besides, we can talk of this property only in a particular experiment. Change the experiment and the opposite property will come to the fore.

On its own, atom or electron or whatever particle cannot exist, in the sense we are used to talk about. It is unnecessary for the atom to 'really' exist. It is not observed during the decay process. It is only 'needed' for certain purposes, at certain levels, at certain times. Most of the matter is without it, more than 96 per cent. It does not constitute much except some accidental bodies like the planets, etc. This is the real reality.

"In other words, 'atom' is simply a convenient way of talking about what is nothing but a set of mathematical relations connecting different observations."[19] In their practical work, many physicists continue to think of the microworld in the common-sense way.[20] The same applies to us too.

Many of the mathematical concepts have been applied so commonly that they have assumed an air of reality in their own right. Let us take for example the concept of energy. It is a purely an abstract quantity. But we have become used to consider it as a tangible entity with an existence of its own. In reality, energy is a set of mathematical relationships connecting various observations.[21] The same applies to the arithmetical and mathematical numbers.

Niels Bohr suggests that atom, electron, photon and so on should also be regarded as useful models that consolidate in our imagination what is only a set of mathematical relations. How do we, for example, observe electrons? What do we 'really' see about these 'particles'? In Young's experiment, we either see an interference pattern on the screen, indicating the wave nature of the electrons, or we see the particles' trajectories. In other words, we see the *results of the actions* of the electrons, but never electrons themselves. We can never *actually* see them. We only see the results of certain interactions.

Our View of Matter: Past, Present and Truth

We are under the impression that we are all the time moving forward as we discover and observe new things. We think that every new act is a step forward, one after the other. This is a serial observation of an orderly world in succession of developments and events. It presupposes that one thing has evolved out of the other and the next will emerge from the previous one. That is how things have developed on the earth, and that is how we human beings have evolved since they were born. We have certain time frame, order and succession. There is considerable truth in this.

Now let us consider this. When we look at the earthly events we find that the things are all the time moving forward. And this is correct. *But as soon as we look upwards into the skies, we find things are exactly opposite.* Many things are not so simple; they are even complicated in terms of time and space. When we look up, what do find? This is very important, and we have ignored certain simple truths. Whether we look at the sun or at the stars, we really look at the past. The rays of the sun take 5 minutes 8 seconds to reach the earth. So it is long past. The sunlight we see on the earth surface is already 5 minutes 8 seconds old. The stars we look at are actually one light year or 10 or 100 or more light years away (meaning light has taken one year or ten years etc. to reach the earth at 3 lakh kms per sec). So the star we presently are looking at may be ten light years old. Thus, we are really looking more and more into the *distant past*. That is *progress* of human knowledge and intelligence. *All* the great discoveries in the skies, in the outer space are about the past, no the present. The present may be only when we study an atom or a planet after reaching it. So, its present is our past.

When we look into the atom and its particles or the waves in the space, we either look at the past or the future, *no present*. We can't catch the present. Time and matter easily move backwards or forwards within the atom; this is the logical conclusion we have to reach, whether we like it or not. There take place electron-photon conversions where time moves backwards and forwards simultaneously. That which is forwards for one particle is a move backwards for another.

This paradox is due to the fact that time congeals on the earth and planets. We are in fact out of time with the outer space. Our view of the space reflects the backwardness of our knowledge. Our view is limited by the earth conditions, by the limits of the earth. We are safe here, bounded as we are by the atmosphere, and therefore still living. Yet this way of living also restricts our knowledge, puts certain conditions on us. The atmosphere binds time and space, within which we continue our life journey. It is only now, due to STR and ICR, that we are able to penetrate this cover of restriction on time and space. Satellites, communication revolution and the internet are making time and space collapse and bring in line with the outer space of astronomical proportions. Reality out there is quite different, not bound by the laws of the earth as discovered by us. We, so to say, see 'the other end' of reality when we look at the universe or take a look inside the atom.

The universe has been formed differently, and here on the earth we are only the end result of the process of evolution. Out there in the universe we see the world of transformations. *Here on the earth we have to discover transformation as hidden in the objects and their series.*

Are the stars going forward or backward? Both. They are going forward, but we approach them *from the end result* and therefore *we go backwards.* Ours is a universe on the earth, and therefore upside down, and that is why our universe is going backwards. That is the only way to know the universe: to go backwards. That is because of light. It is light and related radiation that reach as signals to us. Therefore the information reaches only after the light has reached us. Consequently, our entire information and knowledge is going in the reverse direction as we progress with our instruments. Our view therefore is old, of the past and will always remain in the past as we progress. In this case, to progress is to go into the past, go backwards, to know the past of matter. Progress, its meaning and direction is reversed in scales of the universe as we go out into the space, because we have traversed with movement and development only in the conditions of the earth. Our ambience is made up of the past, though we are all the time moving forward, but *moving forward only on the earth.* The earth being has limitations. It thinks rightly and wrongly that succession of events is change and progress. This is the greatest mistake committed by the human being and its history, through and in form of the greatest achievements, but a necessary and essential mistake in human progress. Because of this mistake, *most of our concepts are upside down.* Hegel was correct in saying that we, the humanity, are bound by concepts. The concepts play a progressive role in unearthing reality. Later, it literally turns into 'un'-'earthing' i.e. separating oneself from the earth, the earthly conditions, in order to reach the truth. For the truth lies, now, out there and not here. Here, it is the reverse of truth. If we had traveled with truth from a star 10, 000 light years away, we would have reached here after human beings had reached certain levels of development. Thus we would have travelled along with truth, *and not in opposition to it.* In that case all the laws would have been reversed, that is, corrected and stood on their head, and the movements had corresponded with each other.

But we are not used to travelling along with truth, its motion and direction. We can't move along with truth, its speed is too fast; therefore, we must take a devious route, go back, move right across to and in opposition to light. The stars we saw as part of us centuries ago, as part of life as children and peasants and poets, are really already the things of the remotest possible past, and therefore are becoming even more remote. Now the two ends of truth must meet together. But for that we must give up the notions created during the centuries and millennia, the truth that shaped us and our brain and consciousness, and reverse the whole thing. We have to relive and re-evolve. That job has to be done by the brain. For that our consciousness has to detach itself from the earth-related and bodily conditions and limitations, and go into the space and into the atom with the help of the latest instruments to rediscover itself, that is rediscover the laws of motion of matter in universe, and to rediscover humanity. In fact, it is not the laws of the motion of matter; it is the motion itself. Consciousness detaches itself from the body and attaches itself to matter as existing in form of motion in the universe. It is the change that has to be captured in order to fulfil the act of comprehension, and comprehension can in no way be limited by the earth. Therefore the earth is nothing but small speck of reality, *which is now exhausting itself in the course of comprehension.*

Particle, Space and Visualization of 'World'

We have already discussed certain things about particles and their nature.

The word is rather used in the sense that the object is '*like a particle*'. We talk of particle because ***we are bound up with the past.*** We still want to take the help of the past concepts in order to understand the present and the future. Similarly we talk of wave-like attributes; we have to because when we talk of particle then its opposite, the wave, comes into picture.

Why this problem of wave and particle? This is because unlike on our dear earth, the particles and the waves do not really constitute anything substantial. We are having to deal with world composed of waves, particles and the like.. We want them to really form 'something' so that 'we' can understand them. But that does not unfortunately happen. In fact the reverse happens. What has happened so far is cancelled out or 'de-happened'!

This is an important conversion, necessitating one in our own consciousness. Our concept of matter, its definition and structure has to change. Should we use the word 'structure', or nature? Does this material form have fixed structure or build up or qualities or attributes that really sustain for any length of time? What is, any way, the 'length of time' at this level of existence or non-existence?!

The particle known as pion, a result of the decay of muon, exists for a mere one billionth part of a second! How do you apply the concept of tangibleness and structure to it? How do we redefine the attributes of matter to it? In what concrete ways? In what concrete ways do such particles have a structure and constitute other material structures? At this stage what do we observe and how do we observe? What is experience and objectivity? Does this particle exist entirely out of our reach, independently or it is partly or fully *a creation of our observation*, that is, of our interaction with the forces of nature? These and others are very crucial questions that cannot be taken lightly.

The quantum theory has this importance and advantage that it calculates quantum of action, and thus enables us to translate the world into that of action. *This brings about a fundamental change in our concept of the world and matter.* The world or the universe is made up of action and not of 'material objects'. This better describes the quantum world. The pion is just not a tangible 'thing' which we seek in our positivism. For we are habituated to positivism and existentialism because we want to feel and experience all the time. Only then we reach, always want to reach the 'final conclusion'. Can there be a final conclusion about a particle or a wave? They cannot be 'experienced' or touched or *even caught on the screens* and apparatuses etc. They are only probabilities constantly happening in the vastness far out there, and we humans are only wondering as their 'being'. They are reality, yet not reality.

Do these waves really exist, as they are found to be in that micro-second? This is a great physical *as well as a philosophical question*. They are all the time crossing the limits of existence.

Every, almost, quantum particle has mass, energy, momentum, position etc. An electron at rest raised to the state of 1000 ev has an energy of one thousand volts. What do all these mean: what is energy, volt, state etc? Can we catch hold of them? Has electron a structure which 'contains' energy? Is it a receptacle or not or is it a sphere? Etc. These are the questions that go beyond the limits of earthly materialism and physicism. What exactly are these concepts of energy and so on? Are they material; if yes, how?

At least this much is obvious that the world we have entered is full of energy conversions and motions. Time 'passes' very quickly. We are beyond the pale of that time, and therefore find it very difficult to understand astronomical motions, particles, waves and so on. Action has a direct relationship with the time spent, which is really very small, and therefore nothing can exist intact, there is no time to 'remain intact'!

One can say a wave is an expression and a measure of energy and work done. Work done in the micro-seconds cannot allow any material form to exist. So we can apply the concept of matter only with great modifications. There is no way we can avoid the conclusion that there is an obvious separation of motion from matter.

Waves connect distant bodies and events. The particles and wave then appear as qualities of space, that is, motions. Space spreads out and time bends; consequently, matter-energy conversions become distorted and assume shapes. This is the inevitable result of the speeds reaching out and becoming independent as the motions of energy or the energy form of motion.

This is *a complete inside out of the matter* acquiring motions and then bending back on itself. Space determines the rest of the reality, which is released from time determination.

The high speeds and new spaces themselves become the stratum of new and unusual events, acting as space themselves. The spaces are vast because the events, waves and the particles are moving at breakneck speeds, appearing as no more than accidental phenomena. It is these speeds that provide new substrata for new events. High velocities come out as new spaces. Time is reduced to virtual nothingness. Spaces have high gravity and therefore can bend events including light, time and matter. The best example of this is the *black holes*, providing border regions for events and their reversal. They can absorb light itself, and thus time, space and events themselves. The black holes are the best examples of the reversal of time and events, and of extreme bending of the space. It is a world where the events non-occur and time and space are non-done.

The black hole traps the light and does not allow it to escape. With the trapping of light, all the events too are trapped. This is a classic example of how all our concepts of reality and philosophy also get trapped there! There is a massive curling of space-time in the vicinity of the black hole and matter is poured in billions upon billions of tons in it, matter disappearing at speeds even faster than light. Since the black holes do not permit the escape of light, they are *anti-event* and appear as black empty spaces in the universe.

It is clear that in the world of high speeds it is not possible for time, space and matter to remain together, and in the black holes, not remain at all. Time and space are no longer the attributes of matter. They become each independent entities. Black hole is 'anti-matter'.

We can visualize that world through the following example. Let us say that an atom ('electron') is making transition from the excited state to the ground level. A photon is emitted in the process. But let us not think that this photon is something spherical and that the atom is shooting it like a bullet from a gun. We may say that it is as if a spherical wave is spreading from the atom. It is a '*probability amplitude wave*', and *not a wave of the classical optics*. If a photon detector is placed in its path, it can be detected as particle because at the point of detection, the probability wave *collapses* to a *local wave* packet.

Now this provides part of the picture of the world we are discussing. That is a world of waves and particles, in which an *emitted photon moves away as waves of photon*. Thus there are easy transitions between particles and waves, imperceptible, almost without borders. This change in the states of the particles and waves are taking place millions of times every second or micro-second. This and such other matter *condense* at various points and various times in the space intermittently to produce atoms, stars and other objects.

What will happen when we enter the territory of such a world to 'understand' it? Is it possible to know it, know it *as it is*? It is not possible to know that world 'as it is'; we can only know a modified version of it. It now appears most natural to see it as modified due to our interference. An observer will only change the events in that world. Only then he/she will be able to 'see' it, as we have already discussed.

To observe means to modify. For example, how will you 'observe' the events at the periphery of a black hole? Is it possible to observe them at all? All the events at the border or near border are happening at the light speed or near those speeds. How do we reach any conclusions whatsoever about them? So the black hole is exactly the **opposite** of our earth conditions, also in terms of emanating information.

Yet what is the meaning of those events and existences without observation? The meaning is the dialectics of motion! What is the meaning of light moving at 3 lakh kms per second? The meaning is the separation of frame of references and observers. What happens after a second? Uncovering of the source of motion in dialectics. What does it mean? Simply that the universe has to be taken as constant transformations, and not as the change of this or that particle or wave. We cannot know about this or that 'constituent' simply because the constituents do not *exist* or need not exist. It all is quite different from knowing this planet or that. Knowing a planet is to know space, time and matter almost at a standstill, moving very slowly. This is what one has to understand. We are living in a different world altogether. We have to derive new laws about an entirely different world, made up of the most unexpected events.

In the Newtonian world, the motion is *internalized* in the matter. Max Planck at one place talks of the Newtonian force identified by Hertz in matter and of potential and kinetic energies.[22] This does give some clue to the internal and external motions in matter. *That is an important point.* The motion is internalized in the Newtonian world of tangible material forms.

It is these motions that form/constitute various objects, material forms etc., giving rise to the concept of matter, both in science and in philosophy. Motion as such has no chance to express itself. It has to express itself in and through concrete material forms. Since motion is internalized, it has to be discovered as the *quality of* that particular material form and of matter in general. Since it has no scope, motion takes the form of tangible realities like the atoms, molecules, solid forms like rocks, plants, animals and so on. The motions have levels inside, *expressed* outside but often appearing *motionless* or in slow motion and as stable. Time is slowed down, as we have discussed elsewhere. The light and near light speeds have to conform to and are confined within *exceedingly* small spaces, and therefore take up various forms and structures to express their motions. The internal motions are converted continuously into various structures and external forms. *Tangibility is the expression of the intangibility of motion.* Electron within the atom is something different from that outside, free in the outer spaces. The atom and molecules and compounds, as also the rocks and trees and rivers and so on we can identify and confine within certain laws, as also the electron in the narrow confines of these objects, but the forces deep inside do not follow those rules when put outside or even when inside. Within the atom or with the forces in the outer spaces, our concepts and notions about the tangibility of the world are destroyed, our concepts are destabilized. The entire world crashes down. The picture we built up of the world based upon the laws of tangibility just disappears.

It is these confined motions that are released from the limited material forms at very high speeds as light and other radiations and wavy 'particles'.

It is a transition and transformation of and into the opposites. There are two worlds. One momentary, the other stable; one is inside the tangible, but the other outside and intangible. The existence of *the being* is in crisis. The world is upside down. *Matter approaches the fineness and abstractness of philosophy.* Concepts are torn from the tangibles and are converted into the intangibles. Finite concepts suddenly become infinite because no concept can exist at the infinity and indeterminateness. Concept of the concept has to change, has to give way to motions and the concept of change. Conversion is the rule. The *first conversion* is carried by the civilization in the material objects that is in their concepts, liberating the internal forces, which come to stand in opposition to the internalized and internalizing objects due to thinking. Thinking is upside down in the sense that matter is increasingly derived from and in motions. The concept of motion, and of matter in motion, has emerged in thousands of years; the concept of motion outside the tangible objects has come within years, hours, minutes and seconds.

The *second conversion* releases space, time, motion and dimensions of matter. Philosophy de-philosophizes itself, transcending into infinity.

Time and space, bound so far, are unbounded, and become abstract and infinite. This contradicts the existence of brain and the consciousness, which have their biological as well as the historical limits. One thing is clear, and that is the dialectics cannot be bounded.

In Einstein's general theory of relativity, space and time no longer provide a fixed, absolute background. Space is as dynamic as matter, it moves, changes, transforms.[23]

Thus space and time, wave/particle duality and energy rather than atoms and molecules etc., become the makers of matter. *Thus the 'attributes of matter' begin to have matter as their attribute.* This is a complete transformation and reversal. The material forms had been and are the expressions of matter because light emanated or reflected from them and we could grasp them. But now light itself becomes dissociated into rapid conversions, thus freed of the trappings of material 'forms'. A material form without the qualities of material form: what do we call such a reality?!

Is photon or electron or a wave material form? They are not material forms but are expression of matter in different, 'non-tangible' ways. That is the only way one can describe these three and all other similar phenomena. But how do they exist as 'matter'? Because they continue to influence our brain, and now they interact with it too, which is a new phenomenon. They are the bases of the material form but now torn aside, inside out. Thus separated, they can only give rise to motions, in 'disintegration', to the most momentary existences nearing no-existences. They therefore create *a crisis* for philosophy and epistemology.

The epistemological problem is related with the nature of the object under observation. One can observe the material forms but not the separate attribute of theirs. How can you measure something moving at light speed or near light speeds? What guarantee is there this is not this particle but that and the other, and that it is particle and not the space vacated by it? The high speeds also mean that we are identifying the paths of the particles and the waves *rather than* the particles themselves. After all, as we have already seen, an electron is made up of amplitudes of waves that coincide. This is applicable to other particles too. This negates any possibility of identifying a particle at all.

What do we observe? In one second there could be three lakh 'particles' or wave concentrations passing through. It is a kind of non-observance. Therefore we only observe the way they move, the motion itself, and not the particle or the material form. It is the motion of the action or the event that we catch hold of or deduce. It is like inside out of the particle.

Consider this. By combining the constant of gravity, Planck's constant and the speed of light (these are the three fundamental constants of physics) it is possible to obtain the quantum length, the basic unit of length. It represents the smallest region of space that can be described meaningfully. It is 10^{-35} meter and is known as *Planck's length*. Similarly there is a fundamental *Planck time*, equal to 10^{-43} seconds. There can't be time shorter than this or a shorter length.

They are length and time of what? Of events and processes. Is it possible for 'matter' to exist at such distances and durations? Our picture of the world is based on the solid world, to the exclusion or negligence of the empty spaces. But all the solid material are made largely of empty spaces: table chair, trees, book, rocks etc. The proportion of solid material is like comparing a grain of sand to a massive hall. But this 99.99999... per cent of the empty space is actually *seething with activity*, it is full of *virtual particles*. The energy density of the empty space is infinite.

This space actually is full of distorted space-time, which we perceive as particles. It is made up of the quantum length and quantum time. This distorted space-time is actually tossing and turning and producing and undoing all sorts of things.[24]

The photons exist for only 10^{-15} seconds but they are popping in and out of existence around the electrons all the time. It is as if each electron is surrounded by a cloud of virtual protons. These virtual photons only need a tiny energy to become real. An electron moving from an excited to a lower state gives off excess energy to a virtual photon which then flies off. An electron absorbing energy traps a free photon, and thus these processes hold the nucleus together.[25]

Two protons are held together in the nucleus by repeatedly exchanging pions weighing a fraction of the proton's own weight.

Thus, continuous exchange of particles and energy, or *instability* in other words, become the source of *relative stability* and life of certain other particles and processes.

In such a space there are areas where we can't have uniform or the same time and the same direction of time. It may even go backwards. Does time go forward or backward in the motion of a particle? Suppose an electron is in motion. It at certain point gives out another particle, say photon. It can equally well be the result of a combination of proton and other particles like positron or neutrino. Has it gone ahead or backwards? *The conversion of one particle into another is no indication of future or past.* The whole process can be repeated *in the reverse.* ('reverse' compared with the one just described; the example can as well be used *vice-versa*). When a photon or an electron is moving, is it going forward or backward? The question is senseless. The particles in motion are all the time getting converted into something else in all the directions simultaneously. And this happens times without number. There is no question of *successive* events in this case. There are continuous, not successive but simultaneous and continuous, events in the outer space and inside the atom. They have no successive times, each one having its own time, which is reversible *all the time.* In fact, for each forward move (time), there simultaneously is a backward move; not only this; each forward move itself is a backward motion in time. It all also depends on where and how and in which frame of reference one is measuring time. The light rays coming to us indicate time for us as the earth goes forward. They also indicate time lapse between earth and sun. But for the particles themselves, this time or these times are meaningless, as they collectively and individually have their own time. Each photon released from sun has its own time which also is its own reversal! They have a world of their own (!) separate from that of the earth and the sun.

That is the point: the world of particles *have their own time, which a reversible time*, an example of unity, identity and conflict of opposites. The opposite poles of time (the reversibles) are exactly opposite, mutually exclusive, and yet are inter-penetrating, identical, convertible and the same! The separate individual histories of the particles are all the time separating and merging with each other, and are each moment reversible and reversing. After all what 'history' can there be at one billionth of a second or even less? Each billionth of a second is reversible, this is a history of non-history, an event of non-event, which itself is an event!

Wheeler and Feynman have much to do with 'backward-in-time' action of the particles.[26] A gamma-ray photon colliding with an atom produces an electron-positron pair; the electron flies off, but the positron may run into an electron, and the pair then instantly annihilate, reversing the pair-creation process and creating photons again.[27]

The commonsense interpretation would be to follow the particle/ s in time, one after the other, but it is not really like that. The electron travels back in time, absorbs a photon and then flies off into future. In fact, even while we say the electron is moving forward, its mirror, positron is moving backwards. So the reverse process is simultaneous. According to Feynman, to the observer placed in a particular position, three electrons will be seen, which actually are one! The electrons and the particles keep bouncing back and forth to give off and absorb waves and particles.[28] Going forwards in time is going backwards, and vice versa! The problem is whether we should consider creation of this or that particle, its annihilation, giving off of waves, recreation of particles 'again' as events going ahead in time or back, 'moving ahead' or back, using our usual commonsensical earthly expressions. No! They are all the time 'moving' here, there, everywhere and nowhere! It is not two-directional time, it is multidirectional and the merger and crystallization out of different times!

Instead of using the word 'moving', it is better to say 'conveying' events.

"A proton proceeding quietly on its way can explode into a buzzing network of virtual particles all interacting with one another, then subside back into itself..."[29] And it may or may not be the 'same' proton! There is no 'same' wave or particle in the quantum world! 'The proton' is constantly emitting and re-absorbing virtual mesons and virtual photons, disappears by giving up mass energy, and 're-emrges' by absorbing energy and so on.[30]

Is it the same proton? *By no means!* Then how can you apply *the concept of time* to it at all?!

The same thing applies to the electrons, popping out and in all the time, and that can only be back and forth, and back and then again forward!!

When two particles are exchanging a third particle, through wave information, they are not *particular* particles, not 'this' electron or 'that' but only particle-like qualities or aspects or events, or wave-like events. It may even be one particle *simultaneously at two places*! And *a* wave has no identity.

Nuclear forces, waves, electric forces, particles, etc. are all constituting and de-constituting events *all the time* without succession, here and there and everywhere, in micro-seconds and parts thereof! Our questions regarding time succession and 'forwards or backwards hold no meaning in this context.

But, for photon, time has *no meaning* because it moves *at the speed of light*!

Cosmos and Matter

A news item appeared recently in the newspapers to the effect that the laws of physics are not the same everywhere in the cosmos.[31] Defying the equivalence principle, according to which the laws of physics are applicable everywhere, new evidence supports the idea that we live in an area of the universe or the cosmos that is just right for our existence.

This conclusion comes from the observation that one of the constants of nature appears to be different in different parts of the cosmos. What is more surprising is that the change in the constant appears to have an orientation towards a preferred direction, an axis across the universe.

The new study focuses on the 'fine structure', constant or the 'alpha'. This number suggests the strength of the interaction between light and matter.

The data has been taken from the Very Large Telescope (VLT) in Chile. The alpha varies in space but not in time. Around 300 measurements of alpha in light have been made from various points in sky, and they suggest a structured variation, not random, like a bar magnet. The universe seems to a large alpha on one side and a smaller one on the other. This 'dipole' alignment matches that of a stream of galaxies moving towards the edge of the universe. Earth is somewhere in the middle of the extremes.

These discoveries confirm our conjectures about the distribution of matter in space and time and its nature. The universe cannot be limited, both in space and time. It has no limits, ***unlike*** what is suggested by Albert Einstein and Stephen Hawking. As the new discovery suggests, our view is limited by the conditions obtaining in a particular region of the universe we live in. Our view, the human view, is always limited by various factors. That is a great limiting factor that has to be overcome. The time for different regions is different. It rolls on due to events that are breathtaking and momentary. But even they differ hugely from the region to region. There are extraordinary forms of matter at extremely high speeds in the various regions, and obviously they each have their own time, each clashing with the other and even moving in directions different and opposite to each other. The region time unites or unifies the endless time for the particles, waves and spaces. Thus time is a unifying factor, but a disunifying one at deeper levels.

There are vast spaces in the universe or the cosmos, but these spaces are created of the energy conversions, of the conversion of matter into motion and energy and vice versa.

Hawking had to admit recently that there is no God involved in the creation and expansion of the universe. He so admitted because he gave primacy to the scientific laws operating at the cosmic levels, which are being unraveled more and more. He is great scientist and has given new direction to the 'origin of universe' and the 'arrow of time'. When a scientist discovers laws, the conclusion is firmly grounded and rational and scientific. The 'God' is momentarily invoked to explain certain facts, contrary to scientific approach, but new discoveries force the 'divine' to recede and take a back seat; it has been going on endlessly since the discovery of reality.

The ghost in the atom is well and truly out, enveloping the whole reality and existence. Reality is more and more being explained from 'the other end', from the end of the conversions and energies and the qualities of matter. The other end, the dark side of matter and the dark matter, constitute the main factors of existence. The earth and its position in the universe are only superficial expressions of this reality. These expressions happen only when the cosmic speeds are brought down.

We have now to speed up, truly.

NOTES

1. Based on Manjit Kumar, *Quantum,* Hachette India, 2009, Note no. 10, p. 388.
2. A.S. Eddington, *The Nature of the Physical World,* Macmillan, 1929, p. 1.
3. Ibid., p. 2.
4. Ibid., p. 186.
5. See Roger Penrose, *The Emperor's New Mind,* Oxford, 1999, pp. 364-65.
6. Bruce R. Wheaton, *The Tiger and the Shark: Empirical Roots of Wave-particle Dualism,* Cambridge University Press, 1991, pp. 287-88.
7. Ibid., p. 288.
8. Ibid., p. 289.
9. Ibid., p. 287.
10. Sir James Jeans, *Mysterious Universe,* Penguin Books, 1938, pp. 51-52.
11. Ibid., p. 53.
12. Ibid., pp. 53-54.
13. Sir Oliver Lodge, *Beyond Physics,* George Allen & Unwin Ltd, 1930, pp. 60-61.
14. Ibid., p. 124.
15. Ibid., pp. 124-25.
16. Ibid., p. 126, emphasis added.
17. P.C.W. Davies and J.R. Brown, *The Ghost in Atom*, Cambridge University Press, Canto edition, 1993, p. 110.
18. Sir James Jeans, *op. cit.,* pp. 152-53.
19. Davies and Brown, *The Ghost in the Atom,* p. 25.
20. Ibid.
21. See, Davies and Brown, p. 26.

22. Max Planck, *Where Is Science Going?* George Allen & Unwin, 1933, p. 43.
23. Lee Smolin, *The Trouble With Physics*, Allen Lane, 2006, p. 4.
24. Based on John Gribbin, pp. 259-61.
25. Gribbin, *In Search of Schroedinger's Cat*, Wildewood House, London, 1984, p. 196.
26. See, Paul Davies, *About Time: Einstein's Unfinished Revolution*, Simon & Schuster, 1995, "The Arrow of Time" or Chapter 9 and some others.
27. Ibid., p. 205.
28. Ibid., pp. 205-07.
29. John Gribbin, p. 200.
30. See, ibid., p. 198, etc.
31. *The Times of India*, September 10, 2010.

10

Postmodern World and Discourse of Subject

In this book we use the word 'postmodernism' in a sense considerably different from that used by the postmodernists themselves, although we do make use of several of their concepts partially. Postmodernism is used here not in a pessimistic, disintegrative sense but in an optimistic, constructive sense. In this and the next chapters, we try to trace how new individual as well as larger social, noospheric and independent (mainly internet) consciousness is emerging. The chapters will also try study the impact the spread of consciousness is having on human society. The postmodern consciousness is closely related with the development of post-industrial and information society, and basically represents ***the new subject.*** The postmodern consciousness and concepts basically critique the increasingly obsolete 'modern' concepts, and show the growing limitations of the consciousness created by the industrial revolution. In other words, postmodernism is the result of the post-industrial STR and ICR. It is subsequent to the industrial age and consequent upon the new technological, electronic revolution.

Electronics play a decisive role in the creation of the postmodern subject, not to be confused with the subject dealt with by most of the usual postmodern literature, which though inadvertently and accidentally do reflect some of the related developments. The analyses in the postmodern literature is derivative in nature, and do not reflect a conscious scientific effort.

One of the major distinguishing features of post-modernism is the new way of looking at the subject/object relationship, of tracing how the subject was and is being constituted, its history and the present, and the how the subject disintegrates and gets reconstituted, and how the object itself is constituted.

Thus, in many ways, post-modernism is the study of constitution, destabilization, dispersal and reconstitution of the subject, particularly in the wake of the electronic communication revolution as well as the quantum revolution. The question of the subject has been among the foundations of philosophy and of human thought in general, as also that of its relations with the object. The quantum revolution has *reopened* many of the settled questions in the subject-object relationship. This revolution has given rise not only to a post-modernist *position* of the subject but also, and more importantly, to a subject which itself is *postmodernist.*

Why should the question of the subject/object relationship be reopened? The industrial revolution and certain events preceding and accompanying it such as renaissance created a world of what has come to be known as *modernism, the modern and modernity*. For the present we will not try to differentiate between these concepts, will broadly treat them as inter-changeable.

The modern subject has *a clear-cut and direct* relation with the object. This subject is, broadly speaking, industrial, stable, 'fully-formed', so to say, and stands in direct, clear-cut and dialectical *opposition* to the object. That relationship constitutes a dialectical unity of the subject and the object. This is a typical Cartesian relationship of the industrial age. The world (object) is reflected, and ideas are formed, in succession and order, and therefore orderly histories are constituted. *History* and causation are important aspects and characteristics of the modern objective and subjective events, processes and transformations.

The subject is *given* in the modern world, and has evolved over centuries and millennia. Otherwise the world 'out there' cannot be contextualized and reflected. It, the subject, goes into the layers of the object one by one, systematically, in an organized manner. The subject 'is'. The object also 'is'. Therefore, there is no room for confusion, as they are *presupposed, we can take them for granted even in our/my own absence, we are confident about their reality.*

But the post-modern, post-industrial era has brought about certain crucial, even basic, changes in the nature of the subject as well as the object, in the nature of their relationship. Post-modernist theories, directly and indirectly, bring to the fore these changes.

There are certain trends/events even in the industrial, modern age which provide launching pad for subsequent developments. These events/processes/phenomena provide favourable grounds which the electronic revolution works upon and transforms first. We will consider some of them and proceed further.

The Postcard

Postcard displays certain features that anticipate events of the electronic age in nebulous form.

The postcards address the question of language as non-communication: who is writing? to whom? to what address? and the reply of Jacques Derrida (whom we refer to a little further on) is – I do not know! While the postcard begins its journey as a definite medium of communication, it begins to dissipate most of its features in the course of travel, which becomes more and more indeterminate, a piece of paper, non-carrier of texts, even losing meanings of the texts. The postcards are transformed into a terrain-less terrain.

Derrida comes closest to thematising electronically mediated writing in his book *The Post Card.*[1] The first part contains a series of 'postcards' from 1977 to 1979. Derrida says, and John Phillips explains,[2] that the Envois is the most important part of the book.

Derrida in the "Envois" and other chapters of his book[3] uses the 'post card' as a symbol of communication evolving through the ages. For example he says that outside the 'postal system', Plato and Freud, like Socrates and Plato, would be without relation, "*at an infinite distance*".[4]

Postcard (PC), like writing, is a means of not saying in the form of saying. PCs have the quality of being addressed to someone, being 'destined'. *But they disrupt the* logocentric *reason precisely when they do not reach their destination.* Here Derrida does not clarify as to what happens when the postcards do reach their destination.

The book jacket of Derrida's above-mentioned book reverses the order of Plato and Socrates,[5] indicating that the relationship between speech and writing is inverted. Derrida's theme is that writing *precedes* speech. Postcards are a form of writing, and as such play a disruptive role in the logocentric tradition. The postcard acts as a disruptor of writing/speech.

Freud (*Civilization and its Discontents,* referred to by Poster in *The Mode of Information*) regretted the advance of technology: while the telephone allows one to speak with distant friends, it also makes it possible to be far away from each other, thus *needing* the phone. The telephone thus fills in or is used to fill in the gap between the individuals.

The chief metaphor for Freud was the wax tablet instead of phone. The tablet functioned as a writing tool by preserving traces but also consisted of layers acting differentially upon writing, preserving and erasing marks, not controlled by the writers.

In *The Post Card* Derrida extends the field of textuality of writing. The 'tablet'-like unconscious is beyond instrumental reason and therefore similar to the "textual" effects of the postcard. (And also pencil writing! – AR)

The textuality of writing with its spacing and marks, includes an account of the medium of the P.C. It, the P.C. (postcard), has the nature of 'tele'-messaging because the messages cover distances, even vast distances. This 'tele'-messaging, according to Derrida, fundamentally impacts writing, as writing upsets the rational subject's ability to control the coordination between thought and utterance because material traces are introduced in between, and thus a fissure opens between the author and the idea.[6]

The movement of the postcard creates two opposite poles or rather two opposite poles crystallize in the course of its motion, and it is these poles that maintain its motion. The P.C. leaves the writer and reaches the receiver. In between is the space, the whole world of events, the medium, expressing the whole societal relations, which are further expanded and created in the course of motion.

The writer of the PC has a set of meanings and purposes, in the words used. Every word has a nuance and meaning, not necessarily the usual ones. The sentences have to be necessarily crammed, the words crumpled, to be used economically. The expressions are short and crisp, at least they try to be so. They can be properly and fully understood only by the receiver, for whom it is meant and to whom it is addressed. For an outsider, many of the expressions are meaningless and useless. But in fact they express a whole range of socioeconomic background and times. They often express the deepest feelings, yet suppress and hide them as much as possible, as there is very limited time and space.

The postcard is necessarily intended to be clear and precise, and the receiver is supposed to understand it properly, and as it is. The receiver is also supposed to understand much that is not written, and the PC often acts as a set of codes.

Postcards and letters have a great value of waiting, and therefore float in time dimension. They are cover spaces to connect the two tensionised poles, and therefore are of great spatial value.

But receiver receives and reads it with an enhanced value, several times more than the sender's intention and than the intended words. The postcards in particular, and letters in general, almost always are read with more meaning and value attached to and behind and between the words. We try to read intentions, whether contained or not, intentions different from the intended, relief or unhappiness or grief, love or absence of it and so on. The polar transition always multiplies the meaning. In the process the PC becomes a referable, valuable document, to be kept safely. It cannot be easily erased; in that secure place it is almost *the opposite* of what it was with the sender.

We have described above the 'material traces' of writing mentioned by Mark Poster and Derrida and the impact of 'tele'- messaging. What are these traces? This is a crucial point. These are the traces that come in between thought and utterance. They delay the utterance of thoughts and change them in the process. *This is one of the sites of the operation of the information revolution and of the formation of the mode of information.*

The postcard introduces lot of complications. It has to travel lot of distance; therefore it might be misdirected or even lost. So the intention of the author to send a message might be thwarted. Derrida goes to the extent of saying that it is always so.

A letter 'never arrives' at its destination, he says. Derrida gives much importance to the relatively rare occurrence of the lost postcard: this is because it upsets the view that it is a mere tool in transmission. This is known as the "instrumentally rational" view of the P.C. Derrida wants to stress that the chance of losing the card is inherent in 'tele'-messaging.[7] That means loss of message is part and parcel of messaging. This point is not clear, nor is it clearly explained. It does not stand scrutiny even if extended to the electronic transmission or any other form of tele-messaging.

'Letter never arrives' at its destination may also mean that it may not arrive in the form and with the content when it began its journey.

Another important point has been mentioned above, and that is the P.C. is not merely a tool in the transmission of message.[8]

But this point is not explained at all. It is just mentioned. The point hides much important information.

Perhaps this point wants to stress that the P.C. in its wake creates a series of relations and impacts the subject(ivity) and the object(ivity) and their relations in particular ways. Derrida stresses some features: the information on the P.C. (the P.C. itself) goes to a post or station, and then to several of others, from one to another, and so on. The post is a place of power. And it also involves a network of posts, and thus a power network. The post changes the message of the PC in a maze of communicative positions. Does it mean losing/suppressing the message in a maze of communications, letters, PCs etc., i.e. ignoring it altogether? Throwing it 'away'? The pinpointedness is lost? Etc.

'Post' also means 'after'. It suggests deferral and thereby alteration, a temporal connotation. Its configuration changes. It is an 'open' message, which anyone can read. Therefore, it is communicated not only to the addressee but to an unpredictable readership. If the writer wants it to be read only by the addressee, it must be suitably encoded for privacy. Thus the PC is both public and private.

From Mark Poster's point of view, the chief importance of the postcard is its presentation of a fragmented and disoriented subject.[9] Derrida shows how writing is a distancing, one that multiplies and decenters the subject, to the extent that the reader cannot specify the author or the subject; neither the receiver of the postcards nor their senders emerge as coherent individuals.[10]

This point again is not clear and remains unexplained. On the contrary, both the sender and the receiver of the postcard are established as coherent, well-defined individuals. Both the individuals at the two ends are clearly defined by the PC by shearing them of their details to the barest and the most essentials. So, instead of being fragmented and disoriented, the subjects at both the ends, using the postcard, become more focused. The travel from PC (postcard) to PC (personal computer) is the transition of the subject from the firmly centred to the decentred. When there is difference and changes in the media, then indeed the individuals undergo drastic changes. Here both Derrida and Mark Poster appear to take a highly subjective and wishful stand.

The postcard (PC) uses the most abbreviated expressions to carry the most meaningful and loaded messages, that establish direct and unambiguous relations between them. In fact PC writing becomes a highly developed art, in which the writer virtually creates a well-organised receiver of the message for an exact and particular transmission. The postcard organizes and even creates the subjects so well.

It is these individuals who are subjected to the process of transformation and expansion under the subsequent systems (modes) of communications.

One can establish a direct relationship between the postcard, and such other means of transmission and communications, and the modes of production as well as information. This has to do with the relative under-development of mode of communication under the mode of production, including the industrial one.

It is only with the conversion of mode of production into mode of information that communication becomes *the central* human activity.

Poster says Derrida is indeed sensitive to differences in the media, to the central issue of the materiality of the trace. The post, according to Derrida, is distinguished from every other telecommunication by "the transport of the 'document', of its material support".[11]

This is a very important point, as it provides the site for the subsequent transformations. The material document itself is transported, the PC along with the material traces of writings. In the postal writing, one does not keep copies, the whole material document itself is transported by a particular subject to another particular subject. The postcard has every chance of falling into someone's hands; in fact, it is so constructed that there would be 'no harm' in others reading it. On the other hand, envelopes, inlands, closed posts etc. are more liberal and open; they can be 'hidden'.

Another important feature is that the postcard creates a distance between the writer and the receiver as well as connects them. By writing down on the PC, more as a document, the writer parts with his/her ideas, takes a highly guided and controlled attitude to expressions. Through the postcards the writers, so to say, disseminate their ideas in the economically cheapest manner. That is why, the postcard is the most common and effective means of communication. In this sense there certainly is some amount of spread, but not dispersal, of the subject. The subjects at both the ends are consolidated, in their individual, social and even political meanings.

Both Derrida and Poster *ignore* these crucial features; why, it is not clear. But one point may be identified, and that is they do not take up an evolutionary and logical viewpoint. They seem to ignore the fact that the postcard reflects *a whole history* of the modern human beings and of their means of communications.

Poster himself criticizes the remark of Derrida that the transport of material document is a rather 'confused idea', and comments that Derrida is hesitant to make an issue of the 'material support'. Poster says that the cultural configuration of each technology should be problematized. Derrida minimizes it in favour of homogeneity of writing. Yet in the quoted portion from Derrida subsequently, he makes some crucial points. For example, Derrida says (in 1987 in op.cit.) that in the years to come, it is not the writing that will be transported, but the perforated card, magnetic tape, microfilm, etc. They are secret, hermetically sealed; yet they contain not one but several addresses.

From Postcard to the Electronics: Evolution of the Subject

The postcard, letter writing, book or article writing or any other kind of writing creates *a particular kind of subject*. It is wrong to suggest that writing upsets the rational subjects' ability to control truth because it introduces material traces, as suggested by Derrida.[12] This is relative proposition.

In fact, it is with writing that subject or the author begins to 'control' truth. If the roots of hegemony and domination are to be sought, they partly lie in writing and putting down thoughts. Derrida argues, and Poster concurs, that the traces of writing come in between the thought and the utterance.[13] But this point becomes significant only later. The main, logical point is that thought has to evolve to a point to be put down in form of writing.

Writing is an act that *consolidates* the subject; it is a stage in the development of the individual, and is not a backward step.

At the same time writing creates a distance between thought and utterance. The unity has to be seen here. As Hegel says we are not able to say what exactly we want to; we end up by saying something else.[14]

The subject establishes relationship with the object through writing, which makes the relation permanent. Writing makes thoughts stable, lasting and communicable even without mutual talks/ conversations. When writing comes "in between the thought and the utterance", it contributes to thought and utterance, enriching them, rather than delaying or postponing, as Derrida maintains.

This does not mean that there is no delay; but this delay is permanence of thought. Concepts evolve, and now can be used in written form. Every concept is a separation and removal from thought process; it is a final product, a tool to grasp the world, the tool is kept aside, and is used whenever needed. And the best way to store concepts is to write them out. A concept or expression can be used even without the author, in his/her absence. That is enrichment of thought, which in turn expresses an evolution, consolidation and shaping of the subject.

At the same time, what is written does not exactly tally with thoughts. Writing changes thoughts. What is spoken and written is a selection from observation. And in this sense writing does come in between thought and utterance.

Crystallization of the Subject

The subject is the subject because he/she represents the object by standing in opposition to the latter. Writing and printing spreads the subject beyond the body, far and wide, while conversation only keeps it confined. Conversation and talking renders the subject temporary, as the words/expressions are generally, though not always, lost forever. Some are carried through the generations, particularly as exemplified in the Indian systems of thought, practice and traditions. Whatever was, and is being, talked by the millions over the ages, has been irretrievably lost by humanity. Only some, a very small part, has been carried by tradition and habit through the ages.

Here it should be noted that all that has survived needs to be written, has in many cases been written, thus lending permanence to the subject. Here it is also true that all that has been written is considerably or partly changed from what was originally said. This happens even now.

But that is only a shaping up of the subject, as part of the clarification process of the relationship between the subject and the object. The subject evolves, comes into being.

The subject stands in relation to the object. So, how does the 'subject' relate with the object? One of the major ways is through writing, which reflects the object in the subject.

Matter, the objective reality existing outside the consciousness, is reflected in and through various ways in the consciousness. Printing technology took this reflection to much higher levels. Books, literature etc. are reflection of consciousness formation, though inadequate. The process will always remain far from adequate. Postmodernism itself presupposes existence of a developed subject, before it is decentred and dispersed by the electronic communication.

So, the question is how is this subject formed before it is dispersed or decentred, if at all?

The subject has to have a history of formation, evolution and consolidation. This history almost coincides with the entire human history: without subjects/conscious individuals, there cannot be human history.

Gutenberg's press was an important stage in the development of consciousness and the subject. Preceding the industrial revolution, it, sort of, got ready to receive the results of giant events in human intellect in form of the explosion of social and natural sciences. The great discoveries of the machine and industrial age, of the great means of transport and communications, of printing presses and books, only helped consolidation of the subject by developing consciousness on an unprecedented scale. If ever real subject was formed, it was during the industrial age.

Copying one's writings and other books and letters only helped spread consciousness far and wide.

Real discussion and exchange of opinions ensued, that helped growth of both consciousness and subjectivity. The great art works and the works of literature would not become known, would not even have developed without the new communications and printing, because, among others, they presuppose certain knowledge of the tangible and material world. The development of the press helped subjectivity.

How can one deny the role of the great spread of print media and the newspapers in the 18th-20th centuries? Not just individual consciousness, more than that mass consciousness was helped this event. Reason and Enlightenment were not only made possible; they were spread by the new media, the print media including the books.

Reason became firmly established. Reason, awareness and self-consciousness, as also conscious consciousness were spread by the new print media.

It is the reflection of the object that *really creates* the subject, the really conscious subject. And this is a very important and crucial point, as it also provides and identifies the tactual terrain for the revolution in the ways communication is conducted and, in the course of it, changes the subject.

Matter is reflected in the consciousness (the function of the brain), and that creates the subject. The ICR has changed much in the way we look at matter, the way 'matter' and its material forms are conveyed, and the way subject is created and exists, the structure of the subject itself.

The subject must be able to reason, to explain the world around. It must be able to justify the reality and existence. It is the first time, during the industrial age, that real, conscious explanations of the processes around are given. While the subject had been *accidental* and local during the pre-industrial ages, it was really the industrial revolution, which converted the subject into a *rule*, a regular observer and interpreter of the world. It was only this subject that could explain the world, really speaking. The subject is a real, reasonable being. Its relationship with the outside world is that of polar tension and opposites, which are developed to qualitatively higher levels in the modern world.

So, the modern subject is characterized by its ability to interpret the world in an objective manner. It really is able to 'look' at the world and understand it, and not just to speculate. When we describe the concepts of objectivity, and of the object and the subject, we talk about a real relationship between the two. The real subject is the one who is able to interpret and look at, delve into the world. This subject is a stable one, which is why it is a real one. In this sense, in a particular and a limited sense, the object cannot 'exist' without a real and stable subject. It is a typical relationship between the stable subject and the Cartesian world of order, history, succession and evolution.

And what is reason? It is an attempt to explain the objective processes and thus to comprehend them. Without that, the subject is not complete. Theories of postmodernism raise the question of domination. Consciousness and subjectivity are no doubt domination; in reality, they are much more than that: they are superior to objectivity.

Reflection cannot take place without reason and argument. To state a reality is to argue and to reason. For example, to state that it is a tree or a stone is to reason. The entire history of humanity is to struggle to establish this reality and truth ever deeper and wider.

Cosmology and Postmodernism

Every human culture is capable of developing cosmology, primarily as a result of wonderment at the 'cosmic' creation. It tries to place the earth and the human beings in the cosmos and wonder at the vastness of existence and/or superiority of human beings. Cosmologies are integral to our self-identity because they contextualize human existence and the life itself, and thus assign meaning to daily life struggles. Cosmologies help not only socially but also philosophically. They were also used to legitimize social authority and power.

In modern times, Edwin Hubble, through telescopic observations in 1929, found evidence of an expanding universe though spectroscope. The age of space sciences has taken cosmology to qualitatively new levels. The Hubble Space Telescope, deployed in

1990 in the earth orbit, opened entire new horizons. Since then spectacular images of the birth and death of entire galaxies have been observed. The Cosmic Background Explorer (COBE) satellite project of 1992 mapped the microwave radiation across the vast spaces.[15]

Supercomputer simulations and robotic telescopic measurements of more than one lakh (one hundred thousand) galaxies spread across billions of light years are producing absolutely new projections into the space. Orbiting X-ray telescopes may open new horizons on the black holes. Quantum physics is opening a new bizarre world.[16] At present, dramatic changes in cosmology are taking place, erasing the dividing line between physics and biology. At the same time, an evolutionary theory of the universe is emerging, which may impact the human identity. Along with the postmodern turn in theory, arts, sciences etc., a clear shift towards the postmodern cosmology began to take place in the 1980s.[17] Many scientists are giving up hitherto held models of universe. The new models and paradigms reject atomistic logic for relational understanding. Static laws are being replaced with history and evolution[18]; the cosmological theories go beyond simplicity to complexity and self-organization. They renounce realism for a hermeneutic approach to science. The postmodern shift in philosophy, social theory, science etc. is influencing cosmology also.

The monolithic concept of a single, closed "universe" is giving way to that of "many universes" or the 'multiverse', the infinite number of parallel universes. Each of these universes gives birth to another. The idea of billions of galaxies has now become common. According to the 'many-universes or branching universes interpretation' of Hugh Everett, for example, when a quantum system is presented with a choice of outcomes, the universe splits, resulting in several copies.[19]

Thus, our universe is *merely one of the infinity of the universes*. The first discontinuity in the development of modern astronomical science was opened by Copernicus; the fifth discontinuity opens up the possibility of life elsewhere in the universe/s.[20] Thus, since the 1980s a clear shift towards a *postmodern* cosmology is taking place.[21] A galaxy is not a collection of stars: "What is most new about [post]modern cosmology is the discovery that the universe is also evolving."[22] Not only this; there are processes of "co-evolution" in the universes, a postmodernist concept, opening up exciting new possibilities.[23]

Therefore, universe is not simply a place; *it is a process.* According to a postmodernist trend, the universe spawns life, it is 'alive'. According to this opinion, cosmology has taken a postmodern, evolutionary turn: it challenges distinction between physics and biology, between inorganic and organic matter; it raises natural selection, self-organisation and ecology to universal principles. According to Gribbin, synthesis of physics with biology indicates cosmology of the 21st century.[24] Terms like natural selection, competition and self-organization are useful analogies to understand galaxies or the universe.

On the basis of genetic engineering, according to Jeremy Rifkin (1998)[25], postmodern cosmology further radicalizes the modern idea that science and technology can transcend/suspend natural laws and limits. On developing idea into the postmodern form, we find that the nature is completely *malleable*, it can be transformed into anything that science wants. Therefore, there are no limits to the powers of techno-science. "Some make the dubious claim that we are in the age of biological control."[26]

The new 'worldview' is being called 'algeny'; it seeks to alter the essence of things and ultimately to 'perfect' them.[27]

In the biotech era, we can create a designer reality and a qualitatively different, postmodern organisation of knowledge.

In contrast, the *modern* reductionists believe that reality can be broken down into self-sufficient elements; these elements can be manipulated without consequence to their surrounding 'parts'. The genetic sciences resolve material reality into fragmented bits of information to be mapped by computer and manipulated by technology. This gives power over nature and human beings.

One result of the new view is that we are not alone in and separate from the universe. The human beings are, in fact, the consummate expression of the self-organisation of matter and life: they carry cosmic dust and gases in their cells, Gaia's oceans in their blood and the great apes in their DNA.[28] For Smolin, self-organisation cosmology overcomes the longstanding dualities in Western thought between matter and spirit, nature and freedom. It also enables a theory of a complex and dynamic universe without God or teleology.[29] He points out that observations of supernovas in 1998 showed that the universe was expanding, meaning that the cosmological constant had to be positive, creating a new and genuine crisis in this field.[30]

Best and Kellner say that science, which has done so much to alienate human beings from nature, now, at this stage, *connects the two.* This is because of the ecological and life-sensitive issues of the present times.[31]

So, what emerges in the discussion is: 1) a change from the modern to the postmodern, 2) ontological integration of culture with nature.

In this connection, we have to discuss and clarify the following:

(i) Is the 'modern' connected with the alienation from nature due to science?

(ii) Does the postmodern realign the separated or alienated elements?

(iii) How are culture and nature interrelated?

It is claimed[32] that the postmodern cosmologies, through their texts, subvert western anthropocentrism, by pointing out that the earth is only a speck in the cosmos and history of human culture only a nanosecond in the 15 billion-year journey. Yet, the postmodern description puts human existence in proper context and generates respect for life, with human beings joining the community of millions of other species, and also emphasizing that we are not alone in the universe. "Crucially, postmodern cosmologies seek to provide scientifically accurate and life-enriching stones..."[33]

What Constitutes the 'Postmodern'?

It is claimed that science is no more mere principles but reverence for life. Besides, everything is 'co-evolution' for postmodernism: from biology to cosmology. So, the concept of 'co-evolution' is crucial for postmodernism. The relationship between technological revolution and postmodernism is a complicated one but very crucial to the understanding of the transition from modernism to postmodernism. Best and Kellner have raised many points, some of which need critical comments. According to them[34], technology is fundamental to the promotion of ever-new innovations and socioeconomic advancement. Modernity was fuelled by perpetual revolutions in science, industry and technology via printing press, steam engine, factory system, railways and other modes of transport, media, culture, industries, etc.

But the postmodern 'adventure' is driven largely by electronics, new media, bio-technologies, computers, etc. How? What does this mean? The current technological revolution is transforming every dimension of life, work, leisure time, communications, what and how we eat, fast food and genetically modified food etc.[35]

Through co-evolution of science, technology and market, a global reorganization of capitalism is taking place. Infrastructure of capitalism is being unified into a networked society and culture. Certain points emerge in the process, e.g.:

— Dematerialized and miniaturized world, exploring particles, genes, space, etc.
— Transition from Newton's world of solid particles to the non-tangibles of wave/particle duality and of endless variety of particles.
— A whole range of transition from the computers of the 1940s, e.g. Harvard Mark I, Colossus, ENIAC, etc. to the PCs and laptops etc. today.
— From slowdown of time and long time to extra-ordinary speed up to microseconds.
— Speed and power of computation doubling every 18 months: Moore's law.
— Emergence of nano-technology as qualitatively new phase.
— Use of microchips in every field.
— Post-PC era. Miniaturization of the computers. Portable communications. Collapse of time and space in the hand-held electronic sets.
— Electronics has enabled development of technologies which have begun new era in human history.
— Beginning of quantum era in science.
— Emergence of 'quantum philosophy'. Etc.

At the same time, quite surprisingly, Best and Kellner take a critical position towards the very method of dialectics. They are not critical of just this or that aspect of dialectics but are anti-dialectics as such. This stands out even more clearly in the background of their treatment of science and technology. For them "some dialectical and scientific theories have tended to be uniperspectival and reductionist."[36] Which ones and how? They criticize both Hegel and the Marxists (Engels,

Kautsky, Plekhanov, etc.) as also the Darwinians for advocating "overly simplified" "laws" of dialectics and evolution for idea, society, economics, and biological evolution and natural selection. The dialectical method and its laws are supposed supposed to mute and passive victims of the natural physical laws, with humans as the helpless spectators.[37] The authors advance no arguments in favour of their contentions, except stating their views. Thus, the most scientific, that is, dialectical method is ignored even while analyzing scientific events.

In fact, in many places their fine book, the authors unconsciously used the dialectical method of investigation and observation!

With ever-deeper advance of science and technology into the natural world, society, life, our bodies, human beings and technology are imploding. According to some theorists, the age of humanism is over, giving way to the post-humanist condition.[38]

Science and technology and are undermining the boundaries between reality/unreality, natural/artificial, organic/inorganic, biology/technology, human/machine, the born/the made, and so on. *These very important boundary lines getting blurred provide crucial points for the emergence of a postmodern society/world.* It is a world of virtual reality, biotechnology, generics, artificial intelligence, artificial life etc. It is a world of the surrogate mother, of test tube baby, and so on.

We are thus *no more living in the old world, old society.* We are becoming cyborgs and techno-bodies. The machines on the other hand are becoming more 'human-like'.

Today's child is virtually born 'with a computer'. He/she begins operating computer at a very early age, which becomes its inalienable 'organ', a body-extension. The child can teach the adult almost everything about the computers and mobiles. *Is there a change of direction here in the evolution of human beings?*

Shifts in Human Consciousness

The shifts in science and technology are causing unprecedented shifts in the conception of ourselves, philosophy, nature of reality and its concept etc. These are paradigm shifts.

The human beings are step by step getting staggering new powers *to manipulate their world*: atom by atom, molecule by molecule, gene by gene, byte by byte.[39] Humanity has reached a point in technological progress where it threatens life and planet's resources. Human beings have begun to shape up further evolution through the creation of transgenetic and artificial species. Techno-science and capitalism are devouring the earth, and they have even ventured out into the space with the same aims.

Humanity in the present phase is creating *artificial intelligence* with the help of increasingly sophisticated computers and robots. They have the potentials to open up new lines of evolution far exceeding our powers and expectations. We stand on the verge of the unexpected and the unprecedented. "Intelligence" is *no more a strictly human property*. The *traditional* concept of the machine is giving way to the newer one/s, and 'machines' are taking the place of the machine. The machine 'learns', uses logic, leads our way forward, and so on, and thus move away from being machine.

Today, the machines are becoming similar to the operations of the brain: through neural nets, parallel computing/processing, evolutionary hardware and software, etc. Is the self-ascribed 'essence' of the human beings being stripped away? *The human beings are beginning to merge with the machines; the flesh is getting fused with silicon chips and steel, and in this setting the human identity is being questioned.*

Thus a *post-humanist* scenario is emerging out of the humanist one, which encompasses, assimilates and includes the latter, and brings it to new levels. *Both the subject and the object are in question.*

Now onwards, the machine will be an *inseparable, inalienable part* of the human being in the course of evolution. One reason is that the machine is becoming smaller, even minuscule. Thus, it can easily fit in the living bodies. Microprocessors and electronic miniature components can fast receive and send signals, and therefore are more efficient and effective than human nervous system in terms of speed, time and space. They therefore take over increasing number of human functions.

Besides, there is a *convergence* of sorts. Microchips and nano-parts are more and more acting as biological microorganisms, while microorganisms now tend to act as source of computing and computers. Atomic and even particle computing systems are being visualized. Nanomachines are more akin to bacteria. They perform several functions in our bodies that can be discharged by the microorganisms. But the advantage, particularly with the microprocessors, is their extremely efficient and ultra-quick communications, which use both the biological and the non-biological paths of communications.

These and other postmodern developments are increasingly putting a question mark on human identity itself, as also on the surroundings that create humanity. For the first time, the conditions that created the human beings are qualitatively different: we are witnessing emergence of Homo electronicus.

Communication Technology and Electronic Culture

According to Marshall McLuhan, communication technologies are creating an electronic culture, ending the era of print technology and 'mechanical man'.[40] They are also bringing the entire humanity on the earth together. In his opinion the print technology made possible modern science and technology, capitalism, nationalism, individualism, etc., thus providing the foundations of modern civilization.[41]

But now the rise of novel media and computer technologies has caused a *rupture in history*; this is due to the innovative forms of society and culture, and eventually a mutation in human species.

Media revolutions in TV, film, video, ads, etc. have transformed politics, economics, identities, life, entertainment, etc., and among others, have created a world of hyper-reality. The computers originated during WWII for decrypting German military codes and building atom bomb, and gradually became more important for society in general. By the 1980s, the PC revolution had begun; then arrived the age of internet. As the whole world is being computerized, all other technologies are being absorbed and transformed into the process of digitalization, and the world of atoms is being transformed into the world of 'bits'.[42] Objects, activities and experience are becoming 'virtualized'. Online activities are spreading, creating a network society.

All the processes are being converted into numbers. *Digitisation* is a very important phenomena. It is becoming universal, through its binary language. Everything is being simplified, reduced to simple numbers and quanta (digits). A distinguishing feature of the present-day world is the increasing use of numbers in all the fields; i.e. the increasing *numberisation* of life, electronics, bar code, forms of various kinds, and so on and so forth, i.e. the growing codification.

This fact has far-reaching implications for the future, particularly for the consciousness. Do the numbers express endless relations?

Computers helped the new genetic sciences ushered in by James Watson and Francis Crick. The current era is that of 'bio-cybernetic reproduction', and computers play a crucial role in it. Storage and manipulation of massive amounts of data is involved in the mapping of the human genome simply to print the names of the 3 million nucleic acid base pairs making up tens of thousands of human genes, and it would require as many as 13 sets of *Encyclopedia Britannica!* Once their nature and interrelationships are established, genetics would undergo promising qualitative leaps.[43]

Baudrillard and Postmodernism (and Post-modernity)

We have dealt with some of Baudrillard's concepts in the chapter on mode of information.

In fact, Baudrillard's positions on postmodernism continue to be quite contradictory, which may confuse the readers, who may draw opposite conclusions if they read his individual writings. One may state briefly that though he opposes the use of words/terms like 'postmodernism' etc., in effect he deals with several crucial transformatory points of the electronic and information society, e.g. TV, virtual reality, impact of electronics on subject formation etc.

"Baudrillard does not believe postmodernism has any viability as a conceptual term. He says that 'one should ask whether postmodernism, the postmodern, has a meaning. It doesn't, as far as I am concerned..."[44] Paul Hegarty concludes that he is actually not interested in postmodernism, and talks about it only when asked or interviewed.[45] At the same time, as we have seen elsewhere in this book, Baudrillard has done great work on impact of TV ads and TV in general on subject formation, on problems of 'simulacra', as also in other related fields.

Baudrillard's views on postmodernity and postmodernism have evolved over time.

Baudrillard's concept of post-modernity is based on three main ideas: simulation, implosion and hyper-reality.[46] Following an anti-foundationalist line of Derrida and Lyotard, he develops a narrative of the end of modernity, an era dominated by production and industrial capitalism and by 'political economy of signs'.[47] By implication, the concept of 'industrial' capitalism means there can be non-industrial and non-production capitalism.

So far, we know mainly of industrial, production capitalism, consequent upon the great industrial revolution. We do know of pre-industrial merchant, circulation and small scale, even manufactory, capitalism. But they were only preparatory stages to the industrial capitalism.

Is non- or post-industrial capitalism, capitalism in the *strict sense?* Several laws of the industrial capitalism are step by step suspended in this phase, as the society moves away from the industrial phase. Capitalism involves industrial production. By becoming post-industrial, the society sheds more and more features created during the industrial age, and acquires aspects in which capitalist and new post-capitalist features merge together imperceptibly. This could be a transition to a new society in which there is *less and less of capitalism.*

This very important point needs a separate and detailed treatment.

Another feature that Baudrillard points out in the context of post-modernity is the '*political economy of the sign*'. This is another crucial concept as a turning point, and can be contrasted with the political economy based on the commodity production. This point also needs a separate and detailed treatment.

Since signs are produced as commodities, semiology (the way signs are produced) also needs treatment in the same way as the political economy, according to Baudrillard.

According to him, post-modernity is characterized by the 'simulation', and by new forms of culture, technology and society. The earlier cultures depended on face-to-face symbolic communication, then on print; the present culture is dominated by the images of electronic media.[48]

The related question is that of the political economy of the sign, instead of the political economy of the 'thing' as commodity. How can cost and the economics of the sign be determined? Sign dissolves the system, as the commodity is transformed into a *system of signs.*

This creates a world of simulacra, models, signs, codes, digitalized reality, etc. Our lives are more and more being shaped by simulated events on TV, computers, video, etc. There are virtual stones, virtual shopping, etc.[49]

Baudrillard claims that we have entered an era of simulations governed by information, signs and cybernetic technology. It is these signs and simulations that structure and create experiences; consequently, the distinctions between the image and reality are erased or reduced. Simulation is where the image or the model becomes *more real than the real.* Therefore, the distinction between image and reality *implodes.* Along with this collapse, the very experience of the real world disappears. *Simulation is the central concept in Baudrillard's conception of history.* According to it, in contrast to the earlier positions, signs now bear no relations with the reality. "With simulation there is a 'generation by models of a real without origin or reality'."[50] The word *hyper-real* means *more real that the real.* The real here is produced by the model. Hyper-real covers the blurring of the distinction between the real and the unreal. It is a state where *the distinctions between objects and their representations are dissolved.* One is left with what Baudrillard calls *simulacra.* The media messages are the prime example, where the self-referential signs lose contact with the things.

Modernism and Postmodernism

How is one to understand the term 'postmodern'? The prefix 'post' suggests that postmodernism is inextricably bound up with modernism; it could be the replacement of the latter or could be placed chronologically after modernism. The 'post' can be seen to suggest a critical engagement with modernism, rather than the end of modernism, or it can be seen that modernism has been overturned, superseded or replaced. The relationship appears to resemble a continuous engagement, implying that postmodernism needs modernism to survive. Therefore, a prior knowledge and definition of modernism is essential.[51]

Modernism was generally the name given to the upheavals in European culture in the first-half of the 20th century. It undermined many aesthetic tenets of arts. It is affected areas like architecture, music, visual art, philosophy, literature, etc. From about 1910 until about the beginning of the Second World War, a large number of writers and artists ushered in and experimented with innovative modes of representation.[52]

Tim Woods catalogues some of the characteristics of modernism.[53] Among others, it includes a commitment to find new forms to explore *how we see* the world rather than what we see in it. A break is made with the realist modes of narrative in favour of consciousness. Cubism emerges, which represents objects as a series of discontinuous, fractured planes, *all equidistant from the observer*, rather than using light and perspective to suggest pictorial depth of solid, three dimensional objects.

Basic geometric shapes like cubes and cylinders in towers are used as expression of a rationalist, progressive society. Use of fragmented forms in art (collage, etc.) and deliberately discontinuous narratives in literature emerged. They were ideologically inspired, and represented the fragmentation of the accepted thought and belief. Aesthetic self-reflexivity with novels with narrative comments and forms, unfinished or blank spaces in the canvas, etc. emerged. A clear demarcation between popular and elite forms of culture emerged, e.g. jazz and rock, rock and pop etc. A gradual growth of interest in the non-Western forms of culture emerged.[54]

In the above explanation of modernism, Tim Woods confines himself, while explaining the concepts of modernism and postmodernism, to art and culture alone. But do modern and modernism not cover the entire industrial era? How are art, culture, literature, etc. related to socio-economic and political changes, and what about the modern trends in the socio-economic and political fields? Why these changes in art, culture and other fields have taken place *at all*?

These question need to be tackled.

Tim Woods further discusses as to what extent does postmodernism emerge out of the modern situation and react to it?[55] At first glance, the 'post' suggests a cultural era after modernism. That suggests some linear or historical periodisation. The relationship between the two is more complex than this. Habermas and Callinicos argue that postmodernism is no different from modernism in certain formal respects. Many theorists argue that postmodernism is not a chronological period, but more a way of thinking and doing.[56]

Here the question arises: how, in what respects?

Zygmunt Bauman regards post-modernity "as modernity conscious of its true nature".[57] Thus, it is a social and intellectual self-reflective mood within modernity. He makes the important point that "the postmodern worldview entails the dissipation of objectivity."[58] This point can become a launching pad for a new turn in analysis of the problem at hand. Postmodernism is a knowing modernism, *a self-reflexive modernism.*[59] It does not agonise about itself. Postmodernism does what modernism does, not in a repentant but in a celebratory way. Post-modernism does not lament the loss of the past, the fragmentation of existence and the collapse of the selfhood. It embraces these characteristics as a new form of social existence and behaviour. Thus, according to this view, the difference between modernism and postmodernism is that of mood or attitude.[60]

Here, postmodernism is sought to be explained in terms of moods or attitudes, and not *as social objective processes.* It does not, to conclude from Woods, follow the socio-economic processes leading to the said fragmentation. How exactly does it celebrate the event, and why? This is not made clear. Besides, these claims are neither explained nor do they stand the scrutiny of facts of historical developments and their causes.

Legacy of Enlightenment and Modernity

Enlightenment is at the centre of the debate between modernism and postmodernism. Rousseau, Kant and Hegel at the beginning of the enlightenment placed a great deal of faith in human ability to reason as a means of ensuring and preserving humanity's freedom. But many of the 20th century philosophers, particularly those living through and after the holocaust, felt such a faith in reason misplaced. According to them, human reason and logic can equally lead to the Nazi concentration camps, as it leads to liberty. Lyotard is the leading exponent of this view. According to Sabina Lovibond, enlightenment pictured the human race as trying for universal moral and intellectual self-realisation. Therefore, the humans were the subjects of a universal historical experience. Enlightenment also postulated a universal human reason in terms of which social and political tendencies could be assessed as 'progressive' or otherwise. The goal of politics was defined as the realization of reason in practice. Postmodernism rejects this doctrine of unity of reason. It does not regard humanity as a unitary subject striving to achieve the goal of perfect coherence.[61]

[Authors refer to the poststructuralist philosophy's claim that ideas that maintain there are centres of truth standing outside the logic of language are merely convenient or ideologically motivated illusions.][62]

Bauman, in an interview with Richard Kilminster and Ian Varcoe in 1990, makes the point particularly clear in the context of the collapse of Communist regimes in the USSR and east Europe. He considers that they were extremely spectacular dramatization of the Enlightenment message. Their collapse was not only the collapse of communism, but more than that "it was the collapse of a certain modern idea of a 'designed society'".[63] The interview clarifies a number of points regarding place and role of reason, enlightenment and global perspective in the context of modernity.

Post-modernity and Postmodernism

Here Woods clarifies the absence of the socio-economic in postmodernism by including it (the socio-economic) in the concept of 'post-modernity'. Thus, post-modernity and postmodernism are two different concepts.

Post-modernity is a concept describing the socio-economic, political and cultural condition. The present-day world increasingly lives in postindustrial, service-oriented economics; the daily, mundane activities like shopping are increasingly mediated through computer networks, email, voice-mail, fax, tele-conferencing, net, mobiles, high speed image bombardment, etc.

Postmodernism on the other hand describes the broad aesthetic and intellectual activities/projects of the society, on theoretical plane.

Postmodernism is a term used roughly since the 1960s about certain characteristics of the cultural forms. They include:

— Undercutting of an all-encompassing rationality;
— suspicion of metanarratives, totalizing discourses, and of any discursive attempts to global or universalist account of existence; etc.
— Rejection of modernism.[64]

In and through all this, postmodernism represents a loss of faith in the main concepts of enlightenment, such as: belief in the infinite progress of knowledge, moral and social advancement, reason, and in teleology, legitimacy, coherence, etc. Therefore, postmodernism seeks *local or provisional*, rather than absolute and universal, forms of legitimation.

In the opinion of many, postmodernism/deconstructionism points a way out of *cultural and epistemological crisis*. Various disciplines have lost their sense of direction, are in crisis, and are getting disrupted. It seems, postmodernism appeals to the societies gripped by frustration and nostalgia due to the demise of their former economic, cultural and political projects/superiority.[65]

The term 'postmodernism' is not understood in the same way in all the disciplines. Besides, the same words and concepts may even mean different things in different areas and subjects. Postmodernism arose at different times in different disciplines: in the 1950s in art, 1960s for architecture, early 1980s for cultural theory, late 1980s for many social sciences, etc.

One of the principal problems is the relation of postmodernism with hegemonic or dominant culture, however implicit, a reality that cannot be denied. For example, the MNCs use ethnicity or tribalism or traditions for money-making, thus subverting these cultures and communities while appearing to propagate them. So this complex and contradictory phenomenon has to be put in a proper perspective. To stress only the radical or reactionary side of postmodernism is to reduce the complexity of the cultural debate.[66]

The political and ethical implications of postmodernism are not easy to demarcate. This is one of the principal reasons for disagreement about the postmodernist interpretation of history, representation, subjectivity and ideology. Postmodernism makes a virtue of its politics of demystification of structures like patriarchy, imperialism, humanism; these concerns interconnect with those of Marxism, feminism and poststructuralist analyses. Marxism and feminism bear theories of political action and agency that often appear insufficient or absent in postmodernism. Another question is that of gender. Though postmodernism claims to represent the suppressed voice of the women, and other groups, it remains dominated by the masculine in many areas. Besides, the postmodernist theorists have often been criticized for confusions, the collapse of certain ideologies of the real and the social with the collapse of reality and society. This point is crucial because the politics of culture is based upon the relationship between the two.[67]

Postmodernist writings generally are opposed to reducing things to bare essentials, to clear-cut definitions; they are obsessed with fragments, pieces, fractures, with no clear-cut beginning or end. They make sudden turns and abrupt shifts from one point to another without explanation, the points having been simply stated and not clarified. These characteristics and habits often make it difficult to understand as to where postmodernism stands on this or that question. Their writings resist clear-cut, rational, consistently argued explanations, all the time trying to avoid what they call 'totalization'. Instead of 'totalizing' essays, the postmodern writings are generally fragmentary.

'Discourse' in Postmodernism

The term 'discourse' is one of the key words in the postmodernist literature. It is a *slippery word.*[68] But generally it is taken to mean the institutionalised practice, through which signification and value are imposed. Discourses are a variety of different linguistic structures used in dynamic exchange of beliefs, attitudes, sentiments and other expressions. These expressions are specific configurations of historical, social and cultural power. Thus, postmodernism is recognized as a 'discursive event' covering a wide range of disciplines.[69]

The concept of discourse has evolved over time as multisided and complex, yet overlapping one. David Howarth[70] has allowed full play to the motion of these concepts over time and with authors and contexts or even in the absence of context. To trace out discourse, he brings together three anti-positivistic traditions of intellectual enquiry: post-structuralism, hermeneutics and post-Marxism.[71] The treatment covers a wide range of field. It involves use of knowledge and its language, institutions, growing divergences of the meanings as the language travels over social terrain, constitution of meanings into a system of symbolic meanings/indications, imparting particular aspects to the subject, going to the extent of constituting *the subject itself.*

Ultimately, discourse appears to constitute a symbolic system of signs, meanings and interpretations traceable to the growing complexity of movement of language and its independence. Here post-structuralism appear to contribute substantially, and both Howarth and Poster tend to draw upon it more than on others.[72]

Woods tries to emphasise that he positions cultural concept precisely as a *cultural* concept.[73] Accordingly, it covers the entire swathe of subjects, and not simply a word debated by the ivory-tower academics.[74] He tries to position a concept within the specific manifestations of the particular discourses including within their fluidity and constantly changing boundaries, whether in literature, architecture, music, politics, law, sociology, geography, business and management systems and so on. Such definitions place people within certain contexts, in specific concrete existences, and thus does not delimit them as specifically either this or that, does not absolutise them. They are thus balanced within the sum total of a wide variety of cultural explorations, cognitive experiences, historical tensions, scientific structures or aesthetic forms.[75]

The problem here and elsewhere in the postmodern literature as well as in the literature on postmodernism is that the term 'cultural' has never been explained: what exactly is meant or what do they mean by 'culture' or the 'cultural'? When such a key concept goes unexplained, it is very difficult to precisely explore postmodernist or any other concept. The concept of culture appears to be a broad but unclear ground of non-economic activities dealing with art, literature, behaviour, language, indications of the subject, and in general endeavour to preserve the individual.

What are the 'nuts and bolts', as Woods puts it[76], of postmodernism? They are, according to him, as follows, at least some of them: thematic issues of: functions of history and representation of the past in contemporary culture; the political role of the aesthetics; representation of the body and the emergence of new concepts of the human or self; metaphors of space in contemporary social experience; textualism of modern knowledge and life.[77]

Obviously, these issues are only some of the themes and areas of postmodernism. These are the issues that directly affect, and constitute and/or deconstitute the individual or the subject. Thus, the postmodern deals directly with the condition of the subject (and self, individual etc.) as constituted and as existing in the generalized cultural terrain. Seen from this point, the concept of culture becomes clearer. *Culture is the domain that sustains and creates the self (subject).* In fact, a key function of culture is *to create* the subject. Creation of the subject is, more than anything else, a cultural activity. If we take the society as given, as a product of forces at points of history, the job of culture is to create that vehicle, which sustains the human, not just the human being, but all that is human and humanly possible.

When we say 'human', we do not refer to just eating and drinking, which activities are not entirely human; they are common to animals too! The concept of the human is much superior; thought, culture and economic and material production distinguish human domain. So, culture is a vast domain, which is always creative. It is here that the real human is created. This leads to the emergence of the individual or the subject, who is always doing something, all the time transforming his/her surroundings, and thus himself/herself. That is how he/she reflects the object and objectivity in a dialectical tension. From philosophy to art and architecture is the vast field of creation of the subject as well as of individual identity. But it is also a field where the cultural becomes non-cultural, that is, goes against the grain of the subject and destroys and disintegrates it. The creations themselves become oppressive, leading to the oppression of the subject, *the domination by the created.*

Massive buildings, for example, are a wonder of human creative powers, yet dehumanized and anti-humanized in direct proportion to their creative giant scales. Individuality suffers immensely, giving rise to pessimism amidst optimism. That is the dialectics of alienation due to cultural creativity, leading to a culture of escape the realm of creativity based upon logic, science and reason. Things are put upside down. Culture is the field where alienation and oppression is felt most.

As an example, one may have a look at one of the premier libraries of Delhi, the Lok Sabha library. In the old circular building, it was more homely, accessible, direct, relatively informal. Everybody knew what is what and who is where. The situation had much to do with architecture. The colonial building meant for domination and exclusion became a place of freedom, informality and knowledge, a place of quiet search for information and truth. It became a truly great place for human endeavour.

But now, it has been shifted to an extraordinary new building, next door only. The building is truly a pinnacle of human achievement, several floors below the ground too, with giant floors and domes above, planned for the future, where you can't see anything or anybody! No records, no books, no human beings – you have to search for them! Onlt stones and wood. One of the leading and finest libraries is lost in this giant space, absolutely modern (and 'postmodern'!), no one seen sitting on chairs; where have they all gone?! And you will truly be lost in it if you are looking for a particular place or room or person. Doors are shut: where do they lead to? Where is this particular number or that? You won't even find a person to ask! The human is truly lost in this maze of ultramodern structure. It is oppressive, made doubly so by continuous air-conditioning of the whole giant structure. You would rather feel avoiding the place than visiting; so oppressive, dehumanizing and antihuman it is!

Truly, a curl back of dialectics of architecture, scaring away the humans!

The modern flat system has a similar effect, causes a similar experience. Modernism has somewhere led to a break in the human and the individual. Electronics has a great potential to overcome it.

Fredric Jameson has much to say about the conversion of space in postmodernist culture and architecture. They go through the processes of self-reflection, spacing out and re-positioning of the individual subject.[78] In his view, postmodernism raises questions about the appetite for architecture which it then redirects. Architecture is a relatively late taste among the North Americans.[79] Postmodernism went on to abolish something more fundamental, that is, the difference between the inside and the outside of 'the building' and within the building. For example, the former streets became so many aisles in a department store.[80] Jameson provides examples and analyses of structures like the 'Westin Bonaventure' building in Los Angeles built by the architect and developer Portman. It has novel kinds of entries leading to some of the floors direct from the street. The usual difference between the surrounding areas and the building is much less marked. The entry or the entries have lesser meaning than usual. It appears to be a total space, a complete world, a miniature city; it has a collective crowd, with individuals moving in free space.[81] It is almost that it does not want to be part of the city, while at the same time trying not to be different.

Jameson describes some other buildings including those of Le Corbusier. He presents interesting details and analytical narration of the reflective capacities and resultant effects of the reflective glasses of the new buildings.[82] He describes houses like 'Frank Gehry House', Santa Monica, California, and others, giving an account of their dialectical evolution.

We certainly need postmodernism to restore the unity of the humans, their culture and environment, because their cultured culture has decultured them!

Postmodernism and the Late and the Latest Capitalism

In the late 20th and early 21st centuries, there have been several interventions in the rapidly changing political and social climate, which may be termed post-modernist ones.

One of the great substrata of change is the nation, nationhood and the concept of 'country'. After the end of the cold war, breakdown of the Berlin Wall, disintegration of the USSR and of the Soviet-era regimes in the Eastern Europe, big changes in the concept of nation and nationhood have occurred. These changes have been facilitated by the new and faster means of electronic communications and by the rapid emergence of a fast-integrating world market. In fact, many of these changes have been caused by the electronics revolution.

Significant changes have taken place in the place and role of states ('the state') and nations. State sovereignty can no longer rely on the modern concepts of classification, identification and spatial separations. The very concept of state sovereignty needs redefinition. For example, how do we look at the emergence of the phenomenon of the European Union (EU)? It needs a separate treatment. Capital quickly stretches across the globe, new problems of locating and policing financial operations arise, electronic media and the worldwide nets pose new problems of regulation. As it is, the electronic communication respects no state boundaries.[83]

What is or what can be postmodern in these events and in today's citizenship? In the course of the political sanctions against Iraq in the late 1990s, one of the measures adopted was denial of Internet access.[84] In other words, that was a denial of *world citizenship*.

There is no doubt that a credible construction of identity, democracy, community etc. without the presence of a territorial space and boundaries *has already become a feature of present times*. The concepts of 'nation' and 'country' have become weakened, in particular due to the electronics, information and communication revolution.

In such a situation of immense possibilities of the way forward, the dominant forces led by the giant MNCs, state of giant finance capital and the big capital use the concepts *both ways* for their benefit. They want to crush the weaker nations, as exemplified in Iraq, Iran, Afghanistan, Libya and elsewhere in the world, using the big national momentum of the past. For this, they want to impose their own status of big and powerful nations to crush others, yet maintain their 'own' nation, nationhood and status of strong countries or super-power, using, among others, the pretext of threat to their 'security'. Thus maintaining 'nationhood' by the powerful has become *a means of national oppression in* the age of electronics. The big business and finance dominated giant capitalism (imperialism) wants to deny the fruits of internationalization, globalization and weakening of national boundaries to others, yet wants to take full advantage of these processes *to keep the past, i.e. the modern in tact*.

In this world of fast changes, postmodernism is trying in its own way and with its own interpretations, to build a critique of the modernist elitism. There could be *two interpretations* of this approach. As a new radical, one might view postmodernism in this context as an attack on modern elitism. As an old radical, one might tend to support modernism as an approach of emancipatory consciousness, and thus attack postmodernism.

But a differentiated approach at this juncture might help sort things out. Modernism as dominated by giant vested interests seeks *to prevent* mass transition to postmodernism. So, the task of the rest of the modern is to transit to the postmodern conditions.

But postmodernism makes the mistake of recoiling from rationality on the pretext of Hiroshima and Holocaust.[85] *There is rationality and rationality*. Hiroshima is both rational and irrational;

the question is, by whom and for whom? Hiroshima and Nagasaki are totally irrational for the overwhelming majority of humanity, in fact even for the oppressors. That is why a giant movement got unleashed to prevent a third world war. A nuclear war is madness, irrational, for everybody. So, here the existing postmodernist attempts to jettison rationality have to be critiqued and negated. Oppression is rational and product of the rational, and resistance to the oppression is also rational. While postmodernism and its roots look upon the Second World War and fascism as the result of 'rationalism' and of the breakdown of the project of Enlightenment, they fail to take into account the opposite rationale of opposition which led to the defeat of fascism and the end to the war.

After all, a post-second world war society did come into being, including postmodernism itself, on the basis of rationalism, and it is quite different from the pre-war era. It is the post-war society that makes possible a transition to a new, 'post' society, making a new world war almost impossible, due very much to the development of technology, a technology of non-use of nuclear weapons.

Every pessimism, including that of postmodernism, has its own logic and rationale, *expressed though the critique of rationalism.* A critique of logic and rationalism itself has a logic.

Concept of Experience

How do you experience the world? And how do you *express/reflect* the experience? We experience the world through our senses directly as well as through the use of progressively more efficient instruments, tools, etc.

The whole phenomenon produces an entire world of words, text, writing, speeches, communications, etc. that enable the subjects to both to experience and express the objects, the outside world, other words and practices. So, it is complex world which we are trying to explore through various theories and practice. It is in this way that the postmodernist 'discourse' is created and which is rapidly expanding. The user develops a number of concepts and methods in linguistic and literary theory and practice in accord with ontological notions/ assumptions, that is, about what exists outside and how, in what order, etc. They include Derrida's deconstruction, Foucault's genealogical and archaeological approaches, Saussure's linguistic distinctions, Wittgenstein's concept of rule following Laclau and Mouffe's logic of equivalence and difference,[86] Baudrillard's and Poster's (Poster, *The Mode of Information*) electronically mediated communication and consequent linguistic configurations with construction of ever new subjects.

This leads us to a very important point of the role of words and texts in social development, and also to the changes brought about by the electronics communications. Word and text are among the key centres, substrata of the STR and ICR, leading to the postindustrial and postmodern society, and to the mode of information.

Can we not assume that the word and the text are acquiring a relative independence, from both the subject and the object? We can certainly assume a growingly autonomous and independent world of electronic communications (e.g. the internet) where they do assume relatively independent existence. Such an assumption solves several *epistemological and practical* problems. In fact, this is not just an assumption but a reality. The growing internet and computer-mobile-satellite networks with expanding capacities are the examples.

How does electronic word (and text) differ from the pre-electronic, industrial, pre-industrial word, etc.? Electronics both erases as well as creates an independent existence for the word. As luminescent light signals, the word is very temporary; yet it is independent in existence, as we can call it into existence any time, and because of other facets too. Such a word, in contrast to the printed word, can instantly spread in no time, throughout the computer networks. The word instantly crosses the time and space barriers. *This does not happen with the printed word.* The multiplication and transmission is instant. Therefore, though, the word disappears from our view, it remains in existence as an independent representation throughout the electronic system like the internet, etc.

Language and Writing

According to Saussure, sound is closer to ideas and thought, whereas writing is at one further remove.[87] Writing simply represents speech. Speaking always presumes presence of a speaker and hearer/s. But writing can function without hearer and speaker, and even writer. At the same time, he considers writing as a transparent medium or expression of ideas. It is simply the means by which ideas are transmitted in the absence of speakers and listeners. On the other hand, writing is able to distort speech/thought; it subsists in the absence of the speaker/writer: the living presence of the spoken-voice is lost or forgotten.[88]

Saussure's theory of language emphasizes the decisive role of meaning and signification in structuring the human life. As per Saussure and his extension by Levi-Strauss, society itself can be understood as a symbolic system. Society is not seen as a product of laws of economic production or of human spirit or individual interactions.

Here we will leave further details of these theories and point out that the electronic revolution has worked deeply upon the sites of speaking, hearing, reading and writing, and has produced speeds of these acts to a point where their stable nature is threatened and transformed. These sited create a new postmodern mode of information, where the subject is partially sidelined as well as changed, and new configurations of texts are produced in no time and all the time.

At the same time the impacts are also resulting in the creation of new kind of spread out subject. This is a distinguishing feature of the postmodern world dominated by information.

NOTES

1. Mark Poster, *The Mode of Information: Poststructuralism and Social Context*, Polity Press, 1990, p. 124.
2. John Phillips on Derrida's *The Post Card*, www.google.com
3. Jacques Derrida, *The Post Card: From Socrates to Freud and Beyond*, University of Chicago Press, 1987.
4. Derrida, ibid., "Envois", emphasis added.
5. See, Jacques Derrida, *The Post Card:* ... etc.
6. Poster, *The Mode of Information*, p. 125.
7. Following Poster, ibid., p. 125.
8. Ibid.
9. Ibid., p. 126.
10. Ibid.

11. Derrida quoted by Poster, ibid., p. 127.
12. Quoted in Poster, ibid., p. 125.
13. Ibid.
14. See, G.W.F. Hegel, *Phenomenology of Spirit*, Motilal Banarasidass Publishers Pvt Ltd, Delhi, 1998, Para 110, p. 66.
15. Based on Steven Best and Douglas Kellner, *The Postmodern Adventure: Science, Technology and Cultural Studies in the Third Millennium*, The Guilford Press, New York, London, 2001, pp. 134-35.
16. Based on Best and Kellner, ibid., p. 135.
17. Ibid., p. 137.
18. Ibid.
19. P.C.W. Davies and J.R. Brown, *The Ghost in the Atom*, Canto, Cambridge University Press, 1993, pp. 34-36.
20. Best and Kellner, *The Postmodern Adventure*, p. 137.
21. Ibid.
22. Lee Smolin, quoted in, Best and Kellner, ibid., p. 134.
23. Ibid., pp. 140-41.
24. Ibid., p. 138.
25. Ibid.
26. Wilmut et al., 2000, quoted in Best and Kellner, ibid.
27. Ibid.
28. Ibid., p. 138.
29. Ibid.
30. Lee Smolin, *The Trouble with Physics*, Allen Lane/Penguin, 2006, p. 154.
31. Best and Kellner, op. cit., p. 139.
32. Ibid., pp. 139-40.
33. Ibid., p. 140.
34. Ibid., p. 149.
35. Ibid.
36. Ibid., p. 141.
37. Ibid.
38. Ibid., p. 151.
39. Ibid., p. 152.
40. Ibid., p. 154.
41. Ibid.
42. Ibid.
43. Ibid., p. 155.
44. Paul Hegarty, *Jean Baudrillard: Live Theory*, Continuum, London/New York, 2004, p. 5.

45. Ibid.
46. Tim Woods, *Beginning Postmodernism*, Manchester University Press, 2007, p. 26.
47. Ibid., p. 25.
48. Ibid., p. 26.
49. Ibid., pp. 25-26.
50. Ibid.
51. Ibid., p. 6.
52. Ibid., pp. 6-7.
53. Ibid., p. 7.
54. Ibid., p. 7.
55. Ibid., p. 8.
56. Ibid.
57. Ibid.
58. Zygmunt Bauman, *Imitations of Postmodernity*, Routledge, 1992, p. 35.
59. Tim Woods, op. cit., emphasis in the original.
60. Ibid., pp. 8-9.
61. Ibid., p. 9.
62. Ibid., p. 10.
63. Bauman, *Imitations of Postmodernity*, p. 221.
64. Tim Woods, *op. cit.*, p. 10.
65. Ibid., p. 11.
66. Ibid., p. 13.
67. Ibid., p. 13.
68. Ibid., p. 14.
69. Ibid., p. 15.
70. David Howarth, *Discourse*, Viva Books Private Limited, 2002.
71. Ibid., p. 5.
72. See, Howarth, *Discourse*, "Introduction" and Poster, *The Mode of Information*.
73. Woods, *Beginning Postmodernism*, p. 15.
74. Ibid.
75. Ibid.
76. Ibid., p. 16.
77. Ibid.
78. See, Fredric Jameson, *Postmodernism or the Cultural Logic of Late Capitalism*, Duke University Press, Durham, and Verso, 2006, pp. 39-45, 95-115.
79. Ibid., p. 97.
80. Ibid.

81. Jameson, *op. cit.*, pp. 39-40.
82. See, for example, Jameson, p. 42.
83. Also see, Woods, p. 252.
84. Ibid.
85. See Woods, ibid., p. 253, who provides the examples but not the criticism.
86. See, David Howarth, *Discourse,* p. 10.
87. Ibid., p. 36
88. Ibid., pp. 36-37.

11

Electronic Communication, Destabilization/Dissolution of Subject and Layers of Postmodern Consciousness

The relationship between thinking, speaking and writing on the one hand and the subject on the other has become extremely complicated and transformed in the wake of the electronic communication revolution. The relation between subject and object also is undergoing big and qualitative changes. As a result, the constitution of the subject is acquiring ever new features. Writing, speech, thinking and such activities, texts and materials of various kinds, narratives, language, words, etc. provide crucial sites/objects for the ongoing STR and ICR to work upon bringing about fundamental changes in their nature. Words, language, their meanings, connotations and interpretations are undergoing drastic conversions, changes and transcendence. These processes are leading to *a transformation and transfiguration of subject* and of the subject/object relationship.

Below we will consider some of the aspects of the problems and the changes taking place.

Opposition between Thinking, Speaking and Writing

Plato distrusted writing. He defined truth as mental experience in which the reality corresponded perfectly to the mental experience. 'Truth' was mental reflection of the ideal reality, ideal world. Writing, on the other hand, *distanced us* from truth. Writing is in opposition to speech, and *therefore to truth.* There is a growing distance *from the author*. Writing is a mere copy of a mental reality; it is supposed to be so. Writing is by nature rational.

The rationalist thought, rationalism, is also 'bound' by reason, and therefore is taken as a fetter on the development of thought. The Hindi word for the rational is 'tarkbaddha' or 'bound by reason' or 'according to reason'. The word reflects the problem very well. Thought is bound by reason, and reason by series of arguments. Thought, as a result, acquires the form of concepts and moves in that form. This aspect is taken in isolation by many thinkers, particularly the postmodernists, to oppose reason and rationalism. Things are presented as if an opposition to reason is the hallmark of new thinking or postmodernism.

What is 'Writing'?

Writing is not only 'writing', i.e. on paper or whatever. Writing is also spacing, and that is timing and gaps in timing. Thus, writing is connected with space and time. It is in a serial form, which is very important reflection of human development. So, once the human beings began to space their voices and later words, they began 'archi-writing'; then come speech/language, then writing proper, in contrast to writing in general.[1]

Writing/archi-writing = differentiation. This is very important as it brings out the dialectics of expression through speech and writing. Hegel brings out this differentiation very well. He says in *The Phenomenology of Mind* that we do not exactly express in accrual language and words what we really think. Quite often, the particular is expressed through the general and the universal, and is thus limited. When we say 'this thing is here', we do refer to a particular thing existing before our eyes, but actually we allow it to be expressed or express it only through a universal, that is, 'this'. The 'this' could refer to anything.[2]

It is important to note that the aspects of expression, language, their inner dialectics, the consequent texts etc. assumes importance as objective/subjective sites for the reorganization and restructuring of language under the impact of information/communication revolution. Language and speech assume independent existence to such an extent that they are in self-motion and open to endless meanings and interpretations. Millions of copies and multimillion receipts render language and meaning totally out of the context and propel them into the new context, with their own separate world. The internet and the satellite systems are becoming distinct world of words, texts images in suspension independent of time and space. In this dispensation, the context disappears. The context is created whenever words and images are invoked according to necessity. The context itself is becoming highly fragile and transitory.

Narrative and Discourse

In the face-to-face exchange between the speaker and the listener, the narrative is direct and unambiguous, and therefore it is widened and involved. The discourse has a limited, direct and temporary nature, closely attached to the narrative: the discourse directly "legitimizes" the narrative. The discourse creates a system of meanings and signs, which provide terrain for narratives. This fact is of great significance, and as we shall see, the STR and the ICR play a decisive role here: they work on this particular point and transform it in a way which changes the very nature of human communication.

In the non-direct, non-face to face narrative, discourse takes an involved, complicated path. Meanings and interpretations appear and emanate by the time the narrative reaches the reader/listener. This is truer of the reader. The reader reads all the frozen time and space in his/her own time and space, and constantly so. This is not so true of listening, but then listening has lesser authenticity. Narrative becomes involved, and takes the form of meta-narrative, e.g. science, allegedly, becomes a one-way imposing affair, whose imposed interpretations, it is alleged, have to be accepted by the 'listener' or the receiver.

Dialectics of Observation, and the Image-subject

Observation is the negation of observation as well as its affirmation. These oppositional sides move in a complicated dialectical inter-relationships and evolution, which is nothing but leaving behind and assimilation.

If we observe an object, we at the same time deny observation to some other object. An object is an object because it is carved out of the object, the reality, by isolating others, 'cutting them out'; otherwise an object won't be an object but only an empty concept. Since an object is identified, others are simultaneously 'non-identified' and even 'de-identified'; the identity of the identity and non-identity takes place at a higher level, when the thought moves forward.

We observe what is to be observed, and we non-observe what could have been observed, in order to observe. The identified, the observed creates direct images, the non-observed, the implied, the related, form indirect images. So, the reality exists in the unreal, implied images, and these images we try continuously to dispel, trying to make them non-existent, like so many myths. Reality expresses through images in rapid motion, due mainly to the electronic configurations.

It is these aspects of observation that are magnified and built upon in case of postmodernism created by the electronic communications. Electronic communication is an unity of observation and non-observation.

Birds' Chirping

Birds' chirpings reflect serenity, echo certain balance of natural forces, an optimal best of the best in existential symbiosis of the living and the non-living. Its fragility is its strength. It is difficult to upset, yet easy to upset. Once upset, its strength comes to the fore, because its fragility is nothing but the meticulously built fragile balance of balances that cancel out the brute strength. Upset, this fragile balance strikes out and strikes back for having disturbed the whole history. The present is thrown back into history, and history as reflected in being is sought to be relegated to non-being. The destroyer, the human, must be prepared to be non-being by negating its own being because being cannot negate, certainly not destroy, being.

The birds' chirping here is the echo of human endeavours, constantly reminding the latter of the role of consciousness. The chirping is magnified many times by instant communication around the earth. Sound is merged with speech and existential crisis. The ICR has a new site to dissolve and crystallize.

Pencil as a 'Computer' ('Word Processor'): History Through Human Learning

Pencil is the nearest non-electronic thing to the computer. One can write and erase at will. One is confident of writing without bother (of change: one can erase with eraser whenever one wishes or needs). In fact, we become more bothered about its writing getting erased. There is every chance of its being lost or faded over time. What is written is not meant for preservation, except in the prison! Often some of the great works were written in prison and smuggled out, and they were written with pencil. It is one of the closest friends of the writer, and very clean!

In the pencil, subject fades imperceptibly into the object through self-effacement!

Pencil generally gives an impression of, represents, an uncertain, tentative, sporadic subject. Pencil-writing is meant to be temporary, always, particularly in the age of production of millions of ball points every minute or so! It makes you look childish, because only children use it, or the artists, at the most. Even the children have grown more 'mature'; they would rather give it up for all sorts of highly attractive and interesting pens and gadgets.

The act of erasement is always there, inherent in the pencil. This is computer-like! So, the negative, the weakness, the inferiority, turns into a positive! The subject and the object are closely inter-related, in fact one growing over into another. Both are temporary but closely inter-related, even merging with one another. Therefore, the author is free, and that freedom is very important: it is a freedom from necessity, which becomes a broad concept here. One is unbound, not committed to anything, to idea, discipline or whatever. Not only writing is erasable but also the idea. And you can keep on writing limitlessly on limited number of pages/sketches! You can mark books or papers, which markings, though unimportant, can turn out to be extremely important.

Do you write at all with pencil? This is the moot question, that should be investigated deeply. Writing is *never* the aim of pencil-writing! It is non-writing in the sense that it must end immediately or taper off, since it is in conflict with the pen, ball points, all sorts of gadgets and, of course, with that universe known as the computer. So, even if we began by calling it a 'sort' of computer, it is no match for the latter.

The pencil is something that you just pick up in the absence of something better. So it is *the worst possible* alternative. You don't even write letters with it, not to talk of writing articles and books. That would be madness!

The pencil is simply meant to make some markings, some tick-marks, notes etc. It is never meant for a serious work, generally, normally speaking. But then suddenly the markings take the form of very important notes and references for research, become important historical documents.

The role of the pencil becomes more clearly demarcated when it comes to making calculations, addition, subtraction and so on. That brings it nearer to the computing. This is simply because we all, the common man, make too many mistakes! So, we are free to make mistakes with the pencil! That is why, it is most friendly to us! It therefore contains the whole history of human learning!

Pencil merges imperceptibly with the postmodern textual world, providing comfortable relief from the complexities of electronics in its simple, yet effective, behaviour.

Second World War, Modernity and Postmodernity

The end of modernity and the beginning of postmodernity has been much debated, without of course clarifying grounds for postmodernism. In an interesting study of Thomas Pynchon's novel *Gravity Rainbow*, the phase between the modern and the postmodern has been portrayed. It depicts the rise of the socalled "roceket state" after the end of the war and intensification of scientific and technological culture facilitating 'the postmodern adventure'.[3] The Second World War stands as a transitional stage to a late modernization and postmodernisation. Modernization turns people into things, depersonalizes individuals, sets objects and bureaucracy over freedom, and breeds fear. Societies are crystallization of power and charisma (of leaders or technologies) that must be tamed. These powers can be converted into wars. The WW II led to an immense scientific and technological growth as well as corporate organisation on a massive new scale. The dominant corporations solidified their hold on the economy, and giant government machineries evolved along with new modes of control and dominations (OSS, CIA etc.).[4]

Nearly all cultures kill; European civilization became *obsessed* and addicted with it. What it could not use, it killed. The military-industrial complex is the latest and most technologically lethal phase of the death culture. It is a mega machine for death. Millions of bureaucrats run thousands of departments of intricate nature, involving corporations, scientists, universities, military, and so on: components of a huge system of domination.

In the global organization of power and knowledge, as described above, the "normal" subjective response is paranoia.

The whole approach of the chapter in the above-mentioned book is that of pessimism and nihilism. While it is true that unparalleled destruction happened in the War, it is not clear how it led to the 'rise of postmodernism': it has not been made clear at all.

Yet one point of departure for our investigation can certainly be taken up, and that is the disintegration and re-emergence of the subject, though not exactly in the sense that Best and Kellner take it up in their otherwise excellent book referred to above.

Culture

Baudrillard considers culture as hyper-real, just as the social is: it comes to prominence when it has lost all meaning and reality.[5] The Pompidou Centre (Beau Bourg) in Paris crystallizes his views on today's culture. At one level, it is an analyses of a new building. It is also a critique of a government trying to gain symbolic capital by chasing after modern art as it disappears or becomes something else.[6]

At another level, the building expresses new vacuity and populism of the society. The building precedes the art. Therefore art is residual for the building. In this sense, modern art loses all the meaning. This situation is described by Baudrillard as the building being (or should be) empty.

The Centre is a contribution to the downfall of the art. It has open access, huge free public library, service points, encouragement to the masses to come, absence of interior walls. It cannot withstand being successful. The resistance is not a refusal but a hyper-participation.[7]

The above was described in 1977; the building had to be reduced in 1991. Walls were put up, as the people working there found open spaces disturbing, library and gallery were separated, free access to the lifts closed, structure support strengthened, queues added but controlled, etc.

According to Baudrillard, the world is synecdoche i.e. the part is in whole and vice-versa. But today this distinction is gone, "so we cannot talk about layers of representation".[8] "The part is the whole is the part."[9]

The series of objects generate resistance. For example, system: it follows this path in a structural fashion, in which furniture, clock, car etc. are not examples but locations of theory. The traditional sociological perspective is collective parts and derive theory, truth on the whole. Symbolic exchange is about the superficiality of the world, expressed in various events meant to express that which the world is not.

This attempt to express that which is not is very interesting. It emanates from the world of images, while the world is that of the objects. Thus, *postmodernism is about the movement of and in the world of images, not about the world of objects. Therefore, post-modernism has an antagonistic relationship with the real world,* as the world of images is growing and people are more and more living in the imaginary world, with moments of connection with the real.

TV reality shows: presence of cameras distorts the reality; the reality is too dull, so needs spicing up with adventures. As a result, the medium prevents the real from ever occurring. The 'falsity' of the TV shows provides a convenient alibi for the supposed non-falsity of 'real life'; it is the search for authenticity in the hyper-reality.[10]

The reality show is an attempt, using cameras, camcorders, nebulas, CCTV, and other instruments, to make people participate. These shows, as others, create hyper-reality, in which people participate, away from the real world. They, dramatize, the banal is main subject. It is the banality that is interesting for the public, and also the real object of the program, as the banality itself and the assistance reduced to its realness, have so far eluded control, as they all the passive resistance of the masses.[11]

So, the TV shows actually are a Hegelian contradiction between the real, the unreal and the hyper-real. In a match, the spectator/s is/are focused on by the camera; so, the object, in order to impose, gets extra-active, and thus out of real, and the camera shifts away. Does the system 'control' the image?

These questions must be gone into details to penetrate the electronic world of images and the culture created by them. They also provide us clues to the constitution of the 'subject'.

The reality the mass participation TV shows could be praised for democratizing access to the media, and for democratizing the masses themselves.

We may compare notes with comments in Chapter 10 of the present book.

The Individual, the Subject and Electronics

We have invented new domains of the social. The social is not a unified society or community. It is a set of network, circuits, and images. It constructs its hyper-reality from statistics, data, electronic figures and imagers, computer models, etc.

The subject or the individual has historically been constituted in a more stable manner, imparting him/her a stability over a long period of time, a permanence in society, history and philosophy. So, when we talk of the subject it/he/she is something permanent, given, with the role of creator of many objects of history. Such a relation between subject and object is permanent.

The nature of subject and its relation with the world outside undergoes changes down the history, particularly in the course of the ongoing electronic revolution and communication.

The individuals are no longer members of a community, and increasingly no longer individuals, but *a set of data,* categories, types. The individual is defined by information, numbers and data. When a shop-loyalty card processes information about purchases, they (the processes) are not interested in you but *in breaking you down.*[12]

This is a very interesting point made by Hegarty and Baudrillard. It can be extended to the relationship between the individual/subject and the whole range of electronic devices and cards, which 'observe', analyse, 'break down' and reconstitute the individual. The subject develops to a point today where its electronic representation can help dissociate it, show its constituent parts/particles/waves and associate and *reassemble* it as easily. Credit/debit cards, bank accounts, all sorts of I-cards and licences and other electronic cards, even e-mail identity, passports and so on, 'break down' the subject, the individual into 'its' constituent elements, and then only he or she functions as part of the system, a system which is becoming more and more imaginary and hyperreal.

The important point is that the subject is constituted in the course of communication, and disappears when the communication is over. This is a historic change. It renders the structures of society more and more temporary and momentary.

The body is no longer an effective limit of the subject's position, we can say following Mark Poster[13], who follows Teilhard de Chardin, and says that the nervous system extends allover the earth, enwrapping the planet in a noosphere of language. Here it would also be relevant to use the Russian scientist Vernadsky's original contributions to the concept of noosphere, whom others followed. We have mentioned him in the previous chapter.

This expansion of electronic information system, and of the system/world of images it creates, *produces a mode of information.* When we talk of the mode of information, a whole new concept of subject and of subject's relationship with the world of objects comes to the fore.

The subject and the subjectivity, themselves are put in question in this mode.

The new subject may be defined and delineated by the following features, which are not exhaustive:

In the mode of information, the subject is no longer located in a point in absolute time/space. That means he/she is no longer located at a fixed point, a vantage point, from where he/she can 'look at' the world; decide on the options, steps, perspectives and so on in an interrelated, orderly world. That would be a Cartesian world; it still is, but is already in rapid transition. Now the subject is losing both 'its' space and time. Electronic signals have abolished that orderly space and time sequence. Electronics becomes part of the subject, as also of the object.

Therefore, the subject is destabilized. 'It' or he/she is not just a receiver of signals and information, enjoying a fixed, physical point. He/she is no longer at one point or place or in one point of time.

Since the nervous system goes out, the subject itself goes out and spreads out allover. It is simultaneously connected to so many times and so many spaces. It can shift from one time/space to another in matter of seconds or moments, and is therefore unstable. The subject more and more wanders about. This is truer of his/her subjectivity.

This is the first time ever that it is happening: the dispersal and the temporary reconstitution of the subject. It is in fact partial jettisoning of the biological (physical) being. The process takes place with the help of another physical/material phenomenon, that of the electronics, which has considerable similarities with the world of nerves, of sensations and ideas. Therefore, it is helpful in partially liberating electronic, light/electro-magnetic signals.

The independence and sovereignty of the subject, inherent in the above-mentioned process, has lot of significance for the future of the human race, even for the species of the *Homo sapiens.*

What does reconstitution of the subject mean? For the subjective subject, it is difficult to remain in one place, as it is constantly dispersed in time and space. The other aspect of the subject is that it spreads out everywhere. It is out of this spread, this everywhere and anywhere that the subject can be reconstituted anytime, anywhere. This is because the mind and brain, the bundle of nerves, have increasing similarities with the spread of electronic communication systems. Both are becoming increasingly similar.

Reconstitution of Subject

What is reconstitution of the subject? What exactly constitutes a subject?

A subject is constituted by its relationship with the object. The two form an inseparable dialectics. The subject/consciousness is related with the outside world through sense organs. It looks upon the world outside, is related with it, reflects it, and that is why it is a subject. The subject also changes the latter.

"Heidegger connects the crisis of humanism to the end of metaphysics as the culmination of technology and moment of passage beyond the world of the subject/object opposition."[14] The crisis is spreading to the institutions of *the late modern society,* and on the other hand "*taking leave of subjectivity* developed in... twentieth century thought."[15] Spengler and Junger are credited with developing these and related ideas.

These are very important points, very crucial. The concept of the 'late modern society' speaks volumes of the basic transformations in the contemporary world society. The late 'modern' society transits imperceptibly into the postmodern society, and provides grounds for basic and novel investigations as never before. The 'liquidation' (dissolution?—a conflicting process of dissociation and association—AR) of the subject at the level of social existence may not be destructive alone, which calls for the 'critique of the subject'.[16] And the 'critique' is a dialectical process. In the course of the theoretical critique of the subject, it has to be recognized that the subject need not always be defended, and has to be negated and evolved. "The subject that supposedly has to be defended from technological dehumanization is itself the very root of dehumanization", because the subjectivity defined as the subject of the object is a function of the objectivity, and thus itself can be manipulated.[17]

The STR and the ICR are playing crucial role here.

The analysis has brought out the great paradox, dilemma and dialectics of the transit from 'modern to postmodern' world. It is not easy to come out of the dilemma. And it has also to be realized that we cannot come out without the study and use of the new technology, electronic communication in particular. Any imagined fear of 'technological determination' should not prevent us from taking up this giant task in transition from one era to another.

Mechanics of subject formation: The subject remains a subject as long as he/she exchanges signals with the object. The only signal that the object can reflect/emit/send is light. Basically, it is light that is reflected on the subject. The relationship is direct. At first, it is this signal that the subject studies.

Then there is the philosophical subject, who is in dialectical relation with the philosophical object. The subject here is the totality of mind in relation with the material, objective world.

In the course of social development, the subject/the consciousness develops tools of progressively higher order that go deeper into the material processes. The subject-object relationship becomes increasingly complex and complicated.

At first, the subject has a fixed and clear-cut relation with time and space. There is a third factor or projection, and that is of language.

The subject always exists in space and time, and is created by them. It has a fixed relationship, relatively speaking, with the reality or the object. It occupies certain space and evolves in time. Its space is the biological boundary as well as the social relationships and boundaries. After all, the subject evolves socially. That way, he/she also evolves in time and space. Means of production and communications and the tools have much to do with this evolution. Thus, the subjects evolve in production and communication.

The subject is most well-organized and well-evolved in the Cartesian scheme of existence. His/her place can be more accurately determined. His language and communication are also highly defined. The context too is clearly defined.

Such a subject is rational and relatively autonomous. It is on the basis of and due to a certain time and space relation that the subject evolves a rational one. The subject can clearly derive events/processes one from the other in a series of historical nature, in a series that is historically determined. The succession and the causes are clear. The subject is clear about time and space and about its place in such a coordinate.

The subject is also autonomous in a Cartesian world. It can place itself outside the object/events and look upon them as an independent observer and draw certain conclusions. Its dialectics with the object in this setting places it a one-to-one relation with the objectivity. The poles are relatively independent and it is difficult to define the interpenetration of opposites, although there are gey regions where the two merge.

Typewriter and Electronic/Computer Typing

When a person types out with the typewriter, his relationship with the tool and the typed word is direct and fixed. He presses the key and the end of the rod types a letter. The material process is clear and direct. The action is solid. The impression is also solid, direct and long-lasting. It would be very difficult to erase what is written or typed out. The language is also clear and direct. The communication is not distant, the written paper is directly before the eyes. It becomes distant only later, say, when the document or whatever is posted, sent, handed over etc.

Such a writing and communication creates a well-defined subject, with no possibility of destabilization and disintegration. Communication is clear-cut, and clear copies can made of the text with intended meaning without disturbing the subject.

Gradually, however, means of communications develop that increase the distance between the subject and the object, between writing and the result of writing.

With the advent of computer and electronic writing, *things undergo a qualitative change.* We again use a keyboard, and we type. In fact, today 'typing' has become common as never before. Typing has spread to the mobiles and many other gadgets. The TV anchors ask us to 'type out' our answers or comments and opinions. People are even finding writing on paper with pens etc. tiresome and cumbersome.

At first appearance, typing on the computer keyboard looks hardly different from typing on the typewriter. People did not realize the difference at first, but gradually they began to feel it. Keyboards of the two are similar, though with important differences. Here the similarity ends and a whole new world begin to unfold: we begin typing out into a qualitatively different world.

A different subject begins to be created. His/her typing involves use of electronic signals, for which the old type of keyboard is used, a survival of the past and also a hindrance in the development of modern machinery. It is the electronic signals that change everything. The subject is in fact not 'writing'; he/she is *sending signals.* The keyboard of the typewriter, at the most, creates symbols. But in the computers, the keyboard and the keys are transformed into creators of a world of signs, signals and characters. It is to be noted that we more and more use the term 'characters' and data rather than 'words'. Herein lies the essence of the change.

These signals (radiation) are not tangible and solid but are emissions. So, *the relation of the subject with something solid is lost.* That begins a series of changes. The distance and intangibility increases: the distance between the subject and the image, and the intangibility of the act.

Here the subject is not working with a tangible tool or equipment.

He/she is working with something that disappears (appears and disappears) instantly. It is not something exists permanently or solidly.

In the course of electronic communication or writing, the relation of subject with object changes. We do not really 'write'; we create *an image of writing*, the written words are not words, they are images of the 'words, whose temporary nature we are aware of all the time and very concerned with: the typed image may be lost anytime; we are not that sure as we used to be earlier with older equipments such as the typewriter. The transformation of *the word into an image* is one of the most crucial events *towards and as part of* mode of information. What is produced by the act of communication is an image, which is temporary or transitory, and can be kept/held back only in another 'memory', that of the computer. So our relationship with the word we have just now typed out on the screen undergoes a change and becomes very temporary. Our object thus is an image rather than something tangible. The subject now establishes a relation with an object, which is transitory, and consequently the subject is also rendered transitory, at least in relation to that particular 'object'. To exist the subject should establish relation with things tangible. While typing with typewriter, the typed page/matter emerges as the product. It is something stable, and can be seen anytime. At least, it does not disappear.

But the product of typing on the screen is an image, just a radiation in a particular configuration. It is electronic image, character, a luminous light, which should become part of an extended memory, nerve system, etc. if they are to be 'retrieved'. To preserve, to be 'on the safe side', we transform what we have typed out, into hard copy, that is we resort to the old methods; we convert the intangible electronic characters into hard signs of the printed form. That provides the subject certain stability or restores its stability.

It is clear, therefore, the electronic signals not only change the object but the subject itself.

Subject: Rational and Irrational, Centred and Decentred

What or who is a 'rational subject'? One, who rationalizes, uses reason, arguments, etc. The whole concept of the rational subject, and of the reason itself, emerged from the Cartesian field-view, with its easy, sequential, well-ordered transformation. Here reason plays a decisive role in the formations of consciousness. The subject too is clearly direction-oriented. Such a subject is basically a product of pre-industrial evolution culminating in the industrial revolution.

But with the modern (with 'post'-modern impacts), electronic means of communication, the subject undergoes a transformation, a metamorphosis. It is not a metamorphosis from one subject to another subject of a different kind. It is a transition from the existence of the subject to its (his/her) disintegration, to non-existences, and then again to a *reconstitution* in new ways. The subject is decentred, divided, dissolved, made temporary, etc., all due to electronic and electromagnetic signals. For this kind of communication, a relatively temporary and transient subject is more suitable.

This phenomenon becomes particularly clearer in the processes like the 'surfing', 'roaming', etc. The continuous shifting (surfing) of the channels of TV have almost become a habit with, an inherent habit of most of the TV viewers. It is as if the person is impatient, restless, in a haste, as also undecided as to what to watch, trying to catch hold of everything (hundreds of channels and thousands of events, occurrences and processes), and in fact catching nothing. He/she hardly settles on one, before shifting to another. The subject does not understand where to settle, unless there is absolutely sensational, explosive event. His/her relationship with time and space is totally lost, he/she is unsettled as the subject, gets dissociated and disintegrated. He/she lives in so many places and in so many events and times, that he/she loses all the rationality and order, and acquires simultaneity, which is unsettling for a subject.

What is the relationship with the object? There is virtually no object all! The subject relates with the image/s of the object/s, not with the object/s themselves. This involves a new kind of relation hitherto not found or found rarely in history. Image replaces object. That transforms the nature of the subject. The image is something that is temporary and transitory, no more than a reflection of the tangible object, and therefore it is bound to disappear instantly. The subject does not relate directly with the object, but in a mediated form, which complicates the relationships. The subject become a unity of different times and spaces, a unity of what is stable and tangible, and of what is instantaneous. The imagery object is that which is not;

it exists only as an instant, can disappear anytime, and therefore can cease to be the object anytime. Thus it renders the subject extremely transitory. To that extent and for that duration, the subject ceases to the subject proper. The other part of the subject is the stable relationship with the stable and tangible object. But this object is receding rapidly into the zone of mediation. Besides, we relate with the tangible more and more through the intangible, thus replacing the former with the latter. It is a kind of subjective subjectivity because we manipulate the image in order to better view the object and to relate with and work upon the object. But working upon the object ceases to be the job of the subject, as the image itself is an active subject, which we simply assign certain tasks. We replace ourselves with our own image and that of the object, an image which is active and even 'intelligent'. The subject is decentred or mechanically depersonalized, to use Jameson's expression.[18]

Such an object, that is the image, is actually an extension of the subject itself. And therefore it is not an object. And that changes a lot in the relation of the consciousness with the world outside. The worker or the programmer-engineer in the steel or paper mill looks at the processes on his/her screen and keeps track of the events through information received. They are nothing else than images; they are not the tangibles, which actually exist on the shop-floor. The worker/ computer operator gives necessary instructions to the computer to manipulate the processes in a particular way. So, the screen becomes an extension of the sense organs of the human beings, even of their consciousness. The electronic system carries out necessary functions even in the absence of concrete instructions, because the commands given are limited and only the essential ones. Otherwise, the computerized system is all the time operating, irrespective of the human interference, as an automatic system, whether person or the overseer is there or not.

The electronic system and the images being created by it in their millions are more and more part of the human consciousness than of the objectivity and tangible solidity of the objects.

Thus, the subject relates with another subject, which is image i.e. subjectivity. Image of the object acts as a subject, transforming the subject into object. This is what decentres and disintegrates, makes temporary, the historical subject.

The historical subject becomes part and parcel of the broader communication system engulfing the earth and the computer systems as the communication networks develop. In fact, the unity between the subject and the image dissolves the subject into as temporary *event* as the communication/information itself. The historical subject is converted from a historically evolved well-ordered tangible with orderly reasoned consciousness into a fragile, brittle and transitory event, which though containing order, is in the disorder of successions. Therefore, the subject now must struggle to relocate itself in time and space and in their unity *independent* of time and space. Rationality has now different connotation and order, which comes into conflict with the well-ordered consciousness.

The material basis of rationality is removed by at least one order. In order to reason and rationalize, an involved path is to be traced.

The subject is dispersed into the growing and expanding electronic signal world, becoming part of the internet, databases and email etc. So, it loses its definiteness, its clear defines, autonomy, to the extent that he/she may rise questions as to where, who, what, how, "am I"?

How does the subject get dissolved and decentred? What does it exactly mean? The question has far-reaching implications. It would be useful to go a bit into history and background of communication/information.

History of Communication, and the Subject

Introduction of telephone not only enabled people to communicate with each other; it also threatened the existing class relations. It extended the boundaries of who may speak to whom.[19] Use of telephone, telegraph, Morse code, radio, electric bulbs and so on opened entire new areas of communications and cultural-social exchange. They spread subjectivity and mass consciousness formation.

At least theoretically, now anybody could come in contact with anybody. The subject becomes more active and, at the same time, spreads out. What is the meaning of inter-continental and trans-oceanic communications (telephone etc.)? Lot of space is covered and different time zones are brought together, interconnected and merged together.

The subject becomes active in the vast terrain of the object. The subject competes with the object, spreads over it and along with it. Consciousness is created by light, basically. Light is spread by the industrial revolution, particularly after the invention of electricity and equipments driven by it.

Light spreads reflection and knowledge, spreads out consciousness. It thus spreads out the subject, both by lighting more and more objects and by helping out our nervous system over vast distances and by shortening time.

The aim of the new technologies, including the electronic ones, is to streamline, simplify and enhance the usual social routines, whose effects and efforts put in are sought to be smoothened and amplified. This simultaneously and consequently amplifies the subject also.

But certain unintended results ensue. The event is not simple quantitative or limited qualitative change. It may produce qualitatively such novel processes or events, which themselves become new events. They do not just enhance the subject's power but change the subject itself.

The cultural and social forms, at this point, begin shaping up new communication patterns, at the point of technological innovations.[20] The nature of new communications or 'new events' are to be recognized through the analysis of nature of communications in modern society. The relations between action and language, behaviour and belief, material reality and culture are to be understood.

To be able to do this, we should be able to decode the linguistic dimensions of the new forms of social interaction. Postmodernism questions the dominant theoretical and disciplinary paradigms in relation to the new communicational forms.

This can be done only be recognizing the fact that the electronic communications is not just an amplification of the existing communication; more than that, it creates a new linguistic dimension of new forms of social communication/interaction. The very structure and nature of the symbolic/linguistic exchange is changed. Cultural transformations and structure changes within these transformations take place.

Every age has certain forms of symbolic exchange and communications. It contains internal and external structures, means and relations of signification. Let us try to trace and identify these stages.

In the earliest times, there used to be direct communication between individuals. Therefore, the word was very important and valuable; it was the depository of all the information and knowledge, so much so that it acquired divine qualities. There was no problem of distance, which was very small: one human being to another. Several social, family, religious, etc. institutions and organizations came into being around this form of communication. Languages evolved.

If the distances increased, the communications took very long to reach the distant individuals or places. Times were immense; it took very long time for communications to take effect; therefore it becomes a specialized job. Weeks, months and years were normal.

In the meantime, and for these purposes, cultural structures came into being.

In such a condition, the word became even more valuable. The subject became all-important in the system and structure of communications, and he/she was very stable, almost infinite and ever-present. The subject represented the totality of relations with the object and objectivity.

How does one define and describe the subject at this stage? He/she is not only very stable, moving or shifting little, he/she also represents all the words. Communication therefore meant taking the help of this depository. And there were very few of them. Thus, communication imparted stability, growth and solidity to the subject. Reflection could take place only if the subject existed and flourished, by the word. This contrasts with the present-day electronic communication.

During the subsequent centuries, the communication tried to overcome time and space. What happens when they are progressively overcome? Let us note that it took centuries. Speeding up of vehicles, building roads and canals and ships, use of other means of communications (birds, etc.), spread of written words, copies of texts and so on, added basically to the volume of communication. It further strengthened the existence, being and tangibility of the subject. The subject began to spread over the object; the former began to be strengthened. One can even say, the subject began to emerge and evolve. Copying of the subject was a new, novel development, conquering, partly, of time and space was a great event. To go out of one's habitation became a great event, and it took years to travel. Therefore, the return was a great event. Important words were spread, and therefore subjectivity became important over long distances and for a long time. The subject thus hovered for a long time, gaining and not losing importance in the meantime. The subject became important in time and distance. Yet, he was shaped by these and other dimensions.

The inauguration of printing through Gutenberg in the 17th century caused considerable changes in the relative position and nature of the subject. Now the author could be copied and his words could be preserved and taken to distant places. A distance began to emerge between the author (the subject) and the words he wrote or spoke. He was carried by his word. And he was also constructed by it.

Third, Electronic Stage of Communication

The third *or the electronic stage* of communication is qualitatively different. It is not a simple amplification or increase in capacities of communication. It does far more than that. We have already dealt with the earlier stages in various places.

No doubt, the electronic communications increase the capacities, speeds, abilities and so on, of the communications many times. In this feature too, it is vastly different from the earlier modes.

But the electronic communication does the unexpected and the unprecedented to the subject. **For the first time in history, the subject is dispersed.**

This causes the beginning of *the mode* of *information.*

Let us analyse this and separate out the distinct threads.

What is communication? Obviously, it is an exchange between two or more subjects via object/s. Communication is an inalienable part of the production and exchange, it is about everything possible in the society: economic, social, political, cultural and so on. Communication constitutes totality of the society minus production. Even production includes communication; more so today.

As we have seen already, the earlier phases of communication strengthen and create the subject. But it is exactly opposite with the electronic communication. **It disperses and dissolves the subject.**

How does it happen? What is its meaning?

The most distinguishing feature of the electronic communication is that it overcomes space and time. This communication is instant. The very purpose of exchange and communication is to connect two or more points distant in space. Communication from this viewpoint means that which connects spaces or points in spaces. That is how it creates, and creates even now, the subject, the talker and the listener. First, there is communication between subject and the object, and, in the second stage, between the object and the subject.

The electronic signals dispense with all this. These signals are instant, and cover vast spaces in no time. Therefore, the space collapses. Now the epistemological and the philosophical question arises: can the subject exist without space, and without time difference? It is almost the situation where communication is not given over, not handed over to the communicated. It is there, instantly. And the next moment, it is not there. It is hardly a communication from the subject to the object and then to the other subject.

What is 'communication'? It is basically a progressive extension of the nervous system through the ages. To communicate means to dominate over nature and society. Social development based essentially over the development (dialectics, evolution through contradictions) of the means of production (and productive forces) arms the human beings with increasingly extended artificial nervous system. The role of the consciousness increases quantitatively and qualitatively over the material world, through the history and outside it. Nature is sought to be won over on the one hand, and society dominated on the other.

To this end, the social/human nervous system must be really very powerful and extensive. Nervous system is basically based in an individual system. But it takes form only in a social system. Therefore, nervous system (consciousness-forming system) can only be social. And that is why, consciousness must dominate matter and overcome it. In social organisation, this takes the form of domination of one segment over another, deprivation of one by another. This deprivation includes that of the means of consciousness formation.

Thus, social development through the ages, history and natural course keeps on not only developing the mental faculties and human consciousness, but also extending them. That is how the subject develops, singly and collectively. Without the subjective, there can be no object/objective, and therefore no social development. History produces and extends vast, limitless consciousness, and the subject is the carrier of that consciousness, through the individual and the society.

At a certain point of development, the subject goes beyond the society, the entire social being. This happens not only collectively but also individually. A point reaches where the human body "is no longer an effective limit of the subject's position".[21] This happens when the "communications facilities extend the nervous system throughout the earth".[22]

Computer communications construct a new configuration of self-constitution of the subject. The subject is changed in the course of electronic communication: it is dispersed in the semantic field of time/space, inner/outer, mind/matter, and it is this that precisely constitutes the postmodern terrain/field. It is different from the modern field, which we have discussed earlier. Roughly, the basic difference between the modern and the postmodern communication and flow of information is the following: modern communications created the subject within the confines and with the help of time and space; the postmodern/postindustrial communications disperse and decentre this subject, reconstructing it in a world of merger of time and space on a different plane. The subject thereby merges with the image increasingly created by the systems enveloping the earth, such as the internet and the computer systems.

Computer writing and communications have definite effects on the subject. Computer 'writing' has features of its own, which we shall deal with somewhat later. What are the effects?

Computer writing and communication plays with the identity. This can at once be discerned in the phenomenon of messaging, which is becoming widespread, ever universal: on mobile, e-mail, message services, etc. The conversationalists reduce or transform themselves into written words, which in themselves are of a different kind. The particular is abstracted as general. So many subjects become reduced to (transformed into) the subject in general, ***which has no particular***

characteristics. This is abstraction of the individual, or reduction in the difference between subject, their mutual collision and dissolution; it is also the mutual dissolution of the subjects in the course of and in the world of electronic information/communication.

Computer writing "degender communications by removing gender cues".[23] This is in contrast to the earlier forms of communications, generally speaking. Electronic communications destabilize the earlier hierarchies, replacing them with new ones.

Computer, TV and internet are in many ways reflection of our own brain! Are we not externalizing over thoughts and brain processes more and more with the evolution of technology, which in fact is a process of internalizing, because what we externalize exist no more except as images, which is no existence, in fact, except as configuration of signals? This precisely is the postmodern status of the subject, which questions its nature: its relation to the external world is internalised, and at the same time spread all over the world. This is a new way to create the subject, an emergence of new type of subject, quite unprecedented.

"Anonymity is complete. Identity is fictionalized in the structure of the communication."[24] With computer messaging or any kind of electronic messaging, e.g. in mobile messages, language use is separated out of the biographical identity. The identity, at the same time, is dispersed in the electronic network of communications.[25]

This is a very important and crucial point. It reveals: 1) Separation of language use from identity. 2) Identity is dispersed in the electronic network.

The electronic communication separates language from identity because of the fact that it (electronics) can make innumerable copies/ images of writing, of the written words, and of the images, in virtually no time. Therefore, what is written is temporary, yet can be retrieved at will, any time. Therefore, the written words assume an independent existence in the form of the internet, etc. that enwrap the earth. They exist in the form of programs, graphics, images of all kinds and composed matter (texts) all the time, and their number and amount is growing constantly, by the minute in fact. It is a reality that is increasingly growing over and threatens to completely take over the society, human beings and the human consciousness. There is no denial that the internet with its whole content, is now an independent reality, and is going to be the single most important factor in human existence and its future history.

Writing, the written words, take on an independent existence, ***independent*** of ***the writer,*** of ***the subject.*** *They now just exist, as if they had been so since ever.* The words, and therefore the language, proliferate, on 'their own', so to say. They are floating all the time, around us. They invite us to use them, to 'download' them! They are becoming more powerful than ever, virtually ruling over human consciousness and the human beings becoming more dependent on them than ever, in every way. Now they are being taken as granted. Admission and job forms, tickets, reservations, informations of all the possible kinds, industrial and agricultural and banking/financial systems and processes, other events including the most obscure kind: the internet words are at our service!

These electronic words are different, both qualitatively as well as quantitatively, from the hand-written or the printed words. The stability and eternity of the latter is gone in the electronic composing of words, sentences and language.

Words are imparted a temporariness. They can only be stored, retrieved on the screen. They are shining, fluorescent lines or structures or shapes that can be made to appear any moment, only to disappear the very next moment. They are made to exist, yet they do not exist. This dissolves the subject, making him/her insecure and fragile. They are nobody's words; it is only through the use of the past (outdated) methods that they are related with the writer.

Mark Poster and some of the other post-modernists are right in maintaining that the subject is disconnected from the word and becomes temporary and momentary. The temporariness and the fragility of the subject, both individual and general, is the result of the electronic nature of communication. The word (text) assumes an independent existence. This communication is mass produced and is rapid and almost simultaneous. This increase in the role of time, in fact the determining role of time destabilizes the subject. Anything that the subject produces, creates, writes, draws, etc. disperses immediately allover, becoming part of the larger reality. Then it can only be retrieved, and retrieval is a transitional and temporary phenomenon.

The subject is related with the object in innumerable ways. The former reflects the latter in so many ways and through so many channels, and simultaneously it influences the objects in increasingly complex manner and with the help of growingly deeper and complicated instruments. Electronics is the latest form of mediation between the two. We in fact 'write' on a huge 'canvass' engulfing the earth itself.

Writing is one of the major ways of contact between the subject and the object. It is also a way of the expression of the latter in the former. We can say, writing also constitutes, creates and configures the subject and its structure.

Writing is a representation of the objectivity, a meeting point between the subject and the object. As we have seen, with handwriting or typing or printing, there is considerable stability, in the nature of writing, which also imparts stability to the subject. The nature and stability of the subject and the subjectivity depends considerably on the nature of the communication. The writing by pen or by typing or printing is difficult to change; in a way, the words, become "a defiant enemy of their author" resisting efforts to change them.[26] The printed ideas in a book can be changed only in the "next edition" of it! So, the author/the subject is transmitted and circulated for long, or kept on the shelves.

But computer writing changes all that. It is only through printing, a survival of the past, that we continue to exist as we have evolved.

So far, the subject has been Cartesian, with things laid out before him/her to be observed; the writing and the subject himself has been Cartesian too. These objects and this writing have been completely different from the mind. As a result, there is tangible and Cartesian stability to the writing and written products.

The screen is the battlefield between the Cartesian and the post-Cartesian scenarios.

The computer brings the Cartesian world to an end. The writer confronts his/her words in momentary, transformable forms. They are there, yet not there. There is a conflict in this transition, between the Cartesian and the non-, post-Cartesian. That is reflected in the screen writing, which reflects this conflict, the dissolution of the Cartesian world. The computer writing, the screen, must dissolve the tangible, stable world in the course of writing (reflection), because it does not just write and reflect the world, it converts the world into the intangibles, into symbols, images, words, etc. A virtual world is created very rapidly, and with accelerating rapidity.

Does it mean that the electronic signals are unable to work with the tangibles? They convert everything into images, ***and then process the images, not the things.***

So, there is such a quantity of images that the subject increasingly deals with the images, the 'unreals' and less and less with the 'reals'. Images become the habit of the human beings. The tangible world dissolves. The subject is left with images! The relationship of the subject with the world changes imperceptibly, and in the process the subject itself changes. The constituent elements of the subject and its structure undergo transformation and dissolution.

For the moment, let us suppose the subject is in contact with the screen alone. In that case, he/she will not miss much of the world! The subject writes the world into the screen, and invites the world onto the screen; the subject in the process also creates the world, maneuvers it, changes it; he/she is in the world of images. The image is only to be created. So the electronic writing is creative, creates a new world. In the process, the very structure of the world is changed. Writing means creating, particularly in the electronic world. The subject stands redefined. We can write many things, create/draw drawings, control blast furnaces or act according to the instructions on the screen for this or that process. And all the time, we are influencing the real processes with the help of the images. The images, without our realization, become almost the real world. Virtual reality replaces the real reality. We are all the time trying to influence the reality via the image. It is not a direct but mediated influence.

Electronic mediation is a world that acts for the real world in order to influence it.

In the process of writing, the writer confronts a representation that is similar to the contents of mind or to the spoken word, in spatial fragility and temporal simultaneity. Subject and object approach each other and achieve a similarity that approaches identity.[27] The Cartesian subject, who thought that the world is composed of things different from the mind, disappears. ***The screen object and the writing subject merge.***[28]

Writing in electronics, on screen, *is a borderline event*, something different from the earlier events. In the Cartesian world, while writing on paper or printing, the subject stands on one side, on the side of subjectivity, opposed to the object and objectivity, facing the latter and justifying its existence. How the subject reflects the object? Through speech, signs, writing etc. They are the reflection of the world. The physical, objective world includes the physical boundaries of the subject. While the ideas expressed in writing, the consciousness created, is subjective, part of the ideal world, the tangible appearance of the written or printed words is the world of the objective. The written words all the time create consciousness.

Electronics brings about a further shift of the written/printed words towards the subject and the subjectivity. In the Cartesian world, the word has tangible and solid form. It is part and parcel, an element, of the well- ordered world. It is 'there', and can be picked up, opened, seen, thought over, and then put back as it is. It is just like any other object. The structure of the words also create structure of thoughts. The words create consciousness; they themselves are both consciousness stayed in its flow, and tangible material.

The printed words, or even the written words, provide certain stability to the subject, keep his/her consciousness safe and well-ordered. They are the safe-keeper of the subject. They represent him/her permanently. The subject can lay claim to the words. And any reader can open the book anytime to have a look at the permanently etched or printed words. The reader has a stable author/subject.

That is how the subject is created, is developed and structured. His/her consciousness and thought and language is structured, is configurated. Cartesian world creates a Cartesianized thought/consciousness. The thought must correspond to the reality. Thought has to think, reflect the world in certain ways, in certain portions, compartments, parts, etc. Motion and dialectics only results from synthesis at progressively higher levels, only as generalization, destruction and transcendence.

Electronics changes all this. The meanings are changed. Electronic writing is writing as well as non-writing; it is writing as well erasing.

Words are intangibles. They cease to exist as soon as the system is switched off. Words are there, floating all around us, but we are unaware, and we have to retrieve and recall them. As distinct from the words in the books, the floating words/texts 'exist' almost as supernatural powers, having their own authenticity. We forget that they are ultimately uploaded by the human beings themselves.

Market is Ideological

Market is ideological in many senses and at several levels. It becomes more ideological as it produces reflections after it is over and its ripples spread through and reign over the society.

Market is, in its simplest form, a place of direct exchange. Therefore, there is no need for ideology. Yet, this exchange continuously produces, emanates, ideology. The exchangers create their own visions and ideas, constantly exaggerate the role and nature and place of market. For them, the rise in the prices of the vegetables is the most important event. The seller is constantly waiting for it, of course within limits, where the buyer is most concerned about the price-rise because it is his very world. The poor will find his expenses stretched to the limits and the better off middle class will find the budget disturbed.

Vegetables, milk, transport, etc. involve daily spending; that is they are most ideological, and create the people's and the individuals daily thought-world. The consumer draws his/her own conclusions. It is most painful; therefore, the 'government' and the politicians are the first casualty, in particular the former. A whole series of reflections immediately ensue from a single transaction of potato or onion or tomato!

Market is the best place for idea-creation. The consumer becomes most active 'materialist' here; only his ideas are invested–they travel from the superstructure to the base, not vice-versa. The buyer blames all those involved in policy-making and governing and this process begins with the known personalities of the country. The market and its price levels are the world of the family; it produces tensions, thoughts and worries about the present and the future, and later, about the future of the country. Such a price-rise is likely to affect education, housing, transport and so on. And the whole world is disturbed, the very future. The individual is like a piece of wood in highly disturbed and turbulent waters. He takes up, even if temporarily, a certain position against the government and even the whole society.

In fact, the commodity is the reflection of the entire society, as Marx put it. It therefore also is the ideological reflection and ideology-creator. If produces widespread fetishism, particularly seen on certain occasions, e.g. festivals. The human beings want to see themselves, want to lose themselves in the sparkling and glittering world of blinking commodities. This world gives them meaning and purpose of life. The motion of commodities creates a whole world, both of things and ideas. The motion creates the society itself.

The electronic transformation of market is playing an important role in the emergence of the mode of information.

What is Postmodernism?

According to Carol A. Stabile[29], postmodernism is loosely identified with a historical epoch, the condition of post-industrial, post-Fordish, or even post-capitalist society. 'Contemporary' relations of production are presented as fragmented. They are diffused and disorganised. The systemic power relations are everywhere and nowhere, pervasive but with no identifiable source, and ultimately unhinged from historical and economic determinants. Consumption has overtaken production, making class struggle or even the notion that society is antagonistically divided, obsolete. People no longer identify themselves with class, but express themselves through various other identities such as woman, gay etc., which are not economically defined. Thus oppression has no material foundation.

Central to the postmodernist concept of society is the notion of totalisation, among them principles like modernity and enlightenment, rationality, progress, humanity, justice, reality etc. Postmodernism opines that these concepts have been undermined.[30]

This line of reasoning emerges from post-structuralist critiques of language, subjectivity and representation. But it is claimed that where post-structuralism refers to theory, postmodernism is the practice.[31] Thus while post-structuralists criticize the foundations of modernism, postmodernists take these critiques as mandates for rejecting foundations totally.[32]

The author of the article gives no analyses, no arguments to prove the abovementioned contentions, and does not show how post-structuralism is different from postmodernism. ***It is also not shown how one is theory and the other practice.***

As per the author, for postmodernists, there is no such thing (system) as capitalism; it virtually does not exist. It is so diffuse and heterogeneous that it not only is beyond understanding, it no longer offers any point from which it can be opposed. It is a media-saturated age in which we can't know what is real; representation has become impossible. Capitalism is so fragmented, lacking any kind of organic unity, that it is no longer comprehensible as a system.[33]

European postmodernists, e.g. Lyotard, opine that Marxism, like the Enlightenment in general, culminated in Stalinism. This was because of totalization inherent in Marxism. Some American postmodernists, e.g. Linda Nicholson, accuse Marxism of generalizing concepts like production, class etc. This de-legitimises such categories as those of women, blacks, gays, etc. who are non-economic.

Here again no further arguments are forthcoming in support of the contentions.

Postmodernism eschews empiricism and quantitative methods. These methods presuppose some form of reality. It relies on interpretive methods of Saussurean linguistics and hermeneutics.

The postmodernists claim absolute victory for idealism, as per the author; materiality and economic base are consigned to the dumps of history, ***and only language remains.***[34]

Here again no arguments are given to prove the point. Though the postmodernists often appear to tend towards idealism, nowhere do they claim absolute victory for idealism or side fully with it. In fact, they appear to give new meanings to idealism and materialism, and this is definitely a positive contribution, and needs to be investigated further.

The above critique, and some others in the volume by Ellen Woods and Foster work mechanically into the system of ideas that goes by the name of postmodernism. They treat the opposition 'idealism versus materialism' extremely schematically and dogmatically. What is idealism and what is materialism in the context of information and communication revolution (ICR) needs to be gone into in-depth, very seriously and in detail. No hasty and mechanical conclusions, no attempt to fit in things in a fixed framework will do. The present volume has tried to treat postmodernism realistically in various places in particular contexts.

NOTES

1. cf. Derrida, *Of Grammatology,* mentioned in Mark Poster, *Mode of Information*, Polity Press, 1990, Chapter 4, p. 99 onwards.
2. Hegel, *Phenomenology of Mind,* Para 97.
3. Steven Best and Douglas Kellner, *The Postmodern Adventure*, The Guilford Press, New York, 2001, p. 23: Chapter 1: "Thomas Pynchon and the Advent of Postmodernity".
4. Ibid., pp. 38-39.
5. Paul Hegarty, *The Postmodern Condition: A Report on Knowledge,* Routledge, 1991, p. 115.
6. Ibid.
7. Baudrillard wrote this in 1977; the building had to be remodelled in 1991. Hegarty, ibid., p. 115.
8. Ibid., p. 112.
9. Ibid.
10. Based on ibid., p. 113.
11. Ibid., p. 114.
12. Hegarty, ibid., p. 94.
13. Mark Poster, *The Mode of Information: Post-structuralism and Social Context,* Polity Press, UK, 1990, p. 15.
14. Gianni Vattimo, *The End of Modernity: Nihilism and Hermeneutics in Postmodern Culture*, The Johns Hopkins University Press, Baltimore, 1988, p. 45.
15. Ibid.
16. See, ibid., pp. 45-46.
17. Ibid., p. 46.
18. Frederic Jameson, *Postmodernism or the Cultural Logic of Late Capitalism*, Duke University Press, Durham, and Verso, 2006, p. 152.
19. See, Poster, *Mode of Information*, p. 6.
20. Marvin does so, see Poster, ibid., p. 5.
21. Poster, p. 15.
22. Ibid.
23. Ibid., p. 116.

24. Ibid., 117
25. Ibid.
26. Ibid., p. 111.
27. See, ibid.
28. Ibid.
29. "Postmodernism, Feminism and Marx: Notes from the Abyss", in, Ellen Wood and John Foster, ed., *In Defence of History: Marxism and Postmodern Agenda,* Monthly Review Press, 1997, p. 135.
30. Ibid., pp. 135-36.
31. Ibid., p. 136.
32. Ibid.
33. Ibid.
34. Ibid., p. 137.

12

Mode of Production to Mode of Information

We have begun to live in a (world) society making transition *from the mode of production to mode of information.*

The term 'mode of information' has first been used by Mark Poster, but in a sense *different* from that used here in this book. In his excellent and incisive work *The Mode of Information.*[1] Poster has tried to explore the theoretical bases for the destabilization and new configurations of the subject, and that is his main object of enquiry. He says that the term 'mode of information' is *not* used by him as a 'totalizing or essentializing' category to inscribe the present age. He visualizes several modes of information, each with its own characteristics.

But I would like to go *beyond* this multiple concept, and take up the term *as really expressing the essence of the new society* that is emerging. This chapter will try to establish that due to the information and communication revolution (ICR), the world society is for the first time shedding the mode of production and transiting into *mode of information.* This is despite Poster's objection that such an approach would be a 'totalizing' effort and will limit and the subject and oppress him/her through reason and rational approach. But I think a restricted concept of the mode of information greatly restricts the chief characteristics of the present phase of social development. We do need therefore an all-embracing ('totalizing') concept. Without this, we cannot explain the new role of the subject and the new subject-object relations.

It is quite clear that the present society has gone beyond the industrial phase and has entered a post-industrial one. Poster and many other postmodernists do not accept the concept of the post-industrial society, which is surprising and misplaced. Poster rejects the concept because, in his opinion it will not only restrict the area of analysis but, more importantly, also be an act of totalisation.

We will discuss this issue separately in another volume. Here I would like to use the concept of postmodernism as a thought reflection of a new, post-industrial, society. The STR and the ICR have changes the productive base of the existing society by creating qualitatively new means of production as well as novel kinds of means of information. As a result, the industrial relations and structure and industrial mode of production is being negated, and in its place a new, post-industrial mode of production is coming being.

The phenomenon of postmodernism can only be explained by assuming the emergence of the post-industrial structures/society. It is the new communicative and productive capacities that can explain the postmodern ideas.

Simultaneously, we are also entering a post-capitalist phase of society, wherein many of the features of capitalism are being suspended or negated and even altogether given up. This we will consider in a separate place in another book.

But there is one more important point I have to make, and that is very crucial. As a result of STR and ICR, *the mode of production is being replaced by or converted into a mode of information for the first time in human history.* And this is *the most crucial point* that is being made in this chapter.

The word 'capitalism' does not explain or does no more explain many new features that are emerging. It is not really able to reflect the new tendencies that have gripped the society. A further and more fundamental problem is that the concept of capitalism is related with and is part and parcel of the concept of the 'mode of production'. Capitalism is taken as a mode of production, and in that sense it has so far been able to cover the existing reality. But several new trends have emerged, and the concept of 'mode of production' does not cover them. And therefore it also does not explain the latest developments in capitalism and as capitalism. This takes us to the broader question of re-considering the very concept. The human society has so far lived in, has been a product of, the successive 'modes of production'. It has been a highly scientific concept, and has really been able to explain the origin and development of human society, it evolution, motion and dialectics.

The human society so far has evolved around and based on the way things were produced. *Production* has been at the centre, the cause and source of social development. Mode of production constituted society; all other areas and forms of life emanated from it. It is production that produced society.

Industrial revolution led to the emergence of an industrial society based upon industrial production. Capitalism was its immediate result, and as history later showed, its one variety, the other later product being the socialist society or at least the concept of socialism as an alternative and continuity without exploitation. Industrial and capitalist mode of production is the highest level of mode of production so far.

But now we have reached huge turn in the social development, a really massive and qualitative change in the way society is produced. Industrialism and the technologies and sciences it produced has led to a qualitative transformation in the nature of production. The industrial age produced, along with others, information on increasing scales, so much so that today it has come to influence not only society and its activities, the way we produce, live, exchange goods and information, create culture and so on, but also to increasingly determine and decide the nature and source of these activities. So, information not just influences but influences decisively, not just influences but even *guides the social development.* The massive quantities of information are leading to the spectacular qualitative conversions into new kind of society and causes of social development. Besides, the way information is produced is more and more impacting various aspects of human existence, such as the nature of the subject and the object.

So, the industrial production of tangible goods necessary for human existence has led to at this point of time to increasing production of intangible information, which in turn has led to non-industrial production of information as well as of goods, and which in turn now guides and directs production itself as also the formation of the 'mode of production'. Information has penetrated, cut down and subverted *the entire edifice of production, the production system itself.* Very soon, we will be questioning the concept of 'production' itself.

Thus, the concept of 'mode of production' is fast becoming outdated.

The human society has always depended on the tangible goods and commodities for its existence, however much it has taken recourse to the intangibles like ideas, philosophy, culture, religion and ideologies. Now, production is slipping away as the basis of the social being. It is receding into the past and is no more important.

Constitution, Deconstitution and Reconstitution of *the Subject*: Impact of Electronic Communication

Mark Poster takes from poststructuralism the theme that subjects are constituted in the course of communication, in its acts and structures. Here, we should not miss the crucial point that the subject is a crucial and key element of the modern society created mainly in the course of industrial revolution and in the era opened by it. The subject has always been an important element of the society, but that is another matter, not so relevant here. The industrial revolution created a particular kind of subject in a particular way. This is a well-formed subject in direct and clear relation with the object, with the objective world. This world is a clear succession of Cartesian structures, some high, others low, of various shapes and sizes, with spaces and without them and so on. It is a world and the consequent world-view of 'as far as one can see'. Things, objects are spread over, giving more or less view up to the horizon. The scenario creates a relationship with the subject in and of a particular kind.

This subject is the product of industrial production, production relations and of the sciences and technologies of the industrial age. The subject basically has been created/constituted by the mode of production. The subject/object relationship has been created in the course of production in world of terrain known as the 'Cartesian world'. Even the communication revolution started by Gutenburg through printing technology reflected this kind of world. Therefore, the ideas formed were of relatively permanent and orderly nature, and basically represented the mode of production.

The point is how this subject is transformed *into a subject of the mode of information or of the age of the electronic communication?* What exactly does this change mean? Poster rightly formulates that the "changes in communication patterns involve changes in the subject."[2] But how? What are the implications?

In the mode of production, and in the Cartesian world, the subject is located in point, has limits of body, as also of mind; from this vantage point the subject tries to look at and manipulate the world.

But in the mode of information the subject is *no longer* located at a point in space and time. Its relation with space and time almost disappears. This is a great historic *leap*, the qualitative transformation that grips the subject. The electronically mediated communication multiplies, disperses, dissolves the subject and puts it beyond and out of context. In other words, the subject is constantly thrown out of the space and time. At the same time, it is constantly constituted, reconstructed from endless number of spaces and times, which are thus congealed in one specific of the consciousness of the subject at a given point of space/time coordinate. The subject is the product of so many times and spaces. It is multiplied by the databases and other means, dispersed by the computers, mobiles, etc. not only locally but all over the world, particularly in and as the internet. The very identity of the subject is thus constantly questioned. The internet is the spread of the subjectivity far beyond the subject, and is now a permanent entity. Out of this subject, any number of subjects can be recreated and constituted anytime anywhere. *The subject is depersonalized.*

This subject is the product of electronic communication, and no more of production or even of the earlier stages of communications. The content of the subject contains less and less of production, and more and more of information. He/she is the product of a conflict of the two, with a historic shift towards information and the mode based upon it. Communication, primitive, medieval or modern, has always been associated with the subject. Without that the subject cannot be created. But the main point is that the historical subject obtaining so far has been the product basically of the production activities of the human beings, with information, knowledge and ideas only as derivatives.

Even if we take the simplest and most direct example, it will be clear. When I see an object, stone or tree or chair, I see it direct, without mediation. But today, what I see is no more the object itself but its 'image'. Thus the objectivity is split. The image here becomes the object and objectivity representing the split object/s.

The objectivity contains the subjectivity, the object the subject. The layers of the internet, of the extended consciousness, constitute the new objectivity. It is out of this objectivity that the subject is freshly constituted each moment. The ways the subject is constituted now is novel and unique. The very nature of the medium imparts the subject a particular nature: the subject is constituted at one moment and vanishes at the next. Its constant reappearance is its reconstitution.

"For the subject in electronically mediated communication, the object tends to become not the material world as represented in language but the flow of signifiers itself."[3] It is increasingly difficult in the world of electronic communications to identify a real world behind the world of information. *This constitutes one of the major features of the mode of information.*

The subject has a certain configuration and structure; it is 'configured' *every time* electronics mediates or intervenes.

Configuration of Subject at Two Levels

The configuration of the subject takes place at two levels. One is the relation of the subject to the solid objects. Here it is interesting to note that the subject himself/herself is a tangible being, with that most important thing: brain and the consciousness. This subject now is becoming more and more intangible and 'de-solidified' with the extension of nerves via the electronic medium, computers and mobiles etc.

Thus the subject increasingly consists of two opposites: subject and object; subject and the image of object. The subject increasingly comes to consist of a combination of consciousness emanating from the objective world and the electronically generated consciousness. The consciousness is generated from the world of particles and waves, and this is a very important point needing further elaboration. The subject is now a reflection of and is at loggerhead with two forms of object, one pure object, the other the world of the images of the object. The world of the subject is increasingly shifting towards the world of images, and therefore will need redefinition as the process proceeds further.

The relation between the consciousness and the electronically mediated communication, particularly the internet, is a more complicated and a novel one, as both the poles are intangibles. In what process is one intangible (subject) is formed by another intangible (communication)? This is a very crucial question thrown up by the electronic communication revolution. This question and its solution are the basis of the mode of information.

The concrete subject/s has been fashioned by the entire human history. Of late, in the course of the last few centuries, the communicating capacities of the subject have been expanding exponentially. The communication between the subject and the object, and between the subjects mutually have increased as never before, and in a very short period.

Even then, this communication and its history have more or less *left the subject intact*, even while the subject has grown and developed by leaps and bounds.

What happens when communication takes place between the subject and *the image* of the object, not the object itself? That qualitatively changes the relationship between the two. *For the first time in history*, this form of communication *destabilizes* the subject. Now onwards, the dialectics is established *between an unstable subject and instable object increasingly consisting of images.*

It is more and more a world of images that we begin to reside in, and less and less of objects. Simultaneously therefore, it also is a world of a growing extension of our nervous system throughout the earth. The nerves and their system have for the first time *gone beyond the confines of our bodies* on such a large scale to really create a relatively independent system or 'consciousness', a 'noosphere', to use Vladimir Vernadsky's term[4], at a higher level, enveloping the earth. It is this layer of consciousness which is increasingly driving us and our society. Technology has taken a new and decisive leap, and from now onwards it is this '*objective consciousness*' that increasingly guides human development and shapes human beings, who soon will need redefinitions.

Human and Brain/Computer Interface

While this process is going on, all sorts of gadgets and instruments in form of computers, mobiles, chips/microchips, microprocessors and so on are attaching themselves to our bodies and are on way to becoming our inalienable part (of our body). They and their functions become more human-like. They are being made to suit human needs, so as to free us from more and more functions. According to the newspaper reports of February 23, 2012 (e.g. in *Rashtriya Sahara*) clothes like the jeans pants are being embedded with or being made of electronic keyboard, mouse and other accessories of touch-screen variety, which can be used to operate laptops etc. Very soon we may see the whole of computer on our clothings or even right on our bodies! In that case, will they be independent computers or part and parcel of our bodies. Obviously they are shifting to become part of our biological conscious being, with the software getting integrated with our bodily functions, particularly the nervous conscious system.

This is a great historic shift.

In other words, we are increasingly transferring our mental functions to the electronic systems and processors. These objects are fast becoming so small that they can be fitted anywhere, including on to and within our bodies. Soon a time will come when we will not be able to live without them, and they will become an inseparable and constituent part of what is known as the 'human being'. *The humans thus have already taken a turn into a new path of development.* These gadgets are run on information and logic; they produce and communicate information. They began their journey as any other normal gadget and machine. Today, they are *crossing the limits* of the 'machine'.

The machines and the apparatuses are shedding their hardware, which are already becoming smaller, and are retaining the software. The solid material like the micro-chips etc. are turning minuscule and more efficient. So much so that these micro pieces themselves are becoming living organism-like. The quantitative change has led to a massive quantitative change of historical proportion. *The means of information are becoming one with the human beings.* This constitutes a major historical transformation and one of the crucial starting points for the emergence of the mode of information. It is mode of information that provides an entry into the mode of production.

A major development in the history of human society and of the consciousness itself is that the limits of time and space of the subject and of the subject/object relationship are broken down. I can talk to somebody from my town or place, to somebody sitting in another town or place far away, even across the globe, even on another planet!. I, in the course of this communication, cross the limits of 'I', of its space and time; the 'I' or the subject breaks down and is extended far beyond its body limits. This is now a common occurrence.

The electronics communication has spread and dispersed the communication network and the information all over, and has broken down *the subject* in real terms. This dispersal has led to the dispersal of the subject itself. This subject had been formed historically, over centuries. I have become consolidated as the 'I' through prolonged processes of production and communication. Electronics spreads and destabilizes it as never before. By talking to somebody on mobile or computer, I also impart a temporariness to the one I am talking to.

Thus, a strange situation is created here. This kind of subject disappears as soon as the communication is over. What remains is a throwback to the older or earlier kind of subject. So, it is revived, reverted/restored to the old position once the communication is suspended. It is the restoration of the subject as it is, but it is fact going back into the pre-electronics communication, and does not fully explain its further expansion. Use of the electronics suddenly reconstitutes the subject and disperses it; it is no more and is spread all over the earth. The subject ceases to exist as it was and becomes part of the larger ever expanding consciousness enwrapping the earth. As an individual, it can anytime take its constituent parts from the world of the electronics images and create *a new subject,* which at the same time also is the deconstruction of the subject.

For deconstruction, the subject should be broken up into its constituent parts. But these parts belong to both the pre-electronic, industrial processes as well as to the post-industrial processes. With the passing of time, there is a conversion of each part into electronic signals/images. The subject is further destabilized. The constituent parts/elements have evolved over time in and due to various productive and cultural activities, and now due to the electronics revolution.

Our consciousness is being fashioned by talking on mobiles, writing on computers, use of mobile functions, TV screens, iPods, e-tablets, e-music systems and other gadgets, and otherwise through discharging increasing number of functions on the screen with greater speeds. *Our own memory is being shifted more and more to the memories of the electronic systems.*

Our brain and its functions are being united in a system with the electronic memory or 'brain'. Thus, the new electronic systems are increasingly brain-like in their function, and this is of great significance for the future of humankind. The most striking feature of the new world is that the consciousness enwrapping the earth acts as *the memory of the entire humankind*, and on rapidly increasing and expanding scale. This 'brain', the one outside our own, consists of electronic and such other speeds and phenomena. It is this speed which is decisive for the further development of the human society and its consciousness.

Speed more and more determines everything, and that is the *decisive* thing/factor in the development of our consciousness. *It is this that guides all our actions/activities of humans and the nature and direction of the society.* Production is also being guided by the internet and computer and program speeds increasingly. Information at high speeds and the software at progressively higher levels force the production and productive processes to acquire greater speeds, convert into information first and at crucial points to change their configurations and efficiency.

TV and Impact on Individual

Watching TV has similar effects. The subject is broken down the moment he/she watches TV, particularly the ads, which are like being in suspended animation.

A habit generated by the increasing number of TV channels and their easy accessibility is their surfing. It is an extremely destabilizing process, in the course of which the viewer loses all the focus and constantly keeps slipping from one to the next channel; the process can go on for hours without even the viewer realizing it. The viewer never settles at one channel, and consequently on one narration, and becomes a bits and pieces individual. Electronically mediated communication cancels out all the contexts, and thus the subject is suspended in thin air or even in vacuum!

One can trace the stages of the evolution of the subject and the reasons thereof. Speech constitutes the subject as the member of a community by solidifying ties between individuals.[5] Print constitutes the subject as a rational, autonomous being, making logical connections with the symbols.

In contrast to this, media language replaces the community of speakers, thus undermining the subject and its relation with the subjects. The subject becomes self-constitutional, as the media language is non-contextual and self-referential. The subject is repeatedly remade as the electronic communication keeps on changing discourse. The subject has no defined identity as the pole of conversation.

Mobile collapses the individual/subject to a small focal point of exchange of symbols, information and images. It is a two-way or multi-way process of destruction and dissolution, and at the same time a reconstitution/reconstruction of the subject/s. The touch-screen creates endless possibilities of reaching the individual without ever reaching it.

The touch-screen is *an interesting development* in human history. It is the *borderline* between the hardware and the software. The hardware, particularly the keyboard, is a *survival of the past* and a real hurdle to the development of the electronics machine reaching the liquid state. *The touch-screen does away with that hurdle*, dialectically overcoming the limitations in form of the machine and therefore in form of the machine age. Information by its nature *does not fit* in with the machine. *With the touch-screen, we cross over into the unknown and the unlimited world of electronic consciousness,* in which the human being is just a point of arrival and departure of information.

TV: Discourse of Consumption and Constitution of Subject

"When an individual watches a TV ad, the chief social relation of society is reproduced."[6]

The TV ads occupy a central structural position in the economy. They are means of consumption: they consume the watcher and at the same time are consumed by the watcher. In the process, they destabilize and recreate the watcher, the subject. The TV ads spread and multiply these relations of consumption. Thus, the watcher of the ads turns out to be a subject of a particular kind: it is constituted by the ad/s, as it turns out, to watch, consume the ads. There has to be someone to watch, to consume. This is not the case with the non-electronic ads. The ads in print are permanent information, acting even as reference. On the contrary, the electronic screen is a very temporary and fragile medium of expression, and at the same time a very effective one. It really 'creates' the watcher in the sense that he/she is transported from one world to an entirely different one. The subject becomes deeply involved in and one with the world created by the commodities, a fantastic world of make-believe events of the weirdest nature. It is in continuous motion. To watch it the subject is transformed into someone else, *an unreal one*, not as the consumer of the day to day tangible life, where he really consumes the commodity proper, but where he is consuming the *fantasies* created out of an absurd images of it. He/she is not the usual subject/self, the normal one but a special one meant only to consume the images. That brings about a change in the consciousness over time, and the subject is constituted by a unity of the 'normal' and the 'fantastic' electronic subjects.

The subject is in transition, there is a leap in its evolution.

An average person watches tens of thousands of ads and any number of other programs every year, and the number keeps on increasing. He/she is virtually shaped by them, and of course by TV watching in general. TV has become part and parcel of the modern life, an inalienable part of it. Today it has become a major social activity, particularly in the advanced industrial societies. People switch it on as soon as they enter the room, that is, as soon as they get the slightest chance and time, and are soon transformed into another subject.

The system of communications constructs an unknown group of receivers that are an abstract audience. Media are centres of information distributing discourses and images to the broad public.[7] In this case, they are somewhat similar to Foucault's 'universal intellectual' in contrast to Gramsci's organic intellectual. The media are systems of cultural transmission without ties to any community. They are simply the emitters of signals received by a tele-anomic society. According to Meyrowitz, media rearranges its relation with the audience, thus drastically rearranging the social order by cutting across the social stratification. The TV nullifies the effects of time and space distances. The electronic media alters the time-space parameters of social interactions. The electronic media do not simply expand and multiply communications; they alter the structure and conditions of the symbolic exchange.[8]

Thus, watching TV and TV ads is an important part of mode of information.

Language has so far been contextual, but the mode of information defaces and destroys the contexts and establishes an independence of language from their context, an independence from the context in which they originated. In their place, it introduces new contexts and new meanings. This language occurs at places unrelated to the material limitations of normal existence. Words begin to acquire new meanings and connotations, and they keep developing into an independent system. This can be seen in the present evolution of English, Hindi and other languages.

Why do people prefer the monologue of the TV over interaction with other people and with the print? People sit for hours together at the screens and watch programmes on a wide range of channels and other facilities in the latest series of technological developments, including on the mobiles? Is it that they try to escape this way the anxieties and boredom? The answer provided by Poster is interesting and crucial. According to him, watching TV *is not a simple passive activity.* It is in fact a process of "*self-construction* by viewers that profoundly engage them."[9]

This is a very interesting point and provides one of the clues to the process of the formation of temporary and transitional subjects. It is also interesting to note that in contrast to the TV, *the print media does not constitute this kind of subject.*

This kind of monologic and non-contextual relation with the media is self-referential. This is because here there is the distance from the concrete context and character/s. The face to face relationship is absent, and therefore the stability of culture is also absent. In contrast to the dialogues, the TV monologues reproduce the contexts from within itself and thus simulate the real context. Thus the TV absorbs the functions of culture differently from the speech or mutual exchange of words and from print. Speech solidifies the relations within the community. Print arranges thoughts in serial series, and constitutes the meanings in a rational, organized and linear form, forcing logical interpretations and creation of thought systems.

It reminds one of the conveyor-belt system of the factory. Print also reproduces thoughts in linear, organized manner.

But it is different with electronic information systems. TV and electronic media and interaction with other forms of screens *radically transform all this.* The viewer unknowingly creates his/her own context by a continuous conversation with a series of discourse created by the TV. Contexts and audience is all the time created. There is no definite and known recipient and no determinate references to act as a standard; the viewer has to create his own meanings. Thus "the subject has no defined identity as a pole of a conversation."[10]

Change from Production to Consumption: Role of TV Ads

The world capitalist economy gradually shifted from production to consumption roughly during the 1920s. The shift and later its combination with the STR and information revolution created a new mode of social existence, which is reflected in the act of watching TV ads in particular and TV in general. Mark Poster's contentions in this regard are fully corroborated by the actual events. We spend huge amounts of time before the TV every day. We follow news, songs, entertainment, films and so on. Now we e-buy commodities, and this is very important as both as a virtual and actual act.

We have, now, serials that run, not once or twice a week, but almost every day, for weeks, months and even years! As if they are our real life events: we seek to find out 'what will happen today?' or 'what happened in yesterday's episode"? Etc. They run at real-time pace in keeping with the rhythm of the real everyday life, and we are eager to know the 'events' which are purely fictional. It cannot be denied that these TV events are mingling imperceptibly with our day-to-day life, and we cannot separate ourselves from it despite best efforts, even granting some exceptions.

It is a combination of the real and the virtual worlds that ultimately affects our economic activity and the money-commodity exchange and economic relations. It is the sphere of consumption, including and increasingly the consumption of information that begins to dominate our life and ultimately decides the way the subject is created/constituted. STR/ICR provide new terrains for the emergence and constitution of the individual/the subject. They have caused new ways where the conscious activity of the human being constitutes the subject.

This is a historic shift in the terrain and medium where and through which the subjective world is being created rapidly. Here the TV and such other screens play a crucial role. It is a world of information, consumption and of the manipulation of the world itself. Poster states significantly, and intriguingly, that "when an individual watches a TV ad the health of the economy is at stake."[11]

Here information drives the economy. It is all about knowing the commodity and its various forms and transformations. This is the discourse, the field of constitution that guides circulation. "The complete circulation of commodities is concentrated in the single act of TV watching."[12]

According to Baudrillard and Poster, TV ads are not about moving the objects in a Newtonian world of the tangibles and rationality. In such a world, the resultant cause-effect phenomena become the object of knowledge, which create a particular kind of subject typical of a Cartesian world. The subject is of a kind who tries constantly to transcend this world; he/she must do so in order to exist as a relatively fixed but evolving point, solving the subject/object tension. It is through reason, analysis and philosophy that the tension is resolved. The subject, therefore, is rational and critical, looking *at* the world. *It is this dialectics that has driven the world so far in the sphere of cognition and practice.*

It is *different* with the new addressees of TV and TV ads. They are not mute and tangible objects; *they are in fact linguistic patterns.* And this is a new development, emergence of a new 'subject-like' subject constituted of and by discourse. They are not subject to *the mechanical laws* of nature but are self-dialectical, trans-material and transcendental.

The electronic communication becomes a sign system, which in turn acts as an action system. It follows the linguistic logic of the communication acts and creates a sign system. When an individual watches a TV ad he/she is watched and shaped by *a discourse*, whose aim is to discipline the consuming subject to the logic of profit, market and production.[13]

So, the point here is that the very act of watching TV or any screen, and in particular the TV ad, leads to *the formation of a discourse, which in turn creates a new kind of subject.* Thus, the subject is not created in direct interaction with the Cartesian object or objective world, but with the images created from it as well as without it. Images are ideas and ideas form a vast structure of views, language and expressions, which create a system of subject, a subject which is a constellation of images and ideas. These images simultaneously create a vast number of subject and thus vast subjectivity.

TV ads are increasingly irrational, absurd, have virtually no aesthetic value, the information they convey has little in common with truth, they create a world of fantasy, they are not true and represent nothing; people get increasingly bored with them and try to leave the screen and the room showering curses on the repetition of the ads, the viewer becomes irritated, the ads are resented and mocked at. "And yet, I contend, they are crucial semiotic indices to an emerging new culture."[14]

This is a very interesting and important observation. The ads and the TV programmes in general create a particular kind of discourse, constituting the subject in a particular way. Despite all the negatives, the ads represent a growing consumerism of the society and economy and of life in general, which need particular kind of subject different from the earlier subject. The ads force the consumer to consume, force the viewer to become a consumer. He/she is no more just a viewer of entertainment; the continuous stream of ads transforms the viewer into a qualitatively different subject, who is unaware of the change. The subject thus created becomes one with the consuming market relations, with consumerism and thus becomes a temporary participant in the entire market consuming process. *Watching TV ads is the concentrated expression of circulation of commodities.*[15]

Thus, *one very important thing that comes out of the discussion is that watching and working with the screen creates a particular kind of world, distinguished by formation of a system of language and its particular structure, includes consumption of commodities and images, and much more important, creates a new discourse of mode of information.* This world of image conveys itself through a structure of language, which is associated with and a product of the software. The electronically mediated language produces its won relations, whose source is the mode of information.

Now onwards, it is this which drives and constricts the mode of production.

Criticism of Ads and the Discourse Behind It: Industrial versus Informational Subject

The criticism of the stream of TV ads has its own problems and creates its own discourse. By implication, a criticism of TV ads has been looked upon as saying at least two things, which are open to criticism. First, there is an unacknowledged anti-feminist tendency inherent in this criticism.

According to the historians of the ads, the earlier ads were informative, direct and clear. They created a rational consumer. But there took place a shift at the beginning of the 20th century. Now the advertisers began to target women as their main consumers. They were assumed to be sentimental and irrational, and their aspirations were utilized and exploited to promote the commodities.

The criticism here, partly correct, is that by so presenting the case you are assuming that the women are generally irrational, anxious, volatile and romantic. Thus, the critics blamed the female audience, the victims, shifting the blame from the emitter to the audience. Thus, there is a difference between a man watching a TV ad and a woman doing the same, according to this criticism. "When a man watches a TV ad, his autonomy is threatened by feminine irrationality."[16]

The second implication of the critique of the TV ads is the defence of the bourgeois male subject, the autonomous, rational ego as the foundation of the discourse. The ads undermine the autonomy of the self which is justified as good. In the liberal accounts, the defence is direct. In the Marxist accounts, a strange conversion takes place. The ideal subject is rational and bourgeois. Here a curious displacement takes place. This very rational and bourgeois individual becomes the critic of the ad system, while the consumer assumes the role of destroying him or her. Thus, here a nostalgia for the rational bourgeois observer emerges, and the present is criticized from the point of view of the past.

This position retreats to a position of the defence of a rationalist subjectivity, and from that position mounts an attack from a moral point of view about the present rather than identify liberating possibilities from structures of domination. So, one bourgeois position is criticized from another.

Althusser goes further and argues that the main result of ideology is to transform individuals into subjects. The viewer of the ad recognizes himself as the consuming subject. This recognition is ideological and at the same time, a misrecognition. It is so because his relation with the real conditions of existence are imaginary. The ad constitutes the subject able to buy a product, who labours and as one who is able to choose. The individual does not receive the communication unless the ad is viewed and is constituted so, as a subject, for the purpose. The process of recognition and misrecognition takes place precisely during the process of viewing the ad.[17]

The ideological effect of the ad is to reproduce the conditions which transform an individual into a subject of the capitalist society, *a legally free*, autonomous worker and a consumer. Such a subject *is in an imaginary relation with the capitalist mode of production*. It is a distorted relation because while the subject believes himself to be an agent of the structure, in reality he is constituted by the structure *as its bearer*. This ideological transformation takes place not in a public place but in the privacy of the room where the TV is being witnessed, far removed from the clamour of history and politics. Ideological effects thus deny that they are taking place as they occur. Thus, this is a place of ideological struggle including that of class struggle. The ideological state apparatus and other structures directly affect our observations. In the course of viewing the TV ad, capitalism is either reproduced or attacked.[18]

Subject in Capitalist and Socialist Modes, and in Industrial and Informational Modes

We will stop here to discuss some interesting points that have cropped up in the course of this discussion, creating a new discourse. The individual is converted into a 'legally free' and autonomous subject. This is an important point, showing the Cartesian independence of the individual, thus converting him/her into a Cartesian subject. This relationship is distant from the object and the world of objects. Mode of transmitting information and the massive unleashing of information destabilizes this very subject like an avalanche hitting a rock. The point to be investigated is how this subject becomes temporary and dissipated? And in that case, what is the relationship between mode of production and mode of information?

Second point made above is that the subject is in an imaginary relation with the mode of production and acts its bearer. This is a very important point of transition of the subject in an age of information. It shows one aspect of the opposites acting upon the subject. The person is far removed from the actual class and other struggles and conflicts going on. His/her other, opposite, aspect is being created ***outside*** the mode of production. *This is a very important point indeed.* They reflect the process where two sides of the subject are created by two modes, one based upon production, the other on information. From the point of view of Althusser and the mode of production, the subject is the product of mode of production, who stands in relation to the objectivity created by himself/herself, while the objectivity creates a particular kind of subject and subjectivity. The important point here is that this subject and the subjectivity is not threatened by the mode of production; on the contrary it is strengthened by it.

Does capitalism, and here we are talking of *industrial capitalism*, ever threaten the subject/subjectivity or is the latter all the time created and strengthened by the former? *Capitalism can be opposed or supported by the subject but never destabilized in the normal course of witnessing it, even on TV.* Capitalism can be criticized but not threatened or overthrown in the course of production, exchange and communication. Thus, the Cartesian world of order and logic is maintained and perpetuated. Capitalism in fact is based upon the very strong basis of subject-object relationship. Without this relationship, it cannot hope to remain in tact.

It is the process of visualization of revolution, a veritable turmoil and transfer of ownership that destroys capitalism, at least that is what is visualised. A separate revolution is needed to alter the relation between the subject and the object. As a result, the subject becomes the owner of means of production, the destroyer of the created object, in order to create a new object, thus taking his/her destiny in one's own hand.

The purpose of socialist revolution is not to destroy the subject and its relation with the object and the objective world. On the contrary the purpose of revolution is to further strengthen the relation, make it more direct, just, stable and non-destabilizing, clear and logical. The Cartesian world becomes more ordered and clearer and thus more 'socialist'. A socialist subject is more active, independent and free from exploitation, so that it plays an active and conscious role in the social development as the conscious creator of new socio-economic and political relations. The purpose of such a subject is *to strengthen the mode of production* by transforming it into a socialist mode minus exploitation. Socialism also is a typically *industrial mode of production.* It is such a mass of individuals that constitute a class or classes.

Capitalism is destroyed by socialism, at least theoretically, but *not as a mode of production*; in fact it is maintained as such, as a mode of production. Herein lies the new problem and the problematic posed by it.

But things are quite different with the mode of information being created by the electronics-based information revolution. This difference results from the fact that the relation between the sign and the object is shattered, leading to a reconstitution of relations between subject and object, between the producer and what is produced.

According to Poster[19] a communication is enacted in the TV ad, which is unreal, which has nothing to do with the real world. An unreal is made real, and a set of meanings is attached. The communication communicated is more real than the real. The object in the TV ad is not the same as taken home from the shop. We may be consuming the object shown and advertised in the ad, and that way contribute to the increase in its sale. *But there is much more to it than this.* The commodity/object in the TV ad is something more, something different, representing quite a different world of unreal objects with their unreal representations. The subject as the buyer of the object and as the watcher of the ad of the same are *two different subjects.* The image is magical, fulfilling and exciting; the images keep one engaged all the time without let up.

This particular subject is the product of objects/commodities which are not existence, yet they are real. They can be real, because we can any time create them. Therefore, they are not outside our realm but very much within our reach. It is linguistic and imagery production, which forces us to create a world of images in which we float much more easily. But to do so, we must use different language and medium. This language creates a hyper-real world; *the screen is the universe in which this world resides.*

With the spread of electronic communication, the world becomes more and more imagery, full of fleeting pictures and images. They represent the real world in form of the unreal. But it should not be taken to be a one to one correspondence: image for an object. The relations change drastically. We are not dealing with objects so much; they are becoming less important. We are living among the images, which now constitute us. The reality itself is hyper-real, as Baudrillard would like to say.[20] We are everywhere and nowhere; we are at once here, there and everywhere, through and outside the mobiles, internet, facebook and so on.

Poster versus Baudrillard

Here Poster takes objection to Baudrillard's position, which itself needs to be objected to. The generalization of the concept of the hyper-real from specific communication practices to the social reality 'is the problematic element in Baudrillard's discourse, the aspect of his position that the critical theory of the mode of information must reject."[21]

But we are forced to *reject Poster's position.* Mode of information cannot remain confined to a system of language within the electronically mediated communication. It spreads all over the society and grips it. The system of signification and constitution of universally spread subject/s is growing fast. Poster says that Baudrillard makes global statements like "We live everywhere already..." This goes "beyond the limit of the situated finitude of their author."[22]

Quoting a Marxist author Gerry Gill, Poster says that Baudrillard grants to the code an almost total sway across economy, politics, ideology and culture. Gill is quoted as saying that whereas for Althusser ideology constitutes persons as subjects, for Baudrillard signs and codes assign subjects to their places.

It is not quite clear as to why Poster objects to Baudrillard's assertions on applying hyper-reality to the whole of society. Baudrillard himself has not clarified anything, only has mentioned the world of hyper and unreal reality in which we live. Nor has Baudrillard drawn any logical conclusions.

On the other hand Poster begins to contradict himself while dealing with Baudrillard. For example, he says that the concept of mode of information is "perhaps a small step" in the direction of understanding a deeply changed social world. Misrecognition of reality stems, he says, from inappropriate theory and limitations of social context of critical theory, as also from "an emerging social formation."[23]

What does he mean?! 'Emerging social formation': so does he really accept that a new social formation is emerging, which of course is a welcome development and which contradicts his attempts to limit the concept of mode of information to certain linguistic configurations without 'totalisation'. He himself is 'totalising' by accepting that a social formation is emerging, without elaborating what it all means.

Now, *this is a peculiar and paradoxical position*, and Poster seems to be vacillating, is uncertain as to whether to "go social" or "to remain individual", whether to totalize or to confine to the linguistic constitution of the modern and postmodern subject.

Thus, Poster is uncertain of the "mode of information" really becoming the mode of information, which should supercede or dominate the mode of production. All his arguments should logically lead him to an analysis of the transition to a new social formation and all-embracing social mode. But he suddenly stops in his own tracks.

Both Poster and Baudrillard lose their way somewhere along. Poster is limited by and obsessed with the linguistic constitution of the subject, and does not want to take the logical steps further. Baudrillard is satisfied with spreading the subject all over but refuses to make a thorough analysis of the implications for the society as a whole, for the mode of information, including for the production system. This is typical of the confused positions of the varieties of systems and schools in postmodernism.

Subject as the Basis of Knowledge

The subject is the focus of modern and postmodern critique as a synthesizing site or centre-point of knowledge. This synthesizing site is the agency of knowledge, experience, culture, thought and activity.[24] That is how we, the modern people, treat or look upon the individual or the subject. So when we utter the word 'subject', it expresses in concentrated form the entire experience of human development. That is how we *the moderns* treat the individual. We expect it to experience and digest reality and to create/process knowledge. Knowledge as well as information is a human product, basically with the help of tools, and on many occasions, without tools, through direct observation and thought processing. Individual is also at the centre of production activity, which in turn produces knowledge.

In this way, the observer and the way the observed is observed are product of *modern* processes. They are securely placed and relate to each other more or less directly and clearly. The industrial tools help them to do so. The observers relate with each other and with the object/s. It is such a human being who is at the centre of the modern industrial society.

"In the flux of modernity, philosophy has often sought to identify a fixed and stable point, from which perspective change might begin to be understood."[25] This is an interesting point, which helps us to unravel the process of development of the subject and of theoretical and practical experience. Modernity accelerates motion of evolution of the subject. As such, philosophy proves to be the stable ground where the concepts help fix reality. This of course may prove to be risky, as one may end up working with finished concepts. That poses us with the task of further developing philosophy itself. It is in philosophy that the subject finds its identity, but that identity at the same time is constantly evolving, with conceptual abstraction posing a simultaneous threat. Thus, a conflict arises between modernity and philosophy. Modernity is process of becoming at one with reality, and therefore tends to go towards *postmodernity*, with philosophization losing firm grounds.

The human subject is the key element in the development of knowledge and experience.

Disruption of the subject is a crucial problem of the modern, and in particular, the postmodern world. The transition from stability to dispersal can only be understood if, along with some other factors, the disruption and decentering of the subject is understood in relation to and as a consequence of the information and communication revolution (ICR). The psychoanalytic and other theories including those belonging to the postmodern schools have tried to show that the subject has been under stress and disintegration even before the STR and the ICR. There have been trends that have questioned the essential core of humanism, which bases itself upon the centrality of the subject. Thinkers like Sigmund Freud, Frantz Fanon and Helene Cixous have challenged modern humanism from various perspectives.[26]

They and others have tried to show that there has been a steady disruption of the modern subject including as depicted by Descartes. Descartes and Kant identify human consciousness with the 'I think' approach. Freud introduces an unconscious reserve into consciousness as a supplement. This element disorientates and disrupts the organizing moments of the consciousness and decentres the subject. Experience becomes questionable.

According to the French psychoanalyst and theorist Jacques Lacan, Descartes' assertion of the 'I think' should be replaced with a more complex formula: "I think where I am not, therefore I am where I do not think. ... I am not wherever I am the plaything of my thought; I think of what I am where I do not think to think." In this complex of formulations, the subject is displaced from the centre of experience, thought and consciousness.[27]

It was Hegel, who really showed the dialectics of the being and proved that 'I is and is not' at the same time; in fact 'I am' itself means 'I am not'. It was Hegel who developed philosophy by transcending Kant's unknowable world, and propelled it forward through his discovery of inherent dialectics in the world, society and human beings. Without his dialectics the modern and the postmodern being cannot be grasped, nor his/her displacement and disintegration explained.

Dispersal of Thinking

We saw above that the subject has been the centre of knowledge and experience. It is subject because it is the concentrated expression of human experience in direct relation with the objective world.

It is consciousness and thinking that the information and communication revolution works upon human beings as a dispersing force. *It is a novel and a most extraordinary revolution that has occurred in human history*. It at the same time, works as a unifying force at higher levels. The sudden acceleration of technology has overturned many features, relations and concepts of social development. In the words of Baudrillard, "the acceleration of modernity, of technology, of events and media, of all exchanges... has propelled us to the '*escape velocity*'..."[28]

This is very well put: we are in the 'escape velocity'; we are escaping everything that is old, past and outdated, in fact escaping the present. And consciousness of the subject is one of them. According to Baudrillard, a certain *slowness and distance* is required for history to be history, for the crystallization of events as history. (We have dealt with this point independently and in detail on 'slowdown of time and history' earlier in a chapter.) But the events are being lost in hyper-reality.

The most important event that has occurred is the dispersal of thought and consciousness. It doe not mean a reduction or loss of thoughts and thought-process, nor a loss in our thinking capacities. It means that the human beings have found means of extending and communicating their thoughts. More importantly, part of their thinking and logical capacities are being handed over to non-human systems, which at the same time function in a brain-like manner. The subject and the individual is no more *the only centre* of thought and experience. These functions, the logical ones, are being *transferred* on a massive scale to the autonomously and automatically functioning systems, basically the electronic ones. Now, we do not necessarily and always 'experience' the events and objects. It is the 'machines' or the electronic/mechanical systems that are also engaged in 'experiencing'.

We are being left with more abstract, philosophizing and generalizing activities. Through our direct and indirect experience we have discovered many stars. But today it is the Hubble-like systems that are doing the 'experience' and also 'drawing' many logical conclusions. We are only selectively picking out of it all what is striking or suitable for us for our general picture of the galaxies and the universe. There is no 'experience' of all of what has the independent system gone through. In fact, we do not know what it really is 'going through' all the time! Yet it is collecting all kinds of data, most of which we will not be using or are not in a position to use. We may even never know all that! Yet, a huge exploration and research is going on all the time, every second and micro-second. This is an unprecedented new situation in the history of human beings.

Part of *our consciousness is being transferred to independently working technical systems.* Consequently, we are forming a unique system in unity with them. Our thought process or part of consciousness has gone *out of our control.* This is *the greatest revolution* ever. *We are no more* Homo sapiens*; we definitely are becoming* Homo electronicus*!*

A new path of historical development has opened up, which also is a new path of social as well as biological development. The human being stands on the verge of a massive qualitative transformation, about to take place or to be completed, in the next few generations.

There is no doubt now that in the last two decades, a layer of consciousness has enveloped the earth, and much of human development henceforward depends upon this layer. It is a unique development. It is turning out to be *an independent information processing zone*, at first as an adjunct to the human society but now increasingly dominating and replacing its conscious activities. This may sound absurd to many, but it is the reality that cannot be ignored. We are now reaching a position or have already reached a position where *we cannot survive without this layer.*

The human activity (consciousness) now is more and more relying on the internet and other self-acting systems, which is continuously processing information. A massive part of the logical activities have been handed over to the computer and internet systems. Therefore, human logic is now split between the human and the non-human activities. The electronic system has the advantage of high speed, of what Baudrillard called the 'escape velocity'. The speeds of technological systems are too fast, and are becoming faster. Therefore, the human brain cannot simply cope with information and logic, and therefore has to give way to the auto-working intelligent electronic systems. If in future, bio-processors and bio-sensors are added to this development, we may see the emergence of independent bio-mechanical systems, far more efficient than human beings and leading a parallel existence along with us. In fact we have already taken the first steps in that direction.

Add to all this, the micro-organisms made of the tiniest processors, systems working at the atomic and particulate levels, nano-system or 'beings' working at and going into the deepest recesses of the minutest parts of the world, and auto-systems guided by and at the speed of light, combination/embedding of the software/electronic processing on and within our body parts, and the picture of the future is complete: the human being lives in a world of and surrounded by non-biological micro-beings of vastly efficient processing capacities, becoming at one with them.

Speed and smallness has become the decisive factor in human and social evolution and development.

Time, Space and Matter

We are living in times of accelerating time and shrinking space, which also opens up a world of limitless space before us. Therefore, the concept of matter is rendered much modified. The qualities or characteristics of matter like space and time are changed, so that we look at matter from different perspectives.

It is time that has taken a superior and dominating position in the world of matter. What do we look at? We look at certain things and events with a certain order of space and certain order of time. And we draw conclusions from this kind of observation.

"The reality of the external world is not so material, as was held by materialism, which got its bearings from the ideas of classical physics of impenetrable, fixed, extended and well-defined bodies."[29]

This truly applies to a world which is transiting from mode of production to mode of information. This mode covers the growing domination of information and discourse created by it.

Mode of Information Drives the Mode of Production

For the first time in human history, mode of information has become the driving force of human development, and the mode of production has lost its primacy.

What does the mode of production do? And in what way and what sense is the mode of information dominant now? Mode of production is the method or way to produce material goods or commodities. It becomes progressively better and higher through the refinements in the instruments, tools and machines. Human society so far has depended mainly on the production of goods. The world of consciousness has been the product of the mode or modes of production, and has emanated from the latter. Transmission of information and knowledge has accorded with the mode of production and has been progressively helped by it.

At a certain point, at the present, there is a qualitative transformation in this state of affairs. *The mode of production begins to produce more information than goods.* This can only be the result of very high efficiency and levels of development of productive forces and of their productivity, where the material goods are produced in no time. The means have become qualitatively transformed into producing not only tangible goods but information and images and signs. As a result, mode of production is, at a certain point, transformed into *mode of information*. It becomes the mode whereby *first* information about the product and process of production and about many other processes are produced, and only then the material goods for consumption are produced. Production is now becoming increasingly information-driven. Communication has rapidly gained domination over production, and is now all-pervading. Information directs and drives production. We need images, and goods are taken for granted. Electronics has the capacity to easily produce images before anything else can be produced. It is the flow of electrons and photons, which are not the tangible things in the usual sense. Image of every process and material object can be instantly produced, *and herein lies the great historical advantage of electronic signals*. The images reach the consumer much before the article itself. Earlier, the images of the article or the commodity or the goods were printed in the newspapers, spread on the cinema screens and information broadcast through the radio and transistor waves. The radio waves made a break to an extent, in the sense that it could reach the consumer before the material object.

Electronics has changed all this. Everything is getting converted into images or has the potential to do so before it is produced and consumed in material form. *The material form has fallen behind* and the image has gone ahead as the maker of objects and of the society. The *image must first be consumed* before the material good is consumed.

Much depends on the nature of technology, even decisively. Some people object to such an approach, saying that this is 'technological determinism' and a surrender to reductionism by sidelining human beings and the class point of view. Let any label be put, technological determinism or whatever, that should not deter us from pointing out the truth. The present electronic technology is such that it has to, it must, *first* produce the image. The electronic technology *is such* that it operates through information and production of images. It has the capacity of converting everything into images and information. This is because this technology operates at first mainly and then exclusively through software. This is *the distinguishing feature* of electronic technology. Software, the language of the computer, converts everything into images, luminescent letters, pictures etc. It is this software that commands the conversion of images into solid, tangible and usable goods. That is *the chief function* of the new technological revolution today. It is easy for the images at the production line and the internet or computer and net systems to get inter-connected. Therefore, production gets connected with the world of images and begins to fall behind and trail the world of images. It must follow the image and in the process change itself and speed itself up in order to keep pace with the electronic speed and its demands.

Baudrillard on Objects and Signs: Constituents of Mode of Information

In the context of this discussion, Baudrillard is right in taking a broader view of consumption, stating that it is not a material practice. He signifies it by organizing all the things into a signifying fabric. Consumption is the virtual totality of all the objects and messages, *constituted as a coherent discourse.* "To become an object of consumption, an object must first become a sign."[30]

As Baudrillard puts it (Ibid., p. 1), our civilization is witness to an endless and ever-accelerating procession of objects, products, appliances, gadgets and commodities, so much so that no encyclopedia can cover them. It becomes impossible even to name them.

So we may safely state the situation as that of fleeting objects, which are in constant change and which can only be grasped at techno-electronic level. Their qualities, varieties, the smallest characteristics, models and forms and so on change almost with the moment.

These moments can only be captured in the mode of information, *and not in the mode of production.* The moment the mode of production captures it, *it becomes mode of information.*

Conflict of Software and Hardware: Dissolution of Keyboard, a Borderline Event

The transition from mode of production to the mode of information is evident in *the conflict* between the hardware and the software, their highly interesting *dialectics.* The former is proving to be a hurdle in the development of the latter. While the hardware represents the *industrial age*, the software represents the *post-industrial, postmodern age.* The software is constantly becoming more efficient and concentrated, almost in geometrical progression, while the hardware is trying to reduce its size and modify itself to keep pace with the former. In fact, the software, so to say, is trying to get rid of the hardware altogether. The hardware is disappearing. The software is a logical system and therefore not the part of the machinery as such. *It is not machinery at all, but antithetical to it.* It is trying to get liberated from the machinery and thus to act as and in an independent mode. The mechanical-technical objects like the keyboard are a hurdle to *mode of information* and therefore must themselves be transformed into software in the course of their major and final *leap into the mode of information.*

There are clear signs of such tendencies in development.

The touch-screen, including in particular the touch keyboard, is a major transition, where the border-line between the tangible and the intangible *comes to an end.* The keyboard, the hardware, finally becomes part of the software. Now onwards, the software as an independent consciousness takes on an autonomous line of development. Step by step other parts of the hardware like the mouse etc. are also being converted into signals alone, into software. This is *a major step* to the success of the mode of information where mere touch or look or *even a thought* can be 'written out' on the screen or whatever and it can act as a command and get converted into the tangible objects of our use. The software will be playing the decisive role, and not the material objects. ***The era of material objects as the driving force has come to an end with the touch-screen.***

The 'keyboard without keyboard; becomes a borderline event. The keyboard, which was a hardware so far, has now become a software, or rather a combination of both: *software discharges the functions of hardware!* This is a great historical transition, with deep impact on the proletariat and on work itself. Work is bound to grow into non-work. *Software dissolves 'work'.* That is why we are able to hand our mental functions to the electronic systems, and that is where the proletariat loses relevance. This point needs further discussions.

The mode of information has finally been established with the touch-screen. The conversion of hardware (hard, tangible tools, objects, operating gadgets, etc.) *into software* is a qualitatively big leap forward into the world of mode of information and the world of consciousness. *It is not a simple change of means and tools,* mere improvement or improvements, where one is replaced by much better and efficient ones. It is a complete qualitative transformation of the tangible material means into non-tangible system of signs and signals, which have the dual functions of means of production and of information; they discharge the functions of solid bodies and are at the same time soft temporary signals. It is these signals that now are taking over the functions of the means of production as well. The means now are more and more intangible and non-material, and this is a historic qualitative change *for the first time* in human history.

This change makes possible the transition to a new world of discourse, concepts, dialogues, information, facebook, emails, internet, twitter, flow of information and bits and bytes about production and exchange and other processes, a new terrain of events. Everybody is wired with everybody else, potentially, and every process is networked with every other, one convertible into another. The flow is abstract, of abstract processes, convertible into particulars on demand or necessity. The abstract dominates the concrete, through independent discourses, direction from human consciousness and *by the commands from the software.* The discourse is created and structured, increasingly, by the software, and the human consciousness and the human subject are being structured accordingly. It is in fact emergence of a *new human subject,* in direct communication with the world of signs and signals creating a terrain of novel kind for the emergence of new consciousness. This world of signs/signals is *both the object and the new subject,* and that is the greatest dramatic novelty thrown up by the upheavals of information. Therefore, the consequent language is different, which is participated in by both the subject and the object, individual consciousness and the noosphere.

From now on the laws of social development take on new and qualitatively different nature; in fact, qualitatively new paths of social development have opened up, with unforeseen implications. It is the thought-process and thought layer (noosphere) that determines the human activity, with the material objects relegated to the background. This is a process where every process is getting converted into an external consciousness, and at the same time it is a convergence of the internal as well as the external consciousness.

It is a new stage of matter-idea relationship that drives social development and imparts new aspects to historical materialism.

We have to rework the society, almost from the very beginning.

Quantity of Information Leads to the Quality as Mode of Information

Mere numbers and some data will show that we really are enveloped by a growing noosphere, discussed above

The planet earth is being rapidly engulfed by layers of information. So much so that we will soon have *to reassess our identity!*

When the Sloan Digital Sky Survey began to function in 2000, its telescope in New Mexico collected more data in the first few weeks than in the entire history of astronomy. At present, a decade later, its archive contains 140 terabytes of information; one terabyte is equal to 1000 gigabytes. Its successor telescope, to be established in Chile in 2016, will accumulate this quantity every five days.

Such scales of information can be found on the ground also. The retail company, Wal-Mart, handles more than one million customer transactions every hour, feeding databases more than 25 petabytes, that is equivalent of 167 times the books in the American Library of Congress. One petabyte is equal to 100 terabytes. Facebook is home to 40 billion photos. Decoding the human genome took ten years the first time in 2003, but can now be done in one week![31]

The world contains unimaginable amounts of digital information getting vaster ever more rapidly. They can be used to do newer things in all fields of life, not possible earlier, if put to proper use. Yet despite the abundance and types of tools, e.g. computers, mobiles, sensors etc., the information already exceeds the available storage space. Besides, the security and privacy of data is becoming a big problem. Storage capacity is half the information created, making it impossible to access much of it. In other words we are going through a rapid and extremely rapid *data revolution.*

The business of information management is growing extremely rapidly. It helps organizations to analyse, interpret and make sense of data. The industry of data management and analytics is growing roughly *twice* as fast as the software business as a whole. A new kind of professional has emerged, who combines the skills of software programmer, statistician and artist-story-teller, whose job is to make sense of the mountain of data available.

Information Explosion

There are many reasons for this explosion, the most important being qualitatively new advances in technology. With the advance in technology, every available information, past or present, is being digitalized. The capabilities of the devices are soaring and their prices are falling rapidly. Besides, many more people have access now to the devices than before. There are, for example, 4.6 billion mobile phone subscriptions all over the world. It is a huge area which is growing, even after adjustments made for various factors like one person having more than one connection etc. 1 to 2 billion people use the internet.

Many more people use the available information. Between 1990 and 2005, the population of the middle class grew by 1 billion. People are otherwise also becoming more literate, which means many more using information.

"Revolutions in science have often been preceded by revolutions in measurements."[32] Microscope transformed biology, electron microscope changed physics; similarly the present data are turning the social sciences upside down.[33] Researchers are now able to understand human behaviour, not only at the individual level better, they are able to understand it at the population levels.

According to the Moore's law, processing power and the storage capacity of computer chips double every 18 months. At the same time their prices halve in the same duration. As a result of this and other factors, the amount of data increases ten fold every five years.

Vast amounts of information is being shared over the internet. By 2013 the amount of traffic flow over the internet per year will reach 667 exabytes. One exabyte is equal to 1000 petabytes or equivalent of 10 billion copies of the journal *The Economist.*[34]

Quantitative to Qualitative Change

The society is shifting towards an information society. There is a surfeit of information, and it is the new raw material of the economy. Managing data better is becoming the basic necessity today and in near future. Sophisticated quantitative analysis is being applied to almost all the aspects of daily life. Not just economic or financial policy matters or the rocket and missile technologies, but increasing number of aspects of daily are being analysed with pinpoint accuracy using unlimited data. For example, a part of the Microsoft search engine Bing, known as Farecast, can advise the customers on buying a particular day's ticket by examining 225 billion flight and price records. These methods can be extended to reservations of hotel rooms, taxis and so on.[35] The micro- and macroeconomic trends of individual as well as social banking can be identified by dipping into the pool of information and identifying the trends.

The trail of clicks left by the internet users is becoming one of the mainstays of the *internet economy*. Value can be extracted from these trails. This is known as the 'data exhaust'. The Google search engine, for example, is partly guided by the number of clicks on an item to determine the relevance of a particular query.

Computer, Science and Work

A worker in a computerized factory is quoted by Shoshana Zuboff in 'The Age of the Smart Machine'[36] as saying that being in the groom with the computer is more mind work; the longer you work with it, the more you come to trust it. As computers are introduced into the factories, a new worker/subject is constituted. The new worker-subject is working with logic of the object and its motion. The motion is too fast, and therefore computer *takes over* from him/her. They both now constitute *a unified system*, in which the commands on the screen increasingly ask the worker (observer) to act in a particular way or discharge this or that function.

For example, data about the processes in a blast furnace or in a group of such furnaces are being continuously displayed on the screen, stating the position of various chemical elements, compounds, gases, pressure, temperature and so on, which is all too complicated and complex, so much so that the engineer, worker or overseer cannot find them out and solve them his or their own. These calculations and performance of vast number of jobs will take long time for the humans. The computer acts as a quick processor, and responds by itself suggesting or giving commands time to time, say about adding this or that gas or chemical etc. The worker/observer/overseer is the one who gives commands on the basis of information/s received, but increasingly there is shift from the person to the computer as far as giving commands is concerned, or there is closer relation between the combination of their commands. These processes apply to any big industry like that of steel, paper or textile mill etc.

So, the operator emerges here as *the manipulator of information* and not of the solid 'jobs' or articles at the shop floor of the factory. So, he/she is really 'not working' but observing, keeping a watch over the proceedings, as if he/she/they are the 'owner' of the means of production *and* information! 'Work' stands redefined. Work shifts to logical aspects. The 'worker'/operator/overseer is so detached from the actual work/production/labour process that he/she forgets what he/she is working with; the individual is concerned only with and deeply immersed in information, the symbols, images and letters appearing over the screen. 'Work' stands dissolved into 'non-work'.

If I want to print a file, I *do not* actually 'print' it; that is done *by the printer* machine. I have simply to give 'command/s'. This is nothing but a manipulation of information. It is not work; the act *breaks out of* the confines of work. I control information, and therefore I control production process, which is not done by me or less and less so. I am actually the owner of this 'information'. Every 'worker'/operator is owner to such an extent that the owner of the means of production and information has to depend almost entirely or considerably on him/her. So, there is a split between the ownership of the *means* of information/production and the ownership of *information* itself. This is a great historic split with far-reaching implications. Earlier too there was, to an extent, such a difference and split but now *it is the rule.*

Similarly, the xerox or copying machine of today is a complex of information of various types, which is manipulated and as a result the objects/images are produced or manipulated.

In the above-mentioned processes, it is *the text* that the operator or the 'worker' is working with, not the object or the article itself. So, Mark Poster is right in postulating that the textual and linguistic configuration of *the subject itself* is emerging and changing due to the electronic intervention. And it is this that constitutes a crucial element of the mode of information.

It is not the worker-operator and the machine which are at the centre of productive and informative processes/events anymore; it is the human/computer and brain/computer interface which is at work in the centre. *The worker is being replaced by the human/computer and brain/computer interfaces*; similarly, every human being working with the computers actually constitutes a system of human/computer interface. Mind it, when we talk of this interface, the software emerges as the *key constituent* of the whole productive and communication system.

Stating these things have several implications. "The mode of information signifies the end of the proletariat."[37] The new worker has a different relation with the 'machine', if we can use the word here. It is debatable whether we can use the term at all, because computer and other electronic gadgets are *no more machines,* neither in the usual sense nor otherwise. Human being is in logical interaction with the software, and the result is manipulation of information, leading to the tangible and intangible productive processes. Computer, mobile, etc. are not machines but a system of logical processors (software), which act more like 'intelligence'. The modern ('postmodern') electronic gadgets are attached more to our brains and are increasingly becoming a part of our brain, body and consciousness.

Another point that emerges is that the worker no longer works in the usual sense of term. In industrial capitalism we impart certain meaning to 'work'. But the mode of information is characterised by the fact that the software absorbs, discharges and dissolves work, and therefore there is no question of the 'worker' existing as the operator of the machine.

Artisans and assembly-line workers had an active 'hands-on' relation with the tangible materials in the process of production. Their bodies were directly involved in the change of shapes and size of the materials with the help of tools and machines. In the process they changed the raw material into finished product. They had particular kind of 'experience', which constituted a distinguishing feature of their lifetime.

"Now, since the introduction of computers in the workplace, a new worker is being produced, one who sits, away from the place of production, in front of monitors, switches, lights, an interpreter of information."[38]

This fully accords with what Marx wrote in *Grundrisse* on workers in the automated systems becoming overseers by standing ***beside*** the production process and the labour process becoming dissolved in the production process.

More discussion on the point is needed. We will take up this question in another volume.

Scientific knowledge is more and more being used in production, and thus *science is becoming a productive force.* Its consequence is that the worker is being shifted *out of* the production process. This participation also takes the form of research and development divisions of the corporations, university laboratories, public and market surveys, policy research, use of high technology and so on.

The problem of production is no more that of shaping materials and coordinating labour etc. It is now of design, simulation, modeling of material objects and after production, attaching them to the imaginations of the consumers. Production is now more and more becoming working out the logic of information, so that precise information leads to better commodities. This can only be done by software, and therefore human beings and software have to form an unity. *The discourse of science has become the chief productive force.*[39]

But having stated this, Poster goes off and is diverted into secondary issues.

The postmodern world works on the basis of individuals constituted through their place in the circuit of information flows. "Staying tuned in is the chief political act."[40] Guattari and Deleuze make an interesting point about the extraction of surplus value by new means, though it is difficult to agree, also because no detailed explanation has been given of such an important and crucial point. They say that the capitalist organization works less and less through the usual concept of 'physiosocial' work, and more and more through a generalized 'machine enslavement', "such that one may furnish surplus value without doing any work". Among such categories of 'workers' are included children, the retired, the unemployed, TV viewers etc. Capitalism according to these authors now operates less on quantity of labour and more of the 'semiotic system', which includes transport, urban models, media, entertainment, ways of perceiving etc.[41]

Now, while some of the points are to be thought over, others are not clear at all and are unreal. First, there is a confusion and combination of 'transport' etc. with production. Second, the point that semiotic methods are used for production and circulation has to analysed; it is not clear how they still produce 'surplus value'. The surplus value is either produced or not at all.

The point has to be investigated *whether the mode of information produces only **surplus** and **not surplus value**.*

Motorised Machines, Electronics and Exchange of Information

Deleuze and Guattari visualize motorized machines as the second age of technical machines, and cybernetic and informational machines as the third age.[42] This is the age of a reconstruction of a 'generalised subjection' of humans to the machine. The human-machine system of subjection is recurrent and reversible, in contrast to the non-recurrent and irreversible relations of the earlier period. With automation a new kind of enslavement comes into being. One is enslaved by TV as a human machine because the viewers are no longer consumers or users but become its intrinsic component parts.

Here he makes a crucial point, that the human-machine relation is now based on *internal and mutual* communication. Earlier it was based on usage or action. This is a very crucial point to understand the mode of information. Here we may ignore the expression of the human having been enslaved to the machine. This provides only part of the picture and gives a wrong impression about the role of 'machines' and the humans. The objection presents itself as to if the humans are really enslaved, how they constitute the dialectics of exchange of information. The point is not clarified.

One point can be said in favour of enslavement and that is this: the human being becomes a mute and passive spectator of the TV. But this is also not fully true in the long run. And this expression does not fully represent the state of affairs. It was truer at the initial stages of the emergence of TV but this apparatus has evolved as a complex interactive system in the course of time, with growing accessories, attendant developments and spread of electronic networks.

Deleuze and Guattari further make a crucial statement to the effect that the TV viewers are no longer consumers or users or *even subjects*. They are intrinsic component pieces of the TV programmes, with them reduced to 'input' and 'output' as their function.

Here in the midst of several negatives, an important positive point is made, though accidentally and as a secondary point. The functions as 'input' and 'output' are intrinsic component pieces of a system that is "no longer connected to the machine", no longer meant to produce the machine as such, in order to produce it. This is a very important point, but unfortunately, Deleuze and Guattari stop here. But we can logically develop it further.

The subject is not connected to the machine to use or produce it, to the machine as such. It becomes part of an intrinsic system of input and output of information. The subject is changed, transformed and assimilated into a system of information produced by that very/those very TVs and computers. The subject is not only a part and parcel of a system of exchange of information but also is constituted in the course of information exchange. This is *a revolution* with unforeseen results.

Having made a significant point of what human/machine interface is not, Deleuze and Guattari retreat into the modern version of "enslavement", as Poster rightly points out.[43] They use the lexicon of 'enslavement' to explain the events. They state that with automation comes "a new kind of enslavement"[44] without explaining it. The subject in fact returns to the earlier positions. The two parts of analyses, inherent and expressed, are in contradiction with each other in these two authors.

In fact, the TV-computer/human relationship is *a revolution* in the subject-object dialectics.

Modernism, Postmodernism and Mode of Information

The development that changed everything was the television.[45] It was the first technological invention of importance in the post-WWII period. Radio had already come in the inter-war period and war-time and it was more potent than the print media. That was because it had lesser demands on the educational qualifications, greater immediacy of reception, but above all because of its temporal reach. The broadcasting went on round the clock, and the borderlines between the waking and sleeping hours were blurred.

Besides, the waking and hearing hours could be the same. One could go on working even while listening. It was possible because of the dissociation of the ear from the eye. In other words, so many activities could be carried on with the radio in the background.[46]

Here something more has to be described about the radio and its transformation and replacement by the transistor radio. The radio was generally a fixed box, whose voice and broadcast filled the house. Then came the transistors and consequently the transistor radio in the early and mid 1950s. That was a new stage of communication revolution. It s distinct character was that it was not fixed to a point near the electric connection or the plug. The use of the transistors made it possible to carry it with oneself, even if one had initially to attach it to the plugs in various places. Use of batteries completely liberated the equipment of any attachment to a particular place. One could carry it at will to any place anytime. Rapid reduction in size was a wonder of its time. One could simply carry it in one's pocket. The individual became one with the transistor, with a direct access to the news, information and music.

Each individual became *a unit in himself/herself*, as far as information was concerned. The individual became powerful as never before. This was contrary to the very nature of the bourgeois capitalist society, where the system works through the class and the mass conflict and exploitation. Here then, there was a serious break, a penetration in the bourgeois solidity was made, which became porous. It is the individual who becomes 'bourgeois'! Monopoly was broken, as far as information and thought was concerned.

The handing over of the transistor to the individual was *one of the greatest* democratic events ever. The society never remained the same; it never looked back. Democracy became all-pervading, as every individual received or could potentially receive a small, handy transistor set.

The transistor prepared grounds for the emergence of the television and computer revolutions and their accompanying impacts.

Television (TV) was first marketed in the fifties. At first it was black and white, therefore the impact was not so palpable. It was considered, in popular estimation, as inferior to the coloured cinema. The arrival of the coloured TV in the early seventies in the west produced a crisis for the films and cinema.

TV lies at the watershed of *postmodernism*, at the *borderline* of modernism and postmodernism. There was a time when the arrival of the machine was celebrated, "modernism was seized by the images of machinery".[47] To be modern was to appreciate the machine to work with it to own it. "Now, postmodernism was sway to a machinery of images."[48] According to Jameson, these new machines are sources of reproduction rather than production; they are also not very attractive solids.[49] Perry Anderson is right in saying the computer and TV terminals are peculiarly blank solids.[50] They generate no confidence in the onlookers, when 'lifeless' or inactive. It is only now that the computer has come contain a whole world, particularly after the emergence of the internet.

The new machines pour out a torrent of images. This is *in contrast to the usual job* of the machine. The industrial machine is at its best in the production of print, which are tangibles. There is no basic difference in nature of the two. Camera and the photography shows some transitional features. There is a transition from the machine to the non-machine, as it more and more takes up the production of images. Production of the image is not the job proper of the machine. Its job is to produce material and tangible objects for our consumption. That precisely what the industrial revolution was about. The industrial revolution made it possible to transfer the physical labour to the machines in order to produce the objects of our consumption.

But now the machines have begun producing images, and thus have *ceased* to be machines. It is not an industrial act. We cannot consume images, we do not need them. Yet, we are producing them in the growing millions! We are now consuming them more and more. That is in order to drive the production process better. Image is driving production. But in the course of it, a basic change is coming over us and the production. That which drives production is becoming our main concern and activity. We are losing sight of our main, industrial, activity and are rapidly shifting to the secondary activity of producing images and information. The secondary becomes the primary. *It is a shift from the industrial to the postindustrial.* Simultaneously, it is a shift from the modern to the postmodern. The postmodern is the *reflection* in image of the postindustrial. The postindustrial here is a historic shift in the job and the nature of the machine.

Consequently, we are living in an age of images. We are surrounded by them. We convert everything into the images first, and only then look at them and understand them. In the process, we begin to erase the difference between the material and the imaginary world. It is now the imaginary world and of virtual reality, the world of information which is driving production and society.

The machines of the industrial age said little and created small measure of *ideology* themselves. Most of the ideology, theory and impression was created *outside, on the terrain of the society*. This was outside the machine itself. It was a specialized field.

In the postmodern setting, *the machine itself is theory and ideology*. Therefore, the machine is now a 'machine', with reservation. It has to be realized that the postindustrial machine produces tons of ideas, and that is why it is past the industrial nature, leaving it behind and acquiring *non-industrial, imaginary nature.* Our focus shifts from the tangible machine to the images that are and can be created inside and by the machine, with the help of the software.

The software is manipulative, overbearing and replicable as nothing else. We are in relationship with the software, and that is why it is a postmodern world in the sense of the consciousness and subjective creation. We have already given over the mental activity to the software. This is a postindustrial and a postmodern act. It is a historic turning point; it is the end of the old history and the beginning of new ones. Modernism is at an end. Modernism cannot deal with the image and information. Why do we say so? Because the modern always deals with the tangible; it is an extension of the tangible productive processes. The modern human being was the highest development, the very culmination, of the whole history based on and driven by production.

No more so; today the human being is not driven by production; it is its secondary activity, even if unwittingly, unknowingly, and unknown to himself/herself. The human being is now driven into a new direction or directions of development. And that is not based upon and driven by production. The humans are now onwards driven by the image, of the world and of themselves. This is the postmodern consciousness. It is an involved and indirect consciousness, not of the tangibles produced by and in the process of production, but in the process of production of the images of activities and beyond, of those activities which are yet to be. Therefore, it is a self-consciousness achieved through self-reflection, something that is possible only in the images of the image.

The virtual reality brings to real life that which is not in order to decide upon the future shape of things. It is possible to create a world on the screen, even take out its prints, and then dismantle the same. We manipulate that which does not exist. These are precisely *the postmodernist act.*

The software programs are rapidly coming out of their hardware limits and casings, and are acquiring almost an independent existence, a driving force at one with our consciousness, more or less existing outside.

Capitalism as an Industrial System *Impedes* Mode of Information

In many senses capitalism can be shown to *impede the growth of mode of information,* as the former is the *product of industrial revolution.* There is a conflict between capitalism produced by industrial revolution and that by the electronics revolution. The two are qualitatively different. At the same time, capitalism increasingly is being imbued with post-capitalist and non-capitalist features, which needs a separate discussion. Industrial and existing capitalism slows down reconfiguration of electronically mediated identity of the subject, a characteristic feature of postmodernism and post-industrialism.

The concept of hegemony was introduced by Gramsci to explain many of the unexplained and supplementary phenomena of society. Class consciousness in itself, and the theory of forces and relations of production, were not enough to cover events taking place in the wide body of civil society. The Gramscian theory of hegemony has to be further revised to explain the growing complications and continuous upsets in the state of objectivity which is increasingly not self-identical.

Laclau and Mouffe do so by introducing post-structuralism into the social analysis of the existing reality, which happens to be a state of mode of information. What is the relationship between this introduction and mode of information? It is the *suppressed absences* that are the problematique of the mode of information. The electronics revolution brings out into the open the suppressed information about the neglected aspects and movements and role of individuals. Electronics brings out what is not to be found in the industrial terrain or are deep down it. The self-identity of the social reality/structures, which was developing under industrialism, is upset much before it evolves and matures. A new evolutionary, identity-shaping factor emerges in the society, and that is the mode of information. Not only the suppressed identities and events but the entire society is transformed rapidly into information symbols and texts. It is these that are being worked out by the human beings in interface with the electronic systems and electronically mediated communications.

And here precisely lies the great historical problem. Now information fills in the existing texts, which occupied secondary historical positions uptilnow, subject to fixed interpretations; the texts now appear with new meanings constantly, defying interpretations. This is partly because we try to interpret them from the industrial positions. Besides, new texts are constantly created in the course of rapid motions while causing new discourse, a discourse basically created in the course of electronically mediated communication. This happens because existence, objectivities and material figures take the form of floating and temporary texts, subject to interpretations as they are transmitted to the subjects, who in turn are destabilized. This is typical of the mode of information.

Earlier, the texts were related with Cartesian appearance; they were produced from the fixed, material reality. Now text is produced from text, and acts as the driving force of society and the individual consciousness.

The hegemony of categories and concepts is thus lost and what emerges is the constant formulation, interpretation and conversion of the concepts, imparting an 'escape motion' to the concepts and to the subject itself, who interprets the text not as a stable subject but being themselves in motion. Simultaneously, the objects too acquire 'escape velocities'. The relation, it has to be realized, becomes increasingly three-way post-industrial postmodern one, rather than the two-way industrial one: instead of between material object and ideas/images, it is now between objects, images of objects and images of images. Images and texts are being copied in endless numbers as never before in the history of human society. We are virtually being drowned in images! The relation between concepts, categories and objects is far more complex now.

So, society is operating at *a new terrain*, that of text, and at the same time is being formed and driven by it. This is a revolution in human consciousness. Poster criticizes Laclau and Mouffe as having closed the non-discursive texts by advocating spread and thus 'totalisation' of text, and thus postmodernism recedes into modernism, because this approach generalizes (totalizes) both the non-discursive (institutions etc.) as well as discursive (texts) events. In other words, this is an effort to control the object.[51]

Mark Poster wants to strengthen the mode of information by introducing contexts as a consequence of the electronically mediated communication. These contexts are momentary, produced in the course of electronic exchange of information, and disappear as soon as they appear. The social world in this way is textualised in a form that can be read through poststructuralist strategies, that is by going beyond the study of fixed structures.

We have entered another world through the collapsing screen, a complete reversal of social relations and events, the world of 'text'.

Human/Computer and Brain/Computer Interface: Computer Science and Postmodernism

There is a basic difference between computer science and other sciences. While other sciences study nature or human beings, the 'object' of computer is the computer itself. It has its own language, program and text, and delves into a world created by, through and in itself. "The computer stands as the referent object to the discourse of computer science."[52] Therefore, it stands in recognition of its false image with great signifying powers, and is known for its transluscent magical powers.

That is why people almost take the computer as some magical force, which can discharge any function or perform any act, complete any of their jobs. One can conclude that the earlier sciences dealt with human's study of objects, and computer science deals with objects, symbols and the study of the scientist himself/herself by the computer.

A scientist, Maurice Wilkes, is quoted as having said that what keeps these scientists together is not some abstraction but the actual hardware with which they work everyday.[53] The logic should be taken further to state that it is increasingly the software that is keeping people together as the common linguistic bond on a growingly new terrain. It has to be realized that the hardware is *a receding reality in the world of computers.*

"If the essence of computer science is a machine, how is the boundary between the science and the scientist to be drawn and maintained?" is the question posed by Poster.[54] Peter Denning expresses anxiety about the loss of boundary between machine and computer scientist. He says that unknowingly, we are becoming the subjects of the objects we created as our subjects. Newell and Simon define computer science as the unity of man and machine. "The machine—not just the hardware but the programmed, *living machine*—is the organism we study." For them, for these two scientists, language is material intelligence residing in physical symbol system.[55]

"Computer science then is a discourse *at the border of words and things.*"[56] Thus there is 'confusion' or mutually interpenetrative dialectics between the scientist and his/her object. The identity of the scientist and the computer is very close, so close as to be often *indistinguishable.* Their jobs interchange. According to Poster they are 'mirror effects' of each other. They each project subjectivity as well as objectivity on each other, mutually. The computer is becoming increasingly intelligent and displaces and judges the scientist or the operator on increasingly frequent occasions as the science and technology develop.

John E. Hopcroft makes a penetrative observation about the role of computers. He says that the computer will help us understand intellectual process, learning process, thinking process and the reasoning process. Their structures will become clearer to us. "Today, we are beginning the exploration of the intellectual universe of ideas, knowledge structures and language."[57]

Computer science is more and more penetrating the domain of what is called the 'spirit'. Artificial and human intelligence are coming closer rapidly together, so much so that it will become impossible to distinguish between the two very before long; in fact, the artificial intelligence has already begun to dominate human one in more than one way. Poster is qu right in stating that "The electrification of science in the form of the computer generates a discourse *at the border of mind and matter* and in so doing destabilizes the distinction between the two."[58]

This is crucial statement and a crucial development validated by the subsequent developments, particularly in the field of human/ computer and brain/computer interface. Poster, in fact, criticizes Hopcroft for identifying language of the artificial intelligence with the human language itself, objects to the view that by developing computer language we are not simply inventing new discourse but objectifying human mind; the objection is that this discourse of computer science "is decidedly not postmodern" but firmly logocentric. He stops at the criticism by saying more studies are needed in this field.

The objection is strange and surprising.

What Poster would have liked, it seems, is the delving deeper into the independent working of the linguistic structural evolution and development of electronic language, and here he is right. But at the same time, he is mistaken in disregarding *the objectification of human mind and language.* He seems to miss the giant leap of human mind, detaching language of independent text of the computer language or the software from it.

The event of the objectification of the human mind is a giant step in human evolution. The developments in human/computer and brain/computer sciences in the recent time point clearly to this trend. We can get attached to the screen through our brain and manipulate the images, write characters and letters without the keyboard. Now, we can just look at the screen and simply get the letters or images appear on it. Our brain and the consciousness itself it becoming part of the 'consciousness' of the computer: they are becoming one system.

A new kind of subject and subjectivity is coming into being, as part of the mode of information.

NOTES

1. Mark Poster, *The Mode of Information: Poststructuralism and Social Context*, Polity Press, UK, 1990.
2. Ibid., p. 11.
3. Ibid., pp. 14-15.
4. See, *On the Road to Noosphere*, Novosti Press Agency, Moscow, 1989, p. 1; Arbatov, Bogolyubov, Sobolev, *Ecology*, APN Publishing House, Moscow, 1989, p. 2; Lapo A.V., *Traces of Bygone Biospheres*, Mir Publishers, Moscow, 1982, p. 37; Balandin, R.K., *Vladimir Vernadsky*, Mir Publishers, Moscow, 1982, p. 106. The term was also used by Edouard Le Roy and Pierre Teilhard de Chardin but there is some controversy over sequence.
5. Poster, *Mode of Information*, p. 46.
6. Ibid., p. 47.
7. Poster, following Baudrillard, ibid., p. 44.
8. Ibid., pp. 44, 45.
9. Ibid., p. 46.
10. Ibid., p. 46.

11. Ibid., p. 48.
12. Ibid.
13. See, Poster, ibid., p. 49; the analysis provides some clues to the concept of mode of information.
14. Ibid., p. 47.
15. Ibid., p. 48.
16. Ibid., p. 51.
17. See, ibid., p. 54.
18. See, ibid., pp. 54-55.
19. Ibid., p. 63.
20. Ibid., p. 63.
21. Ibid., p. 64.
22. Ibid.
23. Ibid., p. 66.
24. See, Simon Malpas, *The Postmodern,* Routledge, 2007, p. 65.
25. Ibid., p. 57.
26. See, ibid., pp. 66-67.
27. See Malpas for some points of discussion, ibid., p. 66.
28. Ibid., p. 94, emphasis added.
29. Aloys Wenzl, "Einstein's Theory of Relativity viewed from the Standpoint of Critical Realism, and Its Significance for Philosophy", in *Albert Einstein: Philosopher-scientist,* ed by Paul Arthur Schilpp, The Library of Living Philosophers, Volume VII, Carus Publishing Company, New York, 2000, p. 603.
30. Jean Baudrillard, *The System of Objects*, Navayana/Verso, New Delhi, 2008, p. 218.
31. *The Economist*, February 27, 2010.
32. Sinan Aral, *The Economist,* February 27, 2010, p. 4 of the Data Supplement.
33. Ibid.
34. Ibid.
35. Ibid.
36. Quoted in Mark Poster, *The Mode of Information*, p. 129.
37. Poster, ibid.
38. Poster, ibid., p. 130.
39. Poster, ibid.
40. Ibid., p. 136.
41. Ibid.
42. Ibid., p. 136.
43. Ibid., p. 137.

44. Ibid., p. 136.
45. Perry Anderson, *The Origins of Postmodernity*, Verso, 1999, p. 87.
46. Based on ibid., p. 88.
47. Ibid.
48. Ibid.
49. Quoted in Anderson, ibid., p. 89.
50. Ibid,. p. 88.
51. See, ibid., pp. 139-40
52. Poster, *op. cit.*, p. 147.
53. Ibid.
54. Ibid., p. 148.
55. Ibid., p. 148, emphasis added.
56. Ibid., emphasis added.
57. Quoted in Mark Poster, ibid., p. 148.
58. Ibid., 149, emphasis added.

Conclusion

The post-industrial and postmodern society being created by the STR and ICR is reorienting the way we look at and explore the world, particularly the new world. It is quite clear that the quantum discoveries, relativity of Einstein, genetics, bio-informatics and a whole range of events in science and technology have fundamentally changed the way we lived and thought so far. We are in for drastic and shocking surprises in the coming decades, and by the middle of the 21st century the world will have changed so much as to be unrecognizable. This is, among others, because all the sciences are more quickly getting converted into the energies of means of production and information. Let us not ignore these developments. These are not figments of imagination but events taking place right before our own eyes.

We are going through the most drastic changes ever in human history.

Among the futuristic events already set in motion are the human/computer and brain/computer interface. These are events at the borderline of matter and idea. To think is going to mean to see and to change. You look at the screen or the wall or the unfolded 'paper' and written words or images appear. The screen is becoming part and parcel of our body organs as it converts into software. Electronics makes it possible to incorporate the electronic systems as part and parcel of our body and mind.

A world is emerging where the 'touch-screen' or touch 'anything' is going to be the driving force of our information- and production-related activities. We may see walls built up or coming down, shapes changed at will, 'cars' and other modes of transport and machines being run with remotes, nano-'machines' pervading every nook and corner of our body and surroundings, objects created with just 'look'-commands, i.e. just looking at the screen at distances and so on.

It is going to be a world where we and the electronics are inseparable whole.

It would be a world of the dissolution of the machine, disappearance of the hardware, which hardly would exist; such a world is already emerging. It would be a world of signals, electronic messages and images, and thus of unprecedented extension of our nervous system. Newspapers are already reporting looking glasses with internet and messaging. We are already operating more and more with the electronic software and less and less with hardware. Touch-screens on the garments and even bodies are being experimented with. Light-driven software is among the future events.

Matter and Idea: Interpenetration and Identity of Opposites

Certain extraordinary things are happening in the world of thought, ideas and consciousness and their relation with matter. What is 'thought'? The question has popped up afresh in the age of information revolution. Obviously, thought is a function of brain as reflecting the material reality. But now this appears as a simplistic and inadequate explanation. Thought is a function not only of the human brain but also of the high speed electronic and other systems. When we say 'thought', it extends to non-biological systems as well, which act increasingly like consciousness. 'Artificial intelligence' is a reality, demanding explanation.

Electronics and light speeds have a great advantage over brain in exceedingly high speeds, which our brain cannot match. Therefore, brain must cede part of its functions to the automatic self-acting systems that process information too quickly, even at logical level. The moment logic comes into picture, thought takes shape. Besides, these self-acting systems are not the old type; they are the products of the electronics revolution. Here software is involved, which is a new factor in the development of human consciousness.

We must realize that software is not a machine but antithetical to it, and is fast coming out of its tangible confines mainly created during the industrial age. It is something that is unmachine-like. And it is fast spreading, emerging both as a cooperator and opponent of the human being. Machines are no more the basis of development of human society; it is software which is becoming the driving force with the passing of time.

This adds new dimensions to matter/idea relationship.

So, this new logical system must at some point become interconnected with and become part and parcel of the human brain as well as consciousness.

Software can be stored anywhere in any amounts, and it is self-acting, much like our brain. It can, in some senses, act as independent depository of brain functions. So, a huge chunk of brain function is fast taking shape outside our brain. This is a giant step forward in human development. At the same time, the software has the potentials to get attached to our brain. The gap and the dividing line between brain and software are disappearing fast, so much so that in the near future we will be unable to differentiate between the two.

Thus, we are confronted with idea having wide ramifications through rapid spread of net systems and various other electronic structures. Matter has so far been almost identified with the material forms. This is no more so. The concept of matter involves existence of reality independent of consciousness. This definition continues to be relevant and broadly correct. But today, it is proving to be inadequate. Matter continues to exist independent of our consciousness. But there are increasing areas of contacts, interpenetration and mutual conversions between matter and idea, and between 'idea-like' matter and idea.

We have seen earlier that our investigations into quantum world establishes the fact that there is mutual penetration of brain, instruments and quantum processes, they often getting identified with each other. Therefore, independence of matter becomes a relative term.

Even earlier, many 'objects' were more a function of brain rather than tangible reality. Colours are more a sensory activity. Triangles and quadrangles are mathematical relations. Numbers are relations rather than objective existence. We have mentioned such examples in the Introduction.

And at the quantum levels, we change the reality when we try to see. Seeing is changing, with 'matter' having little meaning in the usual traditional sense. A particle flying off 2 or 3 lakh kms in a second or micro-seconds is a 'material reality' only in a relative sense. We take it, we are habituated to taking it, as a material reality ('independent of our consciousness') that a particle 'exists'. In reality, a particle or a wave does not exist until observed, and the moment we 'observe' it, it is converted into waves! So, observation is creation. 'Something' certainly does exist; to that extent it fits in with the concept of matter. And added to the larger material reality, it is 'matter'. But in a narrower sense, in the sense of observation, we change it and only then 'see' it. To that extent it is neither matter nor idea.

At this stage of comprehension, atoms, particles and waves of the brain merge with those outside. A new source of idea-creation is formed.

Thus, observer/observed and matter/idea relationships are far more complex and interpenetrative than ever before, particularly in the context of the classical world. When we try to observe the particle, it simply disappears, creating an epistemological crisis. This can only be overcome by giving up the old conceptual tools and by using new tools.

What Has Gone Wrong with Philosophy?

As we have discussed, our philosophy and world outlook have been created during the pre-industrial and industrial ages. Clear-cut concepts, categories and laws were evolved in the course of industrial revolution regarding the nature, society and consciousness.

But things are changing now. Philosophy as a category and discipline had been unprepared for events that have taken place in the last hundred years or so, and particularly in the last 2 to 3 decades of STR and ICR. Philosophy is on the defensive, unable to explain the world events. Interpretation has been left to the sciences, which evolve their own philosophy and categories.

The meaning of philosophy is itself changing, as can be seen from recent events in the world of the quantum.

Even dialectical materialism, the philosophy of Marxism, has been unable to anticipate, analyse and deal with the post-classical developments in sciences and with the STR/ICR.

Why is it so? The earlier philosophies, including the Marxist philosophy, had developed within the framework of means and modes of production. That determined the instruments and tools of knowledge including the philosophical ones. Philosophy has been working with fixed tools and concepts for the last several centuries, including the industrial age. These tools and concepts have evolved over centuries of observation, generalizations and studies and analyses, no doubt. But today they need drastic changes, and here philosophy and related disciplines have failed to absorb the new because of outdated and obsolete tools of knowledge.

Hegel and Marx made great contributions to human thought and philosophy by discovering, developing and perfecting the method or science of dialectics. Their contributions are unparalleled.

Yet, Marxism too has failed to assimilate STR and ICR. It has not been able to absorb the discoveries of quantum, special and general relativity, genetics, bio-informatics and so on in its philosophical and thought system. Marxism fully absorbed the essence of the industrial age but has failed to anticipate the scientific, technological and information revolution and to develop itself further by assimilating the revolution. Even after some 3 or 4 decades of the ICR/STR, Marxist and materialist thought, as also philosophy in general, continue to miss the essence of the new revolution. They have not been able to go into details of it and generally ignored it, except stray mention here and there.

The non-Marxist thoughts have not fared any better. They have also not made any radical break with their past, and it is not expected of them, as they are not scientific. But it is certainly expected of dialectical materialism to assimilate the quantum revolution and the STR.

Why Is It So? Historical Reasons

One important historical aspect of Marxism is its under-emphasis on the active role of idea, and this has been pointed out by Marx himself. He explained that he and Engels had to defend materialism from the sharp criticisms of the idealists and opponents during their times. Consequently, they did not get ample opportunity to develop this active side, the side of ideas, and thus a lopsidedness emerged. Thus,

Marx and Engels were quite conscious and clear of the one-sidedness and drawbacks of Marxist philosophy.

Over time, this aspect developed into reductionism, whereby everything was sought to be explained within the rigid framework of given and final concepts of a materialism lacking active role for ideas, even though Marxism contributed most to the development of theories and concepts. This fixity and tendency of finality increasingly became mechanical. Marxism gradually became a set of fixed formulas and concepts, gradually losing momentum. Often, the explanation/interpretation of dialectical materialism itself took the form and then essence of mechanical materialism.

In this context, Lenin's great work *Materialism and Empirio-criticism* has to be mentioned. It is an extraordinary work, particularly in view of the fact that Lenin is more well-known as the leader of Russian revolution. What is less emphasized or even lost sight of is the fact Lenin was a giant of a philosopher, and as we have seen in this volume, he was one of the handful of scholars who really understood Hegel's dialectics and his philosophy.

After the defeat of the first Russian revolution of 1905-07, Lenin set about writing *Empirio-criticism.* He took it as a very important task, insisting that the copies of this work be distributed immediately among the social democratic and other circles. That was the time when quantum had just been discovered, though its full import was yet to be grasped even by the physicists and scientists. That also was the time when Einstein's special theory of relativity was announced.

It is interesting to find that Lenin used a wide range of scientific data and literature of his time, and thus his ideas were not just free thoughts of his own mind. He mentions works and discoveries of Poincare, Mach, Einstein, Avenarius and a host of other scientists. He goes threadbare into the discussion on the discoveries of more particles within the atom, the socalled 'split of the atom'.

Lenin's *Materialism and Empirio-criticism* is one of the greatest books of philosophy in general and Marxist philosophy in particular.

But it also has a serious drawback, which became more serious as time passed. Lenin was more concerned with *defending* materialism, which is understandable in the context of intense debates between the two camps of philosophers, broadly known as idealism and materialism. Lenin rightly considered that many of the philosophers were using the 'split of the atom' to declare matter dead. He ably defended materialist point of view and showed that the discoveries of science had only shown the 'inexhaustibility of atom' and thus of matter.[1]

But in the course of time, this defence became a mechanical act, detached from concrete contexts, with new developments being ignored as 'idealist'. New aspects were ignored or did not get adequate attention, and the overall significance of new discoveries was lost sight of. This became a practice subsequently, and dialectical materialism ceased to be 'dialectical' and became mechanical.

Even in this work of Lenin's, adequate attention is not paid to the new discoveries like the quantum, relativity and some others. He concentrates mainly on the 'split of the atom' and its fall-out. But Lenin cannot be fully blamed for it. Most of the scientists themselves were yet to understand the significance, even meaning, of the new discoveries, such as those of quantum and relativity and others. There was as yet strong resistance to give up the traditional classical approach among the scientists, and this resistance continued for several decades subsequently. Lenin does not discuss Max Planck, Einstein and some others in detail. Perhaps it was too early. And his purpose was also quite different.

Yet this lacuna became serious in the subsequent years in the Marxist philosophy. It was not taken up further to evolve the materialist philosophy further in any substantial manner. This was mainly because of the rise of the bureaucratic and Stalinist Soviet state, with its own interests. There certainly were some stray attempts like those of Christopher Caudwell on crisis in physics and others. Butthey worked with pre-determined limits and ideas. Deep imprint of Stalinist approach can clearly be seen in them.

Louis Althusser and several authors have written about some historical aspects of Marxist philosophy. Brothers Roy and Zhores Medvedev have also dealt with these the developments in Soviet science and philosophy in detail, including the damage done by Lysenko and his 'ism'. Despite lot of advances and development, Soviet science including physics, genetics, quantum mechanics and other fields suffered heavily at the hands of the ruling bureaucrats.

Among the major trends in the Stalinism was to classify the new developments and theories in sciences as 'idealist' and 'bourgeois'. This included genetics, Einsteinian relativity, quantum theories and interpretations, and many other fields. Einstein himself was long considered a 'bourgeois' scientist and his theories as 'idealist' in the initial decades of the Soviet Union.

The 'ideological' state, to use Althusser's term, suppressed or interpreted and mis-interpreted latest developments in sciences and philosophy to suit it own interests. We will not go into their details as that is not our subject here. We are only pointing to some of reasons why new sciences and philosophy based upon it could not develop even under the state professing Marxism, while Marxism, as the most dialectical and scientific theory was supposed to have developed it. This is among the great tragedies of history of philosophy.

Consequently, Marxism and its component, dialectical materialism, was turned into a mechanical collection of finished statements, concepts and formulations, which had to be repeated as if by rote to explain any new development. Motion and dialectics was lost to philosophical analysis. Thus, despite great scientific and technological advances in the USSR, Marxist method suffered heavily and was unable to anticipate and assimilate the new technological revolution and the discoveries in quantum mechanics and relativity. Dialectical philosophy was thus deprived of its lifeline.

'Mode of Production', New Technology and Philosophy

One of the major problems with contemporary social scientific theory including Marxism is its preoccupation, even obsession, with the concept of 'mode of production', which by extension sets a limit to scientific investigation. Mechanical strait-jacketing has led to attempts to fit in any new development in science, technology and philosophy into the fixed concepts. There is a serious methodological problem here. Nothing must exceed the existing 'mode of production' including the socialist one. All the analyses rebound from the walls of mode of production of capitalism, imperialism and socialism. Capitalism/imperialism is always 'in crisis', and therefore is not supposed to develop new productive forces or necessarily destroys them. This has to be the basis of any observation and analysis. Consequently, anything new is underestimated, even denied existence. Socialism automatically means development of productive forces, and this voluntarism led to actually preventing the growth of technology and sciences and thus to a refusal to see the actual events in the fields of STR, ICR, quantum sciences, relativity, genetics and so on. In the meanwhile these sciences kept on developing at a break-neck speed, leading ultimately to a crisis in and collapse of the bureaucratic socialism in many countries.

Even today, many radical and Marxist analyses of modern science and technologies just stop short of drawing logical and necessary conclusions even while doing a great job of studies in these fields. This is because, for example in philosophy, they are not ready to develop the concepts like 'reality', 'matter', 'existence', space and time and such other. It does not mean that those who propagate the new theories are necessarily correct or final; but it does mean that in the present phase of scientific and philosophical development, there can be no limits on concepts and developments, and one has to be prepared to evolve absolutely novel ideas. The nature of the quantum world itself demands such an open-ended approach: we cannot be bound by any fixed concepts. For example, one cannot base one's study on the assumption that 'imperialism' or 'capitalism' do not develop sciences etc. One has to base oneself on the fact of science and technology in the world as a whole, and events show that these developments are unrelated to any particular society, capitalist or socialist. Science and technology in form of the STR today have become independent of the nature of any social system. That is now an established fact.

'Idealism', Capitalism and Philosophy

That is one of the reasons why we have developed the concept of 'mode of information' in the present book. The present day is guided by information, by the way it is produced and used. Information belongs to the field of ideas and images, which are being mass-produced, and guide increasingly the direction of mode of production. We will be taking up this question again and in greater detail in one of the next volumes of this series. Presently, the book wants to emphasise that a mode of information is definitely emerging and that it is guiding the social development along unexpected new directions.

So, capitalism also cannot be spared sharp criticism for failure to freely allow the development of science, scientific outlook and philosophy, as we will argue further.

Besides, it is also true that many scientists and philosophers try to guide the discoveries in sciences into backward-looking and even reactionary direction and espouse kinds of mysticism and agnosticism. They use inapplicability and obsoleteness of many established concepts to prove correctness of idealist philosophies, even going back to Taoism, 'exotic' eastern mysticism and belief in existence of 'God'. The present writer totally disagrees with such attempts. Science should be treated as science and not mysticism, and there is no place for any kind of 'god' in it. God and science have always stood in direct opposition to each other and will always do so.

The fact that the quantum science and its discoveries open new world of investigations only means that science and scientists have a whole new world to begin with on a *scientific*, not a mystic, basis. In fact, this world is an endless vastness, before which the present planetary world of us 'poor' earthlings appears to be too small and limited. We have a whole universe to explore.

While socialism has failed on many counts, capitalism too has not fared any better several areas, e.g. attitude to the people's consciousness, use of STR for the masses and freeing philosophy from mysticism. In fact, STR/ICR and the mass electronic media are often being used to spread mysticism, sensationalism, and idealism and religious agnosticism among the common people. This is in direct contradiction with the actual and objective process of growth of atheists and non-believers in the advanced industrial/capitalist countries.

Yet, the media and several official organs are advocating weird and mystic forces through various means, and are trying to deliberately spread the belief in 'god' instead of clearing it. Not only this; some official circles in the US and other countries are even trying to prevent, for example, teaching Darwin's evolutionary theory etc. in the name of the discoveries being 'anti-religious' and 'anti-Christian'. It has to be emphasized that Darwinism and other scientific theories grew in the face of stiff opposition from the religious circles and religious orthodoxy and bureaucracy during the previous centuries.

Thus, bureaucracies and centralized administrations of various kinds within many capitalist countries, including in the most advanced ones, are often found to hinder the growth of science, technology and philosophy. Such hindrances also come from the giant MNCs (multinational corporations) and financial institutions. We do not have the space to deal with them in detail nor does it form a part of the present analysis. But these trends do relate to some of the aspects of new sciences and philosophy.

Growth of Science Cannot be Hindered

The growth/development of science, technology and new world outlook cannot be hindered by the conservative forces mentioned above. STR and ICR have found their own ways of going beyond the hindrances and removing the hurdles. One of the ways is the emergence of the 'mode of information', which is replacing the mode of production and opening new avenues of development of human thought.

Information penetrates the state, government, classes, parties, countries, and all forms of structured bureaucratic hindrances. It has given rise to new forms of thought and of propagation of thought. Its rapid envelopment of the planet earth is breaking down all forms of conservative philosophy, concepts and notions, and has started new directions and dimensions of human evolution.

Information is now directly related with the human being, who is now information-driven. Thus, consciousness takes on new dimensions. The difference between individual and social consciousness is getting narrowed. Not only this, and this is more important, extra-human 'consciousness' or 'artificial consciousness' is going to play a far more impacting role than we realize at present. Added to this is the concept and technology of virtual reality. All this makes up a society which was unheard of and unexpected. And more than society, it all makes up a world of consciousness which recycles realities into new realities.

Quantum science and the new particle open out new and unlimited vistas of growth of human consciousness.

Dissociation and Realignment of 'Philosophy'

Not only the Marxist philosophy but philosophy in general has failed to really grasp the new world to satisfaction.

As we have discussed, the constituent elements of 'philosophy' have got disjointed and dissolved, partially or fully. Why is 'philosophy' unable to interpret the world? This is because its basic dimensions and tools have gone haywire and are no more applicable. We are entering a world where the dimensions and categories of time, space, motion, subject, object, laws, causation, observation, reality, and so on are all topsy-turvy. They have to be realigned and re-developed, and the new ones evolved.

But the traditional, existing, philosophy is proving more and more to be a conservative force, refusing to change itself, trying to fit in things into fixed concepts. That is why philosophy is failing badly.

We have many hopes and energies of development in the quantum 'philosophy'. That only underlines that we have to redefine philosophy and begin the comprehension of the world afresh. Philosophy is no more direct one to one relationship. It is a unification with the exceedingly rapid motions, which determine our conclusions.

To comprehend motion and dialectics is to understand and interpret the new world. Motion is the centre-stage of this world. We have to catch up.

NOTES

1. See, for example, Philipp G. Frank, "Einstein, Mach and Positivism", in Ed. Paul Arthur Schilpp, *Albert Einstein: Philosopher-scientist*, Carus Publishing Company, USA, 2000, p. 272, for discussion on Lenin's comments on Mach's philosophy.

Index